Protestantes/Protestants

Protestantes/ Protestants

Hispanic Christianity Within Mainline Traditions

Edited By

David Maldonado, Jr.

Abingdon Press
Nashville

PROTESTANTES/PROTESTANTS
HISPANIC CHRISTIANITY WITHIN MAINLINE TRADITIONS

Copyright © 1999 by Abingdon Press

This book is printed on elemental chlorine–free paper.

Library of Congress Cataloging-in-Publication Data

Protestantes/Protestants : Hispanic Christianity within mainline traditions / edited by David Maldonado, Jr.
      p.   cm.
Includes bibliographical references and index.
ISBN 0-687-05509-1 (alk. paper)
      1. Hispanic American Protestants.   I. Maldonado, David.   II. Title: Protestantes.   III. Title: Protestants.
BR563.H57P75   1999
280'.4'08968073—dc21   98-31142
                                                                                                              CIP

Scripture quotations are from the Revised Standard Version of the Bible, copyright 1946, 1952, 1971 by the Division of Christian Education of the National Council of the Churches of Christ in the USA, and the New Revised Standard Version Bible, copyright © 1989, by the Division of Christian Education of the National Council of the Churches of Christ in the United States of America. Used by permission.

99 00 01 02 03 04 05 06 07 08—10 9 8 7 6 5 4 3 2 1

MANUFACTURED IN THE UNITED STATES OF AMERICA

Preface

In his book *Mañana*, Justo L. González calls for a new way of doing theology. He calls for the theological task to be a communal enterprise in which the community joins in the process and owns the outcome. This book is the outcome of just such an effort. Over a three-year period the writers of these chapters met twice a year in seminar sessions, which consisted of in-depth discussions, sharing, and dialogue. Each member took responsibility for his or her work, yet that work evolved during a series of presentations, exchanges, and sharing with the group. This book is offered to the rest of the community so that it too may enter the conversation and offer its insights.

Justo González played an important role as mentor and consultant. He was an active participant in all the sessions and offered helpful advice to all the writers and especially to the editor. I am indebted to him for his wise counsel, supportive spirit, and encouraging words.

The participants in the seminars and writers of these chapters form the core of the project. Their faithful attendance, mutual support, and especially their serious participation in the seminars made this project a rewarding and enriching process. Each brought a unique perspective and unselfishly shared with the others.

The project was ably staffed by graduate students from Perkins School of Theology at Southern Methodist University. I am thankful for their able assistance and support. Paul Barton played an important role, first as a leading research assistant and later as a participant in the process. Early in the work of the project, Laura Brewster provided important assistance. I also want to thank Martine Stemerick for her help in the early editing work.

This project, however, would not have been possible were it not for the generous support of the Lilly Endowment. I am especially grateful to Olga Villa Parra, who as a staff consultant at the Endowment, offered effective advice and encouragement. She guided this project and lent much moral support during her tenure at the Endowment. Craig Dykstra was most helpful with his sense of the big picture and with suggestions for the direction of the project. Sister Jean Knoerle, likewise, has been a helpful friend to the project and supportive in her spirit and actions.

Robin Lovin, Dean of the Perkins School of Theology, has been supportive of this project and helpful in guiding my research leave throughout the university. I am also thankful to Jim Kirby, who as Dean when this project started encouraged me to initiate the project.

In short, this project owes much to many persons at the Lilly Endowment, Perkins School of Theology, and the Hispanic theological community. It was indeed a task performed in community. It now belongs to the rest of the theological and Latino communities for their consideration and reflection. It also serves as an invitation to join in a wider conversation and appreciation of the Latino Protestant.

Contents

Protestantes: An Introduction

Hispanics? Protestants? How can we speak of Hispanic Protestants? The two terms almost seem contradictory or incompatible. To speak of Hispanics as Protestant might appear just as incomprehensible as speaking of Protestants as Hispanic. Yet, the Protestant faith has been part of Hispanic Christianity for well over a century in this country and in Latin America. Today, dynamic religious life and growth can be found within Hispanic Protestantism. However, very little is known about this religious population and there is much to be explored. Who are the Hispanic Protestants? What are their origins? What is their story? How can we understand their experiences and perspectives within the context of American Protestantism and the broader social and historical realities?

Hispanic Protestants have long been overlooked or regarded as an insignificant exception to the U.S. Hispanic religious reality. Because of the central and influential role that the Roman Catholic Church played in the exploration and establishment of Spanish Catholic rule in the Americas, and in the formation of the mestizo cultures of Mexico and Latin America, Hispanic populations have long been associated with Roman Catholicism with regard to culture, religious identity, and faith. As a result, there arose a long-standing assumption that to be Hispanic was to be Catholic. Hispanics were assumed to be a monolithic religious community, Catholic from their birth as a people, and Catholic in all aspects of their lives.

Facts gathered over a century and especially during recent years contradict widely held perceptions and assumptions. A significant number of U.S. Hispanics adhere to non-Catholic religious identities and actively participate in Hispanic Protestant congregations. Their religious faith is a Protestant faith. Their identity is Protestant. Recent research suggests that Hispanic Protestants may well represent between 25% and 33% of the Hispanic population.

Unfortunately, little is known about Hispanic Protestants—their history, theology, perspectives, leadership, and congregational life. What is their story and how can it be understood within a broader context? It is important to consider their origins and inception. What historical dynamics motivated Protestant missionaries and their denominational strategies? What theological and cultural factors shaped the process and outcome? How can we understand current theological perspectives and religious manifestations of Hispanic Protestantism?

What does it mean to be Hispanic and Protestant? What does it mean to be Protestant in a Hispanic culture which is predominantly Catholic? What is it like to be Hispanic within Protestant denominations that are predominantly Anglo? Does this mean that Hispanic Protestants are essentially at the margins of these two realities? What does it mean to be at the margins?

What is Hispanic about Hispanic Protestants, and what is Protestant about Hispanic Protestants? How do these two terms relate and interact with each other to form the Hispanic Protestant? Are Hispanic Protestants Latino versions of Anglo Protestants? Are they Protestant versions of the Hispanic reality? How can they be understood and what can be learned from this unique blending of history, cultures, and religious traditions?

Hispanic and Protestant: Self-Definition and Identity

Identity is a central issue for Hispanic Protestants. They have been defined by others in many ways. For example, Hispanic Catholics have referred to these groups as "Protestantes," "aleluyas," and "los hermanos." Hispanic Protestants have been referred to by Anglos as "home mission field," "ethnic minorities," and "little brothers and sisters." These terms are externally imposed and used to describe, define, and distinguish Hispanic Protestants. Some are less than positive or endearing.

The use of such terms has made the question of identity an important issue for Hispanic Protestants. To be defined by others is to be told what and who you are. Defining is a way of controlling the very essence of being. Fortunately, externally imposed terms are not always accepted. They do, however, stimulate the question of identity and being. In an unintended way, they stimulate the act of self-definition and self-identification.

The Spanish term *evangelico* is the most popular term used internally among Hispanic Protestants. However, the English translation "evangelical" has a totally different connotation; using it to describe Hispanic Protestants would have serious and erroneous implications. While the English word *evangelical* primarily has a theological meaning, the Spanish term *evangelico* is used to distinguish Protestant from Roman Catholic identity. "Evangelicos" include non-Catholic Christians from a wide spectrum of theological orientations. The distinction connotes more than doctrinal, theological, or liturgical differences from the Roman Catholic Church. It includes many social, cultural, and identity issues related to having a Protestant identity within a Roman Catholic community.

The terms *Protestante* and *Protestant* are used in this volume for several reasons. To simply translate *evangelico* to *evangelical* would confuse the reader. But most of all *Protestante* is used as a term of confession and affirmation. Although some may use the term *Protestante* in deriding ways, the term is claimed as act of confession of religious faith, an affirmation of experience and being. To confess the faith is to call attention to theological

10

and ecclesiastical distinctions considered important. To affirm the Protestante experience and identity is to claim self-identity as Protestants and to recognize the price paid for being Protestant.

Hispanics: An Ethnic Population

An important aspect of Hispanic Protestantism is ethnicity. This term refers to a broad sense of peoplehood among a population. Because of widely shared historical experiences, a common language, religious traditions, and some overlapping cultural practices, including racial histories involving mestizaje and mulatez, Hispanics share a sense of ethnicity. There is a sense of having much in common and of being Hispanic or Latino. Yet, a shared sense of ethnicity does not do away with identification with nations of origin. The sense of being Puerto Rican, Mexican American, or Salvadoran is important. But on a broad level, there does exist a shared sense of peoplehood—a sense of being Latino.

However, ethnicity is also a personal matter, an element of one's self-identity. Ethnic self-identity refers to a sense of belonging to or being a member of a population with a sense of ethnic identity. It can be a strong element in personal self-identity. However, that is not always the case. To be defined externally as Hispanic does not mean that the individual person perceives the self as being Hispanic or living out life as a Hispanic person. Ethnicity as an individual may or may not be accepted. This consideration suggests that ethnicity is an elusive term to define and use, leading to questions such as who is Hispanic and when is that person behaving or living out life as a Hispanic person.

Ethnicity is difficult to define with uniform and universal precision. Even the use of ethnic terms is widely debated. Some terms are more acceptable than others; some are considered derogatory. For example, which term is more acceptable, Hispanic or Latino? Such questions remind us that ethnicity is a very important issue.

More than a mere reminder that the discussion concerns an ethnic population, or that this Protestant population happens to be Hispanic, ethnicity points to a significant element in the self-identity and understanding of the population discussed. To call oneself Hispanic is a matter of self-definition and affirmation. Hispanic Protestants are quite clear about, proud of, and insistent upon their ethnic identity and cultural heritage. To become or to be Protestant is not to give up ethnicity. In Hispanic Protestantism a unique combination of ethnicity and religious traditions from different sources are blended in such a way that both the religious traditions and the ethnic-cultural sources play critical roles in defining and shaping life. Ethnicity is not an inconsequential element, but an essential and defining factor.

The terms *Hispanic* and *Latino* are used interchangeably throughout the volume. Although both are commonly used within the population in general and the Hispanic Protestant communities in particular, the term *Latino* seems to be increasingly the term of choice. Hispanic is a term stemming from bureaucratic and political need. *Latino* is a term long used in the Americas. Nonetheless, the terms are used to refer to those populations that identify themselves as Hispanic or Latino within the United States.

There is not one Hispanic population in the United States, but several. They trace their histories and cultures to Mexico, the Caribbean, Central America, and South America. An important exception is the historic Hispanic population of the Southwest, which traces its origins to settlements in this geographic area prior to the establishment of the United States.

As populations from distinct nations of origin, each could be defined as an ethnic population. Each has a distinct sense of peoplehood with a unique history and a common language. Their national origins and identities are important to their self-understanding. However, Hispanic populations have much in common with one another, to such an extent that their identities can broadly be shared. These populations share a common language—Spanish—and trace their histories to the Spanish conquest. They experienced mestizaje or mulatez—the blending with indigenous peoples on the mainland and African peoples in the Caribbean. It is at such a level that the terms *Hispanic* or *Latino* can be used and make sense at all. Although there is no one Hispanic ethnic population, as a whole its members compose the U.S. Hispanic population. It must be remembered that the term Hispanic is a term developed and uniquely used in the United States. There are no Hispanics in Latin America! Mexicans, Puerto Ricans, or Salvadorans, along with other populations from Latin American nations, are defined as Hispanic when in the United States. In Latin America, national identities are the identities held and known.

Hispanics: Immigration and Population Growth

Hispanics have emerged as an important population in the United States. Although their history can be traced to the Spanish settlements prior to the founding of the thirteen colonies and United States, their size, cultural influence, and political significance have, until recently, gone unrecognized. Political revolutions and wars in Cuba and Central America, and economic stresses such as in Mexico and Central America, have resulted in high levels of Latino immigration. In addition, economic opportunities have encouraged many Puerto Ricans to move to the mainland. Furthermore, the Hispanic population has one of the highest birth rates in the United States. All of this together has produced a large Hispanic population estimated to be over 22 million in 1990 and 26 million in 1995. It is expected to increase to nearly 31 million by the year 2000. The U.S. Bureau of the Census estimates (mid-level estimates) that Hispanics will number 45 million in 2010, 61 million in 2020, and over 100 million by the year 2040. By the middle of the next century (2050) or about fifty years from now, there will be more than 128 million Hispanics in the United States.

Mainline Protestants: A Definition

The second definer for Hispanic Protestants is the term *Protestant*. As with ethnic identity, religious identity is a crucial aspect of self-understanding among Hispanic Protestants. Because being a Protestant within the Hispanic community is such a critical distinction, its significance cannot be overlooked. Although many refer to all non-Roman Catholics as Protestants, it is important to note that the non-Catholic community is diverse. It includes mainline Protestants, Pentecostals, nondenominational groups, and others such as Jehovah's Witnesses, the Mormons, and Seventh-day Adventists. This volume focuses on mainline or Old-line Protestants. These include denominations such as the United Methodists, Presbyterians, Lutherans, Disciples of Christ, and Baptists. Some refer to these denominations as "Old-line" because of their historical significance.

For Hispanic Protestants, mainline denominations are significant because of their role in the origins of this religious population. Mainline denominations not only brought the Protestant faith to Latinos in the Southwest as part of their westward expansion under the influence of manifest destiny, but also introduced it in the Caribbean and other parts of Latin America. Hispanic Protestants, to a large extent, are the product of historical missionary movements of mainline Protestant denominations aimed at the Hispanic populations during the nineteenth and twentieth centuries. The Methodists and Presbyterians played especially key roles in the Southwest and the Caribbean. The Baptists have also played important roles in this effort. Other historically active denominations include the Disciples and Lutherans.

Protestantes: Toward a Framework of Confession from the Margins

Marginality. To be Hispanic and Protestant involves a unique sense of being and identity which overlaps two realities—the sociocultural reality of an ethnic population, and the socioreligious reality of being Protestant and part of larger Protestant denominations. To be Hispanic and Protestant is to be Protestant in an ethnic reality culturally different from the dominant culture, but which has also been historically shaped by the Roman Catholic tradition. In such a reality, to be Protestant is to hold a religious identity and confess a faith both of which are perceived as different from the dominant and historic religious identity and faith of Hispanic communities. As a result, Hispanic Protestants are defined as marginal in the core religious culture of Hispanic life.

Nonetheless, Hispanic Protestants are part of the broader Hispanic reality. They are defined and perceived by the larger society as members of an ethnic minority population of color, and are subject to the same racial attitudes and social differential treatment as are all Hispanics. As Hispanics they live in the same social, political, and economic margins of the broader society and participate in the struggles for justice and survival along with their Hispanic neighbors.

To be Hispanic and Protestant is to be a part of religious denominations predominantly Anglo. In this context, Latinos participate in denominational realities that reflect Anglo/Celtic histories and cultures. Thus, much of the theology, liturgy, music, and symbols reflect a northern European heritage. As a result, much of Hispanic Protestant music and many of the liturgies and other materials have been translated from English into Spanish. In addition, Hispanics have historically played lesser roles in denominational structures and leadership positions. In essence, they have been on the margins of their denominations as well.

Hispanic Protestants have been shaped by the distinct realities of Hispanic communities, the larger dominant culture, and predominantly Anglo denominations. They are products of the formative influences these realities generate. As Hispanics, they are formed culturally by their ethnic heritage. As citizens and members of this society they are American. As Protestants, they are formed by this religious tradition. Yet, they experience the forces of marginalization in all of these realities.

Hispanic Protestants are products of the predicament of existing in the margins. While they are shaped by their cultures and religious faith, they are also shaped by the experience of marginality itself. They overlap several realities yet are distinct from each of those realities. Hispanic Protestants are both Hispanic and Protestant but not entirely like either one. They are in both realities but are not entirely defined by those realities. They have been defined as different in both settings. They are Hispanic, but in that community they are distinguished by their Protestant faith and identity; they are

Protestant, but they are defined as different because of their ethnicity and culture. In both situations, marginality has been the common experience.

Confession as Ethnic Affirmation. To be Hispanic and Protestant is to affirm both realities—the sociocultural reality of being Hispanic, and the socioreligious reality of being a Protestant. Hispanic Protestants claim their ethnicity and their religious faith. Although their experience has involved pain, loneliness, and misunderstanding, they hold their ethnicity and religious faith as core ingredients of their identity and being. To claim both, therefore, is to claim the heritage of culture and faith. It is also to recognize the predicament of being in the margins and the potential of being in and touching two worlds.

To be Hispanic Protestant is to affirm Hispanic ethnicity. It is to celebrate Hispanic culture and traditions. This affirmation may involve participating in and practicing traditions that have historically been associated with Roman Catholicism. For example, many Protestants practice *compadrazgos* and *quinceañeras,* traditionally associated with the Catholic church. But this affirmation also involves the enjoyment of Latin sounds, rhythms, foods, and certainly the Spanish language. To be Hispanic Protestant is to confess publicly one's ethnic identity—a proclamation of ethnicity as a valued element of one's being and identity.

As an act of confession, to proclaim Hispanic identity is to stand with all Hispanics and their realities. It is to affirm solidarity with Hispanics regardless of religious identification or other social definitions. To be Hispanic and Protestant is to participate in the Hispanic world and to address issues facing Hispanic communities such as poverty, racial oppression, violence, and marginality. It means to be one with the Hispanic community, and to be the prophetic servant within that context. Hispanic Protestants will stand on the Hispanic side.

Confession as Protestant Affirmation. To be Hispanic and Protestant is also an act of confession of religious faith and practice. It is to claim a faith grounded on Protestant theological heritage and a practice of religious ritual and life distinct from Roman Catholicism. Hispanic Protestants are Protestant in every sense of the word, and take their Protestantism quite seriously. Most have paid a price for their religious identity, even after generations of Protestantism. Many have converted from Roman Catholicism and have experienced radical changes in their personal, social, and religious lives.

As an act of religious confession, Hispanic Protestantism reflects central theological tenets of Protestantism such as Divine grace and salvation by faith alone. There is also a leaning toward a more conservative theological understanding of the Holy Spirit and eternal life. The Bible is a central symbol and an important source of authority. Religious life centers on worship as celebration, biblical reading and study, prayer, and witnessing to one's faith. Implications for daily living have historically leaned toward pietistic practices and habits. For many, especially first-generation Protestants, to be Protestant is to stand for specific faith beliefs and religious practices distinct from those of Catholicism.

Views from the Margins: Critical Perspectives. To be Hispanic and Protestant means to exist in the margins of two realities—a Hispanic world in which being Protestant means being at the margins of a Catholic context, and a Protestant world in which being Hispanic means being at the margins of a non-Hispanic context. From such a position of marginality, Hispanic Protestants have developed critical perspectives within these realities. Protestant reality is examined through Hispanic eyes. This involves examining Protestant theology and denominational histories, life, and ministries from the perspective of the Hispanic community and other poor and marginal populations. Advocacy and loyal criticism are common marks of Hispanic Protestants within their denominations.

Within the Hispanic reality Protestants also tend to view that context with a critical perspective. To affirm their Hispanicity does not necessarily mean that everything defined as Hispanic is affirmed and maintained. Many behaviors, values, and other practices associated with Hispanic culture and life come under careful and critical scrutiny: for example, attitudes and behaviors toward women, gender roles, and unhealthful lifestyles are frequently questioned. To view the Hispanic context through Protestant eyes is to ask why, and to seek justice and grace in Hispanic communities.

Life in the Margins as Opportunity. Hispanic Protestants live in the margins of several realities. They participate in more than one world. They live out various aspects of their lives within contexts which not only differ from each other, but are at times at odds or in tension and conflict with each other. This points to another aspect of being Hispanic Protestant— that of being a bridge or connector between several realities. As Hispanic and Protestant, Hispanic Protestants provide an overlapping link between Catholic and Protestant realities as well as between Hispanic and Anglo communities. This adds another dimension to confession. In this context, confession means to be a servant and a means of mutual understanding and respect between worlds that have allowed ethnicity and religion to come between them.

Hispanic Protestants as a New Mestizaje. To be Hispanic and Protestant is to live in two realities: the Hispanic Catholic reality and the Anglo Protestant reality. It means to be in both, to be of both, yet not entirely like either.

Hispanic Protestants are different because they are a new creation—a new blending, a new mestizaje. As such, Hispanic Protestants embody the blending of two significant cultures—Hispanic ethnic cultures and Anglo Protestant religious faith. The future of this country is a multicultural future in which the many people and religions of the world will come together in new and exciting blendings. Hispanic Protestants are a sign of today and of the future.

Organization of the Text

This volume has been organized into four main sections. The first section addresses historical roots and the development of Protestantism among Hispanic populations in the Southwest. Of particular interest is the type of Protestantism which moved into the southwestern parts of the United States and established the initial missionary work among the Latino population already settled there. Ed Sylvest convincingly points out that Celtic Protestantism played a strong role in shaping the initial culture of Hispanic Protestantism in the Southwest. Daisy Machado addresses the history of Protestant missionary work among Hispanics with special attention to social, racial, and cultural forces, which contributed to its peculiar development. Paul Barton offers a specific study of the relationship between Anglos and Latinos in the historical development of Hispanic Protestantism, and Tomas Atencio tells the story of its development in a particular region of the Southwest—New Mexico.

The second section addresses the nature of the theological task within and from Hispanic perspectives. José David Rodriguez initiates this section by proposing that doing theology from a Hispanic perspective involves a critical rereading of recent Protestant theology and denominational practices much in the same spirit as the historic Reformation. Such a new reformation would reflect the perspectives of those who have been silent and marginalized as a religious people. Luis Pedraja follows with an examination of Hispanic theologies using process theology and postmodern tools, and points to the blurring of traditional boundaries between Catholic and Protestant theologies. Ismael García offers excellent insights to Hispanic moral reasoning and suggests that although Hispanics engage in many of the traditional forms of moral reasoning, an ethics of care which emphasizes community and its nurturing and sense of mutuality, is emerging. Francisco García-Treto completes this section with a review of Hispanic hermeneutics by pointing to the significance of social location and the work of the interpretative community resulting in the emergence of a distinct reading of the Bible from a Hispanic perspective and location.

The third section examines sociological and contextual dynamics, which have historically challenged the Hispanic Protestant church. Teresa C. Sauceda opens the section with an examination of the significance of race and racial categorization in the historical emergence of Hispanic Protestantism. She convincingly points out that Latinos have historically been defined racially and subjected to racial mistreatment. As a result Hispanics have had to struggle with racial attitudes, politics, barriers, and challenges. Harold Recinos follows with an examination of the most recent immigrants—Salvadorans—and the challenges they present to Hispanic Protestant churches. Recinos argues that Hispanic Protestantism has much to learn and gain by accepting the struggles and symbols of these newest immigrants. Edwin Hernandez concludes the section with an examination of key social and religious shifts which hold considerable implications for mainline Protestant denominations. He gives special attention to the shift toward evangelical religious groups and the meaning this shift has for mainline Protestant churches and their ministry among Latinos.

The fourth section offers insights into the nature of the Latino church, its ministry, congregational life, and the status of Hispanic clergy. Ruben Armendariz opens this section by examining the character of the Latino church and suggests that church as *familia* offers helpful insights to the life and work of these congregations. Jorge Lara-Braud extends the discussion through reflections of the nature and context of Hispanic clergy. Maldonado completes the discussion by reporting on a national survey that profiles Latino clergypersons. This chapter offers a social, theological, and religious profile of those who serve and lead these congregations.

This volume is an effort to call attention to the Hispanic Protestant reality within mainline denominations, and to begin a more systematic study of and reflection on the history, theology, ministry, and leadership of this religious population. It is not an exhaustive analysis, but merely an initial contribution to a conversation long overdue.

David Maldonado, Jr.

Part I

Historical Roots and Development

Chapter 1

Bordering Cultures and the Origins of Hispanic Protestant Christianity

Ed Sylvest

Three hundred years after the Reformation, in a region remote from the cultural centers of Europe or the Americas, Protestant Christianity at last found an enduring home within a Hispanic context. There were two attempts at establishing Protestantism on the Iberian Peninsula, one, an indigenous movement in the sixteenth century, the other, a missionary effort from British Methodism in the nineteenth century. The sixteenth-century effort succumbed to the Inquisition; the nineteenth-century effort simply could not overcome the obstacles and opposition that developed in the tumultuous political disruptions of the period.

This essay proposes the thesis that Hispanic Protestantism, manifest in enduring institutional structures and faith communities, developed on the frontier between Spanish and British North America in the nineteenth century. That development resulted from Protestant evangelization of Mexicans along the border between Mexico and the United States, and in those territories annexed by the United States as a result of Texas independence and the War with Mexico. It was sustained in a cultural matrix constituted primarily by peoples whose heritage was that of the borderlands of North Britain. Scots, Irish, Scots-Irish, and English borderers shared a common culture formed on the frontier in Britain. These Anglo-Celts and their descendants in North America replicated relational patterns that had obtained among themselves and with three other groups of English-speaking immigrants: Puritans from East Anglia, Anglican Cavaliers and indentured servants from the South of England, and Quakers from the North Midlands.[1]

Incipient Spanish Protestant communities emerged in Seville and Valladolid in the mid–sixteenth century, but by 1562 they were effectively suppressed and eliminated by the Inquisition. Some members of those communities escaped into exile. One of them, Casiodoro de Reina, produced a vernacular text of the Scriptures that has long been the most popular version of the Bible used by Hispanic Protestants in the Americas. That scriptural text perdures as an important contribution to the Hispanic cultural heritage from a courageous community of men and women, many of them *conversos* (persons of Jewish ancestry who had converted to Protestantism), who acknowledged the primacy of Scripture as authority for faith and practice.[2]

British occupation of Gibraltar in 1704 led to circumstances that in the nineteenth century (simultaneously with the movement of Protestantism into the Spanish-speaking frontier of North America) resulted in an effort to extend Protestant missionary outreach into Spain. Gibraltar became the base from which the faltering attempt at such a project was undertaken. Neither in Spain nor in Gibraltar did an enduring Spanish-speaking Protestant community develop as a result of that effort.[3] However, once again, there remains an important legacy from that enterprise for the development of Hispanic Protestantism on the Anglo Celtic-Hispanic border of North America. The English missionary who labored in Gibraltar, H. D. Rule, commended Benigno Cardenas, whom he met in London, to the Missionary Society of the Methodist Episcopal Church in New York. Under the auspices of that Society, Cardenas, in 1853, became the first ordained Hispanic Protestant minister in the territory of New Mexico.

Though neither of these efforts established Hispanic Protestantism on the Iberian Peninsula itself, each of them contributed materially to the origin and development of that tradition in the borderlands of the United States Southwest. These fragile roots, along with the language, provide Hispanic American Protestantism with a delicate, but not insignificant connection to the main trunk of the Hispanic cultural tree. In all other respects the origins of Hispanic Protestantism and many of its defining characteristics must be understood in terms of a dynamic process of cross-fertilization through which hybrid forms of religious expression contribute to the creation of what Virgil Elizondo has called the "new *mestizaje*," the new blend that forms Hispanic American culture in the United States.[4]

The evolution of Protestant Christianity in the United States is as important an element in the history of Hispanic Protestantism as the history of the Hispanic communities themselves. Appropriate and necessary though it is to understand Hispanic American Christianity in all its forms as an aspect of Latin American Christianity, as the CEHILA project does,[5] recognizing Hispanic American Protestantism as an element of what historians call "American Christianity" is fundamental to understanding the Hispanic Protestant expression of Christian faith. The story of Hispanic Protestantism requires knowing its Anglo-Celtic roots.

As in the British Isles, Anglo-Celts in North America predominated culturally in the so-called backlands—the Appalachian and trans-

Appalachian frontiers of English-speaking colonization. That was due in part to their own preference to live in areas that permitted the maintenance of their distinctive heritage, and partly because of the prejudice other Anglo groups held for these "barbarians."[6] Consequently, Anglo-Celtic backlanders constituted the leading edge of contact between English-speaking and Spanish-speaking peoples on the North American frontier.

"Crackers" and "Chicanos," both in their own context, met on the frontier between English-speaking and Spanish-speaking America. In some respects, that meeting repeated an ancient encounter between Celts and Iberians on another cultural frontier. The earlier encounter generated an ethnic stock that became the predominant human population of pre-Roman Iberia; the latter may well generate an ethnic stock that predominates in at least the greater part of the United States Southwest, if not other areas of North America. Hispanic American Protestantism is a distinctive characteristic of that encounter.[7]

Anglo-Celtic Border Culture

"We are a mixed people." Thus did a border immigrant to North America describe his culture in the eighteenth century. They were mixed in many ways. "They were mixed in their social rank, mixed in their religious denominations, and most profoundly mixed in their ancestry, which was Celtic, Roman, German, English, Scandinavian, Irish, and Scottish in varying proportions. They were also mixed in their place of residence—coming as they did from England, Scotland and Ireland."[8]

But for all their mixture, they shared a common culture forged on an anvil of endemic violence. Through a period of seven centuries, 1040–1745, English and Scottish monarchs fought over the territory between the two realms; and, on a smaller scale, the local violence of robbery, rape, pillage, and murder in a region devoid of authority competent to maintain public order prevailed. Even the social transformations set in motion by the Act of Union, 1706–1707, produced new violence as ancient patterns of behavior were suppressed by force and old systems of governance replaced by new. Absentee landlords displaced warlords. The disparity between rich and poor increased as the wealth of the land was exported to southern England. Resistance led to armed revolt and further repression.[9]

Ireland suffered an imposed colonial regime governed by an elite of Anglican plantation owners. Many lowland Scots were forcibly resettled in Ireland. There, they were harassed by English overlords and the Irish as well. Some of these Scots-Irish were banished to the American colonies. Others, fleeing the burden of taxation, collapse of industry, and the continuing challenge of famine and disease, came to America voluntarily in search of opportunity.[10]

The refugees were not well received in America. They brought with them a disposition of belligerence toward other ethnic groups, and although they entered primarily through the colony of Pennsylvania, they created such havoc that the generally tolerant Quakers pushed them toward the backcountry across the mountains to serve as a buffer between the Indians and the eastern centers of population. Many of these Anglo-Celtic borderers moved southward along the mountains into Maryland, Virginia, and the Carolinas. "They gradually became the dominant English-speaking culture in a broad belt of territory that extended from the highlands of Appalachia through much of the Old Southwest. In the nineteenth century, they moved across the Mississippi River to Arkansas, Missouri, Oklahoma and Texas. By the twentieth century, their influence would be felt as far west as New Mexico, Arizona, and Southern California."[11]

In 1787 the Spanish governor of Florida described the American backlanders as "nomadic like Arabs and . . . distinguished from savages only in their color, language, and superiority of their depraved cunning and untrustworthiness. They were a distinctive people . . . called 'crackers.' " In his view, Cracker frontier dwellers "chose the wilderness life of Indians in order 'to escape all legal authority,' and they had inherited the insatiable appetite for land of their British forbears."[12]

Governor Zéspedes's opinion of Crackers within his portion of the Spanish frontier with British America is clearly pejorative, and consistent with descriptions of Anglo-Celtic culture throughout the North American South, including Texas. Grady McWhiney provides a comprehensive list of characteristics:

> Eye-witness accounts of life in the United States before the 1860s . . . generally characterized Southerners as more hospitable, generous, frank, courteous, spontaneous, lazy, lawless, militaristic, wasteful, impractical, and reckless than Northerners, who were in turn more reserved, shrewd, disciplined, gauche, enterprising, acquisitive, careful, frugal, ambitious, pacific, and practical than Southerners. . . . The Old South was a leisure-oriented society that fostered idleness and gaiety, where people favored the spoken word over the written and enjoyed their sensual pleasure. Family ties reportedly were stronger in the South than in the North; Southerners, whose values were more agrarian than those of Northerners, wasted more time and con-

sumed more tobacco and liquor and were less concerned with the useful and the material. Yankees, on the other hand, were cleaner, neater, more puritanical, less mercurial, better educated, more orderly and progressive, worked harder, and kept the Sabbath better than Southerners.[13]

Through the migration of these Crackers, religious practices and values rooted in the cultural experience of the British borderlands became important elements in the cultural dynamics of the southwestern United States and affected the formation of Hispanic Protestantism.

Anglo-Celtic Borderer Religion: Significance and Impact

David Hackett Fischer identifies the primary characteristics of North American backcountry religion as "the camp meeting, the Christian fellowship, the love feast, the evangelical preacher, the theology of Protestant fundamentalism and born-again revivalism."[14] Though certain of Fischer's terms may be subject to discussion, those forms of religious expression that developed in the bordering region of the British Isles and were brought by Anglo-Celtic immigrants to North America define historical trends of belief and practice in American evangelical Christianity that affect the shape of Hispanic Protestantism, whether mainline or charismatic-Pentecostal.

Borderer religion survives, in forms similar to the original, in the mountain religion of present-day Appalachia.[15] It survives, with greater modification, as a defining ethos in Presbyterian, United Methodist, Baptist, and Disciples churches, especially in those areas into which Anglo-Celts moved in great numbers, primarily the South and Southwest. In dramatic ways values and forms evolving out of borderer religion are manifest even more significantly in the burgeoning "spirit movement" expressed in Pentecostal and charismatic congregations all over the Americas.

Ironically, mainline Hispanic American Protestantism represents a significant pocket of survival of significant elements of Anglo-Celtic borderer religion within the historically dominant Protestant denominations of North America. This is not unique to Hispanic Protestantism, but it is instructive. It means, for example, that more members of the Rio Grande Conference of The United Methodist Church are likely to be in sympathy with the evangelical caucus, Good News, than with the denomination's boards of Church and Society or Global Ministries, even though those two agencies often advocate for many of the justice issues that materially affect the lives of Hispanics in the United States.

That Hispanic American Protestantism preserves much of the ethos of

Anglo-Celtic borderer religion does not exclude other influences, nor does it discount the significance of those elements of borderland Hispanic American culture itself that either directly or indirectly define the tradition. There are important parallels between the history of Hispanic American and Anglo-Celtic borderers. The history of the Iberian Peninsula is very like that of the borderlands of northern Britain, contributing to similar cultural developments. Historical reality on the northern frontier of New Spain replicated many of the patterns that obtained for Anglo-Celts as they moved across the North American continent. New Spain's northern frontier was to that colonial enterprise what the Appalachian and trans-Appalachian frontier was to British colonials.[16]

Within the matrix were Anglo-Celtic cultural influences on emergent Hispanic American Protestantism and elements coming from other cultural traditions, all of them "celticized" to a degree. Puritanism, English in origin, but shaped by the American context, formed a value system that motivated some of the earliest Protestant missionaries in the Southwest. Those values not only influenced individual missionaries like Presbyterian Melinda Rankin, and Methodist Nannie Emory Holding, they also shaped institutional values and policies determining denominational approaches to Hispanic ministry.

German Pietism played a similar role, though it is difficult to describe precisely the means by which it became an active influence. Many Germans lived as colonists within Texas, both as a Mexican state and as a republic, but it was more likely the influence of Moravian pietism on the Anglo-Celtic backlanders who lived among German settlers on the Appalachian frontier that was of greatest importance. German Pietism also affected denominational values and practice, especially among the Methodists, who received Pietist influences through their impact on Anglican Christianity, as well as through John Wesley's personal experiences with the Moravians in America as well as in Europe. Those Puritan and Pietist influences became embedded in the Anglo-Celtic matrix, and survive, especially among mainline Hispanic Protestants, as defining elements of that community.

Borderer Religion: Origins and Characteristics

Mixed in ancestry, the borderers of north Britain were also mixed in religious affiliation. Most who came from Scotland and Northern Ireland were Presbyterian, though some were Roman Catholic. Most from the English side of the border were Anglican. But whether Presbyterian or Anglican, these borderers appreciated forms of piety and belief that emphasized religious *experience*, "the working of the Holy Spirit," as opposed to a primary emphasis on right doctrine and rational persuasion. "Many Scottish and Irish Presbyterians called themselves People of the New Light before coming to America. They believed in 'free grace,' and before emigrating they had formed the habit of gathering in 'field meetings' and 'prayer societies,' a custom which they carried to America and established in the backcountry."[17]

The English borderers, though mostly Anglican, were likewise enamored of experiential religion. Many of them became Baptists and Methodists as the latter movement gained momentum in Britain. Whether English or Celtic, most borderers regarded clergy with disdain, calling them "hirelings."[18] The result was forms of Christian faith and practice strongly lay in character. Early Methodism in North America was primarily a lay movement, and it is noteworthy that among the Methodists, it was the Methodist Episcopal Church, South, that led in the advocacy and advance of lay participation in church governance at the denominational level.

As sectarian movements developed within Presbyterianism in Scotland and in America, and as Baptist, Methodist, and Anglican missionaries and circuit riders worked among the backlanders of Appalachia, a strong militancy within the various groups developed. There was much conflict among the groups. Fischer notes the prevalence of military metaphors in backcountry sermons and hymns. "Prayers were invoked for vengeance and the destruction of enemies. When these Christian warriors were not battling among themselves they fell upon the Indians with the same implacable fury."[19] In the Southwest that militancy was directed against Mexicans as well as Indians.

Militancy, anticlericalism, "field meetings," and "heart religion" all influenced Hispanic American Protestantism. A look at "field meetings" and their evolution toward revivalistic piety provides an avenue of approach to the actual meeting of cultures and to some of the consequences of that meeting for the religious life of Hispanic Americans in the Southwest.

The revival on the North American frontier was actually rooted in the religious experience of peoples in the British borderlands. In the 1620s and 30s in the southwest Scottish lowlands and in Ulster, among the Presbyterians, many of them Scots, the phenomenon of revivalistic preaching was born in the context of sacramental festivals. Those occasions were grand community events lasting over a period of several days. Hundreds, sometimes thousands, of people from adjacent parishes gathered for eucharistic celebrations that involved prayer and preaching for conversion as well as sharing the communion itself. Many of the elements of religious ecstasy characteristic of response to American revivalistic preaching were first observed in the seventeenth-century meetings.[20]

By the time George Whitefield persuaded John Wesley to preach in the open air at Bristol, such practices had become common, if not commonplace, events in the bordering region of north Britain. In the same year, 1739, Whitefield came to North America and undertook field preaching in Philadelphia and elsewhere in the colonies. He created quite a stir with his Arminian theology, but the outdoor preaching events were not new to the Scots-Irish, and others, who came eagerly to hear him. As for the revival itself, it had begun five years earlier under the inspiration of Jonathan Edwards in New England, and even earlier than that with Presbyterian ministers in the middle colonies.[21]

This First Great Awakening was followed by another in early decades of the nineteenth century, focused in the heartland of Anglo-Celtic settlement in North America. Throughout the 1780s and 90s in the mountains of western Pennsylvania, Virginia, and North Carolina, James McGready and other Presbyterian ministers celebrated outdoor sacramental festivals that ignited revivals. All of this activity provided momentum for the famous camp meeting at Cane Ridge, Kentucky, in August 1801. The Cane Ridge event included eighteen Presbyterian ministers and some number of Methodist and Baptist preachers as well. Approximately twenty thousand persons attended this gathering, which lasted over a period of days.[22]

Cane Ridge, the "Woodstock" of American Protestantism, gave impetus to the rapid growth and extension of Methodist and Baptist ministry in the trans-Appalachian West, and ironically, to the displacement of Presbyterianism as the leading denomination among backlanders as they moved farther and farther west. Most Anglo-Celts who remained in the mountains retained their preference for particular expressions of Calvinist theology, especially its New Light or New Side modalities. The Methodists gained a momentum that led to their becoming the nation's largest Protestant denomination, a position now relinquished to the Southern Baptists. Methodist and Baptist polity, along with their less stringent educational requirements for ordination, allowed a degree of flexibility that Presbyterians with their emphasis on formal ministerial education could not maintain. Nevertheless, among these three mainline denominations, the Presbyterians were earliest in ministry with Mexicans in the Southwest and in Mexico, an effort they began in 1839 in the Republic of Texas.[23]

The Chicano-Cracker encounter on the northern frontier of New Spain, on both sides of the present international boundary, defined the character of Hispanic American culture in its nineteenth-century origins. The areas inside present-day Texas and New Mexico were the critical points of contact, and it was in these two places that Hispanic American Protestantism began.

Hispanic Borderer Culture

Like the borderers of north Britain, the people of the northern frontier of New Spain were a "mixed people." As the encounter between these two bordering cultures unfolded in the late eighteenth century, New Spain entered its fourth century of existence as a political entity. It was populated by culturally and ethnically diverse peoples who had achieved various levels of accommodation and assimilation with one another: a ruling elite of European-born, peninsular Spaniards; a growing group of American-born Spaniards, the *criollos,* who controlled much of the economic infrastructure, but were deprived of political authority at the highest levels of government; large groups of unassimilated Indians living in many areas, and especially on the northern frontier; a relatively small number of persons of African descent; an increasingly important population of *mestizos,* persons of mixed ethnic heritage, developing as the predominant population of an emergent Mexican nation.

All those groups were present within the region, and by the time Protestantism became an element of the cultural encounter within the frontier between British America and Spanish America, a distinctive culture had emerged. It was a culture parallel in important ways with that of the bordering region of north Britain and the backlands of British North America.

Politically, the region was successively controlled by Spain, the Republic of Mexico, the Republics of Texas and Mexico, and finally the United States and the Republic of Mexico. Remote and isolated from the centers of government and "high" culture, the area was vulnerable to foreign influence by invasion, settlement, and commercial enterprise. That vulnerability resulted in an administrative reorganization instituted by the Spanish Bourbon monarchy as a means of protection. In 1772 the Comandancia General of the Provincias Internas encompassing Alta California, Nuevo Mexico, Tejas, Sonora, Sinaloa, Chihuahua, Durango, Coahuila, and Nuevo Santander (Nuevo Leon and Tamaulipas) was established to secure the frontier and to promote development of the region. Among the important consequences of this process "was the development of a *norteño* Mexican society in Nuevo Mexico, Alta California, and Tejas, which was linked . . . to Mexican society in general. . . . By 1800 the frontier society was Mexican culturally, and by 1822 it was Mexican in its political organization and sovereignty."[24]

Much like the border region of the British Isles, pervasive and persistent violence characterized this North American frontier. The constant threat of conflict with Indians, and an increasing threat of violent confrontation with British Americans intent upon promoting their own interests even in opposition to the law and the terms of the agreements by which they had been permitted to settle within the area were a persistent menace to peace. Miguel Ramos de Arizpe described the situation in an 1812 report:

> These provinces, being by their location the natural bulwark of all the kingdom of Mexico, are in consequence on a frontier exposed to the barbarous Indian nations. Their inhabitants, therefore, are obliged to serve not only as militiamen but even as common soldiers. They are all soldiers; and in Coahuila and Texas, each month they are required to present their arms for inspection. This necessity, otherwise deplorable, has formed in them an extremely commendable character of integrity, honor, and subordination. . . . With this combination of such excellent qualities, which result from the celestial climate and cultivated by such honest occupations, each citizen becomes a worker, each worker a soldier, and each soldier a hero that is worth a hundred ordinary soldiers.[25]

In the same report Ramos spoke of the "salubrious air, the agreeable climate, the exceedingly rich soil," that sustained an agricultural enterprise that formed the character of the population. "They are," he said, "truly inflexible to intrigue, virtuously steadfast, haters of tyranny and disorder, justly devoted to true liberty, and naturally the most inclined toward all moral and political virtues. They are very much devoted also to the liberal and mechanical arts."[26]

Ramos's romantic description of virtuous, hard-working, citizen soldiers parallels the view advanced in 1821 by a Mexican commission established to consider sources from which to encourage immigration to populate the frontier, that of all the Europeans, "the Irish would be the most desirable settlers." "They were loyal Catholics, so loyal to their religion that they had suffered the most cruel persecution without hesitating in their perseverance. They had, in addition, outstanding moral virtues; their industry and love of work had no limits; they were not friendly to England or the United States; and, in case of war against the empire, Mexico could count on good soldiers on the boundary of its frontier."[27] However valid these perceptions may be as descriptive of core values, they tend, in both cases, to belie the actual material circumstances and lifestyle of either "chicanos" or "crackers." Nor were all the Irish Catholics.

A thorough comparison of the various folkways of these two groups yields a remarkably consistent parallel between the cultures of the Spanish-speaking and the English-speaking groups. Cattle and sheep ranching were especially important elements in the economy of the region, echoing traditions of agriculture that had developed on the Iberian Peninsula, as well as among the border peoples of north Britain and British North America. Although in many areas families sustained themselves on small farms, as in the area of northern New Mexico, large haciendas worked by tenants replicated a pattern of landholding and employment characteristic of the British. Yet the similarity of ethos and cultural values within the two groups, a circumstance suggesting the potential for compatible relationships, was undermined by prejudice sustained by religious sanction.

Anglo-Saxonism and Manifest Destiny

English colonization of North America began with the presupposition that their colonies would exemplify for other nations the values of Anglo-Saxon culture and would provide a material base from which to extend those values to other peoples. Massachusetts Bay Puritans led the way. "As American settlements advanced outward, the Puritans not only saw God's kingdom moving to the West, but thought of America as the place from which the renovation of the world would begin."[28]

The success of the Revolution reinforced a sense of special privilege and obligation that grew within the new republic. John Adams and Thomas Jefferson were persuaded, as Jefferson put it, that "our Confederacy must be viewed as the nest from which all America, North and South, is to be peopled."[29]

Many eighteenth-century Anglo Americans, especially those along the eastern seaboard, who were increasingly isolated from the tensions of frontier life, and inspired by Enlightenment idealism concerning human nature, believed that all human beings were fundamentally equal and possessed of certain innate capacities that could be released by education and training.[30] Those who lived in circumstances deemed inferior could be elevated and, in the case of the westward expansion of the nation, eventually absorbed into its population. That was particularly true of attitudes toward the Indians immediately following the Revolution.[31]

But there were other voices to be heard. On the frontier, populated largely by Anglo-Celts, "America's empire builders" rejected the notion of equality and expressed the view that Indians were "violent savages." Their view mirrored one side of the ambivalent perspective held by New England Puritans, who admired native peoples and had high hopes of saving their souls and acculturating them; but who also, when native peoples preferred to maintain their own cultures, regarded them as "stumbling blocks to civilization . . . and agents of the devil."[32] "In general, the Indians, by the latter years of the seventeenth century, were despised because they had tried to remain Indian and had shown little desire to become Christian gentlemen. The Indians could therefore be thrown off the land, mistreated, or slaughtered, because in rejecting the opportunities offered to them they had shown that they were sunk deep in irredeemable savagery."[33]

Westward-moving border peoples, feeling neglected by the cultural elites of the East, expressed their disdain for Enlightenment idealism and Indian policies predicated on education and assimilation. "Scots-Irish in Pennsylvania attacked the pacifism of the Quaker leaders, frontiersmen in the valleys of east Tennessee saw little merit in a North Carolina government that neglected their defense, and Kentuckians were to take matters into their own hands as they despaired of help from Virginia."[34] Of course, all this was prelude to the encounter of these very peoples with the predominantly Indo-Hispano mestizo cultures of the trans-Mississippi southwest, and to the implementation of policies of removal in the Old Southwest of the new republic.

With the election of Andrew Jackson in 1828 the borderers prevailed. The fate of native peoples was sealed. They would be removed to lands west of the Mississippi. Even those Cherokees and others in the South who had assimilated and become Christian, many intermarried with non-Indians, would be moved.

Simultaneous with these political developments, new scientific theories "justifying" the popular idea that some peoples were superior to others were affirmed as intellectual warrants for economically and politically expedient behavior. "By 1850 the science of man was of vital interest throughout America, scientific proofs of racial separation were widely disseminated, and the future of the American continents and the world was thought of in terms of white domination and the subordination or disappearance of other races."[35]

Anglo-Saxonism became fixed in the national consciousness as an operative sociopolitical ideology through the encounter of British Americans and Hispanic Americans on the new southwestern frontier. "In confronting the Mexicans the Americans clearly formulated the idea of themselves as an Anglo-Saxon race."[36]

Horace Bushnell, Sterling Professor of Christian Education at Yale University, maintained that the "British family" of select Saxon stock was chosen to people the North American continent. He contrasted that British family with the Mexicans with whom, if British peoples should exchange character, "'Five years would make their noble island a seat of poverty and desolation.' For Bushnell, God had reserved America for a special people of Saxon blood."[37] Bushnell was certainly not unique in his sentiment, but it is notable that so prominent a figure in the shaping of Protestant Christian consciousness articulated such a view.

Mexicans, like native peoples, were obstacles to the expansion of Anglo-Saxon settlement and culture. British Americans, pressing the frontier of English-speaking settlement ever farther into Mexican territory, "were not to be blamed for forcibly taking the northern provinces of Mexico, for Mexicans, like Indians, were unable to make proper use of the land. The Mexicans had failed because they were a mixed, inferior race with considerable Indian blood and some black blood. The world would benefit if a superior race shaped the future of the Southwest."[38]

The Texas Revolution and the Mexican War were both justified in terms of the presumed superiority and deservedness of Anglo-Saxons, who had a "manifest destiny" to occupy the American continents. Even those who opposed expansion by military conquest were certain that the innate superiority of Anglo-Saxons would, through commerce and other contact, result, perforce, in the eventual displacement of an inferior race by a superior.[39]

Ironically, many of the agents of Anglo-Saxonist expansionist ideology were not themselves Anglo-Saxons, but Anglo-Celts. Many borderers found it possible to accommodate to the ideology by accepting the growing nativist sentiment that Caucasians of north European descent born in the United States constituted a superior white race. Some believed that "Americans" were a distinctive race and superior precisely because they included the genetic heritage of the "best in the white European races." Reginald Horsman observes that "often . . . politicians of Irish or Scotch-Irish ancestry" held such a view. James Buchanan and Stephen A. Douglas were among those who asserted, "'We are truly a mixed race.' . . . Our ancestry were not all of English origin. They were of Scotch, Irish, German, French, and of Norman descent as well as English."[40]

Thomas Hart Benton of Missouri and Caleb Cushing of Massachusetts were among those who took exception to narrowly defined Anglo-Saxonism by embracing the notion of a superior *American* race that carried the traits of the finest Caucasian heritage. Benton specifically extended Anglo-Saxon identity to include the Celtic, creating the concept of the "Celtic-Anglo-Saxon" division of the Caucasian race. He elevated the Mexicans themselves to the status of "the second power of the NEW WORLD [sic]." Cushing, on the other hand, was convinced that the "Hispano-Americans"

were incapable of self-government and that their territories would gradually fall into "pristine desolation," permitting the people and laws of the
United States to enter and prevail.[41]

Border Religion and a New Border Culture

Not by gradual encroachment alone, but by military conquest and pur-
chase did the people and laws of the United States enter and prevail over
Hispanic territories. Along with the imposition of new political and economic systems, new religious systems were also introduced. This was as
true of Roman Catholic as of Protestant Christianity. The culture of Roman
Catholicism in the United States was dramatically different from that of
Mexico. The culture shock of the meeting between new bishops and their
constituencies in the Southwest was severe for the people as well as for
their new leaders. The well-known conflict between Bishop Jean-Baptiste
Lamy and the people and priests of northern New Mexico is but one inci-
dence of a persistent condition, and one, in the case of Benigno Cardenas,
that had important consequences for Hispanic Protestantism.[42]

Initial efforts at Protestant ministry within Hispanic territories were
actually directed toward those Anglo-Celtic "empire builders" who had
crossed the frontier, some of them illegally, to find opportunity for themselves. There was no particular desire to proselytize Mexicans or to
embrace them within the congregations of English-speaking Protestants.
Such outreach as there was at the beginning was the effort to distribute the
Scriptures and other literature. Methodists David Ayres and William
Headen, and Presbyterian Sumner Bacon, were among those who distributed biblical materials to Mexicans prior to the beginning of ecclesiastically authorized missions.[43]

As those missions were undertaken, they were without exception
understood as preliminary in some fashion to a mission to Mexico itself.
Even the ministries to English-speaking settlers in Texas were justified
in part on the grounds that to "let Texas stand beside Mexico, highly
evangelized, . . . the contrast would serve to show the superiority of the
Protestant over the Catholic religion; the tendency of which would be to
constrain the degraded Mexicans to yield to the influence of that system
of faith, which might elevate them to the like happy condition."[44]

Such sentiment as that articulated by Presbyterian missionary Melinda
Rankin, echoed the ideology of expansionist Anglo-Saxonism. Indeed, she
saw a parallel between the military conquest of Mexico and the religious
campaign for which she hoped to rally support:

Mexico is now open for the dissemination of the Word of life. Its conquest to national power, inspired the martial spirit of American freemen, and shall not the sons of peace and righteousness follow up the victory with those weapons which are might through God to the pulling down of strongholds? . . . Texas may be regarded as the outposts of the enemy's camp, and every means should be used to secure such an important fortification.[45]

Acting on the strength of her conviction, Rankin made her way to Texas, arriving finally at Brownsville in 1852. There, she soon found some "thirty or forty Mexican children" to whom she began to teach the Bible and whose parents "were greatly desirous [that they] should learn the English language, and become Americanized."[46] With that early and enthusiastic response, and the challenge of renewed Roman Catholic efforts to provide schooling for the children of the region, Rankin went back East to raise money and to seek ecclesiastical approval for her work.

Among the motivating circumstances for her work was her discovery that the schoolchildren were taking their Bibles into Mexico where families and friends were eager to receive them. That convinced her that "much good might be done, even by this slight skirmishing on the outposts of the enemy's camp." She reported that "although I knew the transfer of Bibles into Mexico to be a direct violation of the laws of the country, yet I felt no conscientious scruples in lending them my aid; for I felt God's Word to be above all human law, and no earthly power had the right of withholding it from any of God's accountable creatures."[47]

Melinda Rankin returned to Brownsville in 1854 with the necessary support and organized a school. She continued her efforts there until 1862, when Presbyterians loyal to the Confederacy took control of the school and forced her to leave. For her, that was providential for it resulted in her entering Mexico itself and beginning her work in Monterey.[48] For Protestant Christianity, Rankin's experience demonstrated the effectiveness of establishing schools on the frontier with Mexico as a means of gaining access and of distributing the Scriptures and other literature in the country. Even after access was made legal, the practice continued.

The Methodist Episcopal Church, South, undertook a similar mission when Alexander H. Sutherland and Joseph Norwood in 1879–1880 succeeded in generating support for a girls' school in Laredo, the Laredo Seminary. That institution later became Holding Institute, named in honor of Nannie Emory Holding, who arrived in Laredo in 1883 to become the administrator of the school. The motivation for the project was clear. Sutherland articulated it: "Every new mission we establish on this border is another star to mingle its rays with the streams of light that are pouring down upon this darkened land [Mexico] of nine millions of souls."[49]

A pattern of Hispanic ministry was established. It manifest Puritan values intrinsic to the sense of mission that had dominated the ideology of the Massachusetts Bay Colony and that had become fixed in the sense of destiny that dominated political rhetoric during the geographical expansion of the Republic in the nineteenth century.[50] Those Puritan values were now embedded in a matrix of evangelical piety that developed through the revivals that began in New England and the Anglo-Celtic backcountry and became so characteristic a part of the religious experience of Anglo-Celtic border culture in the United States. That was especially true of the Methodist Episcopal Church, South, and the Presbyterians, U.S.A., and the Cumberland Presbyterian Church, who also sponsored Hispanic ministry in the Southwest.

The schools themselves became instruments of revivalistic piety and furthered the blending of differing traditions of piety. Nannie Emory Holding's report of an early event in the history of the Laredo Seminary describes one incident in the evolving process. Her account of the academic year 1889–1890 describes a "harvest year," a time when the "spiritual wave" swept with "irresistible power" over the school. Alexander Sutherland, superintendent of the Mexican Border Conference, visited the Seminary "attending to the regular routine of business, which comes to every presiding elder. As a rule, he preached in Spanish. A few hours before the time of his leaving, Mrs. Anderson said to him: 'you are partial to the children; you give them the most of your preaching. I wish you would give us an English sermon.' He smilingly said: 'You should learn Spanish.' 'Yes,' she replied, 'but that is not the question. I want to know if you will preach especially to and for us, the teachers.'"[51]

Sutherland acceded to the request and conducted what could only be called a spontaneous four-day revival. Holding's description echoes Wesley's account of his field preaching and the sights and sounds of Cane Ridge:

> I am sure there never was a holier scene than that which gladdened our hearts on the evening of which I write. Our home had never been so crowded before. Faith Hall had never held, at any one time, so many precious souls in whom we were personally interested. Some were at the altar because of the invitation to draw near; but whence came the whisper of the voice which caused one, another, then another to kneel, until kneeling forms alone were seen? The low sob of a troubled soul broke the almost deathlike stillness; subdued, pleading cries rose here and there, until all the room was filled

with the breath of prayer. . . . Try as I will, there is no language to depict this scene over which the angels made joy in heaven.[52]

This incident at Laredo Seminary demonstrates that the values and practice of Anglo-Celtic revivalism, so pervasively characteristic of Protestant activity in Texas, even during the Mexican period when it was illegal,[53] were joined to the educational endeavors characteristic of Puritanism ultimately to produce the hybrid forms of ministry and faith expression manifest today in mainline Hispanic Protestantism.

"The Methodist excitement" that so worried Stephen F. Austin in 1829 for fear that the eagerness of circuit-riding preachers would compromise his colonization agreement with Mexico,[54] along with a like enthusiasm that tempered hard-edged Calvinism in the South with a touch of Arminianism, prevailed in Texas, if not in New Mexico,[55] as the defining ethos of mainline Protestantism, Hispanic and non-Hispanic alike.

Evangelistic preachers offering free grace and a palpable experience of redemption, at preaching stations and through revivals, carried the forms and values of Anglo-Celtic religious practice onto a new frontier. Teachers offered the values of Puritan idealism, tinged though it was with the shadow of racist sentiment, along with the desire for learning and finding one's place in an old environment, now strangely new. Hispanic men, women, and children responded; and in the mysterious process of convergence by which new cultures, human families, and value systems are formed, Hispanic American Protestantism flourished as one significant expression of the continuing evolution of border cultures and peoples.

Chapter 2

*The Empty Cross: The First Hispano Presbyterians in
Northern New Mexico and Southern Colorado*

Tomás Atencio

Introduction

This chapter explores conversion and Presbyterianism from the Hispano point of view, within a social and cultural context defined by two
distinct historical periods: from Annexation to the Railroad Period
(1852–1880), and from the Railroad Period to the Great Depression
(1880–1930s).[1] The empty cross or the removal of the image of Jesus from
the cross is a poignant symbol of conversion from Catholicism to Protestantism.

My recollection of the idea of the empty cross is of a film made in the
early fifties about the Presbyterian mission work with the Spanish-speaking community. Titled "The Church of the Empty Cross," the film featured
a boy by the name of Alfredo Padilla who had converted to Presbyterianism, had attended the Presbyterian Day School in Truchas, and was then
at Menaul School, a Presbyterian boarding school in Albuquerque.[2]
Epifanio Romero, a retired pastor living in Truchas, tells how the film and
its title came about. His aunt, a Presbyterian, operated the main village
store. While rummaging through the merchandise, she came upon a modern crucifix where the image of Jesus was anchored to a cobalt blue mirror. The thought of giving it to the missionary teachers at the Truchas Day
School conjured images of the glaring contradiction. The crucifix was not
acceptable to Presbyterians. But she wanted them to have the cross, so she
removed the image of Jesus and then gave them the glass cross. Accepting
the gift graciously but recognizing that it was a crucifix with a severed
Jesus, the teachers named it the "Empty Cross." When searching for a
theme and title for a documentary film of Hispanic Presbyterian missions,
the teachers suggested "The Church of the Empty Cross."

Epifanio Romero, reflecting on the frequency of conversions in earlier
days, says that "not too many Catholics convert any more."[3] As a consequence, the Presbyterian Church has weakened. In an ironic twist,
Alfredo Padilla became a Presbyterian minister and recently retired,

bringing to a close a century-old custom of native pastors serving their own communities. He is the last minister in this tradition. Without indigenous Presbyterian leaders, the icon of the empty cross is gradually becoming visible mostly through its shadow cast across time. The further from its origins, the thinner and longer the image of the empty cross becomes.

That the crucifix is central to Catholic popular religion in New Mexico is shown by a legend, which serves both as the archetypal as well as the historical basis for the communities of el Santuario de Chimayó and the Cofradia de Nuestro Padre Jesus Nazareno, popularly known as *Penitentes*. The legend starts with the finding of a miraculous treasure in 1816, when the Mexican War of Independence was being waged and Antonio José Martínez from Taos was pondering whether to enter the priesthood. According to the legend, Bernardo Abeyta, a resident of the village of el Potrero in Chimayó and a Penitente brother, was doing penance when he saw a light shining on a spot near the river. He followed the beam to where it struck the ground and there he dug a hole with his bare hands and found a crucifix. He took it to the Santa Cruz de la Cañada Church about seven miles down the river. The next day the crucifix was gone; it was found back at the place where it had originally appeared. In reverence for the miraculous revelation, Brother Abeyta, evidently a devotee of Nuestro Señor de Esquipulas, built a shrine in his honor. Today it is known as *El Santuario de Chimayó*.[4] A larger-than-life crucifix, carved by a native *santero* a few years after the reported appearance, hangs there over the altar.

The historical account tells that someone brought the idea of Nuestro Señor de Esquipulas from Guatemala to New Mexico around the early 1800s. Although the symbol of a crucifix was universal among Catholics, the devotion to Nuestro Señor de Esquipulas was probably a result of Mayan and Christian syncretism.[5] Among Christianized Mayan Indians, the cross was seen as a representation of the Ceiba tree, which splits its limbs into T's thus making the image of a cross; it is known as *el arbol espiritual,* the tree of life, God himself. The spiritual tree is rooted in the umbilicus of both heaven and earth, whereby it integrates humans and the cosmos in divine unity and renders the earth sacred.[6] The crucifix of Nuestro Señor de Esquipulas is one icon that represents the convergence of Christian and Indian religious beliefs and that gives life to what became known as folk Catholicism. For believers, the spiritual meaning of the miracle in Chimayó was enhanced because the crucifix was revealed in an area venerated as sacred land by Tewa Pueblo Indians. Rooted in the Mayan myth of the tree of life and the mystery and sacrifice of Jesus as the Lamb of God, the crucifix was accepted by the Penitente Brotherhood as a representation of "the passion and death of our Redeemer Jesus Christ." The statue of the crucified Christ was revered, venerated, and cared for by Penitentes much as a priest revered the Eucharist.[7] I will return to this topic later.

The severing of Jesus from the cross represents a dramatic and fundamental spiritual and cultural shift. This chapter examines the possible motives and the social conditions that may shed some light on this change.

Hispano Protestant Conversions. Many accounts of Presbyterian missionary activities and testimonies of conversions have been written, but Mark T. Banker most clearly states the theme that this chapter addresses. Banker's "study suggests that the targets of the Presbyterian missionary effort were neither passive beneficiaries of the newcomers' superior ways nor innocent victims of a Presbyterian brand of cultural imperialism." Banker recommends "additional studies which more fully utilize anthropological methodology and resources from the native perspective."[8]

Yet scholars lament the scarcity of material on Hispano Protestant conversions. Although some biographies are available, no specific study on motives for conversions has been done. Opportunity for social mobility and status, family and friends, and dissatisfaction with the Catholic Church have been suggested as the most obvious motives.[9] Using opportunity and protest as guiding propositions, I have examined the New Mexico Hispano Presbyterian story from written accounts and oral histories, contextualized within the historical framework stated at the beginning, to understand the growth of Presbyterian converts through almost half a century and the reasons for the subsequent decline. A parallel goal was to understand the meaning of opportunity and protest within the historical and social context in which opportunity became available and protest was realized. Although spiritual transformation is an important factor in conversions, it was not included in this investigation; it warrants a specific study.

We turn first to a summary of New Mexico's social and religious history before American annexation.

Before the Americans

Religious work in colonial New Mexico was carried on in Indian pueblos by the Order of Franciscan Missionaries. By the beginning of the nineteenth century there were only three churches that were not Franciscan missions. They were San Francisco in Santa Fe, Santa Cruz de la Cañada, and San Felipe de Neri in Albuquerque. The shortage of secular priests in the region was so critical that even Santa Cruz and San Felipe had Franciscans filling their pulpits.[10] With the expulsion of Franciscans after Independence in 1821, the whole region faced an ecclesiastical crisis. A few secular priests were in the region between Independence and American Annexation. Among them were Benigno Cárdenas, a Mexican ex-Franciscan working in Rio Abajo with Nicolás Valencia, a native New Mexican. Some of the other native priests were Mariano de Jesús Lucero and Padre Antonio José Martínez from Taos and José Manuel Gallegos from Abiquiú. Padre Cárdenas, a Methodist convert, became the first Protestant clergyperson in the territory of New Mexico in 1853.[11] But Padre Antonio José Martínez claimed the largest portion of history as the most important spiritual, political, and intellectual leader in nineteenth-century New Mexico. He also opened the way for Protestant conversions in the northern region of New Mexico.[12]

Padre Antonio José Martínez. Martínez was born in 1793 in Abiquiú, New Mexico, to the Martín Serrano family. New Mexico founding settlers, the Martínez clan became rich in land and livestock after they moved to Taos in 1804. By age twenty-three Antonio José had married and had fathered a girl, who died at age twelve. Martínez' wife died in childbirth. In 1817 he decided to enter the priesthood and enrolled in seminary in Durango. While Martínez was in Durango, Mexico's guns echoed the cry for freedom. The struggle for independence was led by an enlightened priest, Miguel Hidalgo, who became Martínez' role model in later life. Antonio José was ordained in 1822 and returned to New Mexico in 1823. In 1826 he became pastor of Our Lady of Guadalupe, the mission church located in Taos pueblo.

A visionary and innovator imbued with the ideology of the Enlightenment, Martínez became pastor-at-large for the growing landholding peasant community made up of *genízaros* (detribalized and hispanicizing Indians), Pueblo Indians, and mestizo heirs to the Spanish settlement. He became their advocate in politics, nurtured them as religious leaders, and elevated their consciousness. He started a grammar school for boys and girls, a minor seminary to usher young men into the priesthood, and a publishing house. Martínez was in Mexico when the new nation was born, a fact which may account for his burning nationalism. Like his role model, Padre Hidalgo, Martínez, too, opted for enlightenment and freedom.[13]

As a pastor-at-large for northern New Mexico, Padre Martínez' relationship to the Penitente Brotherhood merits a detailed discussion. There are several plausible reasons why Martínez would have been associated with the lay Brotherhood, although documents do not necessarily verify this interpretation. From a practical ecclesiastical perspective, the Brotherhood provided lay religious leaders in the absence of priests. Seen in relation to the mythical power of *Nuestro Señor de Esquipulas*—the miraculous crucified Christ—the Brotherhood's importance in the religious life of the community was even more compelling. Since they could not consecrate the host, the Penitente revered the crucifix as the approximation of the Eucharist.[14] The role and place the crucifix occupied in the *morada* (local chapter) brought the community of penitents to a "state of being in gratitude"—Eucharist—for the sacrifice of Jesus. The sense of community, or communion, extended to everyday life through the consecrated rites and rituals of marriage and baptism, which were reflected in the social roles of *madrinas* and *padrinos*, *ahijados* and *ahijadas*, and *comadres* and *compadres*. The sacrament of Penance, which is for the penitent himself as well as for others, is integrally related to the sacrament of Confession, which, of course, priests administer. Penance, in a state of grace, grants both salvation and forgiveness. Forgiveness is God's pardon; in the context of the penitential brotherhood, penance compelled the brothers to forgive each other as well as to monitor each other's moral behavior, thereby serving as the doctrinal foundation for a social ethic which was manifested in the community's solidarity. In their organizational structure, Penitentes were committed to self-rule, in contrast to the hierarchical structure of the church. After Annexation some *moradas*, local chapters of the Brotherhood, adhered to and sought protection of religious freedom under the United States Constitution. Taking the social concerns further, the Brotherhood conducted a comprehensive welfare program for its membership and their communities.[15] A man who fashioned his social action on the life and deeds of Padre Miguel Hidalgo, Padre Martínez would have supported these aspects of the Brotherhood. Martínez may have been behind the incorporation of *La Sociedad Piadosa de Nuestro Padre Jesús* of Taos County under an act of the Territorial Legislature.

In 1833, Bishop José Laureano Zubiría of Durango banned the Penitentes from the church for their flagellant practices, just as he did native carved *santos* for their nonaesthetic qualities. Padre Martínez ignored the ban. Because of his support of Penitentes, his advocacy for the underdog in church as well as secular matters, and his Mexican nationalism, Martínez was portrayed by later authors as inciting the Chimayó Rebellion in 1837 and the Taos Rebellion in 1847, a topic I will return to later.[16] Headed by *genízaros* and Pueblo Indians, the Chimayó Revolt opposed taxation and the Mexican departmental structure. Their battle cry was "to be on the side of God and Nation and the Faith of Jesus Christ." Penitentes were prominent in the leadership. Although Martínez did not participate in the rebellion—and even condemned it, since it resulted in the beheading of the Mexican-appointed governor—his ideological posture and affinity to the Penitentes made him suspect for fanning the flames of protest.[17]

Americans: A New Nation, a New Religion

Since Mexican Independence in 1821, New Mexico native traders on the Chihuahua trail had vented their frustrations with restrictive colonial economic policies by turning to St. Louis for business. The Pereas and Martínez were among them. On the Santa Fe Trail they met Americans cutting a commercial path to Santa Fe. For America, New Mexico would link United States and Mexican trade routes. From the perspective of slavery, New Mexico was up for grabs by either the North or the South. Texas was already a republic and claimed half of New Mexico. Driven by Manifest Destiny and these very pragmatic considerations, the United States invaded Mexico in 1846 and in two years had extended its boundaries to include parts of Colorado, Nevada, Arizona, California, and New Mexico.[18] Many New Mexicans welcomed the takeover, but others resisted. In Taos, the Revolt of '47 took several lives, including that of the American-appointed governor. Skirmishes took place in Embudo, Mora, and other communities as the rebels tried to stop U.S. troops from moving north to quell the revolt. The rebels lost, but among some the sense of defeat, and ambivalence about a new government and a new culture, endure to this day. As in the case of the 1837 Chimayó Rebellion, Padre Martínez has unjustly taken the brunt of the responsibility for the Taos revolt because of his advocacy for the peasants, his Mexican nationalism, and his enlightened political ideals.[19]

While annexation was a bonus to some, it was devastating to most New Mexicans. The full impact was not felt until the U.S. Government established the office of the Surveyor General in 1854. Its mission was to decide the ownership of the vast Spanish and Mexican land grants, to issue titles to the property, and to turn the rest of the land into public domain. Land grant holders lost large quantities of land to the government and to unscrupulous lawyers, who took in payment land they had ostensibly saved their clients. This devastating experience reduced the land base, but the village and landholding lifestyle endured, while the economic situation worsened.

In the ecclesiastical domain, the Diocese of Durango was relieved of its New Mexico charge in 1851. Instead a Vicariate Apostolic under the Archdioceses of St. Louis was created at a meeting of American Bishops in Baltimore. It was elevated to Diocesan status two years later. The first Vicar and later Bishop was Jean Baptiste Lamy. French-born and educated, Lamy brought along his longtime friend and associate, Joseph Projectus Machebeuf. They came with preconceived notions of New Mexico as an isolated Latin backwater of moral decay and general religious decadence.[20]

But two years before Lamy arrived in New Mexico, Benigno Cárdenas and Nicolás Valencia were leading a schism in Belen. Apparently these two priests broke from the Catholic Church in a move sanctioned by Kearny-appointed Judge Antonio José Otero. His brother, Antonio Miguel, who defeated José Manuel Gallegos in his bid for reelection to Congress, was later identified with the so-called American Party. Cárdenas tried to return to Catholicism after Lamy came to New Mexico. Rejected, Cárdenas next sought out the Baptist Church but eventually became a Methodist.[21] Valencia worked his way into the good graces of Lamy, but was later suspended. No details on the reason for the schism are readily available. One scholar suggests that the possibility of the creation of a Mexican Diocese in New Mexico may have encouraged Otero to support a schism against the Diocese of Durango in order to ensure an American Diocese.[22]

Padre Martínez was Lamy's principal antagonist. Good manners and mutual respect as brother-priests offered a platform for conviviality, but Martínez and Lamy's relationship was marked by nearly two decades of conflict. Martínez not only continued his support of the church-banned Penitentes, but he and his colleague-protegés also continually challenged Lamy and Machebeuf with their lifestyle. Before Lamy even imagined coming to New Mexico, Padre Martínez had fathered several children by Teodora Romero, his housekeeper. With knowledge of canon and civil law, Martínez made life difficult for both Machebeuf and Lamy. He kept Machebeuf on edge for having violated the confessional seal in his sermons.[23]

In 1856, Martínez resigned as pastor of the Taos church. Delighted, Lamy appointed a Spanish priest loyal to him. The new pastor ignored the elder Martínez, by then in failing health, and deprived him of his priestly right to say Mass in his former church. The aging *padre* responded by holding Mass in his own oratory. He administered the sacraments, including marriage and baptism. Some of his old parishioners followed him, mostly friends and relatives, creating a minor schism. Martínez was suspended in 1859, and the marriages he performed were invalidated. The split continued after Martínez' death, led by Padre Mariano de Jesús Lucero, and spread as far as Mora, also under Martínez' Picuris parish. In 1869, Donato Gasparri, a Jesuit priest from San Felipe de Neri in Albuquerque, went to Taos and Mora and healed the schism. Seventy-five marriages were revalidated, and 3,597 confessions were heard.[24]

In a related action calculated to lessen Martínez' hold in his former parish, the new pastor of the Taos church also gained support from *hermano mayores* (elder brothers) of the Brotherhood and altered their rules to give more authority to the local priests. The effect was to weaken the principle of self-rule, incorporated by Penitentes and endorsed by Martínez.

Even before the schism, Padre Martínez opened the doors of Our Lady of Guadalupe Church to Protestant clergymen. In 1851 the Reverend H. W. Read, a Baptist minister, preached in Martínez' church: it was the first Protestant sermon in a Catholic church. Other Baptist ministers had similar experiences with Padre Martínez. E. A. Mares writes, "Reminiscent of Protestant tendencies, Martínez was to exhort the people to elect their own minister because it was a right granted by the new government."[25] It was during the period of the schism that Martínez threatened the established Catholic church, which Martínez never officially left. Because of him, however, the people incorporated their disenchantment with the American Catholic Church into their consciousness and recognized their options in the political sphere. Both ideas planted the seeds for protest and Protestantism. They germinated quickly after Martínez' death in 1867. Their principal propagator was the Padre's own son, Vicente Ferrer Romero.[26]

Another important figure from the Rio Abajo is José Ynez Perea (1837–1910). His great grandfather migrated from Mexico in the early eighteenth century and settled in Corrales, a village north of Albuquerque. By the mid-1830s the grandsons of the first Perea settler had staked their claims in Bernalillo, where they were wealthy *latifundos*. José Ynez was born to one of the grandsons, Juan Perea and his wife, Josefa Chávez de Perea, in 1837. After finishing his first year of school in Chihuahua at the time the American Army took New Mexico, José Ynez left for New York and enrolled in a French Jesuit Academy. José Ynez began to question his religious mentors, turned to the Bible, and began to move away from Catholicism. He enrolled at a military academy; eventually he entered West Point, left after a short stay, and returned home. Later he joined a merchant freighter crew, which took him around the world.[27] Regarding José Ynez Perea's rejection of Catholicism, legend has it that when Perea was a young man at home for a visit, he fired a bullet through the statue of the Virgin Mary during an argument with his mother.[28] According to the story, his father disowned him for his Protestant leanings but a few years later brought his prodigal son back home and gave him a healthy inheritance and made him executor of his estate. It is said that José Ynez' father became sympathetic toward Protestantism and started reading the Bible. Francisco, José Ynez' older brother, is said to have been a Presbyterian even before his younger brother.[29]

By 1862 José Ynez was a Presbyterian. He returned to New Mexico and married Victoria Armijo, the daughter of Ambrosio Armijo, another Rio Abajo *don* from Old Albuquerque. After his bride's untimely death a year later, José Ynez took his inheritance—a large flock of sheep—and his money to La Cinta. La Cinta was a small village located east of Las Vegas, New Mexico, near *El Rio Colorado,* now known as the Canadian River. Perea opened a trading post in Las Vegas in partnership with an Anglo. At the same time, he began his missionary career spreading tracts and Bibles in Hispano villages.[30]

Unlike the Martínez cabal from the Rio Arriba, the Pereas from the Rio Abajo were pro-American in their political sentiments. Soon after General Kearny, the commanding general of the conquering U.S. army, marched into Santa Fe, Juan Leandro Perea, José Ynez' and Francisco's uncle, gave a banquet in his honor. Perea later met with American officials in Santa Fe to confirm relationships for future business: the family's loyalty to the American government was never in question. In 1863, Francisco ran against and defeated José Manuel Gallegos, a former priest associated with Padre Martínez, in a bid for the congressional delegate seat. Perea was identified with the American Party, as were the Oteros, particularly in regard to the Belen schism. Martínez and his associates were of the Mexican Party.[31] José Ynez expressed the sentiments of his family. His mission was clearly to educate Hispanos in the English language and American ways. His choosing Las Vegas as a place of business was not coincidental. He anticipated the railroad coming through there bringing new business. But what he wanted most were Anglo missionaries who could start schools. Although primarily a businessman, Perea received tracts from an Anglo friend from Philadelphia, which he distributed in the Las Vegas region, extending north to Mora and east to the plains, paving the way for the missionaries who were to follow soon.

José Ynez and Padre Martínez shared class background. Both families had achieved a high level of material aristocracy. Perea represented the transition from Mexican to American values. His education was principally in American schools and universities. In contrast, Martínez was educated in Mexico, where he had incorporated Enlightenment ideals into his consciousness through the thought and action of Mexican priests and political leaders. He anticipated the changes but held to his Mexican intellectual and religious roots. In politics, Martínez and his followers opposed New Mexican political forces that supported a pro-American agenda. They reflected a kind of "cultural nationalism." Protestantism may have given Martínez' followers an option to protect their Mexican ideological commitments, which were threatened by the Catholic hierarchical structure and Lamy's aggressive pro-American stance: Presbyterian polity was based on local government. José Ynez, on the other hand, was Presbyterian before missionaries came to New Mexico, and he was clearly pro-American.

Perea directly set the course for Presbyterian conversions in northern New Mexico and southern Colorado; Martínez did so indirectly: their influence is the subject of the next section.

The First Presbiterianos

Some New Mexicans may have protested against the Catholic Church, but their options were limited to "minor schisms" until Protestant congregations were established. The names of three men are usually associated with the first Spanish-speaking Presbyterian mission work: David McFarland in Santa Fe (1866), who originally came to do mission work with Navajos; John Annin in Las Vegas and El Rito/Chacón (1869–1879); and James Roberts in Taos, Peñasco, Ocaté (1872–1878), and in the San Luis Valley. In addition, Alexander Darley from Pueblo Presbytery in Colorado labored in the San Luis Valley. Later John Eastman followed Annin in El Rito/Chacón (1880), Maxwell Phillips was in Mora (1882), James Fraser served in Buena Vista (1884), and S. W. Curtis in Embudo (1888). And Juan Whitlock, born to a New Mexico Hispano woman and an Army doctor father, returned to New Mexico from school and became a missionary minister. All were commissioned missionaries by the Presbyterian Board of Domestic Missions.[32] The following narrative will describe their work in specific communities.

José Ynez knew of McFarland in Santa Fe and yearned for a missionary like him in his area. Perea's prayers were answered, tells Gabino Rendón, with the coming of John Annin and his family in 1869. Perea and Annin joined in building a church with an attached educational building. Perea was a ruling elder in the new church and was ordained a minister in 1880. A list of Spanish-speaking men were among the first to join Annin's congregation.[33] Two of them had been members of a Baptist Church in Socorro. Two were Catholics from La Junta, where Methodists were active. Another Methodist who was staying at the Annin's home, Rafael Gallegos, also joined the church.

The church and school quickly made an impact. Although Gabino Rendon was already a student in a public school in 1871, he was withdrawn and enrolled in John Annin's school instead. Rendon said that the church in Las Vegas "marked the opening of the Bible to the common people and the beginning of religious liberty in our part of the world."[34] Catholic opposition was unyielding. When Rafael Gallegos experienced Catholic antagonism, he left for the Mora areas and started a school in Agua Negra (present-day Holman). Parish priests refused to baptize infants with siblings in Protestant schools. The seething conflict led to a healthy competition between Annin and the Jesuit priests who came to Las Vegas to open a school in 1872. Promising students like Rendón were taken out of Annin's school and enrolled in the Jesuit school. In addition, the Jesuits published *La Revista Catolica* that gave rise to a competitive paper from Annin, *La Revista Evangélica*. This led priests to make an active effort to introduce the Bible to the layperson. In a more mundane vein, the Jesuit presence in Las Vegas instigated a boycott of Don José Ynez Perea's store. Rather than reacting, Perea turned to full missionary work and eventually settled in the Albuquerque area, expanding Presbyterian work among Hispanos during the boom days of the Railroad period.[35]

The Jesuits were effective in their defense and affirmation of Catholicism, as they had been in healing the Taos schism. By 1880, when the railroad reached Albuquerque, John Annin had left, dismayed at his perceived failure. He was replaced by John Eastman, who changed the missionary focus from Las Vegas to the Mora area. In Chacón and Ocaté, Eastman linked with indigenous Presbyterians nurtured by Annin and supported by Roberts from Taos, whose work is discussed next.

In the early seventies, while in Santa Fe in transit from his missionary post among Navajos, the Reverend James M. Roberts received a letter from a group of Spanish-speaking men urging him to come to Taos. One of the men was José Domingo Mondragón, who was a Penitente, a former Territorial legislator, and a follower of Padre Martínez. The other man was Vicente Ferrer Romero, son of Padre Martínez. The story goes that while Mondragón was a legislator in Santa Fe, he had attended a Baptist service in 1856 and came home with portions of a New Testament. Even before Padre Martínez' death, Romero had moved against the pro-American Catholic Church led by Lamy. Both men became founding members of the Taos Presbyterian Church in 1872 and were licensed lay preachers; neither was ever ordained.[36]

The town of Peñasco was under the jurisdiction of Padre Martínez' Picuris Parish, which extended as far as Mora. Many of the first settlers in the Mora Valley had moved from Chamisal and El Valle. These two villages were southwest of Peñasco proper, and Embudo, fifteen miles down the watershed. Peñasco was known then as Santa Bárbara. Mora was used by these Peñasco and Embudo people for high country farming and stock grazing; some families began to make the Mora Valley their permanent home. The first Presbyterian congregation in this area was organized around 1880 by Roberts in El Valle at the home of Gregorio Ortega. As bad feelings against Protestants mounted, the people retreated from El Valle and Chamisal and started moving to the Mora Valley, especially to Chacón.[37] The isolation of Chacón may explain its use as a refuge by persecuted Protestants.

Martínez' followers went in other directions as well, and Roberts stationed at Taos was close behind them. A story is told of the Maes family who were ostracized in Taos and settled in Ocaté, northeast of Mora. The elder Maes bequeathed a Bible to his son, Amadeo. Village dwellers accused him of heresy and burned down his house along with the treasured Bible. Later Amadeo purchased another Bible. Fearing that the same thing might happen again, the Maeses cleaned out their cellar and read and studied the Bible clandestinely. Roberts came in 1875 and found a group of more than twenty persons ready to become Presbyterians. In 1878, Roberts and his wife organized a day school, which lasted into the next century.[38]

Early in the 1870s, Manuel Sandoval and Juan José Argüello were among five men from El Rito (Chacón) who came to Trinidad, Colorado, to haul freight to New Mexico. According to the story, they came across a Protestant service where they got Bibles and religious tracts, which they took home. Argüello held secret services and taught students how to read in Spanish in a cellar, much as Maes in Ocaté. The objective was to make people literate so that they could read the Bible. The small group grew, and in 1879 Annin from Las Vegas organized the El Rito Presbyterian Church. Two men from Chacón—Juan Policarpio Ortega, a carpenter, and Manuel Sandoval—became licensed evangelists.[39] Neither was ever ordained.

In Agua Negra (Holman), Rafael Gallegos found a place to build a school. He had been forced out of Las Vegas. Looking for a carpenter, he was referred to José Emiterio Cruz, a skilled woodworker who had been introduced to the trade by his brother-in-law, an English-speaking New Yorker. In the course of his work, Cruz came upon a Bible, studied the New Testament, and soon refused to attend Mass and go to Confession; thus, another important person was drawn to Presbyterian work. Gallegos' school did not last, but it was reborn as the Agua Negra Presbyterian School in the next decade.

Alexander Darley was in the San Luis Valley of Colorado early, but the inspiration for a Presbyterian Church came from within. Pedro Sánchez had a Spanish Bible that he had acquired in 1857. His wife's brothers were Pedro and Pablo Ortega, both Penitentes living in Cenicero, between present-day Antonito and San Luis, Colorado. Through Sánchez, the two were introduced to the Bible. In time they quarreled with the priest over the appointment of *el hermano mayor* of the Penitente *morada*. They left the Catholic Church and became good friends of Alexander Darley. From their accounts and from Pedro Sánchez's records, Darley gathered the material for his book on the Penitentes, *The Passionists of the Southwest* (1893).[40] This is one strain of San Luis Valley Presbyterianism.

Another lineage starts at Embudo. Antonio José Rodríguez learned to read from his father, who was said to be a Penitente. Rodríguez came across a few pages of the Bible while herding sheep on an Embudo hillside. He read the passage until he had committed it to memory. When José was nine, his family moved to the vicinity of Cenicero, where the Ortegas lived. There Rodríguez saw Sánchez's Bible. He became a Presbyterian. This Bible, later known as the Sánchez Bible, has been credited for the spread of Presbyterianism in this area. Seven churches trace their origins to the Sánchez Bible.[41]

In 1865 in Conejos, at the southern border of the San Luis Valley, Juan de Jesús Gómez bought a Spanish Bible published in 1828. He was impressed by the message, which "stressed matters of belief and service rather than custom and ceremony."[42] A small group of extended family members and neighbors formed a Bible reading and study group. In 1879, Alexander Darley heard of the group, made their acquaintance, and organized La Luz Presbyterian Church. That Bible is known as the Gómez Bible. Petra Gómez, a granddaughter, and M. D. J. Sánchez, a grandson, were well-known Presbyterian leaders in the region.

Protest against Catholicism during this period was realized by becoming Presbyterian rather than following the path of minor schism. This seems to be the case with the Ortega brothers. They quarreled with the local priest over the selection of an *hermano mayor*. In short, this disagreement disclosed that the pastor was interfering with Penitente self-rule. The greatest opportunity availed by Protestants was the Bible. It is not clear why the Bible was so significant. Not all Catholics who read the Bible on their own became Protestant, however. Catholic observers have suggested that the Bible became central to conversions because Protestant missionaries exploited the absence of the Bible among laypersons. Since the Bible was interpreted to Catholic congregations by the priests, the Protestant missionaries lured converts with the promise of reading the word of God for themselves.[43] The most obvious influence in conversions during this period, however, was the movement inspired by Padre Martínez. Had the Jesuits not healed the schism in Taos and Mora and started schools in Las Vegas, the Protestant impact might have been stronger. The work in Las Vegas with the Perea and Annin team was less a protest movement than Martínez' work; it was an effective missionary activity to expand educational opportunities and make the Bible available.

The next period shows a decisive shift toward education; schools and churches were organized in tandem in many communities.

The Railroad Period

The railroad passing through New Mexico integrated the territory into the national and international economy and changed the makeup of the population. Extractive industries boomed. New Mexico coal, lumber, metals, cattle, sheep, wool, pelts, and the like, were exported by rail; on the way back, railcars brought different people who were carriers of different values to manage the developing economy. New Mexico was yanked into the industrial capitalist world.

A promoter of the railroad, William Hazeldine, delivering an address at the celebration welcoming the railroad to Albuquerque, said:

> Today the new civilization of the East is brought into direct contact with the ancient civilization of New Mexico, today the bell of the locomotive tolls the death knell of . . . superstition and ignorance and proclaims that henceforth knowledge, education, advancement and progress shall be the right of the people. . . . The capitalist will come to swell his gains.[44]

In the real world, the upper-class *hacendados* who had achieved material aristocracy during the Mexican period dropped to the upper-middle class as their vast fortunes were eroded by the industrial capitalist economy. Subsistence farmers abandoned their small plots of land and became industrial and agricultural wage earners. Illiteracy had jumped to 78 percent by 1870 from a much lower rate in 1850.[45] The landholding peasant became part of a unique marginal group of Indohispanics. They were loyal to folk Catholicism, bonded to the land, uneducated, and at the mercy of the growing mercantile capitalist, who settled in the villages as the new *patrón*.[46] Padre Martínez' flock was in real trouble. And it was the Presbyterians and other Protestant denominations that were taking up the challenge to realize part of Hazeldine's promise.

The missionary teachers were women, a shift from the evangelist-preacher missionaries, who were men. Reflecting in the hinterlands the growing American progressive movement of the turn of the century, missionary teachers were to New Mexico villages what Charity Organization Society's "friendly visitors" and Settlement House residents were to the cities. Missionaries provided educational, social, and health services to New Mexican Hispanos as the urban "friendly visitors" did for their immigrant clientele.[47] But New Mexicans were not immigrants; they were Mexicans annexed to the United States by virtue of conquest. Yet they were as different from mainstream Americans as immigrants, and more threatening, for the Southwest was a threshold to the rest of the Indohispanic world. They were mestizos—Spanish and Indian—and they were Catholic, obvious vessels for very different values that had to be brought in line with dominant American Protestant values.

In 1877, the Home Board created the Department of Schools. Brackenridge and García-Treto write that Presbyterian schools grew rapidly before public instruction came to New Mexico. With only six schools operating in 1878, twenty-four schools with forty-eight teachers were in operation ten years later. A law providing for a Territorial Board of Education was passed in 1891. By 1900, only seven new Presbyterian plaza schools were opened. By 1920, eight schools remained, most of which lasted into the 1950s, and the two boarding schools, Allison-James and Menaul. The original policy of the Home Board had stated that schools would be created and run by Presbyterians only until the state could provide adequate education. Therefore, the idea of closing schools that climaxed in the 1950s and 1960s was inherent in the schools' beginnings.[48]

In their prime, these schools made possible the growth of Presbyterian mission work. One of the first products of these schools was Gabino Rendón. First drawn by Annin into his school in 1870, then pulled back to the Jesuits' school, he came upon the new mission school in Las Vegas run by Annie Speakman in the 1880s when he took his sister to class. Inspired by his desire to learn English, Rendón enrolled in school. He was brought into the church by Juan Whitlock, the associate pastor for the Spanish speaking. Rendón finished school, joined the church, and took to the surrounding villages on horseback spreading religious tracts at random, hoping someone would find them and become interested in his mission. After finishing school at Las Vegas, Rendón became a mission teacher and started a school in Las Golondrinas, north of Las Vegas. Rendón chose the ministry as his vocation and attended the College of the Southwest at Del Norte Colorado, from which he graduated in 1897. Joining Rendón from Los Valles near Las Vegas was Manuel Madrid, a relative of one who had read Rendón's tracts. He went to a short-lived Presbyterian boarding school in Las Vegas and on to Del Norte. Rendón's and Madrid's experiences are prototypical of the preparation of native ministers in the early days.[49]

Perea's and Martínez' legacy converged, and native evangelists from both strains spread the Presbyterian message throughout the north-central villages, southern Colorado, and the prairies as schools developed along with new churches. In Ranchos de Taos, José Domingo Mondragón was instrumental in organizing a church and a school. Alice Hyson, the founding missionary teacher, left her name to the school, which it kept until it closed in the 1950s.

From Ranchos de Taos, Martínez' influence emanated to Embudo in 1888. José Domingo Mondragón, Vicente Ferrer Romero, and Juan Martínez, along with Alice Hyson, gathered with a group of potential Protestants at the home of Hemenegildo Salazar in Embudo, now Dixon. Salazar had invited Mondragón to discuss the possibilities of a church. Both a school and a congregation were started in his home, which resulted in conflict with the priest, who refused to perform the marriage of Salazar's son unless the school and congregation were moved out of the house. The problem spread to the extended family, and when the time came to baptize a relative's child, the family called the Presbyterian missionary, S. W. Curtis. Lore has it that curious Catholics who went to witness this unique ritual were impressed by what they saw and heard, and thus in 1889 the Embudo Presbyterian Church was founded.

Following a disagreement with the priest over his attendance at a Baptist class, young Tomás Atencio of Embudo told his father he was leaving the Catholic Church to become a Protestant. His father joined him. A member of the first class at the Embudo Mission Day School in 1889, Tomás Atencio, who married Hemenegildo Salazar's daughter, went on to become a Presbyterian minister and served for more than half a century. A contemporary of Atencio's, Victoriano Valdez, was in an early class as well, and went on to become a Presbyterian minister. He married Francisco Perea's daughter.[50] Eliud Valdez, a nephew, also became a minister.

The Martínez legacy from Taos was carried on by Juan Quintana and his wife, who organized a school and a congregation in Chimayó and a small church in El Quemado, now Córdova. Córdova produced two ministers, Eliseo and Carlos Córdova. Upon Quintana's foundations, Gabino

Rendón, by then an ordained minister, and Manual Madrid, by then his brother-in-law, both of the Perea strain, built the churches in Chimayó and Córdova. In 1900, a mission school was organized in Chimayo; the buildings, which were dedicated as the John Hyson Memorial in 1901, are still used as a community learning center. Chimayó produced two ministers, Uvaldo and Amador Martínez. In 1903, Truchas requested a church, which was organized with fifteen members. A school had been opened a year before.

Chimayó was served also by José Emiterio Cruz, the carpenter from Mora. His name is associated with an aborted debate with a priest over *santos* or saints. *Santos* are one of the cornerstones of New Mexican folk Catholicism. Upon converting, new Presbyterians would burn their *santos*, which to them were now idols and thus violated the decalogue.[51]

The San Luis Valley program had a growth spurt at the turn of the century and then an immediate decline. Of the sixteen schools founded in the region, most had closed by 1906. San Luis Valley got a boost from the Presbyterian College of the Southwest at Del Norte, which was founded in 1890. The Presbyterian college was designed to offer secondary education and theological training. Gabino Rendón, Manuel Madrid, M. D. J. Sánchez, Juan Whitlock, Amadeo Maes, Victoriano Valdez, Eliseo Córdova, Juan Quintana, Tomás Atencio, and more got their training at Del Norte. It closed in 1898 and local candidates continued their ministerial training at Menaul School, which began theology classes in 1901. The Del Norte–Menaul students served New Mexico and southern Colorado up to the World War II period. From around 1904, New Mexican Hispano ministerial candidates went to accredited colleges and seminaries. The first of these were Acorcinio Lucero from Chacón and Carlos Córdova from Córdova. Others who followed were José Inez Candelaria, who served Denver and Albuquerque, Ezequiel Jaramillo from Trementina, and Julian Durán from Embudo.[52]

The story of Alfonso Esquibel, a young man in the 1920s, merits telling since his ministry is another landmark in Presbyterian Hispano ministries. Raised by a wealthy family acquaintance, Alfonso became his benefactor's ranch foreman. He soon discovered that education was necessary and enrolled in Menaul School. Back at the ranch for the summer, Esquibel fell while hunting. He recovered but his days as foreman were over. He became a serious student at Menaul, went on to the University of New Mexico, and on to seminary at San Anselmo. Replacing José Inez Candelaria, who had moved to Albuquerque, Esquibel distinguished himself in Denver as a counselor, a social worker, a group worker with inner-city boys, an advocate, and a pastor-preacher. He cut a new path in social ministries, expanding the earlier focus of pastors who were primarily preacher-evangelists.[53]

José L. Medina from the Mora Valley tells another story. Raised a Presbyterian, he knew no other religion or way of life. He attended the mission school in Holman, graduated from Menaul School in 1932, graduated from the University of Dubuque in Iowa, and then from McCormick Seminary in 1942. He was a member of the largest cohort group of native ministers who were university-educated and seminary-trained. Reflecting on his experience as a Presbyterian, Medina emphasized that pastors were all native men who served as role models and social and moral guides to the younger members of the community. Missionary teachers were in charge of regular schooling as well as Sunday school and Christian Endeavor curricula.[54]

This period comes to an end with the Depression and World War II. What happened next is revealed by the congregation La Iglesia Betel in la Cebolla, in the mountains west of Mora. The records show that in the fall of 1921, Gabino Rendón and Carlos Córdova celebrated founding services in the home of Juan B. Blea, who was a member of the Las Vegas church. Special revival meetings were held in a home the following January and nine joined the church. A grant of $3,000 received from the Board of the Church Erection Fund of the General Assembly financed the construction of the church building. By April 1935 the congregation had grown to a total of thirty-seven members, and it leveled off at that number for several years.[55]

Changes began to affect the little chapel in 1941 when the first letter of transfer was requested by four members of one family to the Albuquerque Second Presbyterian Church. Others asked for letters of transfer to the Mora Church, in the vicinity. Betel closed in 1949 with fifteen members. Trementina mission work, a multiservice endeavor in an almost totally Hispano Presbyterian community, also closed. The church was located in a village near the prairies, which gradually lost all its residents. The remaining members joined the Las Vegas First Church in the 1950s.[56] Urbanization was taking its toll, luring away from the rural churches its younger and better-educated members.

Although the Presbyterian Church's commitment to education expanded and then leveled off during this period, a geographical enclave defined by Mora to the east, Ranchos de Taos to the north, Embudo, Truchas, and Chimayó to the west continued to receive missionary services. The Brooklyn Cottage was built in Dixon, formerly Embudo, in

1914. In 1941 it expanded from a two-bed to a thirty-five-bed hospital and moved to the main highway. It was renamed Embudo Presbyterian Hospital. From the hospital, medical services were rendered to Truchas, Peñasco, and Mora. In 1956 Mora got a resident clinic. It was staffed by the Presbyterian Church.[57]

By the 1930s a new community of Hispanos had formed around the Presbyterian Church. They called one another *hermanos* and *hermanas.* The Christian Endeavor movement brought people from New Mexico and southern Colorado for religious worship and social camaraderie at an annual convention. But this community was different from the dominant Presbyterian community: its members were all Spanish speakers who held worship services and conducted their business meetings in Spanish. Their differences seemed to have affected their community in other ways that may have had long-lasting effects. The first class of ordained ministers and later graduates from Del Norte and the Menaul Training School did not have university and seminary training, yet they were ordained. Lay evangelists, however, such as Vicente Romero, were denied ordination because they had not attended the training schools. Their ministers were neither called nor installed in congregations until the 1950s.[58]

The competition between Presbyterian missions and Catholic parochial schools for the minds and souls of Hispano New Mexicans eventually brought to an end Presbyterian schools. The State Board of Education contracted with the Archdiocese of Santa Fe for school buildings and for nuns as teachers. A committee composed mostly of Presbyterians, among them the Reverend Porfirio Romero, pastor at the Embudo Presbyterian Church, and Lydia Córdova Zellers, daughter of Eliseo Cordova, a Presbyterian minister, filed suit against the Board of Education over its contract with the Archdiocese on constitutional grounds of separation of church and state. In 1951, the New Mexico Supreme Court ruled against the State in the famed "Dixon Case."[59] Although the legal battle created some tensions in communities between Catholics and Presbyterians, the lasting effect of the ruling was that the Presbyterian Church closed its schools. Today only Menaul School in Albuquerque and the John Hyson Learning Center in Chimayó remain. Some attribute the decline of Hispano Presbyterianism to the school closure. In reality, the opportunity for the Presbyterian Church to provide education was removed at a time when it was no longer unique.

The decline of Presbyterianism in the region was inherent in the mission enterprise itself. The pattern of building local churches and schools, which began under Perea's and Annin's leadership in Las Vegas, was expanded by developing a cadre of local lay evangelists and by bringing women missionary teachers from the east. In order to prepare local men for ordination into the ministry, the Presbyterian Church created special training schools that required neither university nor seminary education. By the early decades of the twentieth century, a few men began to attend college and seminary and by the 1930s this was the new pathway to the ministry. Both missionary teachers and local preachers and evangelists were supported by Presbyterian National Missions, thereby making native ministers missionaries and not members of the Presbytery, as other ministers were. The combination of local pastors and external teachers worked well for the Presbyterian cause. But inherent in the mission strategy were the seeds of the decline of Presbyterian strength in the local communities. As local educational alternatives were created by the state, mission support was withdrawn. Simultaneously, urbanization trends drew the younger and better-educated people away from the local rural communities. The local leadership, especially within the ministerial field, withered away. Few men were called to the ministry after World War II, and some who were and became ordained in the 1960s have left discontented with the church and its mission to the local communities as well as its commitment to fully developing local leadership. At issue has been native pastors' relationship to the Presbytery, a subject for further investigation.

Shadows of the Empty Cross: Summaries and Conclusions

Protestantism came to New Mexico as part of the total package of social change. At base was the Reformation, then the Enlightenment, the Mexican War of Independence, and American Expansionism. The isolated landholding peasant mestizo society was caught by surprise and dragged into a world that upheld the value of a free market economy and ideas of freedom of religion. Two different societies came together in one space. There was conflict in all arenas. This essay tells a small piece of the story in the religious arena.

Conversion was a protest against a Church that denied freedom of religion, that did not provide the layperson the Bible, that banned Penitentes from the church, and later eroded their self-rule. Conversion was a protest against priests who suspended parishioners for sending their children to Presbyterian schools. It was a protest against a hierarchical structure. Protest was enhanced by the political process of New Mexico's annexation to the United States. Converts were called *herejes* for their protest and *protestantes* for their conversion all in one breath. Under Catholicism, they did not have the Bible to read the Word of God for themselves, and the possibility of having it was intertwined with American ideals about freedom of religion. But the most obvious lure to Presbyterianism was educational opportunity. Some converted to be closer to the American values of freedom and rationality; they became cultural *mestizos*. In accepting the Protestant ways, converts had to relinquish some of their Indohispanic traditions.

Richard Nostrand, a geographer, argues effectively about the cultural impress that Hispanos stamped on their environment. One is the impress of religion: Catholic churches in every village, el Santuario de Chimayó, religious names, religious shrines, *moradas,* crosses. To leave that world would have been to slice away part of what it meant to be a New Mexican Indohispano.[60] But there is more. The mystery of the sacrifice of Jesus on the Cross, made present in the Mass through food, provided the spiritual foundation for community. The roles of *padrino, madrina, compadre, comadre,* which were rooted in communion and community, were clearly Indohispano characteristics. To leave that belief and its social manifestations, it seems, would have been to forfeit another piece of what it meant to be Indohispano.[61] To some Hispano Catholics it is inconceivable that Hispanos could be Protestant!

Missionaries were, of course, necessary for protest to actualize and for opportunity to become available. The first missionary sent to Las Vegas by the Board of Domestic Missions was an answer to Perea's prayers and to his advocacy; the second one came to Taos on the request of Martínez' followers. Their work as well as Martínez' and Perea's converged in Chacón and Ocaté. With the coming of the railroad, the contrast between the American critical mass which was forming and the existing critical mass of Mexicans crystallized when Anglo Protestants came out in favor of mission and Americanization. Thus the educational and social service programs were founded, to remain active until New Mexico's government provided adequate education. As public schools opened, Presbyterian schools closed.

The exchange of the crucifix for the open Bible merits further discussion and inquiry. The missions of that period operated within the paradigm that beliefs and observances on primordial or archetypal levels—like the miracle of *Señor de Esquipulas, santos,* and even the mystery of the Eucharist—were superstitions and signs of ignorance.[62] The emphasis on literacy, the use of the Bible as a moral guide, as a pathway to discerning God's plan, were all rational and denigrated the intuitive. Perhaps for those who left the crucifix for the Empty Cross it was not a break from their mythical roots, but a change in institutional affiliation, while secretly they treasured original allegiances. On the other hand, to some, the Bible may have been more significant in their ancestral past, but access to it had been denied. Recent investigations into the possible crypto-Jewish presence in New Mexico's history hinge, in part, on the remnants of *converso* practices. Two of the most suggestive ones are the sacred obligation to read the Bible, in Judaism meaning the Old Testament, which crypto-Jews could not possess for fear of persecution and retribution, and the enmity toward *santos*, which were burned by Protestant converts. It is difficult to prove crypto-Jewish presence, since it was a secret phenomenon, but stories that warrant further investigation abound. For crypto-Jewish heirs it would have been the open Bible and not the Cross, empty or full, that was significant.[63] If so, the Empty Cross could have been a symbol of hope and religious freedom as well as the pathway to the Bible.

Inter-ethnic Relations Between Mexican American and Anglo American Methodists in the U.S. Southwest, 1836–1938

Paul Barton

Hispanic Protestants within mainline traditions are a product of the missionary enterprise conducted throughout the nineteenth century and the first half of the twentieth century. Anglo American Methodist missionaries, who were the chief architects of the Spanish-speaking Methodist work in northern Mexico and the southwestern United States, left a legacy that continues to be felt today in the Rio Grande Conference of The United Methodist Church, the successor to the earliest Methodist institutions in Texas and New Mexico. Consideration of that legacy enables Hispanic Protestants to understand the historical foundations of our current theological, social, and cultural struggles.

Instead of addressing the heroic and indefatigable character of the missionaries as they sought to improve the life of Mexicans through the transmission of the Protestant faith, this essay focuses on the Protestant missionary legacy by examining inter-ethnic relations between Anglo American missionaries and Mexican and Mexican American Methodists in the Southwest. The tension that has existed between Latino Protestants and Anglo-dominant denominations has a historical foundation in the Anglo American missionaries' embrace and promulgation of the idea of Manifest Destiny in the nineteenth century. Just as present-day Hispanics find themselves the objects of mission efforts based upon stereotypical views of them, so did the first generation of Mexican and Mexican American Methodists discover that Anglo American church leaders had misunderstandings about their culture and abilities. By examining relations between Anglo American and Spanish-speaking Methodists in the Southwest, we can view our present struggle against racism within the church as a continuation of struggles that date back more than a century.

Manifest Destiny

The concept of Manifest Destiny in the nineteenth century provided an ideological impetus for the settlement of Anglo Americans in lands belonging to Mexicans and Native Americans in the Southwest and for fil-ibustering into Mexico.[1] This concept—based on the image of the United States as the New Israel and as the instrument for the creation of the king-dom of God on earth—held that the United States had a providential des-tiny to occupy the whole North American continent and to establish in that land a nation that would serve as "a light to the nations." This "doc-trine," as it became the predominant ideology among U.S. institutions and leaders, provided a theological justification for the expropriation of lands already inhabited and claimed by Mexico, Mexican Americans, and Native Americans.[2]

Anglo Americans' encounter with Mexicans throughout the Southwest contributed to the formation of Anglo American racial identity. Anglo Americans perceived Native Americans and Mexicans as an obstacle to the realization of their "manifest destiny." As U.S. citizens confronted Mexicans and Native Americans along their westward path, Anglo Amer-ican leaders and pioneers formulated theological and racial concepts that explained the culture of the existing inhabitants in terms of deficiencies and inferiority. As Daniel Rodríguez-Díaz notes in "Los Movimientos Misioneros y el Establecimiento de Ideologías Dominantes: 1800–1940," on the theological level, Mexicans and Native Americans were understood to exist outside the bounds of the exclusive covenant that God had made with the Anglo American people.[3] Belief in their exclusive covenantal rela-tionship with God allowed Anglo Americans to consider Native Ameri-cans and Mexicans as marginal members of God's kingdom on earth. The categorization of Mexicans and Native Americans as inferior beings also provided racial justification for military aggression against Mexico and the subsequent expropriation of lands owned by Mexican Americans in the Southwest.[4] Reginald Horsman, in *Race and Manifest Destiny,* states, "The process of dehumanizing those who were to be misused or destroyed proceeded rapidly in the United States in the 1840s. To take lands from inferior barbarians was no crime; it was simply following God's injunc-tions to make the land fruitful."[5] Clearly, Anglo American Protestants from the mid-nineteenth to the early twentieth centuries embraced the idea of Manifest Destiny.[6]

The Protestant denominations participated in the expansionist program of the nation. Macum Phelan states in *A History of Early Methodists in Texas, 1817–1866,* "The news of the rebel victory at San Jacinto reached the Gen-eral Conference of the Methodist Episcopal Church in session at Cincin-nati, Ohio, in May, 1836, and produced no little rejoicing."[7] Although indi-vidual Methodist preachers, on their own initiative held occasional, and

illegal, Methodist services in Texas during the period of Mexican sovereignty, the leaders of the Methodist Episcopal Church respected Mexico's
prohibition of Protestant religion in Texas by refraining from sending
Methodist missionary personnel into that region. However, as soon as
Texas became an independent republic, Methodists sent missionaries to
the nascent republic's Anglo-American inhabitants. A Methodist missionary circuit was established in 1837, expanded to a district in 1838, two districts in 1839, and became an annual conference in 1848.[8]

Other denominations also established ecclesiastical organizations in
Texas following its independence. The Presbytery of Texas of the Presbyterian Church of the United States of America was established in April
1840 in Washington County.[9] Three ministers of the Cumberland Presbyterian Church met in San Augustine County in November 1837 to organize the Texas Presbytery.[10] Of the seven Baptist churches, three organized
the first Baptist cooperative association in October 1840, the Texas Baptist
Association.[11] These first ecclesiastical organizations were organized by
and for Anglo American inhabitants in Texas; the central concern among
Protestant leaders was the establishment of congregations among the
English-speaking. There was, thus, very limited contact between Anglo
Protestants and Mexican Americans in Texas during these years.

As Protestants slowly awakened to the needs of the Spanish-speaking in
their midst in American and Mexican borderlands, they began to receive a
handful of Mexicans and Mexican Americans into their organizations.
Anglo American Methodists, like those of other Protestant denominations,
endorsed and participated in the subordination of Mexicans and Mexican
Americans within their own denomination. Mexicans and Mexican Americans who joined Protestant churches frequently found themselves
marginalized within the very institutions designed to minister to them.
Mexican American Methodists, unaware of the systemic causes of their
treatment, were nonetheless cognizant of the inequalities that existed
between them and their Anglo American colleagues. As agents of their
own history, Mexican American Methodists occasionally took measures to
mitigate their marginalization.[12]

First Period: Neglect of Mexican Americans in the Southwest

The period under consideration begins with the independence of Texas
from Mexico. The encounter with Spanish-speaking persons during the
period of Texas Independence, 1836–1845, contributed to the racial identity of English-speaking persons in Texas. A smaller number of Anglo
Americans visited and settled in New Mexico during the same period,

perhaps because the New Mexico territory remained a part of the Republic of Mexico until 1848. Reports about the moral laxity of the Spanish-speaking inhabitants by travelers and settlers in these regions validated Anglo Americans' contention that God had destined them to occupy and govern the whole continent. Sporadic efforts by a few individuals to minister to the Spanish-speaking in the Southwest occurred during this initial period of contact. Sustained efforts by Protestant missionary agencies began after the Civil War.[13]

Mexican Americans were peripheral to the denominations' mission strategy. The first Protestant missionary efforts focused on Anglo Americans in the Southwest. The pattern of neglect toward the Spanish-speaking was relatively the same among Methodists, Presbyterians, and Baptists. Following Texas' independence, the bishops and the Board of Missions of the Methodist Episcopal Church, South, decided to establish a ministry within the nascent nation. Sylvest notes, "That ministry, however, was intended primarily for Anglo Texans."[14] Under the auspices of the Methodist Episcopal Church's mission society, the Reverend Enoch Nicholson's first missionary foray into New Mexico in 1851 focused on the Anglo American community in Santa Fe.[15]

This examination of the relationship between Mexican American and Anglo American Methodists is framed within the process of marginalization; it examines the ways in which the institutional and social relationships between Anglo American and Mexican American Methodists contributed to the alienation of Mexican Americans within their own denomination. The idea of marginality serves as an overarching concept that implies exclusion, powerlessness, and subordination to members of the dominant society. Characteristics of marginality include: (1) paternalism and dependency; (2) subordination to those wielding power; (3) inaccessibility to opportunities for self-realization, such as education, leadership development, and employment; (4) segregation and exclusion; (5) inequality of finances, social status, and distribution of resources; and (6) neglect. These characteristics of marginality describe various ways in which Mexican American Methodists experienced a subordinate status within their church.

As the first and second generation of Mexican American Methodists remained within the Methodist church and became subject to the administrative practices of Anglo American missionaries and church leaders, they eventually developed and expressed resentment toward patterns of domination practiced by Anglo American Methodists. Although Mexican American Methodists esteemed the indefatigable character of the Anglo

American missionaries, they eventually desired to assume leadership roles within their institutions. It was only after Anglo Americans had dominated Mexican and Mexican Methodist institutions that the latter recognized their disfranchisement within their own institutions. While they did not yet question the authenticity of the Anglo American and Protestant model for their church institution, they did come to question and oppose the domination and abuses of Anglo American missionaries. They also struggled to achieve a level of equality with other annual conferences.

Ecclesiastical institutions provide for the ordering of ministry and the polity of the church, but more important, they also structure relationships of domination and subordination among clergy and congregations. Relations between Mexican American and Anglo American Methodists are best understood by examining the interaction of these two groups within the institution, the arena in which the two groups had the most contact. The relationships of domination and subordination during the period of 1836–1939 were clearly structured along ethnic lines, with missionaries maintaining control of the institutions designed to minister to Mexicans and Mexican Americans. Tensions between Spanish-speaking and Anglo American Protestants emerged when Anglo American church leaders made decisions about the ministry that directly affected Mexicans and Mexican Americans without including them in the deliberations. At the turn of this century, Mexican and Mexican American Methodists rejected the need for the continuation of Anglo leadership within their institutions and petitioned general church structures for equal consideration in matters of church policy.

Mission personnel of the denominations demonstrated a greater concern for the evangelization of Mexico than for the evangelization of Mexican Americans in the Southwest. Mission efforts directed toward Mexican Americans in the United States were viewed as preliminary work leading to the eventual evangelization of Mexico. For example, the first Latino ordained minister in Texas, the Reverend Alejo Hernandez, was sent to Mexico shortly after he was admitted on trial to the West Texas Conference in December 1871. After having served brief appointments in Laredo and Corpus Christi, Texas, Bishop John Keener, of the Methodist Episcopal Church, South, appointed Hernandez to begin missionary work in Mexico City in 1873.[16] The Reverend William C. Blair, an Old School Presbyterian minister working among the Spanish-speaking in the Republic of Texas, wrote to his denomination's Board of Foreign Missions in 1841:

> Although this mission is for the present located in Texas, it is properly a mission to Mexico. The day is not distant when the intolerance of popery will no longer be able to retain in seclusion and darkness the missions of Mexico and

South America. As well may the attempt be made to stem the current of the Mississippi as to arrest in our hemisphere the progress of civil and religious liberty which already, by the independence of Texas, has reached the borders of Mexico.[17]

In the wake of religious reforms in Mexico in the 1850s, 1860s, and 1870s, mission personnel, excited by the vision of a Protestant Mexican population, began allocating more resources for the nascent Mexican mission field. The consequence of this new evangelistic thrust was the neglect of the existing Spanish-speaking population in the southwestern United States. Alfredo Nañez notes the lopsided allocation of resources by 1889. In that year, "Out of thirty-seven appointments [in the Conferencia Fronteriza Misionera Mexicana] only eleven were in the United States." That same year, "The six American missionaries in the conference were all stationed in Mexico; and of the six presiding elders, only one was stationed in the United States."[18] Mission personnel also gave Mexico a priority in educational missions; all but one of the Methodist schools were located in northern Mexico in 1890.[19] The lack of attention given to Mexican Americans in the southwestern U.S. in the second half of the nineteenth century points to the view of church leaders toward Mexican Americans as an inconsequential group.

Benigno Cardenas and the Mission Society of the Methodist Episcopal Church

Stratified relationships among Anglo American and Mexican and Mexican American Methodists existed from the first encounters between the two groups of preachers. Benigno Cardenas became the first Spanish-speaking person to preach a Protestant sermon in Spanish in the United States in 1853. A former priest in the Catholic Church, he first became involved with Methodism after meeting a Methodist missionary in England. He was en route home from a meeting with Vatican officials in Rome, a trip made with the intent to resolve his conflictive relationship with Catholic authorities in New Mexico. When he arrived in New York, Cardenas offered his services to the Mission Society of the Methodist Episcopal Church. Coincidentally, the first Methodist missionary to New Mexico, the Reverend Enoch Nicholson, had just returned from a missionary sojourn in the region. The Mission Society decided to renew the New Mexico mission and expand its work to include the Spanish-speaking population. The Mission Society sent Cardenas and Walter Hansen, a young minister from Wisconsin who spoke Spanish, with Nicholson.[20]

The hierarchical pattern of authority, in which Anglo American missionaries served as presiding elders over Mexican clergy, was established with the relationship between Cardenas and Nicholson. The Mission Society appointed Nicholson as the superintendent of the New Mexican mission and Hansen as his assistant. Officials of the Mission Society allowed Cardenas to accompany Nicholson and Hansen on a conditional basis. Cardenas would be accepted into the Methodist Episcopal Church through the mission in New Mexico and would be employed as Nicholson's assistant if he complied with certain conditions. The Mission Society's key conditions for admission as a Methodist missionary were that Cardenas "should apply publicly to the Mission for admission and service and [that] his spirit and conduct [be] satisfactory to Brother Nicholson, the Superintendent."[21] This arrangement, in which Anglo American missionaries supervised the work of Mexican pastors and laity and sat in judgment of their character, continued for decades.

After spending less than a year in New Mexico, Nicholson and Hansen became discouraged in their efforts to cultivate a Methodist presence in New Mexico and returned east in June 1854. They left Cardenas behind to continue preaching in the upper Rio Grande Valley of New Mexico.[22] Under Nicholson's supervision, Cardenas' relationship to Anglo American clergy began as a subordinate to the missionary. Left alone in the mission field, his relationship with the Mission Society became one of frustration and discouragement. Still, he continued preaching and visiting families in the region of Socorro. The Mission Society's corresponding secretary, John P. Durbin, credited Cardenas with maintaining an active Methodist presence in New Mexico in his 1855 report:

> All that remains of these efforts are the residence and the active preaching of Rev. Benigno Cardenas, a native of New Mexico. . . . It is a matter of great thankfulness to God that he has been faithful to his great spiritual enlightenment and charge, and has become, as we truly believe, a genuine evangelical Christian. All our private information from New Mexico attests this, as well as the work he is doing. But he is alone, and earnestly appeals to us to send him a superintendent and an assistant.[23]

Cardenas' petition to the Mission Society to send a superintendent and an assistant to help him went unanswered. After Cardenas eventually quit his mission work and dropped out of sight in late 1855, Ambrosio Gonzalez, a lay exhorter in Peralta, guided the only remaining Methodist group in New Mexico from 1855–1871.[24] Sylvest notes that, despite Cardenas' being received as a minister into the Methodist Episcopal Church and proving himself an effective evangelist and pastor during his two years as a Methodist preacher, "there was evidently no consideration given to the possibility of commissioning Benigno Cardenas as superintendent of the New Mexico mission."[25]

To summarize the first period of inter-ethnic relations along the borderlands, ranging from the beginning of Texas' independence to the aftermath of the Civil War, Protestant churches and individuals occasionally attempted to evangelize Mexicans and Mexican Americans, but failed to develop a systematic and committed mission toward this population. Their work produced few lasting results; only a handful of Spanish-speaking Protestant groups existed by the end of this period.[26] The overwhelming majority of Mexicans and Mexican Americans chose to maintain their Catholic faith. Rarely did Mexicans and Mexican Americans become members of the English-speaking churches, and only a handful of Spanish-speaking congregations existed by the end of this period.[27]

Second Period: Institutional Coordination

In the second period, beginning in the aftermath of the Civil War, the pattern of ministry to Mexican Americans in the Methodist denominations changed from that of individualized and sporadic action to one of institutional coordination. In the northern and southern branches of Methodism, continuous and substantial financial support of Spanish-speaking work by mission boards and annual conferences began with the appointments of the Reverend Thomas Harwood as superintendent of the New Mexico Mission of the Methodist Episcopal Church in 1872 and the Reverend Alexander Sutherland as presiding elder of the Spanish-speaking work in Texas of the Methodist Episcopal Church, South, in 1874. The relative success of Hispanic ministry in Texas and New Mexico can be attributed largely to the zealousness of these two superintendents. Each helped establish and expand the first Methodist organizations for Mexican American Methodists. After the Mexican Border Missionary District of the West Texas Conference was established in 1874, with Sutherland as the presiding elder, the Spanish-speaking ministry in Texas and northern Mexico progressed steadily. The West Texas Conference authorized a second Spanish-speaking district in 1880, and the General Conference authorized the organization of an annual conference in 1882. The Conferencia Fronteriza Misionera Mexicana (Mexican Border Mission Conference) reported 1,370 members at its first annual conference in 1885. Spanish-speaking membership increased gradually for the next five years to 1,859 in 1890, the year that the conference voted to divide into two conferences.[28] From

1885 to 1890, Sutherland served at different times as a presiding elder of three of the districts of this conference. He moved his conference membership to the Central Mexico Mission Conference in 1891, where he served as presiding elder of the Mexico City District, and then to the Northwest Mexican Mission Conference in 1892, where he was appointed to the English-speaking congregation in Chihuahua.[29]

The Reverend Thomas Harwood arrived in New Mexico in 1869 and became the superintendent for the New Mexico Mission in 1872. After fourteen years of mission work that included both English- and Spanish-speaking groups, he urged his denomination to separate the work. He was appointed superintendent of the newly segregated New Mexico Spanish Mission the year that the 1884 General Conference granted his recommendation. The members of the new Spanish-speaking mission held their first annual meeting in Peralta, New Mexico, in 1885, with 410 regular members.[30] Membership increased steadily to 1,118 members in 1890 and 2,098 members in 1907, the last year in which Harwood served as superintendent.[31]

Although one could argue that the establishment of these organizations and the participation of a number of Mexican Americans in the Methodist denominations was a testament to Anglo American Methodists' concern for the Spanish-speaking people, a closer examination of inter-ethnic relations among Mexican American and Anglo American Methodists reveals processes whereby Mexican American Methodists became marginalized within their adopted church. Mexican Americans were marginal within their denomination in the same way that they were marginal within the Anglo-dominant society. Anglo American Methodists dominated the coordination of the ecclesiastical institutions designed for ministry to Mexicans and Mexican Americans until 1939. Also remuneration for Anglo and Mexican American ministers was unequal.

Anglo American Missionaries' Views Toward Mexican Americans

Anglo American Protestants' perceptions of Mexican American religion and culture as inferior reveal more about their own self-identity than they do about Mexican and Mexican American life. Anglo American Protestants perceived themselves as the new religious conquistadors, conquering the "blighted" spirit of Mexicans and replacing their Roman Catholicism with what church leaders believed to be an enlightened religion. Sutherland, the most influential Methodist missionary to the Spanish-speaking in Texas and northern Mexico in the late nineteenth century, the

Reverend Alexander H. Sutherland, wrote in 1883, "Age on age of darkness, duplicity, and degradation have left [Mexicans] so full of evil, so prone to evil, that the task of purification and elevation would be utterly hopeless, leaving out the divinity of the agency."[32]

Methodists were not alone in their evaluation of the inferior status of Mexicans and Mexican Americans. Mission personnel from other denominations also viewed Mexicans and Mexican Americans as persons in need of spiritual conquest. R. W. Roundy, the Associate Secretary of the Home Missions Council, wrote in 1921 about the need to employ the same amount of energy that had been exerted in the military and political conquest of the Southwest in the spiritual conquest of Mexicans in the U.S.:

> What may not be done in solving the problem of the Mexican in our midst by a program of spiritual invasion and Christian conquest on a much less impressive plan of personnel and money than that appearing in our political or military expedition to the border? May we not carry the Christian flag to the very homes and hearts of these handicapped sons of old Mexico at our very doors, aye, in our own American house![33]

Even after Mexicans and Mexican Americans converted to Protestantism, Anglo American missionaries deemed them incapable of managing their own institutions. Conversion to Protestantism, which was a way of becoming more like Anglo American Protestants, did not guarantee full acceptance by Anglo Americans. Sutherland expressed his views of the capabilities of Mexicans in his annual report in 1884:

> The Mexican preachers cannot possibly conduct the work or command the confidence of all classes as can the American preachers. Nature and providence, not to say grace, have endowed them [Americans] differently from the Mexicans. The Mexicans can make good preachers and pastors, and some few will rise to the grade of presiding elders; but organizers and managers they will seldom—very seldom—ever prove. They are a "rope of sand" when left to themselves. They are so politically and socially, and will prove so ecclesiastically and break all to pieces unless there be the infusion of an adhesive element.[34]

This assessment of Mexicans' abilities goes a long way toward explaining why Sutherland monopolized so many leadership positions within the church. Apparently, he judged the Mexican clergy incapable of managing the work of the church, so he took it upon himself to do it for them.

Segregation of Spanish-speaking and English-speaking Institutions

Institutional segregation between Anglo American and Mexican American Methodists began in 1874 with the first organization composed of Mexican clergy and congregations—the Mexican Mission District of the West Texas Conference of the Methodist Episcopal Church, South. After years of expansion, it became the Mexican Border Mission Conference in 1885. In 1884, after fifteen years as a unified mission, the Methodist Episcopal Church divided the Spanish- and English-speaking work in New Mexico into two separate missions.

The first institutions designed to minister to the Spanish-speaking in New Mexico in the Methodist Episcopal Church were fashioned along ethnic lines after an effort at integration failed to produce harmonious and productive relations between Spanish- and English-speaking New Mexicans. Thomas Harwood, a missionary of the Methodist Episcopal Church in New Mexico since 1869, notes in his 1882 report that cultural differences created tension between Mexican Americans and Anglo Americans in the Methodist Episcopal Church.

> Generally, when our work is either all Mexican or all English, it does better. We find it difficult to mix the work without more or less clash. Our native work is passing a kind of transit with the American. We cannot tell from any observations yet made what the results finally will be. It seems quite apparent, however, that the time must come, if it is not already upon us, when the American and Mexican work must be separated.[35]

Inter-ethnic tensions within a few integrated congregations, as well as the tendency for most congregations to remain segregated, led Harwood to request a division of the mission work along ethnic lines at the 1884 General Conference of the Methodist Episcopal Church.[36]

Once the missions were segregated between Anglo American and Mexican American groups, Mexican American clergy did not have an option of joining English-speaking missions or conferences. From the first, Mexican American clergy were appointed to minister exclusively among the Spanish-speaking population. Even though the first Spanish-speaking presiding elder became a candidate for the ordained ministry through the recommendation of the English-speaking mission in Bandera in 1876, the Reverend Santiago Tafolla's first appointment was to the Spanish-speaking church in Laredo.[37] Mexican American Methodist preachers never served as pastors to Anglo American congregations during this period. Anglo American leaders could not yet entertain the possibility, as many still cannot today, of appointing Mexican Americans to Anglo American congregations. Whenever an Anglo American minister was appointed to a Mexican setting, it was usually as a supervisor over Mexican clergy or as an administrator, rarely simply as a pastor.[38]

Dominant and Subordinate Relationships Between Anglo American Missionaries and Mexican American Pastors

Relationships of domination and subordination between Anglo American superintendents and presiding elders of the Spanish-speaking missions and the Mexican clergy reveal another aspect of marginalization experienced by Spanish-speaking Methodists. Because of their direct and frequent contact with Mexican preachers, superintendents and presiding elders served as de facto bishops among the Mexican and Mexican American clergy. Bishops, themselves Anglo Americans, presided over the sessions of the missions and conferences, but in actuality, the missionaries managed Spanish-speaking work. Some of the Anglo American missionaries dominated the leadership in Spanish-speaking missions and conferences. Though one would imagine that Anglo Americans would assume leadership positions while Mexican and Mexican American converts became accustomed to Methodist doctrine and polity, one would expect the Anglo American missionaries to cede their leadership positions once Mexican and Mexican American converts developed into leaders. In fact, the cessation of leadership by Anglo Americans to Mexicans was a slow and difficult process. Although Mexican and Mexican American clergy and laity participated in committees and exercised their right to vote on business matters, Anglo American superintendents and presiding elders at times dominated the deliberations of annual meetings and conferences.

Sutherland's missionary career typifies the leadership that Anglo American missionaries exercised in Mexican and Mexican American Methodist institutions. From 1874 to 1891, while Sutherland worked in Mexican missions and conferences in Texas and northern Mexico, he served only as a presiding elder. He served as a pastor of a local English-speaking congregation in Chihuahua, Mexico, the year before he requested a change of his ministerial status to Voluntary Location in 1893. (Voluntary Location allowed an ordained minister to keep his ministerial credentials while remaining unavailable for an appointment as an itinerant minister. His credentials remained "located" at a particular congregation, where he was allowed to continue as an ordained minister.) During his years as a superintendent and presiding elder, he had much opportunity to instruct Mexican American pastors in the ways of Methodism. Undoubtedly, the early years of Hispanic Methodism in Texas and northern Mexico bear his imprint.

A survey of conference journals reveals the dominance of Sutherland in evangelistic and administrative matters as well as in annual conference proceedings. He was the co-editor of the conference periodical, *El Evangelista Mexicana,* in 1887. In 1888, the conference Commission on Publications recommended the publication of two of his books, *Catecismos Nos. 1, 2, 3* and *Manual de Predicador.* He and another missionary, Robert McDonell, were selected to choose hymns and poems for a forthcoming ecumenical hymnal, titled *Himnario General.*[39] He and another missionary, D. W. Carter, served on an arbitration commission that handled difficulties among denominations in the distribution of mission territories.[40] In 1890, he represented the annual conference as a delegate to General Conference and served as the chairperson of the conference Board of Missions, a prestigious position that coordinated the mission work of the conference.[41] That same year, he was also the conference representative of the Book Concern, the conference treasurer, the editor of the conference periodical, *El Evangelista Mexicana,* and the official editor of publications. He was also the presiding elder of the Monterey district from 1889–1890 and of the San Antonio district from 1890–1891.[42]

The Reverend Sutherland was certainly the most dominant, if not the most effective, Methodist missionary among Mexicans in Texas and northern Mexico in the nineteenth century. He was, however, only one of several Anglo American missionaries and clergy who came from the South and the Midwest to exercise their leadership in Mexican missions and conferences spanning northern Mexico and the southwestern United States. Other Anglo American clergy transferred their membership into the Mexican conferences and quickly assumed leadership positions. It is not surprising that, after several decades of Anglo American leadership, the Mexican clergy of the Conferencia Fronteriza Mexicana Metodista in 1914 requested more careful consideration in the appointment process so that they might exercise their ministry in leadership positions.[43] They recognized that the church in Mexico would not achieve an indigenous character until Mexican clergy were allowed to assume greater responsibility in the administration of their church.

Analysis of the Spanish-speaking jurisdictions of the Methodist Episcopal Church, South, reveals patterns of inclusion and exclusion of Spanish-speaking clergy as presiding elders of districts and superintendents of missions. All superintendents appointed to coordinate Spanish-speaking work were Anglo American clergy. There were more Spanish-speaking elders from 1885 to 1896 than during the period from 1897 to 1925. During the latter period, there was one presiding elder appointed in Mexico from 1898–1901 and another appointed in 1923 and in 1924. From 1902–1922 there were no Spanish-speaking elders in any of the Spanish-speaking jurisdictions of the Methodist Episcopal Church, South, in Mexico and in the U.S. Southwest.[44] This would account for the request for greater participation in the leadership circles by the Mexican preachers at the 1914 annual conference of the Conferencia Fronteriza Misionera Mexicana.

No Spanish-speaking presiding elders were appointed in the U.S. from 1895 to 1930. No Spanish-speaking Methodists in the regions of Arizona, Nevada, or California ever served as presiding elders or superintendents during this period of study. In Texas and New Mexico, from 1914 to 1930, when this region became separated from the southern Methodist mission work in Mexico, the mission was directed by an Anglo American superintendent. With the change to a mission conference status in 1930, Frank Ramos, who had functioned as a presiding elder, was appointed superintendent of a district. He thus became the first Spanish-speaking superintendent in Texas and New Mexico of the Methodist Episcopal Church, South, since the late 1800s.

The Mexico Annual Conference (Conferencia Anual de Mexico) took the first steps toward the inclusion of Mexican presiding elders. Following an absence of Mexican presiding elders since 1901, E. B. Vargas was appointed presiding elder of the Chihuahua district in 1923 and continued until 1926. In 1925, he was accompanied by two more Mexican presiding elders. In 1926, for the first time, all four of the presiding elders in the Mexico Annual Conference were Mexicans. This set the stage for the conference becoming an autonomous Methodist church in 1930. The pattern of all presiding elders being Mexican or Mexican American occurred thirteen years later in the Texas Mexican Mission (Conferencia Misionera de Texas) in 1939. The Pacific Mexican Mission (Misión Mexicana del Pacifico), which later became the Western Mexican Mission (Misión Mexicana del Occidente), and eventually the Western Mexican Conference (Conferencia Mexicana del Occidente), never had Spanish-speaking presiding elders.

The Reverend Santiago Tafolla, who converted to Methodism in 1875 while living in Privilege Creek, Texas, was the first Mexican American presiding elder in the United States.[45] He was appointed the presiding elder of the San Diego Mexican Mission District of the Southwest Texas Conference of the Methodist Episcopal Church, South, in 1881.[46] He served as a presiding elder in four districts within the Mexican Border Mission Conference (Conferencia Fronteriza

Misionera Mexicana) from 1885–89 and 1890–94.[47] Other Mexicans and Mexican Americans eventually appointed as presiding elders had to serve simultaneously as pastors of local congregations in order to fund their office of presiding elder. This was not always the case for Anglo American missionaries appointed as presiding elders; the salaries, pensions, and benefits they received from the Mission Board followed them wherever they were appointed.[48]

Unequal Salaries Between Anglo American and Mexican and Mexican American Methodist Ministers

In addition to being in a subordinate relationship to superintendents and presiding elders, who were almost always Anglo Americans, Mexican and Mexican American clergy were also poorer than their Anglo American colleagues.[49] Anglo American missionaries could dedicate themselves to full-time ministry since they received salaries from the Board of Missions. Some missionaries, such as Alexander Sutherland and Frank Onderdonk, also received additional funds from sponsoring churches and individuals. Roger Loyd, in his paper, "Alexander H. Sutherland: Prophet of the Lord," states, "Sutherland knew about public relations to the extent that he kept his sources for income informed about the work, so that he was not dependent solely on the Board of Missions for funds."[50] Operating apart from the Anglo American community, Mexican and Mexican American clergy lacked access to the sources of financial support available to the missionaries. The paucity of Mexican church members and their poor financial condition prevented local congregations from providing sufficient income for their pastors.

Third Period: Responses to Marginality

Lower salaries for Mexican and Mexican American preachers continued into the third period and became a point of contention between Spanish-speaking and Anglo American Methodists. In addition to unequal salaries, the third period was characterized by the gradual development of an indigenous leadership that challenged the influence of Anglo American missionaries. Mexican American Methodists made their desires and intentions known as they responded to decisions made for their institutions by Anglo American church leaders. The period also witnessed the division of Spanish-speaking work along the Mexican and U.S. border and the transferral of responsibility for the Spanish-speaking missions in the Southwest from the foreign missions units to home missions units.

Insufficient salaries contributed to the decline of the Spanish-speaking work of the Methodist Episcopal Church in New Mexico. Referring to Hispanic pastors in New Mexico, Randi Jones Walker states in *Protestantism in the Sangre de Cristos, 1850–1920:*

> The Methodists had an adequate method of training their pastors, but the churches could not pay them what they expected or even needed. In 1914 the Methodist Hispanic pastors received only $400 to $500 per year in comparison to the Presbyterians who received $700 to $800 per year. The Methodists reported most pastors chose to locate where they could buy a farm or make another living on the side. This made them unavailable for itinerant conference appointment, and they ceased to belong to the Methodist conference and to enjoy the privileges of the conference member, although some continued to serve a church as a local or lay pastor.[51]

Mission Board officials of the Methodist Episcopal Church, South, showed interest in extending the Methodist presence in the Southwest and Mexico by allocating a large portion of its budget to this region, but substantial funding for mission work did not include adequate salaries for the native preachers. Loyd states that "in 1880, the Board gave $15,000 to the Mexican Border Missions out of a total budget of $121,248—over 10% of its resources available. The Mexican work appears to have been somewhat of a showpiece to the Board."[52] However, the Mission Board was investing funds in medical and educational institutions rather than in salary support for Mexican and Mexican American preachers. Mission personnel were creating Methodist schools in northern Mexico that were inaccessible to their own Mexican pastors. The report of the Board of Education of the Mexican Border Mission Conference (Conferencia Fronteriza Mexicana Metodista) states,

> The time has come when the ministers' children need to be educated, and with great embarrassment we have to admit that some of the ministers will be taking their children to public schools in Mexico, where they will become unbelievers and free-thinkers, and therefore their tender hearts will become corrupt; but the brethren say that in spite of that they will take this class of education, because there they receive scholarships for the children, privileges which are not available to them in our Christian schools, the case being that their salaries barely provide a living and do not allow them to send their children to Christian schools. In view of this we call attention to the bishop of our Conference to see if it is possible to remedy this problem that threatens the future of our dear children.[53]

Even as the Board of Missions increased its funding of Mexican and Mexican American mission work to $77,445 by 1913, pastors continued to receive salaries substantially lower than those of Anglo American clergy.[54]

The Reverend Alfredo Nañez frequently alludes to a two-tier salary level benefiting Anglo American missionaries within the Spanish-speaking missions and conferences in several places in *A History of the Rio Grande Conference of the United Methodist Church* and "Transition from Anglo to Mexican-American Leadership in the Rio Grande Conference." Disparate salary levels are even more apparent when one compares salaries between Spanish-speaking pastors in the Texas Mexican Conference and pastors in the (Anglo American dominant) Southwest Texas Conference, both of whose boundaries covered south and central Texas. The average contribution by local churches for the pastor's salary in the Texas Mexican Conference was $363.64 in 1930; the amount contributed per church for the same year in the Southwest Texas Conference was $1,865.28.

Division of Methodist Missions Between Mexico and the United States

Mexican and Mexican American clergy had a marginal role in determining the boundaries of the Spanish-speaking missions and conferences, and in deciding policy regarding the church's mission to Mexicans and Mexican Americans. Mission Board personnel made policy decisions regarding Spanish-speaking work without consulting the Mexican and Mexican American clergy. A clear example of the mission board's paternalistic practice is its failure to include the participation of Spanish-speaking representatives of the mission work in its decision to divide the mission work in Mexico and the United States between the Foreign and Interior Missions units.[55] The memorial to divide the work along national boundaries was made in Nashville by the Mission Board in 1913 and signed by five persons with English surnames.[56]

In light of disruptions and dangers caused by the Mexican Revolution in Mexico, and the Mission Board's plans to divide the Spanish-speaking work, Bishop H. C. Morrison convened a meeting of the missionaries and officers of the Mexican Border Mission Conference (Conferencia Fronteriza Misionera Mexicana) to consider the administrative needs and boundaries of future Spanish-speaking work. Fourteen missionaries, three officials of the Board of Missions, and some visitors met with the bishop in Laredo, Texas, on February 10-11, 1914.[57] No Mexicans or Mexican Americans were present in this consultation. The minutes of the 1914 annual conference indicate that dividing the work between the Foreign and Domestic units of the Mission Board was only one of several proposals made for restructuring and coordinating the work in Mexico and the Southwest, including the establishment of an ecumenical seminary and the reorganization of girls' schools in Mexico.[58]

Fifteen Mexican and Mexican American pastors met separately in Laredo, Texas, on February 11, 1914, to deliberate the proposals that emerged from the meeting of the Anglo American leaders. With the Reverend Basilio Soto presiding, the pastors formulated a series of positions with respect to the Mission Board's proposal and to the general improvement of the church's ministry in Mexico and Texas. The ministers agreed with the rationale behind the separation of Spanish-speaking work according to the political boundaries of Mexico and the United States. Recognizing that the work in Texas would be conducted within an Anglo American society, they added a qualification to their agreement. The statement by the ministers concludes:

> This body would lament the incorporation of the Mexican work into any other conference. This would strip the Mexican work of its identity and take away from members of the conference rights that every Christian considers sacred. Therefore, upon approval of the change, and believing it in accord with good reasoning, this body requests that the General Conference form in Texas a Mexican Conference, in the same manner in which other conferences exist in these regions, [which have been] organized by people not native to this region.[59]

This statement manifests the Mexican clergy's identity as a people distinct from Anglo American Methodists as early as the turn of the century. The pastors were aware that incorporation of the Mexican work into the Anglo American conferences would leave them susceptible to the decisions of an alien organization. Working within an Anglo American conference, they would not receive opportunities for leadership and empowerment that were available in a separate conference; they would continue existing as second-class persons within their own church. In their desire for self-determination and equality, they petitioned the General Conference for the establishment of a separate, Spanish-speaking conference in Texas. Instead of creating a separate Spanish-speaking conference, the 1914 General Conference established the Texas Mexican Mission as a distinct unit of the Mexican Conference. The General Conference also established the Pacific Mexican Mission, for the territory in northern Mexico and the southern U.S. along the Pacific Ocean, as a second mission unit of the Mexican Conference.[60]

The Response of Mexican and Mexican American Methodists to the Domination of Leadership Positions by Anglo American Methodists

Another part of the Laredo Resolution refers to the Mexican clergy's desire to exercise responsibility for the mission of their church. The conference approved the following resolution composed by Spanish-speaking clergy.

> This body believes that the day is not far off in which the Mexican people will have to take responsibility for the work of the Evangelical Church, and feeling the lack of persons prepared to head such a movement, it recommends that greater opportunities for leadership be granted to national workers.[61]

This tactful statement implied that Anglo American clergy assumed so much authority in the administration of the Mexican work that leadership opportunities were lacking for Mexican clergy. Rather than expressing grievances, though, the pastors sought solutions; they asked that future appointments and conference nominations be made with consideration for the indigenization of the church in Mexico.

A sufficient number of Mexican clergy and laity on both sides of the border were so discontented with the dominance of church governance by Anglo American church leaders that a number of them formed an independent church in northern Mexico and south Texas. Nañez reports that, around the turn of the century,

> a group of leaders from several Protestant denominations, many of whom were Methodists, left their churches and organized the Evangelical Mexican Church, an autonomous church formed entirely of Mexicans. This anti-missionary movement extended into Texas and for a few years affected the Spanish-speaking work of the Methodist Church in the Southwest, especially around San Antonio.[62]

The formation of an indigenous church is emblematic of the desire of Mexicans and Mexican Americans to determine the policy and direction of their church without the constraints of an Anglo-dominant denominational bureaucracy. This was a case of Mexicans using a separatist strategy to achieve political autonomy and cultural preservation. The establishment of an indigenous Protestant movement demonstrates the willingness of some Mexicans and Mexican Americans to enhance their self-determination when they felt constrained by existing denominational structures and practices.

Tension between Mexican and Anglo American Methodists rose again after Anglo American delegates of the Western Mexican and Texas Mexican conferences at the 1934 General Conference supported legislation that favored the continuation of their dominant status. The General Conference approved legislation that limited the tenure of presiding elders to four consecutive years, but included an exemption for the Texas and Western Mexican conferences, as well as for mission fields.[63] The exemption allowed Anglo Americans coincidentally serving as presiding elders in mission fields and the two conferences then to remain in their positions indefinitely, thereby denying the native clergy those opportunities for leadership. The exemption had not been requested by the two Spanish-speaking conferences.

Nañez, in an interview, alludes to the emergence of a new awareness of a paternalistic decision-making process as he inquired into the matter of the exemption in 1934. He states that the Western Mexican Conference voted against the legislation because the Spanish-speaking members resented the domination of their conference by several Anglo American missionaries.[64] Nañez was impressed with the fact that the Western Mexican Conference was the only conference that voted against the proposed legislation, "essentially against the double standard." He states:

Little by little I was deducing how legislation was done in the Methodist Church. I did not know anything about this, because I did not have experience. I began to study this, and give it more time, [and learn how] the church, the General Conference, makes decisions according to petitions. Who asked the General Conference that there be an exception to the Methodist Church in the Mexican Conference, that the four [year limitation] be applied to all the church, except in the Texas Mexican Conference [and also in the Western Mexican Conference] . . .

So I began to think who recommended this exemption, and my conclusion, in spite of all of the love and respect I had for the missionaries, especially for Mr. Onderdonk, was that our delegates had made this petition, and the delegates were Anglos. . . .

They made the petition that there be an exemption for our conferences. It could not have been any other way. I never spoke with them about this. But it could not be any other way, because the legislation was that [the presiding elder] remain no more than four years in the Methodist Church.

Then, they involved themselves that there be an exception. And when I discovered this, they began to have doubts about me, and I began to dig around more about the way they operated. And then I said, "Part of the problem was that we had a double standard in the ministry."[65]

If Nañez is correct in his judgment, the incident shows how some Anglo American leaders used their positions of power to maintain their dominant positions within the Spanish-speaking conferences. The coupling of the two Mexican American conferences in the United States with foreign mission fields in this exemption sent a clear message to the members of these conferences that, their official status notwithstanding, they were considered missions rather than annual conferences.

Mexican and Mexican American Methodists of the Western Mexican Conference expressed their resentment after their representatives to General Conference unilaterally supported exemptions that favored the continuation of their positions of power in the conference. When the Western Mexican Conference considered the amendment to the Discipline proposed by General Conference, the body voted 26 to 2 against it.[66] The resounding defeat of the amendment to the Discipline was a pronounced expression of the Mexican members' resentment over their exclusion from the normal policy of the church. It could also be viewed as a rejection of the abuse of power exerted by Anglo American leaders. The Texas Mexican Annual Conference petitioned the General Conference in 1937 for the elimination of the exemption to the rule that allowed presiding elders to serve more than four consecutive years within the Texas Mexican Conference.[67] Nañez states that the General Conference's acceptance of the memorial in 1940 "placed the conference on the same level as the other conferences in Methodism."[68] With the exemption eliminated, the conference could claim to be structurally equal to all other conferences.

The Emergence of an Indigenous Leadership

By the 1930s, various events led to opportunities for self-determination. The Mexican Constitution of 1917 forbade the presence of foreign religious workers in Mexico. This statute provided an opportunity for Mexican clergy to move into the ranks of leadership in the Mexican conferences. Thirteen years later, the Methodist Church in Mexico became an autonomous church. Mexican American clergy eventually assumed more positions of authority in the Texas Mexican Conference (Conferencia Mexicana de Texas) as well. The Reverend Frank S. Onderdonk, who had served as a presiding elder in the Texas Mexican Conference since 1914, died in 1936 while in office. His death left vacant the position of presiding elder of the Northern District. The presiding bishop, Hiram A. Boaz, considered appointing other missionaries to the vacant position.[69] Alfredo Nañez, who at the time of Onderdonk's death was the presiding elder of the Valley District, opposed this option. The night before the bishop made the appointment to fill the vacancy, Nañez met with the bishop to express his desire to see an end to the double standard of compensation between Anglo American missionaries and native clergy. Nañez states:

The following day, to the surprise of several missionaries present at the meeting, the bishop appointed the Reverend Frank Ramos, pastor of La Trinidad Church in San Antonio, where the meeting was being held, as the presiding elder of the Northern District. For the first time in the history of the conference the leadership of the conference was entirely in the hands of Mexican Americans.[70]

At this point, the existence of indigenous leadership of the conference ceased to mirror existing social structures, in which Anglo Americans maintained social, economic, and political power in the Southwest.

Nañez describes the changes that occurred after two Mexican Americans held the two positions of presiding elder in the Texas Mexican Conference (Conferencia Mexicana de Texas) in 1936: "The districts were evenly divided geographically; the name of the Valley District was changed to Southern District, and both presiding elders were given only administrative responsibilities, not having to serve a local church."[71] At Nañez' urging, Grover C. Emmons, the Executive Secretary for Home Missions of the Methodist Episcopal Church, South, abolished the double standard between missionaries' and Mexican American pastors' salaries and pensions within the conference in 1936.[72] From that point onward, missionaries were no longer employed in the conference, and Anglo American pastors serving congregations in the Texas Mexican Conference, and later, the Southwest Mexican and Rio Grande conferences, became subject to the same salary levels as their Mexican American colleagues. With a few exceptions, the leadership of the conference has been consistently in the hands of Mexican Americans since the end of this double standard.

With the appointment of two Hispanic presiding elders and an end to the double standard in clergy compensation, the Texas Mexican Conference set the stage for decades of leadership by indigenous members of the conference. With the cessation of domination by Anglo American missionaries by 1936, Mexican American Methodists were eager to assume responsibility for the administration of their conference and the coordination of the church's mission. After the union of the Methodist Episcopal Church, South, the Methodist Episcopal Church, and the Methodist Protestant Church in 1939, the Spanish-speaking churches of these denominations in Texas and New Mexico were reorganized into the Southwest Mexican Conference that same year. The new conference continued to develop the emerging indigenous leadership. Mexican American leaders proved their administrative and evangelistic abilities; the membership of the Conferencia Suroeste Mexicana increased 42% in eleven years, from 6,903 in 1939 to 9,818 in 1950.[73] The first generation of indigenous Mexican

American Methodist leaders achieved the largest increase in the conference's membership of any period.

Inter-ethnic Relations and the Administration of the New Mexico Spanish Mission of the Methodist Episcopal Church

Spanish-speaking Methodist work in New Mexico, primarily under the aegis of the northern branch of Methodism, prospered while under the leadership of Thomas Harwood, but steadily declined under his successors. Following the departure of Thomas Harwood as general superintendent of the Spanish Mission Conference of the Methodist Episcopal Church in New Mexico in 1907, frequent changes in the mission's leadership and structure continued for several years. In an attempt to revive the weakened Spanish-speaking work, denominational officials merged it with the newly created Southwest Spanish Mission in 1923. This mission spanned four states—Arizona, Colorado, Kansas, and New Mexico—and began with twelve appointments, eight of which were in New Mexico.[74] As the Spanish-speaking mission continued to decline, denominational leaders continued changing the structure of the Spanish work. By 1939, when the Spanish-speaking charges of the Methodist Episcopal Church in New Mexico were incorporated into the newly created Southwest Mexican Conference, the Spanish-speaking membership of the northern branch of Methodism in New Mexico had experienced substantial decline, from a high of 3,117 members[75] to 539 members.[76]

Little consultation with the Spanish-speaking members of the Methodist Episcopal Church in New Mexico occurred as the makers of policy frequently restructured the Spanish-speaking work during this period. Only in the 1930 merger of the Spanish-speaking work in New Mexico with the Latin American Mission in California was there any consultation with the Hispanic members about the organizational structure of their work. Equally significant is the lack of strong leadership, both Anglo and Hispanic, following Harwood's tenure. As in the Methodist Episcopal Church, South, Anglo Americans dominated leadership positions of the Spanish-speaking institutions in the Methodist Episcopal Church. Given the failure of the Methodist Episcopal Church to build an indigenous cadre of leaders, the constant changes in the organization of Spanish-speaking work from 1907 to 1939, and the lack of consultation with the native pastors regarding structural changes in their organization, Spanish-speaking Methodists in New Mexico and the rest of the Southwest found themselves even more marginal in the Methodist Episcopal Church than their counterparts in the Methodist Episcopal Church, South.

Assessing the Character of Relations Between Anglo American Church Leaders and Mexican American Methodists

The relationships between Anglo American missionaries and Mexican clergy during the period 1836–1939 can be characterized by paternalism and dependency. While Mexican American Methodists may not have been as aware as current Mexican American Methodists of the systemic causes of the paternalistic nature of their relationship with Anglo Americans, they were nonetheless aware of the injustices and consequences of paternalism within their church. Their awareness of the paternalism of Anglo American missionaries and denominational leaders and their struggle to reject a second-class status within their church is evident in the previously delineated efforts of Mexican and Mexican American clergy and conferences to overcome domination by Anglo American church leaders and establish their own indigenous leadership.

The struggle of the Rio Grande Conference to maintain its semi-autonomous status since 1939 must be seen in light of the struggle of Mexican Americans throughout the Southwest to free themselves from oppressive structures that relegated them to a second-class citizenship. The conference's struggle to maintain its institutional and cultural autonomy, seen from the point of view of Mexican Americans, is rooted in the struggle of Mexican Americans to be the final arbiters of their own destiny. In this regard, the Rio Grande Conference's history fits within the larger struggle of all Mexican Americans to achieve equality, autonomy, and cultural preservation in an Anglo American–dominant Southwest. To the extent that its Hispanic leadership has sought equality and freedom from discrimination, the conference serves as an ecclesiastical counterpart to Mexican American secular organizations, such as the American GI Forum, the League of United Latin American Citizens, and the La Raza Unida Party, which worked for the equal rights and privileges for Mexican Americans in the United States.

Summary

While recounting Spanish-speaking Methodists' relations with Anglo American missionaries and the Boards of Mission, this study has shown that the institutional life of the church provided structures for the establishment and maintenance of patterns of inter-ethnic relationships characterized by marginalization.

Spanish-speaking Methodists in the Southwest experienced marginalization as mission boards and church leaders neglected them in favor of

English-speaking inhabitants and the Mexican mission field. They also experienced marginalization through the segregation of congregations, missions, and conferences, unequal financial compensation, exclusion from participation in policy decisions affecting their institutions and from leadership positions and seminary education. Marginalization was also indicated by a pattern of dependency and subordination of Mexicans and Mexican Americans to Anglo American church leaders and mission structures. In short, inter-ethnic relations within Methodism in the Southwest paralleled the social inequalities that existed throughout southwestern society.

Mexican and Mexican American Methodists occasionally rejected this alienating relationship and struggled within the institution to move from dependence toward equality and mutuality with Anglo American Methodists. The democratic institution of the annual meeting of Methodist missions and conferences allowed Spanish-speaking Methodists the opportunity to voice their opinions and vote on matters affecting their institutions according to their own interests. By 1939, when three branches of Methodism united (The Methodist Episcopal Church, The Methodist Episcopal Church, South, and The Methodist Protestant Church), the Methodist church in Mexico had become an autonomous church and the Mexican American clergy of the southwestern U.S. had finally assumed leadership of their ecclesiastical organizations.

Latinos in the Protestant Establishment: Is There a Place for Us at the Feast Table?

Daisy L. Machado

Introduction

This chapter examines, through a historical lens, how religious belief, specifically evangelism and missions, was reshaped by particular social conditions. The focus is Texas and the method will be a brief overview of the similarities of the missionary experience for three Protestant denominations: Methodists, the Christian Church (Disciples of Christ), and Baptists in the early 1900s and today. By means of critical comparison, we examine how religious doctrine and social conditions came together in the borderlands missions field of the early 1900s and how these forces have left a long-lasting legacy of tense and unequal relations between Latino Protestants and European American Protestants that still exists today.

In his introduction to the book *Christianity in the Twenty-first Century*, Robert Wuthnow addresses how he understands Christians should think about the coming of the new millennium. He writes that, when thinking about the future,

> the idea is not to identify a crisis in the year 2058 that the church should begin planning for. . . . [Instead,] we need to consider the challenges ahead, asking about the directions of present trends, looking at what we have and what we want, and then by considering the future, assess better where our present energies should lie.[1]

In Wuthnow's list of challenges, which includes the AIDS epidemic, understanding the concept of "community," the vitality of fundamentalism, and the public role of Christianity, among others, he mentions the need to expand the insights made during this twentieth century "about the relationships between religious doctrine and social conditions."[2] Wuthnow holds that at the threshold of a new century, social theorists like Robert N. Bellah, Paul Ricoeur, Peter L. Berger, and others, have greatly contributed to the discourse about doctrine and social environment by demonstrating the *"functional importance* [of religious doctrine] in the lives of individuals and for entire societies."[3] The salient benefit of this has been "to recognize the human need for meaning."[4]

The challenge posed by the relation between religious doctrine and social conditions, which Wuthnow discusses, leads to a question: What does it mean to be a Protestant Christian and also to be Latino or Latina? To ask this one, apparently simple question is to open a Pandora's box of other very significant, albeit complex, questions about the core beliefs (doctrines or theology) of United States Protestantism. For example, how have those beliefs been interpreted since the late 1800s to promote support of and funding for the work of denominations in the historical ethnic American communities (Mexican, African, and Native) of the United States? How has the core belief in religious conversion been interpreted to these same communities by European American missionaries? How have the social conditions of the various historical periods of the United States influenced religious doctrine, specifically the denominational work of evangelism and missions?

The concepts of "home mission," "evangelism," and "new congregation establishment" are religious terms used to describe how Protestant denominations have traditionally done ministry at the national level, meaning within United States borders. Each of these terms represents an effort by Protestants to respond to the Great Commission in Matthew 28, "Go and make disciples," yet the Protestant church's obedience to this call has been continually challenged by powerful social conditions. One significant challenge is the existence of a very multiracial, multi-ethnic, and multilingual society that is no longer just overseas but right next door. Since World War II, both Western Europe and North America have experienced the creation of substantial immigrant communities.[5] Translated into demographics, this means that "more than 100 million people today may live in a country that's not their native soil."[6]

For the North American Protestant establishment, this great, recent movement of people means two very important things. First, ethnic and racial diversity is a national reality, demanding attention at the local congregational level. Second, it brings historical denominations face-to-face with the unavoidable change this diversity implies at the administrative level. As this relates to the Latino population in the United States, the social conditions and patterns of migration are not only very recent, but also come fraught with issues of economic interest, national domination, and racial conflict. The immigration of any group of people is no doubt a complex phenomenon based on a variety of factors. However, for Latinos the reality is that "Hispanics from various points in [Central and] Latin America account for 39 percent of total migration [to the United States between 1960 and 1989]."[7] As a result of this great demographic change, which took place in less than three decades, there exists a visible and growing Latino community that is made up of an exceptionally large number of recent immigrants, which some demographers have said is as much as 13%.[8]

The challenge posed to all Protestant denominations by this recent and tremendous growth of the Latino population is not one that Wuthnow considered in his book. However, this is a very real challenge and one that all denominations across the country face. It has become evident that the Protestant church must continue to find ways to interpret doctrine (in this case evangelism) within very particular social conditions, one of which is rapidly growing Latino communities. As denominations have sought to establish congregations for Latinos, a corollary exigency has surfaced. In trying to understand the "how" of new evangelism or church establishment among Latinos, denominations have had to confront the need to reassess a series of important theological understandings about "mission" and "stewardship."

What has made this task difficult and conflictive is that both mission and stewardship are directly connected to denominational administrative and funding concerns. In all U.S. Protestant denominations, administration and funding are controlled by the European American clergy. In addition to this control, racial tensions have also surfaced, but on two distinct levels. On one level, the issues of power, money, hermeneutics, evangelism have heightened the awareness within denominations of the great disparities that exist between Latino Protestant congregations and their European American counterparts. On a second, more profound level, the great diversity among the ethnic communities themselves means that Protestant denominational bodies are facing the need to expand the historical North American black-white discourse on race. Race in the United States is not just a black-white issue. The social conditions of the diversity which surrounds us mean that the Protestant church's discourse on race must be opened, expanded, and amplified to include the hundreds of thousands of Protestants who are also Latinos and who defy racial stereotypes by coming in all shades of pigmentation, from as dark as ebony to as pale as porcelain.

The Issue of Race: A Look at the Texas Reality

The religious landscape of Protestantism in North America has gone through many changes. Each one has posed a unique challenge to denominations to respond to a changing multiethnic world as an inclusive Christian faith community. Yet it seems that the kind of change needed to respond to Latinos has been barely visible. One can argue that the need for inclusion, for open participation, for full support of Latino ministries, is understood rationally by church folks. This is evidenced by the fact that the ideal of inclusivity and the celebration of diversity have been incorporated into the "God-talk" of most denominations. The public claim of mainstream bodies is to be or to become those "inclusive, prophetic, communities of transformation and renewal" called by God to live in faithful witness. However, these hopeful and uplifting words seem only to disguise the tensions and conflicts that are present and very real in today's Protestant denominations.

In trying to understand the discrepancy between proclamation and praxis, we find that in seeking to minister to Latinos in the United States, most Protestant denominations continually falter when it comes to the issues of race and ethnicity. There seems to be an impasse as denominations face these two constants. The tendency in Protestantism has been to try to absorb the pluralism and "tame" it, but when it comes to the reality of race and ethnicity the process proves more difficult. In the United States today race and ethnicity continue to challenge Protestantism in a distinctive way. This can be explained by differentiating between what one Asian theologian calls the "micro" and "macro" identities found in Christianity. He believes that while the

> church has this universalizing, universalist, homogenizing identity, at the same time church members have micro-identities. Macro-identities versus micro-identities, universalizing or universalist identities versus highly fragmented identities are normal experiences of people.[9]

For this author it is "normal" for all humans to experience the dialectic between macro versus micro and between universal versus particular. However in the United States the historical expectation of absorption and assimilation, as well as the goal of forging a sense of nationalism, have led to other very different conclusions. In the United States, minorities, immigrants, the "Other" have historically been perceived as *needing* to be absorbed into the mainstream dominant culture. The basic idea has been to reshape the Other so he or she can become the sanctioned "American." In a culture that thinks this way, immigrants are perceived as a threat. They are a threat to those already "here" because they represent an uncontrolled diversity, which is seen as "un-American," alien, and therefore, ultimately dangerous.

When closely examined, the idea of nation-building through the process of assimilation, which is so common in this nation's history throughout the nineteenth century, has historically been the normative reaction to recently arrived immigrant groups. Nation-building through assimilation is the process of "majoritarian nationalism, in which ethnic relations are ordered in a hierarchical fashion."[10] As a result the outcome has been that "in this ethnic hierarchy the majority community had access to political power and the other [newer immigrant] communities . . . had no avenues for sharing political power. They [are] at the lower levels of this ethnic hierarchy."[11]

In Texas the continued marginal existence of Latinos in the arenas of politics, education, business, and the church is an example of an ethnic minority with little if any access to power in its own community. At the core of this marginality is the issue of race, and for the Latino community it is an issue that has been shaped by a history peculiar to the Texas reality. Why were Mexicans placed at this lower level of the hierarchy when they were the majority population group? How was race a factor in this marginalization?

> Most [European Americans] who first met Tejanos in the 1820s had never had prior experiences with Mexicans nor encountered them anywhere else. Yet their reaction to them upon contact was contemptuous, many thinking Mexicans abhorrent. . . . The latest scholarship on the subject of racial and cultural attitudes [shows that North] Americans moving to the west . . . had much more in mind than settling the land.[12]

These early nineteenth-century North American settlers to Texas carried with them a cultural baggage that included "a strong belief in themselves and the superiority of their way of life."[13] They also believed it was their "national destiny" to take back or "redeem" the "wilderness" from a less prosperous, unchosen, non-Christian people. Newspaper articles and personal correspondence from this period tell a story of racial attitudes toward the Mexicans of Texas in very forthright language.

> But none was more articulate than Stephen F. Austin, who several times before the war for independence [from Mexico in 1836] confessed almost stereotypically, that his intent was to "redeem Texas from the wilderness." In one of his most eloquent expressions, he averred: "My object, the sole and only desire of my ambitions since I first saw Texas, was to redeem it from the wilderness—to settle it with an intelligent honorable and enterprising people."[14]

Racial attitudes and perceptions dating back to Elizabethan England have been analyzed by Texan historian Arnoldo De León as a way to understand the almost immediate racial rejection of the Mexicans displayed by North Americans. De León argues:

> English immigrants to the North American colonies probably brought those ideas with them and were certainly exposed to them through anti-Catholic and anti-Spanish literature constantly arriving in the new society. Men of letters, ministers, and propagandists helped in disseminating such notions.[15]

De León further posits that the fact that most of the North American settlers to Texas came from a Southern (i.e., Alabama, Tennessee, Georgia, Kentucky) and frontier culture (i.e., Louisiana, Arkansas), which had its own very strong racial attitudes toward African slaves and Native Americans, served only to reinforce the deep racist reactions shown toward the people already living on the lands they sought to occupy. Mexicans were seen as Other, and because of this they were perceived as "primitive" and "savage." But they were also perceived as a "mixed blood" people. Miscegenation was further proof that the Mexican had to be inferior to the "pure blood" of the North American settlers.

> Travelers, who frequently came in contact with Tejanos, plainly discerned the Mexicans' relation to the black and red peoples. Thus, whites often likened Mexicans to Africans and Native Americans . . . Sam Houston [in an 1835 address arguing for the independence of Texas] asked his compatriots if they "would bow under the yoke of these half-Indians." . . . The *New Orleans Bee* in 1834 pronounced the people of Mexico the "most degraded and vile; the unfortunate race of Spaniard, Indian and African, is so blended that the worst qualities of each predominate."[16]

For De León, the war for independence from Mexico, from which came the Republic of Texas in 1836, was a revolution which contained distinct yet unexamined racist roots. Mexicans were perceived as a very different sort of people "who did not approximate the [North] Americans' ideal of racial excellence."[17] The Texas Revolution was a move for military, political, and economic control of a geographic area, yet it was also fought ideologically as a conquest on behalf of "white supremacy and civilization."[18] And along with this "civilization" came Protestantism.

Protestant denominations began to make their presence known early on in colonial Texas in the 1820s, when it was still the Mexican province of Coahuila y Texas. This occurred despite the fact that the official Mexican

Constitution clearly stated that Roman Catholicism was the one and only religion of the new Mexican republic. It is believed that Freeman Smawley (or Smalley), from Ohio, preached the first Baptist sermon in Texas, at the home of William Newman in the year 1822.[19] Joseph L. Bays, from Missouri, held the first Methodist worship services in Stephen Austin's colony at San Felipe de Austin in 1823 before being arrested by Mexican authorities.[20] The first Sunday school in Texas was established by the Baptists in 1829, but when the suspicions of the Mexican authorities were aroused, Austin closed the Sunday school.[21] Collin McKinney and his family, who came from Kentucky and who identified themselves with the newly emerging Stone-Campbell movement, were the first Disciples to cross into Texas, in 1831.[22]

These Protestants were not only active in changing the religious make-up of Texas during the colonial period, but with the advent of the Texas Revolution they also played a role in changing the political fortunes of the area. For example, Daniel Parker, a Freewill Baptist, joined W. C. Crawford, a Methodist, and Collin McKinney, a Disciple, in signing the Texas Declaration of Independence.[23] By 1855 there were 35,000 people in Texas holding membership in Protestant communions, including Protestant Episcopalians, Presbyterians, Baptists, Methodists, and Cumberland Presbyterians.[24] The fact that Disciples are not mentioned in this early census may have more to do with the organizational makeup of the Disciples' church than with their absence from Texas. Unlike the other Protestant bodies, the Disciples were not represented by a Presbytery or Conference or Association. But Disciples were indeed making their presence felt in Texas, having organized their first congregation in 1846.[25]

As Protestantism continued to grow, the reality of the Mexican presence came into greater focus, yet it was not a concern that immediately dominated the energies or the resources of any one of the Protestant denominations. This fact may have much to do with the continuous arrival to Texas of North American settlers in the 1840s and 1850s. This growing number of European American settlers became the main focus of ministry for denominations in Texas. However, historians have been able to trace an aggressive marginalization of the Mexican-Texan through the decades right after the Mexican American war of 1846.[26] This marginalization occurred despite the public and political statements of concern made for nonwhite people by the expansionists of the nineteenth century. In reality the expansionist agenda of North America was based on calculations about how best to control the borderlands of Texas and the people who inhabited that land.

When the Mexican–United States border was put into place after 1846, as a result of the Mexican-American War, the issues of immigration and illegal border crossings became of utmost concern for the northern nation. By the late 1800s and into the mid-1900s, secular historical writings, as well as the religious reports of Protestant denominations in Texas, concerned themselves with what was called the "Mexican Problem."[27] Writers of this era, who included social scientists as well as missionaries, were troubled by the large and continuous immigration of Mexicans into the United States. Why?

> The overall sentiments held by secular authors were that Mexicans lacked leadership, discipline, and organization; that they segregated themselves; that they were lacking in thrift and enterprise . . . that they did not measure up to the intellectual caliber of Anglo-American[s].[28]

These ideas about the Mexicans' inferiority and need for "civilization" became more deeply entrenched in the Texan ethos as they were further elaborated in political, economic, social, and religious circles. As a result, Protestant denominations in the Texas borderlands adopted the secular definitions and assessment of the Mexican-Texan, who was categorized as "Other" in race, culture, and religion. It was a category filled with limitations. It was a category that produced marginality. Yet by using a theological lens to reinterpret what was in reality the racist reaction of European Americans against Mexican-Texans, Protestants were able to develop a very useful interpretation of evangelism. The concern was never about the economic and political conquest of the Mexican-Texans that was taking place in these borderlands.

No biblical critique was put forth to question why Christians held racist beliefs. What happened instead was that Protestant missions followed the dominant ideologies being forged on the western frontier. Denominations gave a religious spin to a situation that was really the conquest and displacement of thousands of Mexican-Texans. The national expansionist agenda had become Christianized. For many settlers God too wanted Protestants to make things "right" in Texas. It was now possible for Protestants to perceive the "Mexican Problem" as a providential opportunity that would finally bring to the Mexican-Texan two greatly needed blessings: Christianity and European American civilization.

Like the missionary efforts to Native Americans, the "Mexican Problem" was interpreted as a window of opportunity for evangelism. The Great Commission was now the rallying call that brought Protestants to the Texas missions fields to bring to fruition the two important and related activities of Christianizing and Americanizing. This was how authentic "kingdom building" was understood. Consider the wording of an article written by Disciples missionaries in the 1920s in which they interpreted their work among Mexicans in Texas to church members around the country.

> The "Mexican Problem" is ever present with us. It is inescapable. The border line between Mexico and the United States is 1,833 miles long. It is a political rather than a natural barrier and is therefore artificial and easily crossed. . . . The Mexican population [1928] in the United States is easily 1,500,000 and fully 400,000 of these are living in Texas. . . . The Christianization *and* Americanization of this large body of alien people is a task for the whole church.[29]

Now consider the plea issued by Baptists in 1911 calling for support of their work among the Mexicans of Texas.

> It is our *duty* to save those born on Texas or Mexican soil who speak to us in an alien language.[30]

The words used in both these denominational reports support the idea that the primary task for missionaries was the "uplifting" of a people truly perceived as Other. Notice how in these reports the idea of a "duty" to be performed by faithful Protestants is emphasized. What is being communicated is a forceful theological assumption about evangelism and missions work which directly associates "Christianization *and* Americanization."[31] The great problem in this entire process was its inherent failure, which no Protestant acknowledged. The hard reality was that even when missionaries succeeded in converting the Mexicans or Tejanos to Protestantism, even when they preached about and believed in the inclusivity and diversity of God's Great Feast, the conversion of that Latino did not bring equality or acceptance by European American Protestants in general. After conversion came the task of facing the great test Protestants could not avoid—bridging the great chasm that had been created between word (religious belief) and practice (social praxis).

The History of a Changing Religious Landscape

At the core of the challenge that Latinos bring to Protestantism lies this history of a missions or evangelism theology that has been in service to the social conditions of its time and space. Many denominations have celebrated or are celebrating the centennial of founding a ministry to Latinos in Texas. For example, the Methodists organized the Mexican Border Conference in 1878, which had four districts: "two in Texas (San Antonio and El Paso) and two in Mexico (Monterrey and Monclava)."[32] The first Mexican Baptist church was founded in 1883 in Laredo, Texas.[33] The Disciples of Christ initiated their first congregation in San Antonio in 1899 using Spanish-speaking leaders from Mexico.[34] Yet given this century of missions work the fact is that U.S. Protestantism is still in need of an effective and inclusive ministry to and for Latinos. Why the great resistance?

No doubt, the religious landscape of the United States has undergone profound changes before. From the vantage point of the twentieth century, three phases of change for Protestantism in the United States can be discerned. The first important shift is often called by church historians a "first disestablishment." During this first shift the historical denominations, which were the Presbyterians, Congregationalists, and Episcopalians, had to make room for the other developing denominational bodies of the early nineteenth century. These "new" denominations were the religious expression of the growing United States, and they ministered to people who were part of the westward-moving frontier. These new denominations included the Christian Church (Disciples), the Methodists, and the Baptists. William McKinney describes what happened:

> To use a baseball metaphor, [oldline denominations] were the only teams on the field. With disestablishment in the early nineteenth century, the oldline groups were forced to admit other teams, but they still owned the stadium. They gave up their established status, but retained their cultural and economic power.[35]

A second shift, which occurred after World War I and was called the "second disestablishment," forced North American Protestantism to reexamine the historically accepted self-perception of "the United States [as] a white country in which Protestant Christianity set the norms of religious observance and moral conduct."[36] This second shift brought in Roman Catholics and Jews, the new religious "players." Church historian Robert T. Handy uses the term "second disestablishment" in order to describe how Protestantism now had to contend with the fading away of its cultural hegemony. Yet despite the "disestablishment" that took place within Protestantism, this did not lead to the creation of an open and inviting Protestant establishment. In fact, although religious pluralism may have pushed mainline churches toward a greater acceptance of Roman Catholics and Jews, there still remained repressive elements in the religious culture which stressed the universal elements of faith and in a sense created a forced religious unity. So much so that, for researchers Roof and

McKinney, even Catholics and Jews became "denominationalized."[37] What is being said is that these two religious groups conformed to the norms of religious freedom and voluntarism that have been characteristic of North American Protestantism. The United States was now able to describe itself as a "Protestant-Catholic-Jewish" nation.

Examining how Protestantism has historically understood pluralism is important for our analysis because it provides a tool to help us better examine and interpret the present-day reluctance and hesitancy Protestant denominations have shown toward building ministries with Latinos. What the Protestant establishment has historically understood as "pluralism" has been a United States phenomenon less about being plural than about shaping others to conform to the accepted dominant religious patterns. It can be said that the type of "pluralism" found in the United States religious establishment

> tames religious sects up into denominations bringing them into the respectable middle class. . . . The point is that centripetal forces in [North] American religion propel—"taming" up or down—toward some inclusive culture of non-offensiveness.[38]

Internally the tumultuous decade of the 1960s did much to chip away at Protestantism's ability to bring a canopy of perceived cohesiveness to North American culture. Sociologists of religion Roof and McKinney have called this significant shift in the religious landscape of North America the "third disestablishment." This third shift was the result of myriad trends, which included the rise of secularity, religious pluralism, the flourishing of both conservative and fundamentalist groups, and a more expansive individualism. The bridge between religious belief and culture or social conditions, which was so very strong in the 1950s, was now gone.

> In the sixties and seventies, then, religion was flourishing on the right and left fringes and languishing in the center. There was much experimentation with "new religions" and various quasi-religious and spiritual therapies. . . . At the other extreme, conservative faiths seeking to restore customary ways of believing and behaving were prospering as well. . . . The growing tensions at the center reached deep into the fabric of [North] American life.[39]

Looking back at this landscape from a distance of more than two decades, it is easier to identify other powerful external or foreign forces, which also affected North American Protestantism and which are mostly overlooked by the dominant Protestant establishment. The fact is that political revolutions, military death squads, repressive juntas, pressure from North American multinationals, economic disasters, as well as the continuous military intervention of the United States, all created a twenty-year period, from the late 1960s to the late 1980s, of great instability and immense human suffering for the people south of the Rio Grande.

Because of these external exigencies, the United States faced unavoidable change as it began to receive within its borders a large influx of immigrants from Cuba, Central America, South America, and Mexico, all in a very short period of time. What was quickly discovered was that the extant orthodox pluralism employed by mainstream Protestant denominations was not a feasible tool for dealing with the new wave of immigrants. A new paradigm was needed to provide critical understanding for what was a very new and different situation. This new paradigm would produce a moral, ethical, and Christian response to this mass of immigrants coming north in search of freedom, hope, and life itself. Religious doctrine was once again to find itself pressured from all sides by unavoidable social conditions.

These newly arriving immigrants were mostly Roman Catholic. They did not speak English. They came in a variety of pigmentations. This new wave of immigrants was clearly different from the earlier migratory waves coming from Eastern Europe or Italy or Scandinavia. And not only were they a "mixed-race" people, but the proximity of the United States to their homelands created a migratory group that would continuously "flow" across the spurious U.S.-Mexico border. As a result of these south-north migratory patterns, not only was there created a base or "stock" of 24 million Latinos in the United States, but at the same time the continuous (and historical) flow of Latinos who crossed the U.S.-Mexico border on a daily basis became an alarming reality for many citizens of the United States. The continued crossing between nations and cultures meant that the established notion of "assimilation," which is a secular parallel to the notion of "religious pluralism" (understood as a "taming up or down"), was no longer a useful tool for Protestant Latino ministries. Whereas in the past to become Protestant was understood to mean to also become "American," the migratory patterns of the new Latino immigrants pointed to a reality mainline denominations had never dealt with. This reality took most denominations by surprise and to this day has been little examined and even less understood.

Jorge Lara-Braud, a Presbyterian pastor, has called this misunderstanding of the Latino presence in the United States by Protestant mainline denominations the "tragic miscalculation."

> The miscalculation was this: Hispanics, the argument went, will go the way of all other immigrants. They will learn English and our cultural ways, and those who wish, will join our institutions, as Americans, not as Hispanic-

Americans. There is the flaw. In the strict sense, Hispanic Americans are not immigrants. We were here, in euphoniously named garrisons, towns and cities of the Southwest long before Pilgrims, Puritans or carpetbaggers. And we never ceased to be replenished. Nor will we cease to be replenished as long as the whole of the United States keeps on being an extension of Latin America in huge Spanish-speaking pockets like all of the Southwest, [California], [northern Illinois], southern Florida, and [the Northeast].[40]

Surely the time has come for North American Protestantism to accept the fact of this new "disestablishment." The social conditions caused by the great migratory waves of Central and Latin Americans, of Cubans and Mexicans demands a reexamination of religious belief or doctrine. The reaction of the Protestant establishment to this external pressure has been one of fear and trepidation. Neighborhoods were changing. Older European American congregations were dying, and empty church buildings were a common sight in the many barrios across the United States during the 1980s. Church development meetings or ministerial events became places to express a tragic sense of loss. Yet McKinney interprets the process of disestablishment as one that will not only prove to be of intrinsic value, but will also provide an ultimate benefit for North American mainline churches. He comments:

Accepting the fact of our disestablishment challenges us to rethink assumptions about our own institutions and their appropriateness for the challenges that face our communities and their churches. . . . We hold firm to the old rules as if they were ordained on high. . . . We need to break the chains that bind us to ways of doing things that however appropriate they may have been at earlier points in our history, prevent us today from the new challenges we face.[41]

Today's Voices of Change

The Hispanics of the United States are not problems to be solved, nor statistics to be counted, nor objects to be neatly categorized. We are the mystery of the ancient past of the peoples who have inhabited these lands for thousands of years, freely moving back and forth across the vast regions without the interference of humanly-made borders. We are the mystery of the Spanish conquistadores who came to these lands a few hundred years ago and mixed freely with our native ancestors to produce a new race—the cosmic race. We are the mystery of the Latin American *mestizo* who is today undergoing a new *mestizaje* with Anglo-America.[42]

With these words Virgilio Elizondo begins his foreword to Isidro Lucas' book on the "browning" of the church in the United States. Although the focus of Lucas' book is on the Roman Catholic Church, the existing parallels between the Catholic *and* Protestant failure to respond to the spiritual and religious needs of Latinos signals to us that the problem is not only one of theology or doctrine but also one of culture, class, and race. Surely Latinos are not merely "problems, numbers, statistics or objects," but the fact that this is how the religious establishment of North America has historically dealt with Latinos is a very telling reality.

Elizondo's admonition to look beyond the numbers, to look beyond the problems associated with inclusion, and to look beyond racial categories to actually see the Latino as a person, is one that needs to be taken seriously. The concern being expressed in this comment is that the development of Latino churches should not be based merely on demographics, or fear, or the perception that Latinos are a problem that must be confronted "sooner or later." Instead the call is for developing ministries to Latinos that are based on a genuine concern for the religious and spiritual well-being of that community in the United States. Yet the history of mainline Protestantism shows us that this has not been the case. The main reason for the hesitancy or reluctance to reach out to Latinos (and other ethnic groups as well) is that mainline churches, whether Methodist, Baptist, or Disciples, are religious bodies, which despite their theological distinctiveness, share a cultural heritage.

These denominations were shaped in a particular geographical, historical, racial, cultural context that has permeated religious belief and has provided reworked definitions of "Christian," "Church," and "God." The missionary enterprise carried forth by Protestants in Texas during the first decades of this century provides a clear testimony to this reality. Yet despite the years which have passed and the many changes Protestantism has endured, the legacy of that past is still with us today. Consider how McKinney describes the mainline, or what he calls oldline, denominations of the United States.

> For most of [North] American history the oldline churches were a dominant force religiously and culturally . . . [but] by the early twentieth century the old Protestant mainline gave ground to "newcomers" like Catholics and Jews. And in what historian Robert Handy has called the "second disestablishment" they gave grudging acceptance to religious pluralism. . . . [Now] the relationship between oldline churches and [North] American culture has changed. They are no longer at the center of things. . . . Yet our churches and members have not yet caught up with that change. In most of what we do,

whether in national boards and agencies or in our local churches, we continue to think and act as if we remain at the center of things.[43]

McKinney, when talking about a "center" and what it means to be at that center, is addressing a pivotal issue for oldline denominations. Because of the great changes undergone, especially in the last three decades, mainline denominations have been in many ways displaced. As a result mainline denominations have had to deal with the reality of a "fundamental change in the relationship between the oldline churches and mainstream culture."[44] Not only are mainline denominations no longer at the center of mainstream culture, but the new ethnic composition of North American society has made the situation for Protestantism that much more complex.

How does a mainline denomination, accustomed to being at the center of a mostly homogeneous reality, respond to a people whose language, race, and culture is so unlike its own? What does this response look like if that same group of people lives on the margins of the dominant culture? McKinney posits that the most useful way for Protestantism to respond to this challenge is for oldline denominations to move "off center."

> It is only when we accept the fact of our own new offcenteredness that we will have a chance of partnership with peoples whose experience has not been that of the center but rather of the margins.[45]

This however is no easy task as he himself acknowledges.

> That's something new for churches that have been at the center of things for so long they don't know how to act when they are off-center. It's new and rather scary.[46]

It may indeed be "scary" and it may not be easy. Yet the need for Protestant mainline churches to effectively and morally respond to Latino and other ethnic communities is undeniable. It is also a matter of survival.

The reality one finds in Protestant denominations today is that the focus given to new congregation establishment, particularly in those communities with a large Latino population, has stemmed in large measure from the unavoidable changes that have taken place in the demographics of the United States from the 1970s forward. The doctrine of evangelism and missions has been redefined in order to respond to the new demographics of the United States, which ranks fourth among the nations of the Western Hemisphere in the number of its Spanish-speaking residents. Mainline denominations, like the other institutions of this society, have had to seek ways to respond to a very real population group of approximately 24 million Latinos.[47] It is possible to ignore 24 million human beings only for so long. Yet the issue of Latino ministries within Protestant denominations must go beyond the statistics and the issue of survival.

Perhaps this is why we can find a chorus of Latino voices being raised from within the various denominational bodies with an admonition similar to Elizondo's. These voices call attention to the need for the creation of a specific "Hispanic (or Latino) Ministry," one not only planned but also enjoying full denominational support at all levels. Such a planned ministry would be effective because it can go beyond the notion of "numbers and problems" and thereby seek to serve Latinos by first seeing them as a people worthy of sitting at the Feast Table of God's kingdom. To create a Latino ministry that is seen as "special outreach" or "one-time missions project" is to deny the permanence of diversity in North American society and in North American Protestantism itself. To categorize Latino ministry as "special" or "one-time" also belies the stresses and conflicts that exist within denominational bodies. To better understand this issue, consider this brief sampling of opinions and concerns coming from actual Latino leaders in two mainstream denominations as they discuss the need for a planned and fully embraced "Hispanic Ministry."

In June of 1988, the Christian Church (Disciples of Christ) held a "Churchwide Planning Conference" in Lexington, Kentucky. One of the papers presented at that national event was "Toward a Liberating Ecumenical Church" by David A. Vargas, who currently serves as Executive Secretary of the Department of Latin America and the Caribbean, and is the first Latino to hold that position. He wrote regarding what he understood to be the chief obstacle preventing the Christian Church (Disciples) from reaching out to ethnic communities, not overseas, but right next door. Vargas said:

> It is the abyss that exists between our statements and resolutions and our actual pilgrimage; between what we wish to be and what we really are . . . we are basically an English-speaking church with a white Anglo-Saxon mentality, a middle-class faith community where the Black, Hispanic and Asian presence and concern is approached as a simple program or project and not as an essential dimension for the church's unity and life.[48]

Six years later the slow progress of the Disciples to respond to the need for a Latino ministry is again made evident. This time the hesitancy of the Disciples is expressed administratively through Resolution 9523, presented at the October 1995 General Assembly held in Pittsburgh. In this resolution the concern of the Disciples new congregation establishment committee (called CAN or Church Advance Now) was clearly stated. The resolution warned that in the denomination there "continues to be [a] lack [of] adequate funding and regional initiative for beginning racial ethnic churches."[49]

In an analogous statement, the words of Bishop Joel N. Martínez, the first U.S.-born Latino bishop in The United Methodist Church, seem to echo Reverend Vargas' observation about the Disciples. Bishop Martínez wrote an article which appeared in the Methodist publication *Christian Social Action*. In this article he states that Latino ministry is most often seen by the leadership and membership of a denomination as "'add-on' or 'supplemental' to the mission of the particular denomination."[50] He then poses a difficult question: "What if The United Methodist Church continues to be a principally white institution in a largely multiracial nation?"[51]

Surely the Methodists and the Disciples are quite different Protestant bodies, yet the red flags that are being raised by the two Latino leaders are very telling. Both of these Latino Protestants focus on the common flaw within their denominations and both express their concern that a perceptible Disciples or Methodist ministry to Latinos has not received the necessary support or the acceptance given to other Anglo European ministries. They point to a reality in North American Protestantism that transcends denominational lines. These Latino voices give evidence that despite profound administrative and doctrinal differences between Disciples and Methodists, they continue to share a common trait.

These Latino voices are calling for a reexamination of those shared religious beliefs that seem to dismiss and resist the reality of the social conditions of the nation and society in which they live. They are giving expression to the negative effects of religious belief that is shaped by deeply held notions of what is Christianity as it relates to the idea of nation and racial supremacy that go way back to the first European settlers to this entire hemisphere. Conquistadores, Roman Catholic friars, Pilgrims, Protestant missionaries at the turn of the century—all these may have had divergent nationalities and theologies, but they all shared one common trait. The religious belief of each of these groups was influenced, shaped, and fueled by the social conditions of their day and age, which included culture, politics, economics, and race. Vargas and Martínez are today's voices of change who serve to remind us that history does indeed repeat itself.

Vargas and Martínez are saying that both Disciples and Methodists demonstrate a resistance or hesitancy to embrace the ethnic and racial diversity that has become the reality of life in the United States. They are

101

saying that the religious belief espoused by their denominations, the church as a vehicle for inclusive evangelism, is incongruous with the praxis of exclusion and marginality of Latinos. And what is so distressing is that this hesitancy is still today most visible in areas where ethnicity and poverty are synonymous, as is the case in the borderlands state of Texas where the Latino population is 19.4% of the state's total population[52] or a total of more than 4.3 million Latinos.[53]

Vargas and Martínez sharply criticize the evident discrepancy between proclamation and praxis. For the Methodists, Bishop Martínez says, this has meant that "in spite of all the resolutions, documents, and legislation, Hispanics and other ethnic minorities perceive their interests and concerns as marginal to the future of these churches."[54] Vargas writes that the discrepancy between the "saying" and the "doing" has created "a Disciples third-world church whose participation at the decision-making levels that affect the whole church is still very limited or simply symbolic, not having yet overcome the evil of 'tokenism.'"[55] This statement speaks of the existence of marginality for Latino Disciples whose voice and presence is often missing at the crucial levels of denominational decision making. The reluctance and the hesitancy to embrace a changing society only reinforces the fact that racial and ethnic pluralism in the Protestant church is a nonnegotiable reality that must be addressed.

That is why Bishop Martínez poses a second question in his article. He asks, "What if we are unable to be inclusive of the 28 percent of the national population which will be Hispanic in the year 2080?"[56] This is a question that deals not only with the survival of one particular Protestant denomination, but calls all Protestants to a rereading of the biblical image found in Romans 12:5 where Paul describes the church as "one body in Christ, and individually members one of another" (RSV). How is U.S. Protestantism going to respond to Paul's image of the church as one body? How indeed, in light of the fact that as the nation's fastest growing minority, Latinos pose a great challenge to both the institutional structures as well as to the theological integrity of many North American, Anglo-majority Protestant denominations?[57]

The Next Millennium

I think that Robert Wuthnow made a wise statement when he warned churches in the United States not to look at the future thinking of the problems that will arise. Instead the great urgency is for Protestant church bodies to seek ways to make themselves relevant to the existential problems and needs of Latinos living in the United States. The history of missions work or evangelism carried out by mainstream denominations among Latinos holds many lessons from which much can be learned. Today's denominational leaders, clergy, laity, and denominational seminaries, have at their disposal missionary archives that represent a religious and intellectual storehouse for learning and for promoting change. Yet the sad truth is that the marginality of Latinos in Protestantism has been so strong that few, if any, denominations have had their historians write the history of the many hundreds of Latino Protestants who have shared and who continue to share a faith in Jesus the risen Christ. Is this cloud of witnesses not worthy of remembering and of celebrating? Is not the faith of Latinos, who have experienced conquest, poverty, and racism, not an expression of God's presence and sustenance? Is it possible that the Protestant establishment in this country can continue to ignore the contributions, the ministries, the talents of their Latino sisters and brothers?

A new millennium can provide U.S. Protestantism with the perfect serendipity to use the existing missionary legacy among Latinos to help bring to fruition the paradigm shift that must accompany a relevant and real ministry of inclusivity, dignity, and mutual respect. Theological beliefs will always exist within specific social conditions. Faith and culture have always and will continue to influence each other. The challenge is not to shy away from or seek to ignore this dialectical relationship. What is needed is a reexamination of what has gone on throughout this century regarding missions work with Latinos. How has Protestant theology of missions helped to segregate, marginalize, and forget Latinos? How can the history of our own denominations be used to effect change?

The need is for a willingness to allow the gospel message of inclusivity to engage us so that the church, as a community and as individuals, can commit to the transformation of the world in which we live. This means the application of what Stephen Bevans calls "committed and intelligent action."[58] Can U.S. Protestantism respond to this call in the affirmative? The many voices of Latino Protestants reflect the urgent need for mainstream churches to move beyond the idea that theology is to be understood as critical reflection. The gospel invitation is to praxis. Latino Protestants are sure of their place at the table of the Great Feast. But do European American Protestants understand that they do not own the table?

Part II
Theological Perspectives

Chapter 5

Confessing the Faith from a Hispanic Perspective

José D. Rodriguez

Introduction

Some of the most satisfying experiences during my sixteen years as a teacher of theology have taken place teaching courses from a Hispanic perspective. These courses provide Hispanic students much more than a standard theological education in their language: they also enable them to engage in a creative theological educational process. For some students, this experience helps them relate the tradition of faith to their own historical and cultural religious background more meaningfully. For others, it deepens their commitment of faith and their call to the mission and ministry of the church. For most of them, this educational experience becomes an opportunity to participate in the critical examination of a religious tradition that needs their unique contribution for continuing renewal and development.

In one of these courses, I met a relatively young Hispanic woman preparing for the ordained ministry in the Evangelical Lutheran Church in America. After several years of experience as a Lay Professional Worker in Latin America, she moved to the United States. Leaders of her home congregation who appreciated her leadership skills encouraged her to pursue a theological education to become a pastor. She originally registered for one of my courses because it was taught in Spanish. During the course, she realized that we were discussing topics that she also studied in other courses at the seminary. She felt good in my class and participated actively in our discussions. The other courses were not that interesting for her, and she was not actively participating in their group discussions. When we evaluated our course at the end of the quarter, I became aware that other Hispanic students had a similar experience and we decided to address this matter. We found that most courses at the seminary failed to make references to the contribution of Hispanic scholars, or to the religious experience of Latinos and Latinas in the U.S.[1] Hispanics did not participate actively in these courses because they experienced being treated like outsiders. Their history, their culture, and the religious witness of their people were not an important part of the course. However, in my course, although there was an emphasis on the emergence of a Hispanic theological perspective, the perspective and religious experience of representatives of other ethnic groups were not neglected. The experience in our course gave Hispanic students the opportunity to have a voice in the discussion of issues of faith related to the Hispanic community. It also gave them a voice to participate in a discussion of these issues in the context of a wider community. As they began to grasp this fact, Hispanic students became more actively engaged in the discussion of these issues in their other courses. They also became aware that their contribution was important not just to other Hispanics in the course, but also to those other non-Hispanics who had neglected it.

My experience teaching Christian theology helped me realize that the catholic nature of our faith emerges from the gracious self-revelation of God and the collective witness of the community of believers.[2] Students in my class learned that this community of faith transcends the limits of space, time, and gender, and ethnic, cultural, social, and other boundaries that we have established. My commitment to continue teaching theology from a Hispanic perspective comes from my belief that the witness of faith from this perspective helps us recover, not only those important elements that define our sociohistorical reality, but also some central teachings of the Christian faith that make possible its continuous renewal and obedience to the gospel. Students in my class learned that this prophetic religious witness of Hispanics comes out of our effort at correlating our faith with the sociocultural history of our people.[3] My conviction as a Protestant Hispanic led me to appreciate the confessing nature of our faith and the need for a continual reformation of our religious witness and church's doctrine. Students in my class learned that being Hispanic in a largely white middle-class seminary challenged them to retrieve this confessing nature of our faith. Their willingness to respond to this challenge contributed to renewing and enriching this tradition of faith.

In this chapter I will examine some important dimensions of the religious witness and theological contribution of Hispanics in the United States. Rather than being exhaustive, my goal is to clarify some important trends, articulate some significant contributions, and propose some promising developments. I will also focus attention on the experience of that sector of the Hispanic population that claims to be mainline or oldline Protestant. The main purpose of this focus is to show how the affirmation of some central principles of the sixteenth-century Reformation in Europe by Hispanics in the United States leads to a radical reformulation of these principles, challenging the church to a renewal of its understanding and witness of the gospel.

108

Hispanics, Heralds of a New Reformation

In one of his most important publications on Hispanic theology, Justo González argues that the twentieth century is experiencing a time of vast changes in the church's self-understanding. As a historian of the church and its theology, he finds a similarity between these changes and those which led to the Reformation in the sixteenth century.[4] One of these significant changes is the growing self-consciousness of those who for a very long time were mostly silent. These people are now speaking up and claiming an authority that past centuries denied them. In settings like the United States, this event is manifested in the growing self-consciousness of women, ethnic minorities, and others, whose opinions and contributions have been rejected for reasons of class, nationality, gender, age, sexual orientation, and the like. This event has tremendous social and political implications, for it means that those who were mostly silent until fairly recent times will have a more significant impact on the decisions affecting their lives and the lives of others.[5]

In the specific context of the church, these new voices are leading to a new reformation—or reformulation—of its ministry, mission, and theology. As in the Reformation of the sixteenth century, the "Twentieth-Century Reformation" is leading to a revision of the church and its systems of doctrine that will be radically different from what we have known in recent centuries. This radical reformulation may very well bypass the position established by Roman Catholics and Protestants in theological issues, as well as do justice to some of the basic concerns of parties on both sides of the debate.[6]

For Hispanics, participation in this "Twentieth-Century Reformation" means active engagement in a confession of faith with catholic roots and a prophetic vocation.[7] Surely, the religious background of Hispanics and other Latin American people needs to be traced back to the sixteenth-century religiopolitical conquest of America by Spanish and Portuguese explorers. However, our contribution to the new reformation in the twentieth century challenges us to recover, not only those foundational elements of our sociohistorical reality that give meaning to our identity as a people, but also those basic dimensions of our catholic faith that make possible a continuous renewal of our understanding and confession of the gospel. The main goal of our contribution, rather than establishing the dominance of an ethnic perspective over others, is to call the entire church to obedience in a radically ecumenical context. This ecumenism seeks as its primary goal a dialogue and collaboration with the whole church and the many movements, ideologies, parties, and programs committed to God's promise of human fulfillment and social justice.[8]

Confessing the Faith in Spanish

Hispanic theology in the United States exhibits a rich diversity among those of the Hispanic community.[9] An important challenge to this theological perspective is the critical rereading of our denominational traditions, so that in the effort to evangelize people from traditionally marginalized groups of our population, we avoid conscious or unconscious domination. As an ordained pastor in the Evangelical Lutheran Church in America teaching in one of its seminaries, I have a great appreciation for the Lutheran Reformation of the sixteenth century. However, my experience in Lutheranism and my understanding of its historical development and that of other Christian denominations have also made me aware that for Hispanics and other ethnic groups, participation in the mission and ministry of these various Christian traditions has been one of struggle.[10] Some of the efforts of these different denominational traditions have produced a religious marginalization of our people. Thus, there is a need to engage in a critical recovery of the theological and ecclesial experience of these religious traditions to focus on those elements which would foster an expression of our witness of faith, which would help in correcting past mistakes, which would promote a more evangelical expression of faith in the present, and which would offer a vision for the future more in tune with the promise of life generated by the proleptic experience of God's reign among us.

Likewise, there is a strong need to confess our faith in Spanish.[11] Those with a Protestant perspective may receive this suggestion as an affirmation of their Reformation heritage. Yet, for Hispanics, whether Protestant or Roman Catholic, this confession of faith aims at a more radical and comprehensive goal. It is an effort to recover the perspective that inspired the confessing witness of those early Christian believers who, throughout history, have continually challenged the church to remain faithful to the gospel.

Confessing the Faith from the Margins

An increasing number of individual and collective studies by Hispanic religious scholars in the U.S. continue to document the emergence of a Hispanic theological perspective and its impact on a broader social context.[12] These studies show that this religious experience was the product of two important religious encounters. The first was the Iberian Roman Catholic colonization of the southern American hemisphere in the sixteenth century. The second was the later seventeenth-century Protestant colonization of North America.[13] However, in recovering our religious identity we are confronted with the fact that the elements of this makeup form a greater complexity than traditional stereotypes used to define us. This is a witness of faith, especially present among the most popular sectors of our population, that goes beyond the traditional dogmatic, cultural, organizational, and programmatic distinctions established in Christendom after the sixteenth century between Protestants and Roman Catholics. It is also a witness of faith produced by a process subjecting our people to continuous suffering and violence. Out of this experience emerged a particular expression of faith from the margins confronting the dominant sectors of society.[14]

Piri Thomas, an African American Puerto Rican brought up in the streets of New York's Spanish Harlem, in his book *Savior, Savior, Hold My Hand* provides a compelling description of his religious conversion. The book is an autobiography relating his painful experience of addiction, street combat, the degradation of prison life, and continuous struggle against the various institutionalized forms of religion that have contributed to the marginalization of our communities. One chapter is a moving account of Piri's painful experience in what he calls the White church. Reacting against the racist and patronizing attitudes of suburban Christians toward the faithful who live in the ghetto, he confronts John, who had spearheaded the efforts of the White church among Hispanics in the barrio, with the prejudice of these relations. John, reacting defensively, reprimands Piri for showing lack of respect in his comments and proposes bringing these angry feelings to the Lord in prayer. Piri responds,

> Prayer gotta be strengthened with some kind of action, John. Without disrespect, amigo, if you've read history, too, you'd know many people have been taught to pray and when they finished praying and looked around, their land and respect was gone, taken away by the one who taught them to pray.[15]

Piri's bold resistance and provocative response to John's plea for submission to the God of the suburban Christians reveals an important element of this confession of faith from the margins. Some scholars argue that this popular expression of faith can be traced back to the sixteenth-century defective evangelization of America.[16] Contrary to the religion of fear imposed by the conquistadores who took over their lands and enslaved them, the indigenous people discerned the presence of a different God, who led them into the mystery of the Triune God's redeeming plan for creation, through the experience of Our Lady of Guadalupe.[17] This conversion experience, supported by the witness of Spanish religious leaders such as Antonio de Montecinos, Bartolomé de Las Casas, and a host of others,[18] led to the reformulation of faith and a popular creed establishing the basis for the renewal of the church and its theology in the Americas. More important, it led to the recovery of the fundamental confessing dimension of Christianity characteristic of its emergence as a marginalized and persecuted community in the first century and the stance of some of its prophetic leaders who, throughout history, have challenged the church to remain faithful to God's Word amid ideological manipulation, oppression, prejudice, and idolatry.[19]

The Confessional Dimension of Faith

My theological training and teaching experience have helped me understand the significance of the confessional tradition characteristic of Lutheranism and of most Protestant denominations. Students in our seminary are required to study the Lutheran confessions as part of their core curriculum. The course provides candidates for the ordained ministry and other leadership positions in the church with the content and scope of the Lutheran confessional writings and the manner in which they become normative for Lutheran theology, as well as for Lutheran ministry and church life today. The same expectation is usually established for students of other denominational backgrounds as they meet the requirements of their program of studies at their seminary.

Theologians help us understand the central confessional nature of Christianity.[20] Although their studies of the Christian faith have carefully examined the meaning of its apostolic origin, its trinitarian basis, its evangelical substance, its christological emphasis, and other important related aspects, they have failed to provide an equally thorough analysis of the sociohistorical implications and significance of those who were actually involved in the act of confession.[21] Part of the problem can be traced to the goal of most theologians to focus their analysis on the confessional writings that document these acts of confession and their efforts to avoid a biased perspective in their examination of the subject. However, as we all know, all confessional writings point to an act of confession that precedes them. We also know that every theological perspective, no matter how seemingly objective, betrays a bias of which the theologian may not be consciously aware. What most theologians fail to acknowledge is that this bias, if openly expressed in an attitude of dialogue and self-criticism, may provide a significant contribution to human knowledge.[22]

Next I try to show how confessing the faith in Spanish, that is, confessing the faith in a way that brings our Hispanic history and perspective to bear on our interpretation of the gospel, provides valuable insights into the meaning and significance of the Christian faith that may prove useful, not only to Hispanics, but to others with whom we share this confessional tradition.

Reading the Bible in Spanish

The fundamental features of this confession of faith are deeply rooted in the life and witness of Hispanic religious communities. Since these are living communities rich in diversity and continuous development, any rigorous attempt to define them may merely lead to stereotypes that can only project our prejudices, or deprive these religious communities of their vitality. However there are distinguishing features that help clarify the uniqueness of this confession of faith and its particular contribution to the wider Christian community.

Surely, a significant number of Hispanic religious communities in the United States reflect in their theology and ecclesial practice the teachings and values characteristic of Anglo congregations of the same denomination. This can be explained in part by the marginal status of Hispanics in their denominations and that most Hispanic religious leaders have been trained in the same theological institutions designed to maintain the dominant expression of faith characteristic of the predominant Anglo constituency of these religious groups. Yet, as Hispanics become more radically committed to the struggle of our people, and as educational programs for the training of our leaders begin to incorporate this experience as an essential part of their teaching,[23] the theology and practice of these communities of faith begin to manifest some features that distinguish them from the expression of faith of their Anglo brothers and sisters.

The most prominent of these features is their unique reading of the Scriptures. Some Hispanic scholars have already begun to provide a careful examination of the way in which biblical interpretation relates to theological and pastoral issues confronting Hispanic religious communities in the United States. There seems to be a consensus that, given the diverse nature of our people, there are a variety of reading strategies employed by Hispanics for biblical interpretation. Since my focus here is the experience of mainline or old-line Protestant Hispanics, I will highlight the contribution of some Protestant Hispanic leaders in their efforts to provide an assessment of how Hispanics read the Bible in their religious communities.[24]

In his effort to clarify this distinguishing feature, Justo González argues for a reading of the Bible in Spanish. His proposal is not a chauvinistic appeal to Hispanics to do away with serious biblical research based on the historical-critical method. Nor does he emphasize using a Spanish translation. What he emphasizes is to take seriously a feature central to the Protestant tradition since the time of the Reformation: making the Bible available to the people in their vernacular.

It is common to think that the goal of this approach was to facilitate more people having direct access to something previously reserved for scholars. But there were more significant and profound goals. When the Bible becomes a resource accessible to the people, and the people discover in the Bible their own particular perspective, then the Bible becomes the people's book, that is, a subversive book no longer under the control of the dominant groups in society.[25]

In contrast to the one characteristic of the dominant culture, the point of departure for reading the Bible in Spanish is to read the Scriptures as presenting a history of the people of God "beyond innocence," that is, to view biblical history as "responsible remembrance" leading to "responsible action." Bible stories have great difficulty idealizing their heroes and heroines. Biblical characters are not presented as flawless, but as human beings struggling with ambiguities similar to the ones we have to confront daily.[26]

To be sure, biblical history is a history beyond innocence. The Bible's only real heroes are the God of history and history itself, which somehow continues to move forward in spite of the failure of its great protagonists. Since this is also the nature of Hispanic history,[27] it may well be that on this score we have an interpretative advantage over those whose history is still at the level of guilty innocence and who, therefore, must read Scripture in the same way they read their own history, that is, in terms of high ideals and purity to justify their privileges and interests.[28]

For González, such a reading of the Bible involves a very specific "grammar" with four basic principles. The first principle focuses on issues of power and powerlessness as they are present in the Bible. As noted by other Hispanic scholars, this principle calls into play the notion of correspondence in biblical hermeneutics. In this sense, the situation and liberation of Hispanics are anticipated in the Scripture's account of the liberation of God's people by a God who demands justice in human affairs.[29] The second of these principles highlights the public character of the Bible, stressing the need to read it as addressing the whole community. The third principle points to the privileged perspective of the poor and the simple, urging our attention to their voices. Finally, González insists on the "vocative" nature of this reading. While he stresses the need for a better understanding of the biblical text, he clarifies that the ultimate goal of our engagement with this text is to be led toward greater obedience to the word of God in our historical pilgrimage.[30]

For Harold Recinos, this reading of the Bible in Spanish is actually present in the experience of Hispanic communities in the inner-city barrios of the Northeast, who look upon the whole of the Bible as liberating and make use, once again, of the principle of correspondence. Such a reading of the Bible helps the people of the barrio make better sense of their reality of oppression, enables them to regain a fundamental sense of their human dignity, empowers them to struggle against the forces that dehumanize them, and calls them to join hands with others, striving for a better world and human fulfillment.[31]

A specific example of the impact of this reading on the confessing witness of the Hispanic community is shown in the way the subject of migration has been treated by some Protestant Hispanic leaders. This issue is examined from many perspectives—historical,[32] social,[33] biblical,[34] and theological[35]—to formulate a creative and relevant pronouncement that calls for our obedience of faith. In this sense, when the issue of migration is discussed, not only are the sociopolitical problems challenging the present ministry with migrants introduced,[36] but also the biblical and ecclesial experience of the past, in a search for the inherent dimensions of this faith that may allow for new opportunities of Christian witness. This is what leads Francisco García-Treto to suggest that in our treatment of the migrants in the United States, we should follow the biblical tradition according to which foreigners were considered to be under divine protection and try everything possible to lend them our aid.[37] This also explains González' affirmation that when dealing with the issue of sanctuary, both the Bible and the witness of the early church call our attention to refrain from giving absolute obedience to the state and its laws, when they are in opposition to the will of God.[38]

Preaching Our Faith in Spanish

From this reading of the Bible emerges another important dimension of the confessing witness of our religious Hispanic communities: the preaching of the Word by its religious leaders. In many ways, our confession of faith through preaching recovers another important emphasis characteristic of the Reformation of the sixteenth century. The preeminence of preaching in the ministries of Luther, Bucer, Melanchthon, Calvin, and Zwingli is too well known to need amplification.[39] This emphasis on preaching has also marked the Protestant churches of the past four and a half centuries. However, preaching the Word of God in Spanish today leads to a more radical expression of this reformation heritage, challenging the church to reformulate its understanding of doctrine, mission, and ministry.

In a volume of a series primarily designed as a resource for strengthening the needs of the preaching function of the church and its leaders, González examines the contribution of Hispanic preaching.[40] In this work, he gives a clear and compelling analysis of the concept, dynamics, methods, and forms of this preaching that he describes as liberation preaching.[41] One of the main contributions of this preaching approach is to rediscover some central teachings of the gospel, especially significant in the earliest time of the church's history and at critical points in its development thereafter, teachings that challenge the church to a reformation of its witness of faith.

For the task of listening anew to the biblical text and the church's tradition, González explores some of the obstacles that impede this liberating interpretation and suggests some resources for overcoming these obstacles.[42] Among these important resources are what he calls pointers on biblical interpretation. The first and most significant of these pointers asks the political question, that is, examines the way in which God intervenes and responds to the interplay of power in the relationships established by human beings in their sociohistorical context.[43] For Hispanic preaching this implies a hermeneutics of suspicion that leads to a hermeneutic circle.[44] When this mode of interpretation is made an intrinsic part of our theological perspective, we are able to discern God's actual involvement and liberating actions in the tradition of the church and our own historical experience. It also empowers us to challenge the church to make this liberating witness a central feature of its mission and ministry.

> Once we have gone through the circle and made it a part of our basic theological outlook, we can once again look at tradition, no longer as that which we have to oppose because it is oppressive, but rather as that which, in our struggle for liberation, we are to reinterpret and reclaim. Tradition then becomes a living reality, in which we discover many kindred spirits whose struggle was akin to ours, but who have been forgotten or obscured by an interpretation which sought to preserve the existing order.[45]

Some eloquent examples of this preaching approach are recorded in a recent publication, aimed at making available the present collective homiletical contribution of our people both to the U.S. and Latin America and to a wider audience.[46] In this publication Daisy Machado shares a compelling reflection on the text of Luke 13:10-17. On the basis of her personal experience and her Hispanic preaching approach, she compares Jesus' action at the synagogue in regard to the bent-over woman and the religious Jewish leaders with Hispanic women in the U.S. in their efforts to witness to their vocational goals and ministry. Similar to the prejudice expressed by the ruler of the synagogue against the woman in the story, today's Hispanic women experience the sexism and exclusion exerted by our own religious leaders. For Machado, Jesus' action at the synagogue points to God's call to resist this prejudice and exclusion and to join our efforts with those who participate in the present liberation of others.[47] Elizabeth Conde-Fraizer uses the texts of Matthew 27:57-61, 28:1-10, and John 20:11-28 to reflect on the experience of death and the empowerment of the resurrection for the witness of our religious Hispanic communities in the barrio. By focusing on the reaction of Mary, Judas, and Peter on Jesus' suffering and death present in these texts, she provides a moving account of how this loss, disenchantment, and hopelessness continues to be reproduced in the lives of our brothers and sisters in places like the South Bronx and other urban centers. She urges us to see that this experience of death is being transformed through God's loving power in Jesus' resurrection. Our encounter with the resurrected Christ empowers us to successfully confront these forces and overcome them. This encounter with the resurrected Lord that brings new life and meaning takes place once again in our Galilee, that is, in the humble but faithful community of faith in the barrio where we once met him.[48]

In another publication based on Ephesians 1:9-10, 3:1-12, and 4:11-16, José D. Rodriguez examines the implications of this text for the ministry and mission of the church.[49] For this Puerto Rican Lutheran pastor and educator, an important facet of this text is to remind us of the central prophetic vision of the gospel. This prophetic vision is connected to God's revelation of the divine plan for the redemption of all creation. As a witness to this project taking place in the history of humankind, the church is called to participate in confronting those forces which, in opposition to God's plan, abuse the dignity of human beings by subjecting them to oppression and destroy the beauty and worth of the whole creation.[50]

Celebrating Our Faith in Spanish

It is in the context of Hispanic religious communities that this reading of the Bible and its proclamation are nurtured and developed. The awareness of God's empowering presence in the lives of the faithful also leads to a renewal of these Christian communities in their worship and ministry, as was the case in the sixteenth-century Reformation.

For many of these communities, this renewal is reflected in the rituals and songs that characterize their religious celebrations. Most elements in these rites and celebrative songs emerge from a popular expression of faith in God's gracious liberating presence, calling for a witness of faith that is deeply social and historical, not just otherworldly. They portray a God who sides with the oppressed and works for their liberation. They provide a hermeneutic of liberation that involves the use of the Bible and the tradition of faith as effective resources for social change based on love, justice, and equality. They also challenge the whole church to live out the terms of its covenant with God, immersing itself in the struggle against those forces that violate the lives of the oppressed and the well-being of God's created order. It is in this sense that Edwin D. Aponte argues that *coritos,* that is, little choruses or songs, become active symbols in Latino Protestant popular religion.[51] It is also what drives Roberto Gómez to claim that, after Christmas and Easter, the most holy day in the life of most Mexican American Christians is the celebration of the Virgen de Guadalupe.[52] This is true for both Protestants and Roman Catholics.

In a recent publication, a group of Protestant Hispanic leaders document the richness and significance of these elements in the worship experience of our Protestant communities. The study of María L. Santillán Baert gives us a brief but meaningful summary of leading trends in the historical development of this worship renewal in the Hispanic United Methodist Church.[53] Pablo A. Jiménez offers a glimpse of the variety of this worship experience as it emerges in the ecclesial practice of our Hispanic communities.[54] For Teresa Chávez Sauceda, this renewal in the worship experience of Hispanics leads to the development of a mestizo church in which its expression of faith, rather than marginalizing or tolerating the diversity of our Hispanic background, reaffirms our cultural and sociohistorical identity.[55] Miguel A. Darino reminds us that the most important contribution of this trend in Hispanic worship practice is to lead us again to a better understanding of and witness to the gospel.[56]

While a significant feature of this worship renewal is the incorporation of autochthonous elements of our Hispanic cultural traditions in the liturgy,[57] another important feature is the giving to some of the ancient rites of Christian worship a new relevance, based on the difficulties and challenges confronted by our people. An example of this trend took place during the parish ministry of one of my friends and present colleagues. Shortly after graduating from seminary, he received a call to lead a Lutheran mission with Hispanics in an urban center in the Northeast. In an election-year campaign visit to the city for a seat in the state senate, one candidate publicly denounced Hispanics in the barrio as being responsible for the violence and the escalating crime rate in the city. Abhorring the prejudice of this pronouncement against Hispanics, my friend asked secular and religious leaders to join him in celebrating an exorcism in the place where this candidate had made his statement, to drive out the devil and the forces that had produced so much evil and prejudice against our people.[58]

The Justice of God Against All That Condemns Us

Surely, those who have been raised in the context of Protestantism appreciate the sixteenth-century Reformation emphasis on the doctrine of justification, which highlights the scriptural teaching about the gospel of God's gracious dealings with humanity. This doctrine is described by many Lutheran scholars as the *articulus statis et cadentis ecclesiae;* that is, the article by which the church stands or falls has a compelling attraction for Hispanics and other traditionally marginalized sectors of society. To be sure, God does not bestow blessings upon us in carefully calculated proportions to match what each one of us deserves, but gives with prodigal liberty all there is to give, not because we have any rights to these gifts, but because God sees our need for them, and because it is God's nature to give with ungrudging bounty. This is indeed the heart of the gospel message and a message of hope for the most worthless and undeserving.[59]

However, what this central doctrine of the Reformation fails to convey with clarity and conviction, especially when articulated by those who promote the self-interest of the dominant sectors of our society, is that this justice of God calls for a witness of faith deeply rooted in the life-struggles of our brothers and sisters. It is in this context, and from the transforming dynamics of the resurrection, that God's justice becomes good news, empowering us to a prophetic witness against the forces that trample the dignity of our brothers and sisters and God's broader creation. The pastoral experience and theological reflection of our Latin American Protestant brothers and sisters help us understand some important dimensions in witnessing to this central teaching, when we do it from the perspective of the oppressed and in the context of their struggle for liberation.[60] In one of the recent and most important studies on this topic, Elsa Tamez suggests a radical reinterpretation of the doctrine of justification from the perspective of the poverty, oppression, and death experienced by large sectors of her Latin American society.[61] This reinterpretation, focusing on the revelation of God's justice as an inalienable gift for the renewal of life and dignity of all people, makes human beings subjects of their history, empowering them to transform those forces that exclude, dehumanize, and bring death to their brothers and sisters. For Tamez, this is an important reinterpretation because it recovers some important liberating aspects of the doctrine that were neglected by an ahistorical interpretation, which led to minimizing the challenges of the present historical reality of injustice and oppression for the witness of the believer.

> The problem is rooted in the fact that in Latin America the usual meaning of justification is confusing or misplaced. The historical dimension, which is capable of challenging both conscience and concrete practice, is absent. What does justification say to the poor indigenous peoples of Peru, Guatemala, Bolivia, or Mexico, who suffer both hunger and permanent discrimination? It is shameful to bring them the message that God has justified the sinner with no contextual specificity, or with nothing to distinguish the faces of the sinners. If we accept that sin has to do with social reality, justification also has to be understood within that same horizon.[62]

As a Protestant Hispanic, I have always cherished the act of confession demonstrated by the leaders of the Reformation in the sixteenth century. I am also convinced that our confession of faith is a constitutive element of Christianity that we share with the greater tradition of the church. For this reason, our confession of faith, while being a conscious effort to examine the implications of correlating this faith with the sociocultural history of our communities, will also aim at recovering for today some important aspects of the understanding and witness of faith from those who have preceded us. These aspects have been consciously displaced and forgotten throughout the centuries even by those who brought us in contact with the gospel.

Throughout this study I have documented some important features of the confession of faith characteristic of our Protestant Hispanic communities. In a very significant way this religious witness points to our confession in the revelation of the justice of God empowering us to resist and transform the forces, attitudes, and systems that bring death to our people and try to condemn us.[63] The essential point of reference for this theological perspective is God's supreme act of self-revelation in Jesus Christ. It is there that we encounter the foundation, not only of our doctrine of redemption, but also and above all, of our understanding of God.

Justo González reminds us that from the beginning and as a consequence of their public witness, Christians were subjected to persecution and martyrdom.

> The Lord whom Christians served had died on the cross, condemned as a criminal. Soon thereafter Stephen was stoned to death following his witness before the council of the Jews. Then James was killed at Herod Agripa's

order. Ever since then, and up to our own days, there have been those who have had to seal their witness with their blood.[64]

In the New Testament it is Jews who persecute Christians since from their perspective Christians had emerged as a Jewish sect going from town to town tempting good Jews to become heretics. As Jewish nationalism increased and eventually led to rebellion against Rome, Christians, particularly the Gentiles among them, sought to put distance between themselves and that movement. Yet as the Roman authorities acknowledged Christianity as a religion quite different from Judaism, they also began to recognize the threat of this new religious movement in Roman-ruled territories. This new consciousness became the basis of two and a half centuries of persecution to which Christians were subjected by the Roman Empire from the time of Nero to the conversion of Constantine. Scholarly research on the records of this witness shows that they are among the most precious and inspiring testimonies of early Christianity.[65]

It is important to note that this was a time during which the church established a consensus regarding its sacred texts and rule of faith, on the basis of a trinitarian formula. This process also led to the formulation of the symbols of faith and the emergence of Christian dogma. However, during the course of the church's historical development and as Christianity became a dominant power in the West, the efforts made by many of the church's leaders to make the church a respectable movement in society led, whether by design or not, to compromising its beliefs by interpreting them from the perspective of the dominant sectors of society.

In his critical evaluation of this theological heritage, González challenges us to question the validity of those theological perspectives that dominated the field, in order to raise the significance of a marginalized perspective that leads to a deeper understanding of the Christian message. Contrary to the omnipotent and impassible idea of God that developed from the appropriation of Greek philosophy by Christian apologists, González stresses the importance of recovering the "minority God" of the Scriptures who, as an active participant in human history, breaks up the bondage of Israel in Egypt, raises judges to liberate Israel from its enemies, sends prophets to rebuke the people and their rulers, and, being incarnated in Jesus Christ, suffers oppression and injustice for our redemption.

This fact, well attested throughout Scripture, finds its clearest expression in Jesus Christ, in whom God is carried to and fro by human beings whose victim God becomes. If being a minority means being subjected and victimized by forces one does not control, God is a minority.[66]

Surely this was the perspective that inspired the confessing witness of believers who emerged as a minority and persecuted community in the early centuries. It is also the perspective that led to the prophetic stance of those early Christian martyrs and many others throughout history. The challenge posed by this confession of faith today is to bear witness to God's creative, redeeming, and sanctifying activity in the present. The evangelical understanding of justification by grace through faith so dear to our Protestant heritage leads us to commit ourselves both in word and deed to the incarnation of the gospel in changing social and historical contexts, as well as in diverse cultural situations. Faithfulness to this call in the pluralistic context of the United States requires the recognition that God created us so that even in our differences we might enrich one another. Witness to the continuing saving work of God in the world challenges us to bring down the barriers of gender, language, race, age, class, and any other barrier that has been built by humanity to separate nations, races, and families from one another. We have to realize that no one is exempt from the temptation of using others for personal advancement. Excuses of all types, colors, and forms will be readily available to those, who for lack of integrity, will rationalize their values, attitudes, and actions at the cost of others. Let us remind ourselves that gender, language, race, age, class, or any other element is not in itself an indelible mark of assurance of righteousness. Righteousness comes from God through Christ, who graciously and lovingly urges our commitment to the struggles of those who, on account of their gender, language, race, age, or any other reason, are subjected to prejudice, injustice, and oppression.

While the ministry and mission of the church is ultimately dependent on God's power, as God's people we are invited to participate today in God's creating, redeeming, and transforming experience of ushering in a new reality, a new way of relating as children of the same God and brothers and sisters of one another. I am confident that, as we reflect on this important aspect of our faith and the witness of those who have tried to recover this witness throughout history, we will renew our commitment to a confession of faith with catholic roots and a prophetic vocation.[67] This is my belief and hope. It is also an invitation to action for all who take this confession seriously.

Chapter 6

Guideposts Along the Journey: Mapping North American Hispanic Theology

Luis G. Pedraja

North American Hispanic theologies originate from the experiences, faiths, and practices of different living communities of Hispanics in the United States and develop in a continuing dialogue between Hispanic theologians, their respective communities, and the greater complex of theological traditions. As Hispanic theologians engage in both theological reflection and dialogue with these communities, their theologies parallel both the similarities and differences of the communities that serve as their loci of reflection.

The different perspectives and communities involved in Hispanic theology restrict attempts to simplify or generalize these theologies. Their vital connection to their respective communities also precludes abstracting them from the life that shapes them. In addition, the different dynamics of the dialogues which create Hispanic theologies resist reducing them to rigid constructs. Yet, because they often share similar struggles and goals, there are also some similarities between these theologies. In the case of both Catholic and Protestant theologies, their shared concerns and dialogues often blur the lines between them, even while the different communities from which they emerge create differences within each type of theology itself.

Tracing the similarities and differences between Catholic and Protestant Hispanic theologies requires a strategy that provides us with points of comparison between them while preserving their contrasts. This requires a twofold strategy. First, we need a flexible methodology for making meaningful comparisons between these theologies without resorting to static abstractions. Second, once we devise this methodology, we can explore the distinctive characteristics of these theologies, and the distinctions and similarities that exist between Catholic and Protestant Hispanic theologies. Through this approach I will show how both the dynamic dialogues and the teleological eschatologies of these theologies blur rigid lines of demarcation between them while preserving distinctive identifying features necessary for a continuing mutual dialogue.

Demarcating North American Hispanic Theology as a Postmodern Exercise

The character of Hispanic theologies precludes characterizing them through rigid abstractions and systematic structures. Alfred North White-head, a philosopher of the early twentieth century, warns of the dangers involved in the process of abstraction. For Whitehead, reality is a creative, interrelated, and dynamic activity that brings together diverse elements into a particular concrete actuality. These concrete actualities unite past and future possibilities to create a new reality. Human experience mirrors these complex interplays, creating meaning through contrasting and comparing concrete and particular forms.[1] Like the term *mestizaje*, which characterizes the identity of many Hispanics, diverse elements continually come together to form new realities. Since Whitehead understands reality as fluid and interrelated, he argues against confusing rigid abstractions with reality. As a result, the goal of philosophy is not the "finality" of systematization. The goal is to make progress in describing human experience.[2]

Hispanic theologies describe the theological content of the experiences, culture, hopes, and faith of Hispanics. They examine the theological implications inherent in the culture and practices of the different Hispanic populations in the United States. In addition, Hispanic theologies are not merely descriptive. They also prescribe a theological direction for action. They embody the eschatological hope of the Hispanic community and critique present structures in light of this hope. As they interpret the faith of the Hispanic people, they call for the transformation of society by their critique of oppression, marginalization, and the totalizing primacy of being that subjugates praxis, labor, and life to ontology.[3] These struggles and hopes of the living communities with which Hispanic theologies interact resist strict categorizations, abstractions, and systematization. Concrete human life and practices prevent rigid essentialist definitions and limit our ability to predict the outcome of Hispanic theologies.[4]

Some traits and features do distinguish Hispanic theologies from other theologies. Instead of defining these theologies in terms of rigid categories, it is better to tentatively demarcate them by marking certain distinguishing traits and features. Like a cartographer who charts the features of a terrain so that others can find their way, we can chart the features that appear along this theological journey.

The move away from essentialism and foundationalism in postmodern and poststructuralist philosophies provides a fluidity that facilitates the process of demarcating these theologies. For instance, Jacques Derrida develops his philosophy using Saussure's maxim that language is a complex network of differences placed in relation. He argues that we do not derive meaning from being or from a symbolic correlation to being. Instead, meaning and value emerge from a linguistic interplay of differences, which Derrida expresses by coining the word *différance*.[5] *Différance* is a play on the French words for difference and deference, and presents graphically what is hidden phonetically in the French: the silent "a" that differentiates the word *différance* from the word for difference.[6]

Derrida's philosophy locates reality solely within language and textuality, but new possibilities arise if we extend its premises to humans as the embodiment of text and language. If Derrida is right, and meaning emerges in the interplay of differences that are in relation within the text, then Hispanics are a living embodiment of meaning by embodying both difference and deference. In society, Hispanics are similar to the silent "a" of *différance*. Although they are "graphically" different in their appearance and culture, the differences often remain unnoticed by those who speak about them. In addition, Hispanic voices are consistently muted by those who want to "assimilate" Hispanics into a cultural sameness defined by them—a "sameness" that becomes more poignant by the way "American" history and culture hides and covers up Hispanic history and cultures. When Hispanics are noticed, their differences are hidden in a blending of traits that lumps all Hispanics into categories that eradicate their differences. Similarly, Hispanics often must defer to the powerful both to survive and to work. *Différance* actively captures the diversity, deference, and interconnectedness embodied in Hispanic communities. Thus, we can speak meaningfully of the dynamic interplay of diversity in the Hispanic community within a postmodern context and use a methodology of cultural and socioeconomic deconstruction to disclose hidden agendas of power and oppression.

Another useful tool provided by postmodern philosophy that helps us to move beyond static ontological assertions of essence is the "trace." Both Derrida and Emmanuel Levinas use the trace as a means of noting what is beyond essence. The trace validates the plausibility of speaking meaningfully of the fluid and diverse Hispanic theologies through demarcations. For Derrida, the trace marks the movement of *différance* as a signification that transcends presence. The trace marks something that has already been, but is no longer there. It refers to something which preceded its appearance and which has already gone beyond it. Like a footprint in the sand, it marks the passage of someone who is no longer there and points toward a direction taken, thus capturing its origins and apparent destination. The trace is not a monolithic monument to essence or substance, but merely a temporary indication of something that has moved beyond.[7]

Levinas also uses the notion of the trace, in *Otherwise Than Being or Beyond Essence.* Here the trace appears as a "breaking point" (separation) and as a "binding place" (unity) for the transcendence of the other. The trace appears not merely as a linguistic sketch but as the face of the other which evokes and signals the demand for our response. The notion of the trace grounds our theological language in the ethical demand of the other and in the embodiment of alterity in the human face of the alien. The trace transcends essence and maintains the ambiguity of a mark that does not endure.[8] Using the trace as a paradigm for speaking of Hispanic theologies allows us to avoid essentialist definitions, while capturing its ethical demands and active interplay.

However, we must be careful not to pitch our tents in the midst of post-modernism without some strong qualifications. In *Caminemos con Jesús* Roberto Goizueta warns of the dangers inherent in postmodernism's reaction to intellectualism.[9] The very name "postmodernism" acknowledges the dependence of postmodernity on the worldview of "modernism" and signals a certain indebtedness to the power structures of modernity. Also, the intellectual concerns of postmodernism often ignore the embodied realities of humanity and its struggles for justice, dignity, and liberation. Goizueta warns us of the dangers of a multiculturalism and pluralism often found in postmodernity. These forms of postmodernism can lead to a radical nihilism or relativism in which dialogue breaks down. Dominant groups, asserting the "different" nature of a group's experience, can preclude any possibility of transformative dialogue and criticism of their own status.

Although differences are necessary for meaningful and creative dialogue to occur, references to differences in the Hispanic community could easily lead to arguments for relativism and incommensurability that can further marginalize Hispanics. If Hispanic theologies cannot critique and transform the dominant cultures, the power structures remain unchanged.[10] However, these dangers can be avoided by affirming the teleological character and dialogical dynamics of Hispanic theologies. Hispanics are both outsiders and insiders in the United States. Differences in some areas do not preclude similarities in others, which provides the basis for fruitful dialogue. Furthermore, while Hispanic theologies originate out of diversity and value the affirmation of diversity, they also share a common struggle and hope for the liberative praxis of a new humanity.

The variety of themes that appear under the rubric of Hispanic theologies complicates attempts at noting the marks that differentiate Hispanic

Protestant theologies from their Catholic counterparts. Growing dialogues and shared interest often blur the dividing lines between them. The remaining distinctions are due primarily to their different points of departure. For instance, their treatment of popular religion and the Bible is not identical. However, their shared goals and struggles blur the distinctions when one moves from their points of departure toward their destination. As an emerging theology, the best way to trace their features without reducing them to a system is to note common sources, directions, and shared goals. Underlying these theologies is a shared indebtedness to South American liberation theologies, and three prevalent sources of reflection: Hispanic identity, popular religion, and biblical hermeneutics. They also share similar methodologies and eschatological-teleological dimensions. These common sources, directions, and goals distinguish Hispanic theologies from other theologies while serving as points of comparison and contrast between Protestant and Catholic Hispanic theologies.

Hispanic Theologies, Antirationalism, and Intellectualism

The methodology I suggest resists attempts to reduce Hispanic theologies to a set of absolute and universal categories. Hispanic theologies, with their multiplicity, celebration of difference in unity, and resistance to a universal system of detached absolutes are a postmodern response to modernity in their own right.[11] Modernism values a rationalism which reduces reality to a set of abstract propositions detached from affective and subjective experience. These abstract propositions distort the ambiguity, diversity, and fluidity of Hispanic life and experiences.[12]

To reject an emphasis on detached reasoning is not to reject intellectual reflection in favor of anti-intellectualism. Rather, it is to reject a false dichotomy between intellectual reflection and the work, action, and experiences that are part of life. For instance, Ada Maria Isasi-Diaz defines praxis as a unity of both intellectual and physical activity that rejects their separation.[13] Similarly, Justo González proposes in *Mañana* the "radical" notion that the unabashed acceptance of the intellectual life by academic theologians is an attempt to justify its own status and lack of contribution to the activities that create and preserve life.[14]

Intellectuals create a hierarchical dichotomy between intellectual life and physical work, valuing ideas over the life-sustaining practices of everyday life. Intellectuals assert their superiority over those who work to support the infrastructure of society. They oppress and marginalize the workers while reaping the benefits of the workers' labors. González proposes that theologians differentiate themselves from other intellectuals by doing theology with "dirt under our fingernails," thus recognizing the importance of humanity's embodied existence and the value of physical labor for doing theology.[15] Theologies that separate life and intellect are unbalanced. They oppress and marginalize those who do the manual labor that supports our society and sustains life. Hispanic theologies resist such unbalanced approaches by connecting theological reflection and concrete human experience.

A Genesis of Liberation: Where Does the Journey Begin?

Catholic and Protestant Hispanic theologians in the United States share a common source in Latin American liberation theologies, and on that basis concern themselves with liberating action, justice, and the condemnation of oppression in their communities.[16] However, the nature of the oppression experienced makes Hispanic theologies distinct. While in Latin America oppression appears in very concrete and identifiable forms, it is often more subtle in North America. Hispanics in the U.S. do not always encounter systemic oppression and violent assault as intensely and clearly as South Americans. Most do not have to fear the organized violence of government-sponsored death squads and the radical socioeconomic oppression that leaves the poor of South America in physical peril.

Oppression within the U.S. takes more insidious and less readily identifiable forms, such as the systemic marginalization of Hispanics through prejudice, exploitation, and cultural and educational oppression. National and cultural identities are more difficult to identify in the complex milieu of North American Hispanics. As a result, economic and social exploitation occur at different levels, and class struggles and marginalization take different forms. The situation of U.S. Hispanics is different from that of South and Central Americans. Thus, their theologies are also different.

This does not mean that Hispanics are not in need of liberation from socioeconomic oppression. There is widespread economic oppression of Hispanics, especially of Mexican Americans and of newly arrived refugees from Latin America. The *indocumentados* who come "illegally" to the United States often bear the brunt of this oppression, even though they play a vital role in the economic infrastructure of the United States' agricultural and domestic labor pools. Since they lack "legal status," their oppression remains hidden and obscured. Since their status as illegals prevents them from making official reports, they work lengthy hours for little pay and suffer violence, often at the hands of the authorities. As voiceless victims, they are exploited and threatened with deportation. Although their only crime is hope for a better life and a desire to help their families, they are misrepresented as "criminals" and "parasites" by politicians who often create the impoverished conditions that force their migration. Their "graphic" suffering becomes a subtext hidden by the vocal rhetoric of those in power. Thus, postmodern concerns for deconstructing logocentric power structures to reveal hidden subtexts is more urgent in Hispanic life.

Legal immigrants and native-born Hispanics also face oppressive structures and conditions. Poverty and oppression do not limit themselves to a given ethnic or racial group, but they are more common among marginalized racial and ethnic groups. Hispanics and African Americans often bear the burdens of prejudice, previous injustices, and systemic oppression.

South American liberation theologians affirm their solidarity with North American Hispanics, recognizing their identity as a people and their socioeconomic oppression. However, they also recognize that the situations faced by Hispanics in the U.S. are not identical to those faced in Latin and South America. For instance, Enrique Dussel writes that while Chicanos are becoming aware of their situation, there is still a need for more unity and awareness of liberation concerns. In making this claim, Dussel recognizes that the concerns of the Chicanos are not identical to those of Latin America. Chicanos are oppressed, but they are also part of an oppressive "imperialistic" system of American interests that often contributes to the oppression in marginalized nations. According to Dussel, this places a dual responsibility upon Chicanos. First, they must become aware of both their oppression and of their participation in an oppressive system. Then, they must act for their liberation and for that of others in the Developing World.[17]

This duality of being both oppressed and oppressors is paradigmatic of the Hispanic situation. In recognizing this duality, Dussel captures part of what it means to be Hispanic in the U.S. One is caught between two worlds, participating in both, but never fully belonging to either. Hispanics in the United States are both oppressed and oppressors who participate in an oppressive system. As a result, the call for liberation in the Hispanic communities of the U.S. is not identical to that of South American liberation theologies. Hispanic theologies in the U.S. must work toward liberation on a dual front.

In Hispanic theologies, the inheritance of Latin American liberation theologies is present in the reexamination of the socioeconomic structures and the historical-political dimensions of the Bible. South American liberation theologians call for a reinterpretation of the biblical text that includes the Bible's concern for the poor, its commitment to liberation, and its critique of unjust structures that produce oppression and poverty.[18] Hispanic theologians also read the Bible for its socioeconomic concerns and political impact. González calls for such sociopolitical interpretations of the Bible in what he terms "reading the Bible in Spanish."[19] In solidarity with their South

American counterparts, Hispanic theologians in the U.S. also affirm the need to listen to the perspectives of the poor in their reading of the Bible.[20]

These readings of the Bible point to a unique relationship between Catholic and Protestant theologians. Protestant Hispanic theologians are indebted to Catholic South American liberation theologians for their concern with liberation, praxis, and critical readings of the Bible. Protestants had long considered their study and access to Scripture a part of their distinct identity. Yet their mainline denominations often influenced their reading of Scripture, preventing them from readings that included the perspective of those marginalized by society—a reading derived from Roman Catholics in South America.[21] As a result of this influence, both theologies share a deep concern for issues of justice and empowerment, and a quest for the creation of a *new humanity* free from oppression and a people who are agents of their own history.[22]

Gutiérrez's understanding of a new humanity free from oppression takes on an added dimension in Hispanic theology. Hispanic theologians have built upon José Vasconcelos' understanding of *mestizaje* as a means of creating a new race, a *raza cosmica* that would allow and affirm diversity as a means of enrichment of human life.[23] This new humanity embodies the multicultural celebration of difference at the heart of postmodernism. Diversity and difference become concrete and incarnate in the Hispanic people, whose lives represent this diversity. In the notions of *mestizaje* and *mulatez*, Hispanic theologians recognize the presence and hope of a new humanity that can define itself as a diverse people without the imposition of categories by dominant cultures. This affirmation of difference embodied in the mestizo and the mulatto creates a new reality that does not deny difference, but accepts it. Through this, the barriers that lead to marginalization break down in a new form of existence.[24]

Theologically, mestizaje takes on a further significance for Hispanic theologies that move beyond its indebtedness to South American liberation theologies. It presents a dual affirmation of those rejected by society as the ones chosen by God and the ones embodying a new humanity. South American liberation theologies recognize God's preferential option for the poor as a primary motif in the scriptures, and call for a new humanity in which the poor can live with dignity and the possibility of self-determination. Hispanic theologies move this concern to the realm of identity, and thus join the "preferential option for the poor" with the "new humanity" in the concrete reality of the mestizo. The mestizo embodies those rejected by both cultures, those marginalized and impoverished physically, culturally, psychologically, and socioeconomically. God's preferential option for the poor becomes God's preferential option for those who are rejected by society and marginalized.[25] The mestizaje of these people allows them to embody a diversity that creates a more inclusive notion of humanity, one that accepts, affirms, and celebrates "otherness." Similarly, their suffering and marginal status opens a new possibility for compassion and an affirmation of liberation.[26]

Diversity, Community, and Identity as Loci of Theology

The diversity of Hispanics also serves as a point of theological reflection. Hispanics define themselves primarily by national origin, each bearing different cultural, racial, social, political, and linguistic traits. These differences prevent simple categorizations of Hispanic.[27] The blending of the Spanish *conquistadores* with the Natives and Africans in this continent brought about the racial mixtures we call mestizaje and mulatez. The difficulties involved in defining the Hispanic identity take on gigantic proportions when one considers the mixture of the Spanish and the Moors that predates the conquistadores, the influx of Asians and Europeans into Latin America, and the present mix of cultures and races in the United States.[28] As a result, the question of identity plays an important role in both Protestant and Catholic Hispanic theologies.

Hispanic Protestants often define their identity through opposition to Catholicism. On occasion, the self-definition of Protestants takes the form of a strong anti-Catholic rhetoric. However, for most Hispanic Protestants, self-definition takes the form of a slow withdrawal from the aspects of cultural and family life that are rooted in Catholicism. This withdrawal from their heritage adds to the problems of understanding and building a Hispanic identity. For the Protestant Hispanic, there is a double marginalization. Often they are both rejected by Catholics and alienated from the Catholicism that lies at the core of their cultural and family identity.[29] On the other hand, they are also marginalized by their Anglo denominations and forced to conform to structures, rituals, and practices that are alien to their culture.

The question of identity is not limited to the racial and cultural milieu. It is also ontological and ethical in nature, affecting all Hispanics. In *The Future Is Mestizo*, Virgilio Elizondo writes that the core of Mexican American existence is " to be 'other' or to 'not-be' in relation to those who are."[30] All Hispanics are caught in different levels of oppression that attack their dignity as human beings. Ontologically, they are denied their being and forced either to conform to imposed identities or to define themselves in terms of negations. Anglo Americans do not always fully accept Hispanics as "Americans." At the same time, Hispanics no longer fit into or belong to their country of origin. According to Gustavo Perez Firmat, Hispanics live in the "hyphen" between two cultures. Their identity lies in the crossroads of cultures, races, and nationalities.

The "non-being" of Hispanics is not just about self-definition, it is about marginalization. Hispanics, immersed in the predominant cultures of the United States through education, socialization, and necessity, are denied their culture, identity, and history. The contributions and heritages of Hispanics are often ignored and absent from both education and the media.[31] "English-only" movements further threaten to marginalize Hispanics by denying them a basic aspect of their culture—their language. Language bears identity and values, serving as the principal link to culture and heritage.[32] But it can also become an instrument for persecution, derision, and economic oppression at the hands of those in power.

The resistance of Hispanics to the leveling force of the dominant culture manifests itself in issues of identity as a liberative praxis. The Hispanic quest for identity is a quest for liberation through the right of self-definition. This does not mean that Hispanics lack an identity or a voice. Rather, it means that their differences, uniqueness, and voices are covered, hidden, and silenced by political and social agendas. In asserting their voices and their identity, they are ensuring their place in society and asserting their right to self-determination. Theologically, the quest for identity is connected to our understanding of the doctrines of creation and humanity. It asserts the positive value of both creation and humanity. By affirming their value and dignity, Hispanics oppose the sinful structures that try to marginalize, obscure, and eradicate God's good creatures who are made in the image of God.[33] Thus, Hispanics bear the imago Dei, revealing the diversity and inclusiveness of God, which can never be reduced to a singular image. Furthermore, along with the pain that results from existing as nonbeings, there is also a liberating dimension in the in-betweenness of Hispanic identity. As Elizondo notes, Hispanics are free to move in the in-between and emerge as a new people whose identity is not yet defined. They are neither this nor that, rather, they are fully both.[34]

Popular Religion and the Bible as Distinguishing Marks

According to Roberto Goizueta, a liberative praxis also emerges through the communal and aesthetic practices of Hispanics that are the basic expressions of human praxis as a communal solidarity, a solidarity that is negated by oppression and alienation.[35] These communal practices result in different forms of popular religion that help Hispanics locate themselves as active agents in the world. As a result, the symbols and rituals of popular religion are the principal way for being in the world available to these Hispanic communities. Popular religion plays a crucial role in the formation of Hispanic theology. Both Orlando Espín and Sixto García point to popular religion as a principal locus of theological reflection in Roman Catholic Hispanic theologies.[36]

"Popular religion" is a term derived from the Spanish *religiosidad popular*, which describes innovations, celebrations, and the development of religious expression without the control of clerics or institutions.[37] Espín refers to popular religion as the *sensus fidelium* that is part of all living traditions taking concrete form in the richness of various cultural contexts.[38] It uses the cultural vehicles available to express faith experiences in concrete symbols and forms. But it also expresses the necessity for concrete expression of religious faith. These concrete expressions of faith provide a liberative voice to the community expressing their protest and opposition to their exclusion, marginalization, and oppression at the hands of those in power. Thus, their rituals serve as symbolic acts of resistance against power structures that dominate and hide the voices of the people.[39]

Popular religion is the concrete expression of the religious experiences of a community. However, in most cases, popular religion takes the shape of cultural expressions that are not limited simply to accepted Christian practices. While expressions of popular religion find easier venues for expression within Roman Catholic communities, there tends to be a greater resistance to them within Protestant circles. Protestants reject many of the vestiges of Catholicism and native religions that appear within popular religion as examples of the syncretistic, idolatrous, and superstitious practices of Catholics.[40] At first glance, popular religion may appear to be one of the principal distinguishing marks that separate Protestant and Catholic Hispanic theologies. However, its rejection does not indicate its absence from Protestantism.

If popular religion is a concrete expression of empowerment and resistance for marginalized communities, then it will also be present in Hispanic Protestantism. Mainline Protestant expressions of popular religion are different from Catholic expressions. Instead of using expressions derived from native religions, they tend to use Pentecostal expressions that are often absent from mainline denominations as vehicles of empowerment. They also incorporate music and practices that are closer to Hispanic culture. For instance, Edwin Aponte presents a compelling argument for recognizing *coritos* (little choruses) as a form of Protestant popular religion. According to him, *coritos* are concrete vehicles that express a hope, faith, and empowerment rooted in both the Bible and the lived experiences of the community.[41] They give a voice to the people's hopes and faith in God. Their presence beyond the institutionally bound hymnals attests to their power as expressions of popular religion outside the rigid power structures of institutions. Coritos are usually printed on loose pieces of paper that attest to their transgressions of any given boundary and formalization. The coritos, which are an integral part of Protestant Hispanic services, represent the fluid and living dimensions of the faith found in the Hispanic communities that sing them. In addition, as Aponte notes, coritos also defy the rigid, structured liturgies by maintaining an open adaptability to the community's circumstances.[42] In this sense, coritos transmit orally the traditions and faith of the people in a concrete form adapted to their context.

Another way in which popular religion expresses itself in Protestant Hispanic communities is through the *testimonio*. In the *testimonio*, congregants are invited to speak during the service to give their testimony of how God is active in their lives. *Testimonios* provide a concrete dimension to the faith by articulating how God is active in the present. In this sense, *testimonios* provide a dual vehicle of empowerment. First, they empower ordinary members of the congregation to speak about their faith and life. In the *testimonios* it is not the clergy or the institution that speaks and teaches about God. Instead, they invite the people to interpret everyday circumstances and attest to God's power and presence in them. In this act, the hermeneutical prerogative is taken away from the institution and placed with the people. Second, by recognizing that God is active in the lives of the people, testimonios recognize several elements of the Hispanic faith. First, they affirm God's presence and work in the midst of the people, and move the locus of God's activity and presence away from the powerful and the institutions. In addition, they express an essential element of hope in God's living presence and activity in the world. Testimonios replace the distant and abstract God of philosophy with God's immanence and activity in the world, bridging the gap between God's transcendence and God's immanence. As a result, testimonios empower the Hispanic people by asserting the reality of God in their lives and God's solidarity with them.

The role played by testimonios and coritos in Hispanic Protestantism point to a further aspect of the popular religion of Hispanic Protestants. Where Catholics express their popular religion in concrete symbols, Protestants express it primarily through words. The primacy of the "word" in Hispanic Protestantism takes the place of the icon in Catholic popular religion. As a result, we find that testimonios, coritos, prayers, and Scriptures take the place of images, devotion to saints, and certain types of religious acts. The homes and churches of Hispanic Protestants do not have images of saints on their walls, but they do have Scripture verses. Instead of a statue of *La Virgen*, there is an adorned, Bible-shaped frame with the Ten Commandments or John 3:16 written colorfully in its center.

The primacy of the Scriptures in Hispanic Protestant piety does not negate the concreteness of their popular religion. The words of the coritos and testimonios are firmly rooted and enfleshed in the lives of the people who speak those words, and point to concrete issues and concrete ways in which God's presence and power works in the life of the community.

The role of the Bible takes on an added sacramental significance for those who place scriptures on their walls. The Bible is indeed the *Holy* Bible, serving as a source of insight and strength. As González notes in *Santa Biblia,* the Bible "interprets us in a radically new and ultimately affirming way."[43] For Hispanic Protestants the Bible served in times past as a source of empowerment in several ways. It empowered them by giving access to the Scriptures and their interpretation in ways that were not possible for many Catholics before Vatican II. In this sense, it provided an identity that distinguished Protestants from Catholics and empowered their biblical hermeneutics. For Hispanic Protestants, the Bible was a prized possession that affirmed that God's Word was not a prize reserved for the intellectuals and the elite, but a source for the people's empowerment.

Although the Bible was formerly one of the principal sources of differentiation between Catholics and Protestant Hispanics, the differences are becoming less radical. The centrality of the Bible in the lives of Hispanic Protestants plays a crucial role in Hispanic Protestant theologies. However, the role of the Bible since the Second Vatican Council has changed. For instance, biblical interpretation is a central aspect of Virgilio Elizondo's arguments in *Galilean Journey* and Latin American liberation theologies, both of which have influenced Protestant hermeneutics. This increasingly prevalent role of biblical hermeneutics in Hispanic Catholic theologies blurs some of the differences between itself and Hispanic Protestant theologies, yet differences still remain. While the Bible is always central to Hispanic Protestant theologians, some Hispanic Catholic theologians still minimize the Bible's importance in the lives of Hispanic Americans.[44] As a result, Hispanic Protestants are more likely to use Scripture as a locus of reflection, while Catholics are more likely to use popular religion.

On the other hand, the use of concrete symbols and images in Catholic popular religion does not need to be in opposition to the Bible. For instance, C. Gilbert Romero makes an interesting connection between the Bible and the symbols of Catholic popular religion. Romero builds upon the arguments of the Mexican theologian Raul Vidales, to draw a parallel between the symbols of popular religion and the religious practices found in the Hebrew Bible.[45] In addition, Romero uses cultural anthropology, language theory, and biblical hermeneutical theory to argue for the necessity of these symbols as ways of expressing the affective and mythic dimensions of the biblical text in concrete forms.[46]

Similarly, the importance of the Bible and the "word" in Hispanic Protestant circles does not deny the validity and presence of certain symbols in their midst. The two images that still survive the iconoclastic tendencies of Protestantism are the images of Jesus and of the empty cross. These images present a unique insight to certain dimensions of the Catholic and Protestant Hispanic communities. In many instances, the images of Jesus and the crucifixes in Catholic churches present a graphic image of suffering. Even images of Christ teaching depict the crown of thorns over his heart. These images offer a sense of comfort and hope in the recognition of God's solidarity with their suffering. The suffering of the Hispanic people is graphically present also in the suffering of God, which validates their experience and unmasks the invisibility of their suffering.[47] On the other hand, the empty cross of the Protestants and the resurrected Jesus speaks of the hope and end of suffering. In their symbol, they capture the eschatological hope against hope that the living God will triumph over death and suffering. The importance of these symbols to express meaning and evoke action cannot be overstated.[48] In a sense these symbols in Catholicism and Protestantism express a polarity that requires the presence of both images: suffering and resurrection. The emphasis of one over the other can lead to a denial of suffering or to a denial of hope. Although changing symbols in both groups now portray the cross as a source of suffering and confrontation, both of their theologies require a continuing dialogue that ensures the preservation of these elements in their popular religion.

Doing Theology in Community

Hispanic theologies, unlike many other theologies, emphasize dialogue. Theology does not occur as the work of an individual in isolation. Rather, it comes out of a community in a double sense. First, theology is done in dialogue with one's community of faith. Justo González notes in the opening chapter of *Mañana* that theology cannot be done in the abstract. Instead, theology takes shape within the dialogue that develops between one's community of faith and one's own individual history and perspective.[49] Doing theology as dialogue avoids the Enlightenment's model of doing theology as an abstract observer. Instead, the theologian participates in the community, both influencing and being influenced by it. This prevents theology from becoming a one-way pronouncement made solely by either the theologian or the community of faith. Both remain grounded in each other, shaping and contributing to each other.

The communal nature of theology does not find its genesis in Hispanic theology. Rather, it is a recovery of biblical principles and practices. For example, González notes as a part of the grammar for reading the Bible in "Spanish" that only a small portion of the Scriptures was originally intended for private reading. Instead, the majority of Scriptures are addressed to a community of faith and intended to be read in community.[50] However, the attempt to recover the communal nature of Scripture in Hispanic theologies is not just an attempt to fulfill a biblical mandate or to make a radical return to the Bible. Rather, it is part of the communal nature of the Hispanic population. The communal nature of Scriptures resonates with the communal celebrations of liturgies and festivals in which Hispanic religious experience finds its cultural expression.[51]

Hispanic theology is a dialogue in a second way. It rejects the abstract individualism that characterizes the academy. Since theology is a task done within the community of the church, it cannot be done in isolation. Instead, theology should be a communal exercise. This methodology of dialogue and community pervades Hispanic theology in both Catholic and Protestant circles. Catholic scholars in the Mexican American Cultural Center in San Antonio often engage in collaborative theological enterprises that explore the praxis, faith, and theology of the Hispanic community.[52] Protestants also engage in similar joint projects, one of the oldest being the "Hispanic Instructors Meetings" conducted by the Mexican American Program of Perkins School of Theology. Through that program, pastors, religious leaders, and scholars meet to discuss different issues to produce theological works.[53]

In *Mañana*, González proposes what he calls *Fuenteovejuna* theology: a theology that emerges from all the people as one.[54] This theological methodology, also called *teología de conjunto* (joint theology), is characteristic of Hispanic theologies. Individual contributions made by Hispanic theologians always bear the marks of a continuing dialogue with other theologians that gives guidance to their project. In *Mañana*, González acknowledges his indebtedness to other theologians who have helped him congeal and generate many of his theological reflections. However, even when it is not directly acknowledged in the text, the indebtedness to others can be seen in joint ventures such as this one and in the acknowledgments in books.[55] This methodology that encourages dialogue further blurs the distinctions between Catholic and Protestant Hispanic theologies into a new ecumenism.

Eschatological Hope and the "New Ecumenism"

Hispanic theologies are teleological and eschatological in nature. The movement of these theologies is not a senseless wandering, but a journey toward a specific destiny. Although they originate in different cultural contexts and experiences, they move toward a singular vision. The characteristics that bind both Protestant and Catholic Hispanic theologies are teleological in nature: their shared vision of the future embodied in a new humanity and their common struggle toward a liberative praxis. Both Catholics and Protestant Hispanics struggle against assimilation pressures, against unjust discriminative practices, and against their marginalization by both their denominations and mainline culture. These factors produce a new ecumenism within Hispanic theologies that unites them in a common goal and struggle without dissolving doctrinal differences.[56] This ecclesiastical mestizaje holds the key to the future for Hispanic American theologies.

The opening of a continuing dialogue between Catholic and Protestant Hispanic theologians has yielded a fruitful result. The growing use of the Bible and greater ecumenical and interreligious dialogue engendered by the Second Vatican Council holds the promise of allowing different perspectives in a continuing dialectic that increases our notion of ecclesiastical mestizaje.[57] The increased openness to interreligious dialogue places Hispanic Catholic theologians in a unique place that can foster the recovery of truths conveyed in native religions and that might introduce new perspectives into the continuing dialogue with Protestantism. Similarly the joint struggle of both Protestants and Catholics against injustices, marginalization, and prejudice, along with their concerns for a liberative praxis, has placed a common vision before both groups.

The common vision of a radical new humanity envisioned by Hispanic theologies provides these theologies with an eschatological dimension that affects the present in a radical manner. This eschatological vision is not a transcendent or otherworldly reality that merely serves as a placebo with no real impact upon the present structures of oppression and domination. Rather, they are teleological visions that drive their activity in the present and critique present structures in light of these shared visions of the future. Within Protestant Hispanic theologies, González's *Mañana* is not a deferral of the present to an idealized vision of the future. Rather, it is a radical questioning of today.[58] While it instills hope for a common vision of the future, it also empowers the struggle against those who do not share that vision and a critique against those structures that deny its possibility. Elizondo presents a similar eschatological vision for the new humanity embodied in the inclusive notion of the mestizo and what he calls "the resurrection principle" in which love triumphs over evil.[59] However, these hopes cannot be fulfilled without questioning and confronting the present by taking the risks involved in initiating new ways of life that will eliminate some of the dehumanizing elements of the present situation.[60] These eschatological dimensions of Hispanic theologies point to a common destiny and unity.

Conclusions

Hispanic theologies parallel and share some of the same concerns of postmodernity. As a result, postmodernity can provide some necessary tools. For instance, the dynamics of contrast and the inclusion of diversity can be useful in developing a descriptive language for distinguishing these theologies without reducing them to static and detached notions. Postmodern hermeneutics of deconstruction can also aid in discovering and disclosing hidden texts and structures that hide and oppress Hispanic Americans. However, Hispanic theologies must also preserve their dynamics of dialogue and critique of traditional theologies and structures without falling prey to the incommensurability or relativism that often plagues postmodernity. Hispanic theologies are postmodern theologies in their own right and can set their own postmodern standard.

Although differences remain in the treatment of certain loci of reflection, such as popular religion and biblical interpretations, the continuing dialogue between Catholic and Protestant Hispanic theologians has slowly blurred the rigid lines of distinction between them while preserving their distinct identity. Their mutual concerns, their continuing dialogue, and their eschatological hope have created a greater interaction between these theologies, an interaction that was almost impossible half a century ago. The unique anthropological origins of Hispanic theologies and their continuing struggle toward their goal prevents a simple system for defining or contrasting these theologies. Nevertheless, the impact of their message and power cannot be dismissed. In their call for justice, dignity, dialogue, and celebration of differences, they present us with several unique theological perspectives from the underside of history. In a sense, they reverse the prevalent standards of theology in the academy. Rather than doing theology as a detached and purely intellectual exercise, Hispanic theologians advocate a theology that rises from the people, affirms the value of humanity as created in God's image, and critiques the structures that pretend that only their image and power structures reflect God's image and kingdom. Hispanic theologies reject hierarchies of domination enshrined in Christian dualisms and dichotomies derived from Greek, Gnostic, and Modern philosophies. Instead, they affirm the central thrust of the Christian gospel as an affirmation of a life shared with God in Christ. This life, concrete and incarnated in the people, points us in a different direction from what academic circles typically demand.

Chapter 7

Hispanic Experience and the Protestant Ethic

Ismael García

Although it is simply not possible to formulate *the* ethical theory that dominates Hispanic American Protestant moral thinking, it is still possible to identify common motifs or centerpieces of Hispanic moral reflection. Our moral language reveals our concern and commitments to *moral principles,* a concern with *character formation,* and a commitment to *group recognition and care.* These three motifs inform the eclectic manner in which we engage in moral reflection.

My claim is that the ethics of recognition and care is becoming the preferred, not the exclusive, way Hispanic Protestants articulate their moral point of view. Most of us assume that (1) the needs of people have priority over principles; (2) humans do not exist for ethics, but ethics exists for enhancing the goodness of our life together; (3) familial and group relationships are morally more significant than abstract principles and rules; and (4) the moral systems of subcultural groups are normatively more relevant than universal standards of ethics.[1] When Hispanics express justice concerns such as (1) the commitment to love the powerless and poor, (2) the affirmation of group differences, and (3) the quest for greater recognition among the marginal, the ethics of care assumes a social and political character that enhances its liberating character.

Hispanic Religiosity

Looking at the world from a religious point of view is an intrinsic dimension of Hispanic culture and personality. None of us is free from the formative influence of our religious heritage, which shapes our culture. Religion influences the way we feel, think, and relate to the world. It sustains our courage and strength to struggle, as well as being a fount from which to console our pain. Religious images and expressions such as "hay bendito," "Ave María," "Dios te bendiga," "hay Dios mio," and "Adios" permeate our language. Even Hispanics who are otherwise religiously disinterested display rosaries and statues of the virgin and other saints on the dashboards and rearview mirrors of their cars. Protestants, of course, have a preference for displaying their Bibles or a sticker with a biblical verse. Many among us are named José, María, and Jesús, and we continue to show an inclination to give our children the name of prominent biblical personalities.

Our religious and theological perspective has been shaped by Roman Catholicism, Protestantism, and the religion of indigenous people. Ever since Protestantism became a significant religious alternative for Latin Americans and Hispanic Americans, Catholics and Protestants have been suspicious of each other. Catholics accuse Protestants of being not only heretics, but also cultural traitors and political and social anarchists. Protestants, on the other hand, accuse Catholics of being antibiblical, economically and socially backward, and politically antidemocratic. This has led many Hispanic Protestants living in the United States to define their religious identity as anti-Catholic. And both the Catholic and Protestant criticism of indigenous and African religious beliefs and practices has deprived us of the wisdom of our ancestors.

Fortunately, there is a new ecumenism among Hispanic Protestants and Hispanic Catholics. It is an ecumenism of mutual appreciation, respect, and recognition grounded not in common theological beliefs, but in an attitude of solidarity in the struggle by which Hispanics aim to overcome the conditions of oppression and domination to which they are subjected in the United States. This ecumenism has allowed Hispanic Protestants to rediscover and appreciate those elements of their culture that they mistakenly felt compelled to abandon in order to be good Christians. And it has led Hispanic Catholics to reclaim Scripture as the center of their spirituality. Both communities are discovering how the needs of the larger Hispanic community provide a common ground from which to act and make moral judgments.

There still remain significant differences in the way Hispanic Catholics and Protestants understand the nature and function of moral reasoning. For Catholics, morality is an intrinsic part of the teaching authority of the church. Morality has been and continues to be shaped by, and is intimately tied to the priestly functions of judging sins and prescribing penances. Many Hispanic Catholics also believe that morality is part of the objective order created by God and able to be discerned rationally. They also believe that striving to become morally righteous is part of the process by which we prepare ourselves, in mind and soul, to live in ways fitting those who will be saved. Morality is seen as having both the pedagogical and juridical function of correcting the particular sins a believer has committed. Sins are interpreted as infractions of the objective moral order (natural law) created by God. Sins bring upon us a state of confusion and disorientation from God and God's purpose. The confession of sin and the practice of penance and contrition assist us to come back to the right way, or to act in ways that fit our nature, and to regain the vision of our true end. Catholic ethics, or moral theology, is rationally, practically, and ecclesiastically cohesive.

Hispanic Protestants, however, focus on the general condition of sinfulness and not on particular actions that are sinful. We view sin more as a theological than a moral dilemma. Our pastors do not have the responsibility of judging our conduct or telling us what is the right thing to do to get back on the right track. Moral counseling is done in a more voluntary and informal context and manner. We eliminate the sacrament of penance or reduce it to a general and abstract public confession of sin. Protestant denominational moral teachings are less authoritative, functioning more like counsel with a purpose mostly pedagogical. In general, ethics assumes a more informal connection with the practice of ministry.

For us Protestants, morality and right conduct are secondary to the theological concern that we trust and depend on God's grace for our salvation. It is God, not our acts, who makes us right. And the proper human response to God's free gift of grace is gratitude. We have a certain distrust in ethics and moral development because it entails a legalism that nourishes various forms of self-righteousness. It must be pointed out that different Protestant groups have different interpretations of the role of morality in the formation of our religious personality. Calvinists and Methodists who uphold the theological significance of "the law" or "the doctrine of sanctification" do give moral development a positive value. Lutherans and those of other denominations who emphasize grace as the main source of our salvation see morality as having mostly negative value. In this view, morality helps contain the spread of evil. Thus, within the Protestant family there is greater moral diversity and more ways of doing ethics. It is not surprising that this greater freedom and diversity also lead to greater moral confusion.

Dominant Styles of Moral Reasoning

Principle Ethics

Some Hispanics express their moral views in the legalistic or judicial language characteristic of the culture of modernity. This is particularly true of those Hispanic Americans who aspire to be fully assimilated into this society. But it is also true of all of us insofar as we cannot escape the influence of the Anglo Saxon moral tradition embodied and dominant in the basic social institutions under which we presently live.

This style of ethical reflection, which we will call *principle ethics,* focuses on human action and decision making, and is mainly concerned with determining the right action we are obligated to perform. It proceeds by formulating general and abstract principles which all rational creatures can recognize and accept as universally acceptable and binding. Given our finitude and sinfulness, we acknowledge that equally valid moral principles can and do conflict with each other. This is why, with few exceptions, Hispanics do not claim that moral principles are absolute; we recognize that noncompliance with a particular moral principle can be justified. But advocates of principle ethics argue that the only justification not to comply with a binding principle is that we intend to comply with an alternative but equally valid moral principle. Right choices and judgments, thus, must take into account both continuities and differences that are morally relevant. Moral agents must also assume a discerning attitude and remain open and flexible enough to opt against our presumptions and moral preferences.

To the question, What should I do? the ethics of principle provides two answers: (1) do that which is right in and of itself, independent of the consequences of your actions (duty ethics); or (2) do that which will bring the best consequences and minimize harm for everyone involved (ethics of consequences). Those who choose the first mode of ethical thinking give the principle of autonomy priority. Those who advocate for the second give the principle of beneficence and utility priority in their system of values.

Duty Ethics. Many Hispanic Protestants are scriptural legalists who emphasize rights and duties as the core of their moral obligations. Their answer to the questions, How do I determine the good? and What should I do? is: do that which, independent of its consequences, is in itself right. Doing what is right must take precedence over achieving the good.[2] Our duties and obligations are determined by the inner traits of our actions themselves. For example, murder, torture, lying to parents, marital unfaithfulness, and disobeying authority are actions that in themselves are always wrong, no matter how desirable or positive their consequences could be. The terms used to describe such actions already signify that it is wrong to do them. Lying and disobeying the law can help us save an innocent life; however, in spite of their good consequences, they are still morally wrong acts. That they are necessary and even justifiable for most of us merely reveals the brokenness of our communal life and our lack of recog-

143

nition and respect for the integrity of our being. If we must do such acts, we should at least recognize that they are morally wrong, express and feel remorse, and engage in acts of contrition. Repentance and contrition become more stringent obligations for the religiously inclined who must confess and admit the wrongness of their actions before God as well as before others.

On the positive side, truthfulness, faithfulness, promise keeping, and honesty describe actions that are in themselves desirable, and thus it is our duty to perform them even when they do not bring forth convenient or good consequences. Such actions are right in that they contribute to sustaining and forwarding the integrity of our being and the possibilities of living in community. If one wants to live within caring and loving communities, one does well living in light of the Ten Commandments.

This point of view emphasizes that not any means justifies the end, no matter how good it is. It also emphasizes that each individual is worthy of respect and dignity and should never become a mere means to someone else's well-being. Individuals are moral agents entitled to the freedom to give themselves a life plan and the freedom to carry it out. Duty-based ethics emphasizes the principle of autonomy and the language of rights. Rights language has national, cross-cultural, and international significance and appeal. It has become an acceptable and frequently used language in international relationships and of movements committed to progressive social change.

Hispanics find this language attractive in that it signifies the longing for freedom at the heart of our struggles for justice.[3] This language is also at the root of the Hispanic understanding of human dignity. In our view, dignity is intrinsically intertwined with our being creative agents capable of autonomous decision making. Whenever we feel that our point of view is not taken seriously or that we are treated in a paternalistic manner, we claim our dignity has been violated. Dignity demands not only that we be allowed to live in light of self-given rules, but also that we must be consulted in all matters that affect our life in significant ways. Religiously speaking, autonomy entails our having the capacity to discern truth in the Scriptures and to be authentic in following our understanding of God's will for our lives.

Hispanic Protestants who abide by this style of ethical reflection look within Scripture for the rules and principles that enable us to live a morally good life. Such is the function of the Ten Commandments and the Sermon on the Mount. In this perspective, which is close to the Roman Catholic natural law conception of ethics, God is viewed primarily as a lawgiver and sustainer of order within the cosmos and society. Most Protestant scriptural legalists assume a conservative rather than progressive understanding of the function of moral laws and principles. Even Hispanics who belong to the Calvinist and Methodist traditions, in which there is a more optimistic view of the possibility of improving the web of human relationships, still emphasize the curtailing power of laws rather than their creative possibilities. The laws and principles revealed by Scripture do not make us morally better nor do they make the community more harmonious. More than anything else, these scriptural laws and principles reveal how deep-rooted sin is in our being. Morally and politically speaking, scriptural laws and principles make us aware that we need to abide by prevailing legal structures in order to repress our propensity to sin. The inclination to abide by dominant social institutions, civil law, and prevailing moral mores of the dominant community has a theological rather than moral foundation. Institutions such as the state and marriage, for example, are ordained by God and cannot be undermined, since tampering with them merely undermines another barrier to the ravages of sin. Thus, we find that most Hispanic Protestant legalists are against homosexuality, same-sex marriage, and most acts of civil disobedience because they undermine our personal dignity, social cohesion, and political stability.

There are drawbacks to the ethics of duty that remain a concern for most Hispanic Protestants. In focusing on the *right,* it can make us insensitive to the obligation we all have to enhance the *good.* Always acting out of an uncompromising sense of duty can lead to dogmatic and cold forms of behavior that disregard the negative consequences of such actions. That is, duty ethics does not always take into account what, for Hispanics, is a morally significant question: For whose good is this action taken? Hispanics, given their state of oppression and powerlessness, look for and work in hope of a better future, where a fuller life will be accessible to more members of society. Thus *enhancement* of the good, or minimizing of the evil, is central to their moral sense of obligation and the moral good.

Furthermore, within our dominant political culture the language of rights and the principle of autonomy are biased toward the protection of individual interests. Rights promote social arrangements that protect individuals from undue interference from others and, in particular, from the political state. They serve as moral entitlements that empower individuals and safeguard their capacity for self-determination. Hispanics, however, have a cultural bias toward the quality of group life and a central concern with the cultural well-being of their community, both of which are group-based.

Ethics of Consequences. We find that there are other Hispanic Protestants who are mostly concerned with identifying challenges and goals, and fashioning responses to realize desired ends. For them the morally good is determined by the ends or consequences of our actions. What are "good or worthy ends" are variously defined by different individuals and groups. For some it is the development of reason or spiritual pursuits or both, for others, friendships and community; some claim it is religious political activism, and others argue for the contemplative life. Most of us argue for some combination of these alternatives. However, whatever the end specified, consequentialists determine the morally good action by how that action brings about or denies the end pursued.

Hispanic consequentialists make the principles of beneficence and utility normative.[4] We believe that, given that we derive benefits from the network of social relationships in which we dwell, and from the contributions made by members of our *comunidad,* we are morally bound to enhance the goodness of their lives. This belief is at the root of our obligation to offer hospitality to friends and strangers, and loyalty to family and our ethnic communities. Furthermore, the simplicity and common-sense nature of these two principles makes them inherently attractive. For most Hispanics it is intuitively true that we have a moral obligation to minimize evil and, whenever we are able to do so, to contribute to the goodness of our lives and the lives of others.

For us, beneficence does not entail servitude and undue self-sacrifice. There are limits to our obligation to do the good. Beneficence, thus, is a conditional moral principle. We can only contribute to the well-being of others if it is possible for us to do so. Whenever we (1) are aware of someone in a state of need, (2) have the resources and skills necessary to act in ways that can satisfy their needs, (3) can act in a way to make a difference in their life, and (4) can assist them without undergoing undue sacrifices or disrupting our life plan in any significant way, we have a stringent obligation to benefit such groups or persons. Clearly there are some who might want to do good beyond what is morally required, but no one is morally obligated to contribute to the well-being of others when doing so significantly impoverishes one's life prospects.

Hispanic Protestants who are consequentialists also appeal to Scripture, but rather than lifting up laws and principles, they point to those goals and benefits that underscore God's concern with the well-being of all of God's creatures. For example, the biblical story of the good Samaritan and the love command are used to motivate our concern to contribute to the well-being of others. There is also a lot of attention given to what we need to do to contribute to the realization of God's kingdom. For these Protestants the practice of beneficence is justified theologically, not morally; because of God's providential and beneficent actions toward us we must act in ways that benefit others.

These Protestants believe something which is also true for many Hispanic Catholics: God is not only a lawgiver and a preserver of order. God is mainly a historical actor whose mighty acts create new liberating possibilities for the future. Morality, thus, is not mainly about preserving order and abiding by our need for stability and consistency, but concerns itself with enhancing the possibilities of human relationships. As it is true that humans have the need for stability and consistency, the focus of the ethics of duty, it is equally true that we are incomplete beings who look forward to new realizations of our humanity. Both aspects are important to forward the possibilities of our life together and our personal realizations. Thus, contrary to their legalistic brethren, they emphasize that there are limits to keeping ethical principles, particularly when they are destructive to people.

Overall, most Hispanic Protestants have a preference for acting morally out of a sense of duty, but not at the expense of the well-being of the parties involved in a relationship. The well-being of all the parties is a factor in determining what ought to be done. In biblical terms, the Sabbath is made for humans, not humans for the Sabbath. And given our commitment to the authority of the Scriptures and our attempts to look within them for theological and moral guidance in laws or goals, we have a preference for a morality of rules over a morality of situations. We recognize that the Scriptures do not present us with ready-made solutions for all the dilemmas we presently confront. But we do believe that the human condition is such that there are enough continuities and patterns within the web of human relationships to make it possible for us to find, within our biblical and theological traditions, guidance for the task of organizing our mutual dealings. Scripture provides wisdom and insight, regarding human relationships, that have not only been proved to be good, but that remain relevant to our present situation.

Hispanic Protestants recognize that utilitarianism has drawbacks that prevent us from making the principle of utility our exclusive or dominant criterion of moral action and judgment. Utilitarianism tends toward "the end justifies the means" kind of thinking. It disregards significant moral differences that exist between two actions if they both bring about similar consequences. For example, if we bring about the same good consequences but in one case we lie and in another we do so by telling the truth, both actions are identified as morally equal. For most of us this goes against our intuitive sense of what is properly called morally good.

It also worries Hispanics that the utilitarian mode of thinking allows a social group or individual to bracket or sacrifice personal interests in order to improve the general well-being of other social groups or society as a whole. In ways similar to oppressive notions of sacrificial love harbored within the Christian community, utilitarianism can support practices and policies that call for even higher levels of sacrifice, in name of the common good, from those who can ill afford them.

In conclusion, many Hispanic Protestants are principle-oriented. We affirm the principle of beneficence or the principle of autonomy as central to the moral life. We disagree among ourselves as to which of these principles ought to be given priority, but we do not question their moral relevance. We keep both these principles in tension and balance the demands each places upon us. Those among us who give priority to the principle of autonomy do so because we are convinced that focusing too much on the language of beneficence and providing assistance can create among the needy a social consciousness of being mere victims, or passive recipients of the generosity of others. It makes the needy overdependent on the goodwill of others and deprives them of the joy of knowing and experiencing that they are agents capable of shaping their own destiny. Others among us choose the principle of beneficence because we are convinced that the condition of the needy and powerless will deteriorate significantly if there are no programs, organizations, or individuals willing to provide whatever assistance is needed. In our view, to promote autonomous self-reliance is a legitimate moral end, but not at the risk of allowing an individual or social group to drown in the oppression and domination by which they are victimized. Hispanics are not victims, but too many of our people are victimized in various ways. Therefore, we have the obligation to assist people as a necessary step in the process of empowering them to become agents of their own destiny.

Christian Identity and Character Formation

The value Hispanics give to family life, church life, and the quality of life within their *comunidad* make us aware that we have moral obligations beyond those defined in terms of rights and impartial universal laws. Within these smaller and more intimate contexts, it is not the impersonal and conflict-ridden language of law, rights, and contracts between free agents that makes moral sense. Rather the language of mutual dependence, shared and abiding convictions and commitments, and loyalty communicates what is morally required. In these intimate contexts, obligation and responsibility take precedence over rights. We have obligations and responsibilities toward others not only because they have rights entitlements, but mostly because they are within the purview of our network of interaction, and our relationship with them is what enables us to become the kind of person we can become.

Some Hispanic Protestants, thus, express moral concern with issues other than acting out of moral obligation and engaging in decision making. They argue that the root of the lovelessness and violence our *comunidad* confronts daily has to do with individual and collective defects in moral character. This explains our growing commitment and concern with the character traits of the moral agent who acts and chooses, and with the kind of person we become as we choose and perform particular acts.

More and more Hispanic Protestants (a probable carryover from the influence and attraction of the Anabaptist tradition) are acutely interested in the question of Christian identity expressed through the formation and the development of Christian moral character and the development of Christian virtues, particularly among the young.[5] Their aim is to act morally out of their unique religious convictions[6] even if these convictions go against what is culturally acceptable. The particular beliefs, experiences, and convictions of the community of faith are identified as the source and spring of our moral convictions and commitments. In their view, Scripture provides us not so much with principles and rules, but with a new and alternative way of living that is a challenge to the lifestyle provided by civil society. They lift up the figure of Jesus and the disciples as their mentors, and attempt to mold their communal and personal lives in ways that model a story consistent with the Christian story.

The claim is made that the development of a virtuous character is morally more significant than mere conformity to rules and principles, since rules can always be avoided, while a strong character has permanence and reliability. People of character are internally disposed to do what is morally right, particularly when the going gets tough. And when they commit a wrong act, as all finite and sinful creatures are prone to do, they will be predisposed to correct it when it is pointed out to them. Finally, people of strong moral character exhibit the right balance of caring and commitment.

Motive and emotion, which the ethics of duty tends to disregard or minimize, are central to the ethics of character. When a friend or a caring agent like our pastor responds to our needs, we expect this person to do so not merely out of a cold sense of duty as defined by office or merely out of a rational sense of obligation, but also with care and with a sense of love. Paul expresses this point of view when he states that if one performs the right action and acts out of duty, but lacks the proper moral motivation, neither the act nor the person is virtuous. "If I give away all I have, and if I deliver my body to be burned, but have not love, I gain nothing" (1 Cor. 13:3 RSV).

This commitment to character formation does not entail lack of concern with action and decision making central to the ethics of principle. These two ethics are seen as compatible and mutually reinforcing. Who we become is largely determined by what we do, and what we do is shaped by who we are. Principle ethics stresses the importance of *acting* under the guidance of the principles of autonomy, beneficence, and justice, while character ethics calls us to *be* respectful, benevolent, and just. The virtues of truthfulness and faithfulness are developed to some degree by abiding by and practicing the principles of veracity and fidelity.

These two kinds of ethics, however, are different. Therefore, we must not be surprised if, when we ask the advice of a virtuous person, he or she responds, "I do not know!" One cannot assume that a person who displays a virtuous character will always act in morally acceptable ways or will always know what is the moral thing to do. Virtuous people commit morally unfit acts either because they were ignorant of a significant fact, made an honest mistake, or did not have the skill to make their actions effective.[7] We will always need principles to help us decide what to do, particularly when we must choose between conflicting virtues, and we will also need to learn how to move from principle to action. Principles are indispensable guides of conduct, and knowing how to apply them is a skill and an element of the moral life we all need.

For Hispanic Protestants who focus on character formation, abstract principles provide neither a proper source of moral instruction nor a proper spring for moral inspiration and action. Equally deficient is the individualistic bent of principle ethics and the language of human rights. Life in *comunidad*, the quality of communal life, and the preservation of tradition are indispensable elements of our moral upbringing. Our communal experience is what makes this kind of ethics attractive to us.

Communities shape our vision. They influence the way we look at the world and give us a sense of meaning and the goals we ought to pursue. They structure and define the roles and responsibilities we are obligated to perform, the goals we ought to pursue, and the standard of excellence by which we evaluate these goals. Traditions, which are given, not constructed, provide us with a unique language, symbols, and system of meaning. More emphatically than the ethics of principle, the ethics of character emphasizes the fact that we become who we are through relations with the world and others. It is within community that we learn the virtues of caring for and serving the needs of others and the common good. There is no such thing as an individual morality, nor a universal morality that is applicable to all human beings and is relevant for all circumstances. Morality always belongs to a particular community in which obligations and duties are defined in light of the roles we are called to play within it. To grasp the fullness of meaning of a particular moral point of view, we must, to some degree, immerse ourselves in that community's history and conception of the good life.

For many Hispanic Christians, participation within a particular church community is not an option, but an essential part of what it means to be a Christian. Becoming and acting morally as a Christian (by which they mean following the example of Jesus, our mentor and role model) requires disciplined and continual study and preparation. The virtues are not natural to our being. To develop them requires hard work over a long period of time. We learn them by watching and imitating those persons who represent the best values and moral ideals of the traditions and communities we belong to. Mentors and role models, supported by well-structured educational interactions, are indispensable to character formation. In church we not only read and talk about Christ, but more important we are in touch with today's Christian *disciples* and *saints,* who teach and model the Way to us.

The Christian community of faith provides the context out of which we engage in moral reflection and practical moral decision making. This community provides the resources—that is, the stories, symbols, traditions, visions, and interpretations of God, self, and world—that ground our choices. It delimits what we are and are not able to do.[8] When we make moral decisions we make them not only as individuals, but also as representatives of the faith community we belong to. Furthermore, when we do violate a community precept, it is the faith community that is called to forgive and accept us.

The church is understood as a community of acceptance and commitment and of discipline and sacrifice. Sacrifice or self-giving is always part of a life lived in dependence on God's way. This is at the heart of the story and journey of God's people. Protecting the innocent is a noble and worthy *act,* which we are obligated to practice, but only in ways that fit what it means to be church.

For all the emphasis on community life, Hispanic Protestants who stress the centrality of character formation argue that character formation is bidirectional. As we are shaped by our community, we still are free to choose what within our communities will influence us. No one can represent or do the religious thing for us. We are all called to take personal responsibility for our own character formation. Thus, the practice common among Hispanics, that women carry the religious responsibility for their families, is challenged.

Politically speaking, we have the capacity to change and re-create the world that has been given to us. In fact, we create and choose our own character as we contribute to the re-creation of the social and natural world. We have and must assume responsibility for the moral quality of our individual actions and of our social world. The social structure in which we live can channel our actions in a given direction. An evil and unjust social structure can make us act in evil and unjust ways in spite of our good moral character. An evil structure is a powerful reality, as Paul makes us aware; within society one encounters powers and principalities that make us act contrary to our best intentions. Thus, moral evaluations and concerns have to be directed not just to individuals and their characters, but also toward the social structure that defines the roles and responsibilities we are called to perform and which limits our choices.[9] This is the reason why, for an increasing number of Hispanics, structural transformation is becoming a central and urgent moral matter.

Character ethics is attractive to many Hispanics because it affirms the centrality of communities of moral conviction and mutuality that are instrumental to helping us live the morally good life. But here also lie the dangers of this kind of ethics. Small intentional communities with a strong sense of identity are not without moral problems. They can generate tribal and provincial attitudes and can make our moral concerns narrowly focused and self-enclosed. Internally, they can oppress and obstruct rather than become a means to the realization of our unique individuality; they can diminish rather than enhance our creativity. Politically speaking, they can also encourage separatist attitudes and diminish our social responsibility and contribution to the common good.

In order to be morally evenhanded, intentional communities need help in putting some distance between their particular interests, beliefs, convictions, and commitments. They need to find ways to be more objective and impartial when dealing with strangers. This is one reason why many Hispanics keep their commitment to the ethics of principle and individual rights. Rights give strangers a voice and empower them to demand recognition. They enable us to relate to and include strangers in our field of moral concern and, in so doing, to create occasions to initiate new relationships. And whether or not these occasions result in new intimate relationships, they do make us aware of the importance of contributing to the larger community. If the central question of virtue ethics is the determination of those communal values and traits of character that sustain community, then it is important to emphasize that the protection of rights is a significant way to promote communal values. Rights provide protection against unscrupulous behavior, promote orderly change, and enhance cohesiveness in communities. They allow diverse communities to coexist peacefully within a single political state. Even if life in community is the best kind of life, it ought not to weaken our individual goals or truncate our individual rights. All of these are the reasons why the Hispanic commitment to character formation is accompanied by a commitment to clearly defined and widely propagated basic political rights.

The Ethics of Care

Increasingly the moral language used by Hispanic Protestants reveals an alternative sense of moral obligation, which I am calling *the ethics of care and recognition.* As the ethics of principle stresses what is to be done, and the ethics of character focuses on who we are, the ethics of care emphasizes the creation of nurturing communities of mutual aid. It is an ethic that stresses the importance of identification and commitment to one's ethnic community. It is concerned with the dynamics of group rights, for example, the rights of cultural identity and the related issues of membership and belonging, recognition, and respect, which ensure that each one's needs will be given equal consideration.

The ethics of care is grounded on the experiences of small communities such as the family, the church, and those local social and political organizations that provide spaces for intimacy and solidarity, and on the capacity to assert one's group's unique identity and interests. Hispanic Protestants who are proponents of care ethics claim that we have special ethical responsibilities toward those who are powerless and dependent, vulnerable and frail. In our face-to-face encounters with such persons, we discover that our moral obligations are best expressed through the more familial language of satisfaction of needs and prevention of harm than through the language of claims to individual rights, autonomy, and character. More important than abstract universal principles and the concern with our Christian identity is freeing people from that which harms and dehumanizes them.

Personal encounters with the victims of our violent world put and keep them at the center of our moral concern. It becomes impossible for us to reduce them to mere statistics or to an impersonal wave of the faceless that leave us insecure and fearful. More important, we cannot conceal their flesh-and-blood humanity and suffering under the guise of impersonal and bureaucratic concerns that come with a social cost. For example, when we hear the cry of the migrant for protection and the injustice of the events and circumstances that make the refugees leave their homelands, the personhood of the migrant and the refugee remains the springboard and center of the moral imperative. In this encounter the main issue becomes, How do I share the care and love of God with such a person? How am I to be hospitable to those defined as strangers? How do I make them part of my family? How would I want others to act toward these persons if it so happened that they were my mother, my sister, or my brother?

One of the dangers of the ethics of duty is that, in its zealousness not to be paternalistic and in its desire to honor the principle of autonomy, it overemphasizes not being intrusive and not violating the personal and social boundaries of other persons and social groups. The ethics of care, on the other hand, finds in this situation an occasion for responsible intervention in the life of others. It is through our immersion in the life of strangers, particularly in the life of the poor and powerless, that we unveil quintessential facets of the moral life and what we must do to promote human dignity and life-sustaining communities. Those who suffer unjustly make us aware of the reality and consistency of the power of the sins of death and evil, which deny the purposes of the God of life.

Individual Christians and faith communities exercise the freedom to leave the poor and oppressed alone and expect that someone else will respond to their needs. Apathy and indifference are identified among the greatest sins. Our inclination must be to meddle in the life of all groups who are victimized by our world. We meddle in solidarity, faith, and trust that as God's people we will discern what is the right thing to do. Our assumption is that what the powerless and exploited expect from us is not detached respect for their rights, but emotionally attached attentiveness to their needs.

In this view, God is more than a lawgiver or a goal setter. The God of Abraham and Sarah is a historical actor, a listener and responder to the cries of those who suffer. God's mighty acts create new possibilities of life for those who are denied life. The cries of the poor are embodied by God. In them we find indications as to what has to be transformed in the web of human relationships. And the recognition, solidarity, and care we provide the refugee signal God's presence and care for them. It is in the context of the struggle to overcome suffering and unjustified death that we find occasions for liberating solidarity. The creative power of God is such that it does not rule out the possibility for solidarity between oppressed and oppressors, a solidarity based on mutual recognition and care, intent on forwarding justice for all members of society in a shared life.

To avoid the real dangers of being paternalistic as one purposely and aggressively becomes involved in other people's lives, the ethic of care finds it necessary to stress the importance of justice as a moral commitment. Thus, the notion and models of care that we learn within the family must be extended to include social and political concerns. The ethics of character is right when it points out that we are shaped within community. In care ethics, this entails that more and more communities within the larger political community must be made just if we are to become and sustain ourselves as just people.

Hispanic Protestants who abide by the ethics of care argue that justice entails that we commit ourselves to act *with* the poor and oppressed and not *for* them. We commit ourselves to the task of mutual consciousness raising, and to mutual organization and responsible participation in the re-creation of our social world. One way to do this is to politicize self-help programs and continue to forward the democratization or broad popular control of key social institutions. This focus on active involvement in the struggle for justice gives the poor and oppressed another way to define and understand themselves as other than mere victims, as people who, in the company of others, can express themselves as creative agents.

Hispanic Protestants who abide by the ethics of care express three main justice concerns: a *politics* of empowerment for Hispanic Americans so they have a greater voice in matters that affect their local communities and the national destiny; a *social* commitment to the creation of more spaces and occasions to experience the joys of recognition through leadership and authority; and a commitment to nourishing one's evolving *cultural* identity.

Politically speaking, Hispanics must be able to create a plurality of empowered local communal organizations, each independent from the other and focused on particular issues. Their purpose is to enhance the political consciousness of the community about those matters which affect their life prospects, and to make the larger center of power accountable to the needs of the community. It is equally important to create spaces and structures that enable diverse social groups to encounter one another. It is here that we achieve a more sophisticated understanding of those who are different from us, where we discover common concerns and interests, and where we are able to create more inclusive networks of mutual aid. Autonomy within a particular sphere of influence and interrelationship in structures of solidarity and mutual aid represent the dynamics of the social and political vision of justice central to the ethics of care. This commitment to solidarity among different, small, independent communities is what distinguishes the ethics of care from the ethics of character, which is inclined to be more separatist and exclusive.

Socially speaking, the aim is to redefine the division of labor, ensuring to all who work a fair wage. But equally important is to create more opportunities for Hispanics to participate within all levels of production as owners and managers. It entails recognition of unpaid labor, such as household work, and a more just division of the responsibilities of work that is not remunerated, but that is socially necessary and important. Within the workplace, more democratic control should be exercised and more occasions created to allow all workers to experience what it means to both give and receive orders and thus be looked upon as people who speak and act with authority.

Finally, the quest for freedom and equality central to the ethics of principle and character must go through the struggle for cultural affirmation. True freedom and equality demand that we overcome the distortions Anglo-Saxon culture presses upon us. Hispanics have learned that becoming *derivative* Anglo Saxons impoverishes our life and leaves it void of a viable system of meaning. As members of ancient and honorable cultures, we must be allowed to negotiate a dignified acculturation based on mutual recognition and respect.

Care ethics, politically, socially, and culturally speaking, is an ethics based on the dynamic of true dialogue among groups who are different but who desire to negotiate a life together. It claims that moral formation emerges through the conversations and interactions we have with "significant others," both friend and foe. And like all true conversations and encounters, it depends on our capacity and willingness to listen, understand, and grant one another respect and recognition. In our present social context, recognition is not a matter of courtesy or etiquette, but something at the heart of the preservation of one's humanity and dignity. To be denied recognition is to be subjected to the domination and oppression of other social groups.

Justice is also central to the Protestant Hispanic ethics of care because it saves legitimate acts of caring and nourishing from having to justify themselves ideologically as self-surrender and self-sacrifice. This is the lesson Hispanic women are teaching us. Hispanic women continue to make us aware of how being forced and limited to the function of caregiving and nurturing, in themselves noble tasks, becomes a means of social control and repression. Locked into the task of caregiving, most Hispanic women have been denied fair participation in other social functions within and outside the family and the recognition and respect related to these more public functions. For too long Hispanic women have been forced to live their lives within the private realm performing tasks generally associated with cleaning and servicing the household. Their life energy is spent serving others and following others' orders and visions.

To a great extent, Hispanic women's struggles of self-affirmation have created among all of us a clearer consciousness of the importance of self-love or legitimate caring for oneself and for a more egalitarian share of the responsibility of caring for others.

Hispanic Protestant care ethics is a group-based ethic that claims that one's cultural group is entitled to preferential moral loyalty, and that the needs of the group ought to be one of our primary moral obligations. Not to be morally partial to the group or groups that shape the unique beings we are is understood as an act of betrayal, and we risk becoming alienated and severing relationships with those who traditionally have provided us with support. Lack of preferential loyalty is a way of weakening one's personal identity and one's social and political standing. If one's group also happens to be dominated and oppressed, the ethics of care stresses the importance of the practice of self-love. Self-love among the socially despised becomes a necessary condition for their empowerment and ability to move toward more inclusive social arrangements.

As the ethics of principle adjudicates conflicts between rights, and the ethics of character faces conflicts between the virtues, the ethics of care must balance responsibilities owed the various moral communities that significantly shape our identity. At one and the same time the ethics of care must be biased and impartial. Care ethics must bring together a passionate moral concern for the members of one's own group and a healthy dose of dispassionate consideration for other people and groups. Care ethics shows preference and intimacy for one's own group, while it also recognizes that at times persons and groups who are different from us deserve to be judged more favorably.

The Protestants who assume the ethics of care agree with those who abide by the ethics of character that faith communities are indispensable to the moral formation of their members, and that Christians ought to be faithful to their liberating narratives. However, they also value the creation of ethnic churches as a positive way to affirm the value of their unique identity. And they see the ethnic church as another way to resist cultural assimilation and value commonness and to promote the rich plurality of God's creation. More and more they understand the church in more ecumenical, public, and worldly terms than what is advocated by those who favor the ethics of character.

Hispanic Protestants who embrace the ethics of care believe that as we are called to model the care and love of God within the faith community, we are also called to engage in world-transforming activities to make our world more caring and loving. It fits the Christian witness, for example, to be a partner, with all people of goodwill, in the creation of places of refuge that signal God's will to provide for the poor and oppressed of this world. What is at stake in this world-transforming activity is not the consolidation and strengthening of our identity as Christians but effective service to the poor, or as Scripture says, "as you did it to one of the least of these . . . " Like all effective politics, the creation of islands of refuge for the victims of this world needs and depends on the building of broad and well-structured coalitions among all people of goodwill. A new, ecumenical vision emerges in which the Christian family is one component of God's people. The true church is constituted by all people of goodwill, no matter what the basis of their belief system. What matters is that they reveal a commitment to protecting the vulnerable from the power of death. This ecumenism is political not in the sense of seeking political power, but in the more fundamental sense of making power accessible to the powerless and keeping power accountable to the weakest members of society. This church understands that God is not absent from any place and that we are all God's people. As a church, thus, we have as much to learn from the world as we have to teach to the world.

Among the dangers found within the ethics of care advocated by Protestant Hispanics are the tensions between the loyalties owed to society as a whole (the loyalty to promoting national unity and a harmonious political community) and the loyalty owed to our social group. It recognizes that the politics of difference can encourage and promote a separatist mentality that is pernicious to social and political stability. It wrestles with the question of whether or not Hispanic Protestants can create a society whose members develop the capacity to live in the tension between the communal need for some level of unity and the need for greater group autonomy and differentiation. A related concern is the capacity of this ethic to allow its members to choose outside of the mainstream of the group. Can members question the traditional ways and give expression to their own way of being? Can the social group abide by and respect the right of its individual members to choose another way? Is there enough tolerance within the group for subgroups and critical voices? This is particularly relevant when we consider gender, class, and lifestyle struggles within a social group.

The same tension exists within the church—a tension between the connectedness of the one church catholic and the Hispanic-based ethnic church. Hispanic Protestants, in general, look at church life as being an extension of family life. We seek intimacy with and are inclined to give moral preference and the benefit of the doubt to those who worship and share their religiosity with us. The ethics of care can stress community life and loyalty to—and the intentional preservation of—tradition to the point that it can become chauvinistic and tend toward tribal and oppressive behavior both within the group and toward other social groups. It is important, therefore, to raise the question of the inner tolerance of the community in question. The danger is that we stop extending hospitality, recognition, and respect to strangers and to the future generations that our youth are forging. New voices are emerging within our churches to challenge these oppressive inclinations and practices, but more needs to be done to create within the church an environment which is more welcoming and empowering for all members of the community.

In short, Hispanic Protestants reveal different ways of thinking and acting morally, with the ethics of care being predominant. What we need now is to continue to focus on considerations of justice—such as equal recognition, respect, and the right to speak with an independent voice—to give the ethics of care a more liberating context both within our churches and the body politic. In keeping a focus on justice, we will push the ethics of care beyond the concerns of family life to a more inclusive and diverse public sphere.

Chapter 8

Reading the Hyphens: An Emerging Biblical Hermeneutics for Latino/ Hispanic U.S. Protestants

Francisco García-Treto

Lumped together by Anglo American society as "Hispanics," often as part of a marginalizing or patronizing project, Hispano/Latinos in the U.S. have begun a process of melding into a new identity which transcends without abandoning the former separate national identities and self-images, in order to stress a new Hispano/Latino cultural solidarity, and to empower the community politically and economically within U.S. society as a whole.[1]

The Bible, always of central importance for Hispanic/Latino Protestantism, is beginning to be read in the churches, and by some of the academic writers that serve them, in ways that seek to respond to that condition. This chapter identifies and analyzes current efforts to move forward in community-building, empowering directions toward a hermeneutics which truly speaks to, and from, the life situation of Hispanic/Latino Protestants in the U.S.

A Cluster of Questions

What then are the directions of biblical hermeneutics for U.S. Hispanic/Latino "mainline" Protestants? What important contributions have already emerged? How do these directions respond to the life situation of the U.S. Hispanic/Latino church? How are they likely to affect theological education and the teaching and preaching ministry of the churches? What contextual factors and challenges have begun to shape this hermeneutic and are likely to continue to influence it?

The Interpretative Community for a Hispanic/Latino Hermeneutics

The first step that must be taken in attempting to answer those interrelated questions is to provide at least a basic definition of what "U.S.

Hispanic/Latino 'mainline' Protestant" means today when used as a label for a particular kind of hermeneutics. The concept of "interpretative community," which literary critic Stanley Fish defines as a community "made up of those who share interpretive strategies not for reading (in the conventional sense) but for writing texts, for constituting their properties and assigning their intentions,"[2] and the currently emerging emphasis on contextual or "social location" readings of the Bible,[3] converge at this point in my project. As a very important base for the *teología de conjunto* being developed in U.S. Hispanic churches, new hermeneutical strategies and standpoints are being put in place. My proposal, then, is to investigate the hermeneutics emerging in the "interpretative community" constituted by U.S. Hispanic/Latino mainline Protestant scholars and churchpersons whose work affects the academic community of scholars as well as the church. The three elements of the definition must be examined in turn in order to make clear their meaning and interconnection.

U.S. Hispanic/Latino. This admittedly awkward designation, rather than being an attempt to name a group by race, by national origin, or even by language, means instead to point to a social location in the U.S., and to a growing recognition among U.S. Hispanics of that social location that it is their own. Beyond the "hyphenated American" identities, and transcending them, a new consciousness is emerging in this group, which, if it is still in the throes of self-definition, is nevertheless already a reality. We are not sure yet whether to call ourselves "Hispanic" or "Hispanos" or "Latinos"—for the present, I have chosen to use "Hispanic/Latino," as the title of an important new journal[4] also has it. A broad diversity of group identities and cultures is included in that category, from New Mexican Hispanos to Mexican Americans (or Chicanos) in California and Texas, to Cuban Americans (or Cubans) in Florida, to Puerto Ricans (or Nuyoricans) in New York, not to mention Dominicans, Salvadorans, Guatemalans, or many others. Diverse historical experience, economic factors, and political allegiances, as well as the appearance of generational differences and different degrees of assimilation to Anglo culture and facility with English complicate that diversity even more. More than one denominational jurisdiction has come to grief over the past decades by ignoring these differences and assuming, for example, that a pastor recently arrived from Cuba would be successful in a Mexican American congregation, simply because they all spoke Spanish.

Nevertheless, the fact is that a new, U.S. Hispanic/Latino consciousness (and culture) is emerging, shaped both by pressure from outside and by internal recognition of the deep Iberian/Native American/African heritage that all Hispanic/Latinos share. Justo González has identified as a central element of what may be called the historical aspect of that consciousness the mindfulness of being "a people in exile"[5]—either literally, as many of us are for political, economic, or ideological reasons, or, though U.S.-born like parents and grandparents, as "exiles in the deeper sense of living in a land not their own. Although they are U.S. citizens by birth, they are not full citizens, and therefore they are exiles living in a land that remains foreign."[6]

Virgilio Elizondo's widely used term "mestizaje"—or its correlate "mulatez"—epitomizes the central cultural aspect of that emerging consciousness, that is to say, a recognition that, as Fernando Segovia has recently put it,

> we are a hybrid people, with biological and/or cultural miscegenation at our very core. This indiscriminate mixture, this *mezcolanza*, brings together in many and varied ways the heritage of Europe via Mediterranean and Catholic Spain, of Africa and America, as well as of Asia (though to a much lesser extent). Though it is in large part because of such mixture that we find rejection in our present world, we must emphasize and embrace mixture: for us mixture is life and gives life.[7]

Such mestizaje and mulatez permeates our art, our music, our food, our religion, our very way of constructing and functioning in the world, and of course, our way of reading texts. Thus, "biological and/or cultural miscegenation" lies at our very roots and stamps our very praxis, sharply distinguishing us in a society that still thinks of itself by and large, even today, in terms of black and white. Segovia's words make it clear that he is talking about a total culture, one which finds its venues of expression in the Spanish TV networks with their telenovelas and their commercials aimed at the "Hispanic market," in the music of Selena and of Gloria Estefan, in the ubiquitous *bodegas, mercados,* or *marquetas* where almost any item in the enormous variety of Spanish, African, or Amerindian foods dear to various Latin American or Caribbean peoples can be found in profusion—fresh, canned, or frozen, and more often than not, bearing the Goya brandname. There is a sense that what I would call a second mestizaje, perhaps a *metamulatez*, is developing, to produce the emergent U.S. Hispanic/Latino community, both in society at large and in the church.

Mainline Protestant. Perhaps it will come as a surprise to the reader to be told that this category is the least distinctive and most problematic part of the definition of our "interpretative community," particularly since this article is part of a study of U.S. Hispanic mainline Protestant churches. Yet, to proceed simply by listing the denominational credentials of a relatively minuscule number of U.S. biblical interpreters seems to me to be a major error in trying to ascertain the impact and importance of the interpretative community in question. Stanley Fish concludes that there is only one possible way to determine who belongs to a given interpretative community:

> How can any one of us know whether or not he is a member of the same interpretive community as any other of us? The answer is that he can't. . . . The only "proof" of membership is fellowship, the nod of recognition from someone in the same community, someone who says to you what neither of us could ever prove to a third party: "we know."[8]

Fellowship, in academic terms, is demonstrated by mutual reading and influence; the "nod of recognition" takes the form of citation and review of the other's work. By this criterion, then, the interpretative community in question, already engaged in doing *teología de conjunto* among U.S. Hispanics is radically ecumenical,[9] inclusive of Roman Catholics, mainline Protestants, and Pentecostals in an unprecedented fellowship of scholars who read, are influenced by, and cite one another in their hermeneutical work and who are developing interpretative strategies notably free of denominational baggage, and, most remarkably in service to the church across denominational lines. Although the ecclesiastical history of U.S. Hispano/Latinos is inextricably rooted in the conflicts of a Roman Catholic Church shaped by the particularly intolerant Spanish version of the Counter-Reformation, with "mainline Protestant" churches founded by U.S. missionaries who went to Latin America, or came to the territories annexed from Mexico in 1848 and from Spain in 1898, with openly anti-Roman Catholic agendas, and though old prejudices certainly remain in some places, the world has changed radically, and the churches have also changed. I can remember two reactions to the changes brought about by Vatican II among Mexican American Presbyterians, among whom I was doing research during the late sixties, and Mexican American Methodist pastors whom I taught later: first, a sort of amusement at no longer being officially called "heretics," but rather "separated brethren," and second, a real sense of expectation—as I often heard them say, "Están leyendo la Biblia!" ("They are now reading the Bible!").

Ingrained in every Hispanic Protestant's consciousness is the conviction that when a person or a people begins to read the Bible, change for the better follows. And, in what would have surprised and even dismayed some of the more conservative of these U.S. Hispanic churchpeople, that expectation was even then becoming a reality in the emergence from obscurity to prominence of liberation theology and of the Bible-reading practices of the base communities as a gift of the people of God in Latin America, a gift which Christians of all denominations could value and appropriate.

Today, within the U.S. Hispano/Latino churches, and specifically at the academic-theological professional level, a new ecumenical openness to cooperation, dialogue, and mutual acceptance has developed between mainline and other Protestant and Roman Catholic biblical scholars, to the extent that a true interpretative community in Fish's sense may already be identified. Virgilio Elizondo, Catholic priest and Dean of San Antonio's San Fernando Cathedral, writes the foreword to Methodist Justo L. González' *Mañana: Christian Theology from a Hispanic Perspective*.[10] Arturo Bañuelas, a Catholic, edits a volume entitled *Mestizo Christianity: Theology from the Latino Perspective*, which includes works by Justo González, Harold Recinos (also a Methodist), Samuel Soliván-Román, and Eldin Villafañe (both Pentecostals) among its fourteen articles.[11] Bañuelas makes it a point to indicate in his introduction that the bibliography of the volume represents the work of 9 Protestant and 38 Roman Catholic authors. On the other hand, it is not unusual to see Roman Catholic scholars' work appear in *Apuntes*,[12] and it is Fernando Segovia, a Roman Catholic, who writes the article "Reading the Bible as Hispanic Americans" for the introductory volume of the (United Methodist) Abingdon Press's *New Interpreter's Bible*.[13] Examples could be multiplied almost without end to illustrate the point. Just as a transnational Hispanic/Latino consciousness of being a people is emerging and setting a sociocultural agenda in the United States, so a transdenominational consciousness of being an interpretative community reading the Bible from the social location of our people has arisen and is beginning to bear noticeable fruit.

Scholars and Churchpersons Whose Work Affects the Academic Community of Scholars as Well as the Church. Although it would be very interesting indeed to try to ascertain, through social-scientific techniques such as polling, for example, what hermeneutical directions are implicit in the Bible reading of the "average" member of a mainline U.S. Hispanic church, that is beyond the scope and resources of this study. Instead, I propose to focus on the "interpretative community" constituted by scholars and churchpersons whose work affects the academic community of scholars as well as the church. This is, I think, an important distinctive characteristic of this community: we—I include myself—tend to maintain our ties to both the academy and the church, and to produce texts in the genres required in both of these venues, to a greater extent than many non-Hispanic academicians do. Justo González has put it very well, when he points out the parallel between medieval scholastic theologians, whose "hermeneutic (interpretative) community" was constituted by other scholastic theologians, and modern historical-critical biblical scholars, whose interpretative community is the guild of scholars, and no longer the church.[14] González concludes that

> although one often hears it said that our people have rejected the historical-critical method because it takes away the authority of the Bible, it is proper to ask if there is not another, deeper reason for that rejection, which is perhaps that the method itself, and the manner in which it has been used, takes away the authority of the people, of the hermeneutic community which is the entire church.[15]

A number of factors are coming together in our time to change that situation, not in the least the well-known "paradigm change," which has already substantially altered the tenor of the activities of the guild of academic biblical scholars. Although it would not be fair to say that the historical-critical method has been totally supplanted, or that its conclusions have been overturned, it is accurate to say that it is no longer the only method, or its results the only valid ones, recognized today by the guild of biblical scholars. Literary criticism, the study of the text as a poetic construction, rather than only as a historical artifact, critical attention to the role of the reader in the construction of the meaning of the text, and a recognition of the inevitable plurality of readings given the variety of readers' social locations are emphases in the new (some would say "postmodern") situation in the academic study of the Bible. Just as an example, I cite the two groups within the national structure of the Society of Biblical Literature with which I am centrally involved: the "Reading, Theory and the Bible" group, and the "Use of the Bible in Asia, Africa, and Latin America" group, neither one of which would have been conceivable twenty years ago. As the academy itself begins to recognize that its own historical-critical methods and results are neither the only nor the last words in biblical interpretation, new possibilities arise for a confluence of interests between "postmodern" scholars and a Hispanic church whose readings of the Bible have always been "naively joyous [and] precritical,"[16] as Justo González has recently said. And publications where the academy and the church interact, for example, the introductory volume of the *New Interpreter's Bible,* begin to recognize the importance of social location readings with articles on reading the Bible as African Americans, Asian Americans, Hispanic Americans, Native Americans, and Women.[17] An interpretative space is thus beginning to emerge, where a Hispanic/Latino interpretative community is able to make its distinctive voice heard in both academy and church. A spectrum of genres of literature ranging from the academic scholarly article to the biblical commentary, "popular" books, adult lessons, and Sunday school curriculum forms the written product of this community, at the same time that it gives evidence of its readings of the Bible, that is to say, of its hermeneutic strategies and directions.

The Emerging Hermeneutics of the Hispano/Latino Church

In what directions are the distinctive strategies and approaches of a biblical hermeneutics sensitive to the situation of the U.S. Hispano/Latino churches moving? How is and has the Bible been read in ways that correlate to the divisive interconfessional strife and to the hegemonic agendas rooted in our religious history? What efforts have been made to transcend that past and to move forward in community-building, empowering directions which truly address the needs of Hispanic/Latino Protestants? Two important studies have recently appeared, in which the new hermeneutical directions beginning to emerge in the U.S. Hispanic community are the focus of attention. Fernando Segovia, a Cuban Catholic biblical scholar who is Professor of New Testament Studies and Early Christian Literature at Vanderbilt Divinity School, has surveyed the work of seven scholars, four Roman Catholics and three Protestants, in the two articles which constitute the first of these two studies. The first article, published in 1992,[18] details the hermeneutical work of theologians Ada Maria Isasi-Diaz (Cuban American) and Virgilio Elizondo (Mexican American), both of them Roman Catholics, along with that of Harold J. Recinos (of Puerto Rican descent born in New York City) and Justo L. González (Cuban American), both United Methodists. Segovia more recently (1995) published the second article,[19] a major study which examines the developing work of two Catholic priests, C. Gilbert Romero and Jean-Pierre Ruiz, and one Cuban American Presbyterian, Francisco García-Treto. Segovia distinguishes between the first group of four, whom he identifies as theologians, and the second group of "three individuals whose area of specialization is biblical criticism."[20] As he goes on to observe, in the first group

> all four individuals adopted variations of a basic model of liberation hermeneutics involving a formal analogy between past and present, between the relationship of the Bible to its social context and the relationship of Hispanic Americans to their social context, with a basic correspondence posited between Hispanic Americans today and the people of God in the Bible.[21]

166

Harold Recinos, for example, is seen to take a classic liberationist position when he posits "the fundamental correspondence" between the people of the barrio and the people of God in the Bible, "the God of the Bible and the God of the barrio."[22] Recinos, says Segovia, extends the concept of the barrio to stand for the "vast majority of Hispanic Americans in the United States . . . faced with racial discrimination, cultural aggression, political marginalization, and economic oppression"[23] and as a result of the concomitant high levels of unemployment, crime, and violence, "ultimately yielding to a profound attitude of self-blame and fatalism."[24] For the construction of a barrio theology then, Recinos proposes the model of biblical reading that arose in the Christian base communities of Latin America, "an explicit reading from the perspective of the oppressed" centered on the concepts of God's preferential option for the poor, which can be read in the exodus story, in the voice of the prophets, and in Jesus' proclamation of the kingdom as the paradigmatic narrative of divine action on behalf of the oppressed. The central hermeneutical strategy would, in this case, be to reappropriate "the basic story of the Bible: a God of the cross who identifies with the oppressed and the poor and who participates actively in their liberation."[25] For example, take Recinos' powerful reading of the conclusion of Luke's rich young ruler story:

> The Rich Young Ruler learns through Jesus that radical humanization means obedience unto death—in his case the death of private wealth. He is to take up the shared life (eternal life) in the community of the poor and outcasts which has gathered around Jesus as a sign of the messianic Kingdom of God. The wealth of the Rich Young Ruler was to be placed at the disposition of the poor who had been its victims. Eternal life is an inheritance when one lives in solidarity with the poor and human suffering and one struggles to create God's shalom within human society.[26]

Without question, the essential, central figure for this study is Justo L. González—not only for his constructive work, in particular his proposal for "Reading the Bible in Spanish," but also for his labor as a historian of Hispanic theological thought. In the latter, he epitomizes the developing contributions of others as well as his own, as he does for biblical hermeneutics in his most recent work, *Santa Biblia: The Bible Through Hispanic Eyes*,[27] which is discussed next.

The 1990 appearance of *Mañana: Christian Theology from a Hispanic Perspective* has to be seen as a watershed in the development of U.S. Hispanic theology. Before *Mañana*, it was still possible to think that U.S. Hispanic theology was a subset of Latin American liberation theology, and that in any case "U.S. Hispanic" was more or less an abstraction, such categories as "Mexican American" or "Cuban" (not even "Cuban American") being more to the point, given the diversity of Hispanics in the U.S. Even Virgilio Elizondo's towering contribution of the concept of *mestizaje* as a key to theology more often than not seemed to present it basically as a key to Mexican American theology.[28] While liberation and *mestizaje* are both important, one would even have to say basic, to *Mañana*, they are also transformed into concepts fully rooted in the *U.S. Hispanic* experience. It is interesting to compare, from this point of view, Elizondo's *Galilean Journey*, say, with the important recent work of Roberto S. Goizueta, *Caminemos con Jesús: Toward a Hispanic/Latino Theology of Accompaniment*,[29] a work that deals with many of the same themes found in *Galilean Journey*, but in a tenor that perhaps can best be described as the accent of *"pasado Mañana."*

One of *Mañana*'s virtues is its thoroughness in mapping the ground that U.S. Hispanic theologians will have to cover in their future work, and an essential part of that map is chapter 5, "Reading the Bible in Spanish,"[30] which for me, as a Hispanic biblical scholar, quickly became the most powerful chapter in this seminal book. The chapter begins with an exposition of the dangerous concept of "innocent history," the selectively forgetful readings of the Bible or of the realities of American history in which "the great heroes are depicted as people of pure and unmixed motives, clear conscience, and undeviating righteousness" and "biblical faith and flag waving go hand in hand." Such an "innocent" reading, whether of history or of the Bible, "serves to justify the present order as the result of the great deeds of those past heroes."[31] Hispanic readers have the hermeneutical advantage of knowing that theirs is not an innocent history: "We know that we are born out of an act of violence of cosmic proportions in which our Spanish forefathers raped our Indian foremothers. We have no skeletons in our closet. Our skeletons are at the very heart of our history and our reality as a people."[32] What this means in terms of a hermeneutical stance for Hispanics is spelled out in a "grammar" for "Reading the Bible in Spanish," which by way of summary may be excerpted as follows:

> 1. The Bible is a political book [which] means . . . that it deals with issues of power and powerlessness. . . . Read it . . . as exiles, as members of a powerless group, as those who are excluded from the "innocent" history of the dominant group, and we shall begin to see that it is indeed a political book.
> 2. Only a small portion of Scripture was [meant] to be read in private . . . even when we read Scripture in private, God is addressing all of us as a community of faith.

3. The core principle of scriptural "grammar" is its availability to children, to the simple, to the poor. . . . To read the Bible "in Spanish" means to give attention to what the "babes" find in it.

4. Above all . . . read Scripture in the vocative. . . . with the clear awareness that we are not before a dead text, for the text that we address addresses us in return. . . . [In] the Hispanic church . . . the Bible is most frequently read in a different manner . . . one that disconcerts both fundamentalists and liberals. The reason is that the Bible is read in the vocative, . . . giving us not so much information about correct doctrine or about times past as direction as to who we are in our present time.[33]

A noninnocent and political reading of the Bible, a reading done primarily in the community and by the community, a reading available to all, inclusive and welcoming the insights of the poor and simple, an interactive reading in which the text and the reader are subject and object in turn, "reading in Spanish" calls Hispanics, as Segovia puts it, "to liberation, to peace and justice, social change, and transformation in the world. Hispanic Americans are also called to work toward a new *mañana* in the context of the new reformation unleashed in the church, a reformation ultimately described by González as far more substantial and profound than that of the sixteenth century."[34]

In *Santa Biblia: The Bible Through Hispanic Eyes,* González employs the advantage of a six-year distance from the publication of *Mañana* to survey and summarize the field of issues he mapped out in "Reading the Bible in Spanish." In order to provide an overview of what it means to read the Bible "through Hispanic eyes," he suggests an outline composed of "five paradigms or perspectives that Latinos employ when reading both the Bible and their own situation."[35] Noting that these paradigms are somewhat arbitrary as a set of taxonomic categories, and that they often overlap in practice, he then goes on to devote a chapter of his book to each: Marginality, Poverty, Mestizaje and Mulatez, Exiles and Aliens, and Solidarity. Here I briefly characterize them:

Marginality. "To be marginal means to be excluded from the center. That is an experience with which most Latinos identify."[36] It is clear from the examples that González considers himself among those for whom marginality is an important hermeneutical perspective. Chief among these are his sensitive readings of biblical passages, particularly from the book of Acts, which he offers in this chapter.[37] The chapter does include one reading by another Hispanic interpreter, Loida Martell-Otero's account of Paul's encounter with Lydia of Thyatira, a woman who becomes a leader in a situation where Paul would have expected a man. Paul learns, as

Martell-Otero puts it, that "the church is being made to convert, even as it seeks converts."[38] One of González' concerns in his readings of *Acts* is to trace the dynamic effects that take place when the periphery manages to affect the center: disturbing and at times disruptive, but also essential for growth in new directions. So essential, in fact, is "bringing the marginalized to the very center of God's love and God's community" that the question may be asked: "In a world in which so many are marginalized, is it legitimate for a church to call itself both 'mainline' and 'Christian'?"[39]

Poverty. Rather than treat poverty as a special kind of marginality, which it is, González holds it up as a central and distinctive fact, determinative of the existence of the larger portion of U.S. Hispanics. He concludes that "although the vast majority of us who write on Hispanic hermeneutics are not ourselves poor, we can only write about such a hermeneutics to the degree that we stand in solidarity with the vast majority of our people, who are indeed poor."[40] He insists that the hermeneutical key in this instance is not to ask "what does the Bible say about the poor?" but rather "what does the Bible say when read from the perspective of the poor?"[41] Sometimes, as González shows with the examples of David García's reading of Genesis 22 "from the perspective of the ram . . . for there are many people, even today, who are 'convenient rams' for the sacrifice of the powerful,"[42] that perspective can yield startling interpretations. Sometimes, as in Yolanda Pupo-Ortiz' reading of the "Naboth's vineyard" case in 1 Kings 21, that perspective produces deep insight: "To take away the vineyard was to take away Naboth's humanity: his connection to his parents, tradition, and beliefs" says Pupo-Ortiz,[43] and González sharpens the point: "Poverty . . . is dehumanization. It dispossesses, not only of money, but also of dignity, of tradition, of identity."[44] In his own readings of Jesus' parables of the laborers in the vineyard and of the unforgiving servant as presented in Matthew, as well as in his insights into the economic life of the early church as seen not only in Acts but through such texts as the *Didache* or the *Epistle of Barnabas,* González makes a persuasive case for the validity of the perspective of the poor as an interpretative strategy for today's readers of the Bible.

Mestizaje and Mulatez. I have already referred to the centrality that the concept of *mestizaje* has gained in U.S. Hispanic theological labors ever since Virgilio Elizondo's doctoral dissertation was published in English translation in 1978, followed in 1983 and 1988 by two other books on the theme. González acknowledges the publication of Elizondo's *Galilean Journey* as marking "the beginning of Hispanic theology in the United States."[45] The concept has been extended from its original application to

Mexican Americans as other U.S. Hispanics have applied its explanatory power to their own experience, and used it as a hermeneutical key in their readings of the Bible, as for example in Pablo Jiménez' reading of Philippians 2:7.[46] Elizondo himself, however, spoke of a "double *mestizaje*," what González identifies as "a further *mestizaje* or *mulatez*: our own relationship with the dominant culture." As all people who live "on the hyphen" know, "there is always a sense of belonging and yet not belonging, of being both fish and fowl, and therefore fowl to the fish, and fish to the fowl; but also able to understand the fish as no fowl can, and the fowl as no fish can."[47] A case in point is González' explanation of Saul or Paul as a cultural *mestizo*, his reading of the book of Acts as "the progressive *mestizaje* of the church," and his interpretation of "the process and the goal of Christian mission . . . as the progressive *mestizaje* of the church and the faith."[48]

On the other hand, the frontier or better, the borderland where culture engages culture can easily become a site of oppression, and the Bible is by no means exempt from that fact. González devotes part of the chapter to my reading of Joshua 9, where the Gibeonites, Canaanites whom Israel is supposed to destroy utterly, lie and trick their way into a covenant which ensures their survival. That constitutes an unexpected expansion of the covenant, an unwitting and unwilled extension toward inclusivity, brought about by the wise wiles which *mestizos* of all cultures know are essential strategies for their survival. Following his presentation of Loida Martell-Otero's reading of Esther as a successful cultural *mestiza*, González concludes that "as followers of the *mestizo* Jesus, we shall learn to read the Bible, and life itself, as *mestizos* who have much to offer to the false purities claimed by today's deuteronomists!"[49]

Exiles and Aliens. The experience of being an exile and an alien is of cardinal importance for U.S. Hispanics, among whom, as González puts it, "the category of exile and alienness applies, not only to those who were born in other lands and have migrated to the United States, but also to many in the second, third, and fourth generations."[50] Since the Bible is demonstrably a book written in large part by and for exiles, the Hispanic consciousness of exile provides another important hermeneutic key. González notes as an example the appearance, in the first issue of *Apuntes*, of an article where I pointed out the emphasis that much of the Hebrew Bible (my point of departure was Psalm 146:9) places on Yahweh's protection of the *ger*.[51] I go on to argue, however, that the paradoxical concept of Israel as an "emigrant people," as themselves *gerim* even when they were in possession of the Promised Land, was an important key to their survival of the Babylonian Exile and other national catastrophes. Jorge Lara-

Braud, in the next issue of *Apuntes*, sketched "similar conclusions with regard to the role of Hispanics in the U.S.," based on autobiographical, rather than on exegetical grounds.[52] González briefly sketches the way in which the ambiguity of the exile's experience may be used as an exegetical key to reading such figures as Joseph,[53] Ruth and Naomi, or Jeremiah.

Solidarity. If the first four of the paradigms, insofar as they spring from the sociocultural situation of U.S. Hispanics, provide standpoints not only for biblical interpretation but "for how we understand and experience sin and its consequences,"[54] the fifth, on the other hand, responds more to the way in which, as Hispanics, we experience the good news of redemption: and that is above all in terms of the "family" and "community" expressions of solidarity. González uses as examples readings by Pablo Jiménez (Abraham's call), Frances Mitchell ("honor your father and mother"), and David Maldonado (Jesus' encounter with the Samaritan woman at the well) to show the depth and power of this paradigm. The church, which as this brief survey of his work should already have made clear, is for González the central paradigmatic image, is, as "the family of God," central in the experience of redemption of people "who are either second-class citizens or noncitizens, and who lack and miss the extended family ties that have traditionally given us a sense of belonging."[55] By the same token, "the gospel, the good news, is not only that our sins are forgiven and we have been reconciled with God; it is also that we are now *citizens* and *family* with the saints and with God!"[56]

Finally, if it is true (as González insists), that the basic attitude of the Hispanic church concerning the Bible is best expressed as "the Bible has been good to us!" it is also true that some of us are increasingly aware that the Bible has been used in ways that are the opposite of "good to us." It is apparent that not only has the Bible been read in oppressive and xenophobic ways, but that there are passages in the Bible that lend themselves fully to such readings, and which therefore must be read "dialogically," as I, for one, have recently proposed.[57]

Nevertheless, there remains only to say that the emergent hermeneutics of U.S. Hispanics is remarkably unified, truly ecumenical, carried out in a wide variety of venues in the academy and the church, and already beginning to achieve self-definition and to produce solid and helpful results. Above all, there is a sense of expectation within the "interpretative community" of U.S. Hispanics who, sharing these common paradigms and strategies we have discussed, are turning in their work to the Bible with the certainty of finding there that which González' words eloquently express:

And that is precisely what we are: a new hermeneutical community. We are people who read the Bible as we were taught, and who therefore find in it what we were taught. But if the day comes when we truly dare to face the Bible, not as we were taught but with full openness to the text, affirming and recognizing our own perspective and our particular experiences, and trusting that the Holy Spirit will lead us to truth, what we shall find in the sacred text may well amaze us, and perhaps will also amaze the world hermeneutical community, which will have to acknowledge in the text those elements which we, from our own point of view, will have discovered.[58]

Part III

Sociological and Contextual Dynamics

Chapter 9

Race, Religion, and la Raza: An Exploration of the Racialization of Latinos in the United States and the Role of the Protestant Church

Teresa Chávez Sauceda

Race and religion have both played a significant role in the development of U.S. society, interacting in the historical processes which have shaped the national identity and coalesced the centers of economic and political power around what is "white" and "Protestant." Latinos, *la raza cosmica*, a *mestizo-mulatto* and largely Catholic people of multiple ethnic and racial identities share a particular, alienating, and marginalizing experience of race in the United States. As a social and cultural institution, the mainline Protestant church has played an integral role in the historical construction of race in this society. In the midst of these dynamic forces, Latino Protestants have struggled to maintain their own sense of identity: to be Latino in predominantly white Protestant denominations, and Protestant in a Catholic culture.

It has long been assumed that the movement of Latinos into Protestant denominations was motivated at least in part by a desire to get on the fast track to acculturation and assimilation in the dominant Anglo culture and society. The reality of Latino Protestants today raises questions about this assumption. As David Maldonado observes, "Mexican American families will drive past two or three Anglo Protestant churches in order to reach the Hispanic Protestant Church across town," a fact that points "not only [to] their desire to worship in Spanish, but to the persistent racial reality" in the church and in our society today.[1]

The goal of this article is to contextualize the historical encounter between Latinos and the Protestant church in the U.S. sociopolitical history of race. I begin with a brief look at the historical process of racialization for three groups: Mexican, Puerto Rican, and Cuban.[2] Each of these groups has entered the trajectory of U.S. racial politics at a different point, through different means. Second, I will explore the role of the Protestant church: how has racism and the racial structure of our society affected Protestant ministry and relationships in the Latino community? What impact has the church had on the social construction of race? How have Latinos affected the church?

Racial Formation

Manuel Dominguez, who served as an elected delegate to the California State Constitutional Convention of 1849 and as a member of the Los Angeles County Board of Supervisors, traveled to northern California in April 1857 to enter testimony in a San Francisco courtroom. Before Dominguez could testify, however, the Anglo lawyer for the plaintiff objected to his taking the witness stand. The lawyer argued that Dominguez was an Indian and therefore ineligible to enter testimony. The judge upheld the objection and dismissed Dominguez.[3]

The story of Manuel Dominguez illustrates the fluid, transitory, politically laden nature of racial categories and racial meanings in U.S. society. Though rooted in color difference, race is best understood as a social construction: "created, inhabited, transformed, and destroyed" through dynamic social processes. Race is neither an immutable fact defined by objective scientific data, nor an illusion that we can progress beyond in some kind of utopian color-blind society.[4]

Historically, race in the United States has been perceived as a black-white issue. The experience of Latinos has been interpreted as simply an extension of, or secondary to, the black-white racial encounter. This perspective often renders Latinos without a voice in the public discourse. Although rooted in perceived differences in human physical characteristics, efforts to define or differentiate specific racial groups reveal in themselves the ultimate arbitrariness of racial distinctions. This is especially true for Latinos, who as a people, encompass the full range of the human color spectrum. Racism exploits difference to "create or reproduce structures of domination." Ultimately, racism is about the manipulation of power in society—the distribution of rights and privileges, wealth and material resources. Indeed, racism is about nothing less than "who shall live and who shall die."[5]

Racism permeates all aspects of our public lives, including our public religious life. Despite the racial and ethnic diversity among Latino people, the experience of racism is increasingly recognized as a common, even unifying experience. The specific attention to race in this analysis however, is not intended to privilege racism over other facets of oppression. From a Latino perspective, race is a complex reality, interacting with sexism, ethnocentrism, and economic marginalization. The goal in focusing on this one facet is to better understand this complex web.

The consequences of historical patterns of racial discrimination are measured statistically in higher rates of poverty and unemployment, lower levels of education, and a greater degree of alienation from the political process. Despite years of affirmative action programs, Latinos continue to be grossly underrepresented at managerial levels in government and private industry, including the church. Middle-class Latinos, while achieving some degree of economic security, are frustrated by stereotypic attitudes that continue to perceive them as alien, foreign, and suspect. While Latinos have made significant political inroads at the local level in communities like San Antonio or Miami, they continue to feel ignored or excluded by the political agenda at the national level.

Latina women contend not only with racism, but with sexism in both their own Latino community and the dominant society. The intersection of racism and sexism can render Latinas completely invisible, like the underpaid nanny who works unprotected by workers' compensation, Social Security, or health insurance. Or it can make them public scapegoats, like the unwed teenage mother who has come to symbolize all that is wrong with our welfare system, in a public rhetoric that seldom asks who or where the father is.

In the historical experience of Latino men and women, ethnic prejudice has been closely linked with racism. In recent decades, the English-only movement and virulent anti-immigrant rhetoric have exhibited strong racist overtones. The connection between racism and ethnocentrism is rooted in the expectation of the dominant culture that Latinos must sacrifice cultural distinctiveness and ethnic identity to achieve political voice and economic parity. From the perspective of Latino people, this assumption is inherently oppressive. In the racial politics of this society the maintenance of cultural norms, values, and traditions, the persistence of ethnic identity in the face of tremendous social pressure operates as a strategy of resistance.

The Anglo Saxon conquest of the North American continent marks the beginning of a process in which "white" has become equated with what is "American." It marks the beginning of a racial state where exclusion from full participation has been based on socially constructed racial identities. The Pequot, Iroquois, or Tutelo became "native," just as the conquest took those who had once been Asante, Ovimbundu, Yoruba, and Bakongo, and created "black." In this same process English, Irish, French, Dutch, and German became "white." Racial privilege was first encoded in law in 1790, with passage of the Naturalization Law defining U.S. citizenship as available to free white immigrants only. Westward expansion in the early 1800s brought U.S. whites into contact with people they had not previously defined racially, requiring categorization in the racial structure of U.S. society.[6]

Mexico

In the first half of the nineteenth century U.S. territory expanded tenfold. Claiming simply to pursue their Manifest Destiny, "God's injunction to make the land fruitful, prosper economically, and attain their divinely appointed calling,"[7] white settlers justified the displacement and disfranchisement of the territory's prior inhabitants. As competition for land, power, and wealth grew within the territory, racial categorization increasingly determined access to these resources. White settlers moving west encountered another hierarchical society structured by race, class, and gender. Marriage records kept by Roman Catholic priests in New Mexico note the *calidad* (social status) of bride and groom. From 1693 to 1759 there is little mention of race. In the next decade however, race is identified in 78% of the records, with seven different categories identified: *espanol, mestizo, mulatto, coyote, genizaro, negro,* and *indio.* From 1780 to 1800, with the growth of the white population in the region, these distinctions collapsed as the polarization between white and nonwhite increased. By 1800, the intermediate hues of race, so important earlier, were disappearing from marriage records.[8]

Throughout the West and Southwest the second half of the nineteenth century is marked by the struggle for group position. White privilege was encoded in law and institutionalized through social and economic practices. In 1848 the Treaty of Guadalupe Hidalgo defined Mexicans (including both Spaniard and mestizo, but excluding Indians) as a "white" population, accorded the political-legal status of "free white persons." By contrast, Chinese immigrants to California were defined as "Indian" in an 1854 California Supreme Court, denying them the political rights reserved for "whites." As competition for land, wealth, and power increased racial categories shifted. The story of Manuel Dominguez demonstrates the prevailing attitude among whites as they vied for power within the region. Despite the presumed legal protections, color and class combined to deny the *Mexicanos* equal status in the eyes of the growing white population. A new racial hierarchy emerged that was not simply an extension of the black-white race relationships of the Northeast and South. Within a few short years of statehood, even the landed Mexican *ranchero* elite found themselves politically and economically marginalized—accorded the same status as other racialized groups in the state.

To the predominantly Protestant white immigrants to the West, not only was the Roman Catholic Mexican mestizo a racial anomaly, the Spaniard was also racially suspect after eight hundred years of Moorish occupation in Spain, and both were seen as only quasi-Christian at best. "Semicivilized" and "semibarbarian" were terms frequently applied to Mexicans. Working-class Mexicans were often labeled Indian in order to deny legal rights reserved for whites. The upper class gained only grudging acceptance, by virtue of "their ostensibly European ancestry and formidable class position."[9]

As the white population grew, competition for economic and political control displaced even the Mexican elite. In California the Gold Rush of the 1850s precipitated a rapid transition, but the process is representative of what occurred throughout the Southwest. The Mexican ranchero elite participated in the first state legislature, but an overwhelming influx of white voters into the new state rendered Mexican political influence marginal in just a few short years. Moreover, the economic aspirations of white male entrepreneurs entering California after 1848 "required the undermining of the Mexican economy and its reorganization along capitalist lines." These free-labor advocates, "guided by Protestant values and a commitment to white supremacy," sought rapidly to dispossess the rancheros and dismantle the society Mexican settlers had created in California.[10]

In the conquest of Mexico's northern provinces, Mexican American identity coalesced in opposition to the growing white power structure. Mexican American consciousness, an identification with one another across class and gender lines, developed as an oppositional consciousness, resisting white, Eurocentric cultural hegemony, the presumption of cultural and racial superiority. Even in the most repressive periods of U.S. racism, there is evidence of oppositional identity and culture asserting itself. The folk heroes of Mexican *corridos* (folk songs) are some of the more overtly political examples, but in the violently oppressive environment of the 1800s, media that were not explicitly political—Spanish language newspapers, autobiographical narratives, and cookbooks that recorded community traditions and social history—exhibited the expression of an oppositional identity. In this context, worship in Spanish, whether Protestant or Catholic, became an act of cultural resistance, reinforcing an oppositional identity.[11]

Puerto Rico

U.S. occupation of Puerto Rico and Cuba in 1898 following the war with Spain extended the reach of Manifest Destiny and opened the door on a similar confrontation between a white-Protestant culture and a mulatto-Catholic people. Viewed by the United States as an underdeveloped, over-populated convenient source of cheap labor, Puerto Ricans entered the U.S. socioeconomic sphere essentially as a racialized, nonwhite people. The United States sought political and economic control, without bringing the Puerto Rican people into the mainstream of its social and political life.

For Puerto Ricans, occupation also opened the door to migration to the U.S. mainland. The decades leading up to World War II saw a steady increase in migration to the East Coast. U.S. policies of economic development promoted commercial farming for export that resulted in growing numbers of displaced workers. The resulting increase in unemployment in the island corresponded with a growing demand for labor for East Coast factories, particularly in New York. Early migration between Puerto Rico and the mainland was driven by these economic push-pull factors.[12]

As Puerto Rican enclaves established themselves in New York, the new arrivals re-created family networks through kin and *compadrazgo*[13] connections, which provided a basic support system. Women played a critical role in this process, enabling Puerto Rican immigrants to build a community within an alien environment. The colonia enabled immigrants not only to maintain their cultural identity, but also to create support systems which provided the foundation for the growth of the Puerto Rican community as migration swelled during the 1940s and 1950s.

Ironically, prominent social scientists examining the development of the post–World War II migrant community in New York "blatantly denied the existence of an early Puerto Rican community." Reminiscent of the cultural superiority arguments of the previous century, sociologists like Moynihan and Glazer argued that "the process of community building never existed on the island proper" and interpreted the perceived lack of formal political organization as a failure to build support systems or coping institutions. Neither family or *compadrazgo* networks nor hometown associations were recognized as institutions of community.[14]

Puerto Rican migrants to the mainland found themselves in a "situation of perpetual incongruence," struggling not only with the pressures of acculturation, but with the dynamics of race as well. Eldin Villafane notes the generational differences in the conflict experienced by Puerto Ricans, "a culturally homogeneous, racially integrated group," as they confronted racial attitudes and structures that sought to define them as either black or white, but not Puerto Rican.[15] Not until "the late 1960s does one see developing in significant numbers the 'grassroots,' indigenous leader with interests in electoral politics."[16] Nor does Puerto Rican political identity begin to coalesce as a "racial" group until this period, as the second and third generation born and raised on the mainland reaches maturity.[17] Thus, the creation of Puerto Rican identity as a racial group, in opposition to "white," reflects a high degree of investment in U.S. political life.

Cuba

Cuba's proximity to Florida has meant a long relationship with the United States, but most Cubans in the U.S. trace their history here to one of the relatively recent waves of migration coming out of postrevolution Cuba. The first large group of Cuban emigrés who began arriving in 1959–62 settled primarily in the Miami area. Migration peaked toward the end of 1960, with as many as 1,500 emigrés arriving each week.[18] Most assumed their stay would be temporary. Whereas Mexicans and Puerto Ricans were racialized through the processes of conquest, the experience of Cuban immigrants has been different, due largely to politics of the cold war era. The first wave of emigrés was disproportionately white and middle class; nearly one third were professionals or managers. As refugees of a Communist revolution, they symbolically reinforced the notions of U.S. economic and political superiority. Both church and government responded with humanitarian aid. A variety of programs to aid resettlement quickly developed. South Florida in 1960 was a segregated society and racial politics soon surfaced. The black community watched in disbelief as Cuban black and mulatto children were settled in "white schools." One local minister wrote, "The American Negro could solve the school integration problem by teaching his children to speak only Spanish!"[19]

Another leading source of local conflict was the fact that federal aid to refugees exceeded the amounts of state welfare aid available to residents. African Americans in South Florida, disproportionately represented among the poor, were most often in direct competition with refugees for low-paying, menial service jobs. "Blacks watched in anger and amazement as the 'temporary guests' became the beneficiaries of social and educational programs that the Civil Rights movement had long fought for." They called on the president to remember his responsibility to "the economically oppressed of this community, [not just] the politically oppressed of Cuba."[20]

After 1965, the second wave of emigrés was distinct from earlier emigrés in significant ways. By 1970, in contrast to the first wave, only 12% of

Cuban emigrés were professionals or managers, while more than half (57%), were blue-collar, service, or agricultural workers. Moreover, as "men of working age were the most likely to be held back by the Cuban government, women were overrepresented in this migration, as were the elderly."[21] The third wave, the Mariel boatlift, differed widely both in the socioeconomic makeup and in the reception that met them in the United States as well. This group is estimated to have been as much as 40% mulatto or black, compared with 3% of the 1959–70 emigrés. They were 70% male, and at the average age of 30, generally ten years younger than their predecessors at the time they left Cuba. Like the 1970s emigrés they were more likely to have a working-class background, but had slightly higher levels of education.

U.S. attitudes toward the Mariel boatlift were very different. For the first time since the cold war began, the government denied refugee status to individuals emigrating from a communist state. The United States was in the midst of a recession, with high unemployment, high interest rates, and oil embargoes making daily news. Increasingly, all immigrants were perceived as bringing greater competition for a shrinking number of jobs and placing greater demands on overburdened government services. Rather than a welcome symbol of the moral superiority of democracy and capitalism, these newest immigrants were seen as a burden to the U.S. taxpayer.[22]

Although Cubans as a group have tended to do better economically than other U.S. Latinos, Cuban income on average remains below the national average. A significant percentage of U.S. Cubans live in poverty despite the relatively high level of aid available to the emigrés. The working class, especially women, continue to struggle for job security and better wages. Black Cubans experience discrimination from both their nonblack compatriots and U.S. white society. As late as 1990 their income lagged behind that of other Cubans by almost 40%.

A shift in Cuban self-perception from temporary visitor to permanent resident begins to appear in the mid-1970s, evidenced by increasing numbers of exiles seeking naturalization, and a new interest in domestic politics and civic affairs.[23] Although politics in the U.S. Cuban community has been dominated by the generation that left Cuba as exiles, concerned largely with events in Cuba, the growing numbers of U.S.-born Cubans are articulating a wider sphere of political interest. This shift in consciousness is reflected in a growing sense of solidarity with other U.S. Latinos, and the concomitant racial politics. Racial overtones in the U.S. reaction to the Mariel boatlift, growing anti-immigrant sentiment evidenced in the

English-only movement, and legislative efforts to restrict the access of all immigrants to government benefits and services have all contributed to a growing sense of common cause. Thus, the growing political solidarity among Latinos is driven by the conflict between a sense of belonging in U.S. society and the experience of marginalization and racialization in U.S. society.

Latinos and the Protestant Church

The church, as a social institution, plays a key role in the processes of racialization. Historically, the church has both sanctioned racism and condemned it. It has been a place where Latinos find space to resist oppression, and it has been a place where they feel invisible. This initial inquiry into the connections between the church, Latinos, and race focuses on the Protestant church as the principal religious voice in the dominant culture. In the complex relationship between religion and culture, the Protestant ethos gave its sense of divine providence and missionary zeal to the ideology of Manifest Destiny, literally equating Protestant Christianity with democracy, free enterprise, and modern civilization.

The history of Protestant ministry among Latinos, begun in the context of conquest, has evolved within the trajectory of U.S. racial politics. Protestants heralded westward expansion for extending the tandem benefits of Christian salvation and Christian civilization. God had chosen U.S. Protestants to create a "true, Protestant, scriptural paradise on earth." Later, U.S. military intervention in Puerto Rico and Cuba was driven and sanctioned by the same goals of expanding U.S. economic development, culture, and Protestantism. Indeed, "Concern for mission was one of the determinative aspects of the ethos that led to U.S. occupation of those territories." Church and state pursued this massive historical project together. Their mission was "nothing less than the conversion of the world."[24] For many U.S. whites the success of westward expansion was not just a confirmation of cultural or ideologic superiority. Their claims of cultural superiority were generally attributed to an assumed racial superiority, validated by "the survival and prosperity of the tiny colonies, elaborated by the miracle of a successful revolution . . . , and confirmed by a growth that amazed the world. They were God's 'chosen people.'"[25]

Claims of racial superiority were contested within the church by those who held to the orthodox Christian view of the "unity of man" and the human capacity for "indefinite improvement." On the basis of contemporary biblical scholarship and interpretation of the Genesis story, which dated creation to 4004 B.C.E., they argued that racial differences could not be attributed to human origins in creation, nor was it reasonable to believe that the presumed biological differences could have evolved in the relatively short span of six thousand years of human history.[26]

Despite the theological opposition to the concept of racial superiority, the strong affinity perceived between Eurocentric culture and Protestant faith hampered, even neutralized, the church's ability to pose any effective opposition to the prevailing racial ideology. Whatever their individual motivations, Protestant missionaries were important agents of European American culture, indirectly reinforcing the prevailing racial ideology of their era. Some would become "cultural converts,"[27] moving from zealous advocacy of Eurocentric Protestant culture to admiration, if not advocacy, of Protestant faith expressed in Latino culture. Latino Protestantism in the Southwest, begun in the context of conquest and paternalism, begins a long historical struggle toward empowerment and self-determination.

1830–1910: Conquest to Conversion

Under Mexican rule, Roman Catholicism was the official religion. All other religious practices were banned as heretical. Despite these prohibitions, white Protestant settlers in the Southwest, equally convinced that Catholics were little more than pagans, began openly to assert their own religious practices as their numbers grew in the 1820s and 1830s. By 1833 public revivals were being held and several Protestant congregations were well established in Texas, complete with their own church buildings.

Anti-Catholicism and racism combined in the antipathy felt by white settlers toward Mexicans of Spanish, mestizo, and Indian ancestry alike. The tie between strong anti-Catholic sentiments and racial prejudice stemmed from the sixteenth-century conflict between England and Spain that continued to generate a flow of anti-Catholic and anti-Spanish literature to the United States. "Men of letters, ministers, and propagandists" continued to espouse the notion that the Spanish were a racially "impure" people, "not much better than light-skinned Moors and Africans," engaged in a "demonic" alliance with the pope. Despite the church's public rhetoric concerning the goal to spread Christianity, early Protestant mission effort in the Mexican Southwest was due only to the isolated efforts of a few individuals who worked largely independent of denominational support.[28] The first white Protestant missioners were either pastors to white congregations who became secondarily interested in working with the Mexican people in their community, or missionaries who saw their stay in Texas as temporary, held there "only because the doors of Mexico were then closed by law to Protestant evangelists."[29]

The personal experience of some of the first Mexican "converts" suggests that many were disaffected Catholics. In New Mexico, for example, Bishop Lamy's efforts to "Americanize" the Mexican Catholic church provoked some dissidents to explore the Protestant alternative. Benigno Cardenas, a former priest, and Alejo Hernandez, a former seminary student both turned to Methodism in part because of their own dissatisfaction with the Roman Catholic hierarchy.[30] Although the Catholic church in post–gold rush California was a "prime mover for acculturation," its impact was nuanced by a different racial environment. The rapid influx of European Catholic immigrants formed a multicultural Catholic church, which helped to smooth tensions and foster a more tolerant attitude among white settlers in the annexation period. In this context, "Mexican Catholics were at least a God-fearing people," in contrast to Indian and Chinese "pagan idolators."[31] The lack of an organized plan for ministry among Mexicans in this initial period of expansion effectively marginalized Mexican Protestants within the church. As Ed Sylvest argues, the lack of an organized missionary plan must not be interpreted "as a function of respect and concern for a more adequate Roman Catholic ministry (which was badly needed), but as an expression of the insidious racism and sense of cultural superiority that were unfortunate characteristics of the Anglo-Saxon Protestant ethos of the United States."[32]

By the 1880s, Protestant-run schools were flourishing in the Southwest. The schools, which emerged after the war with Mexico, became one of the church's most effective mission strategies. A critical factor in their success was that they met a recognized need in what had been the remote frontier of Mexican territory. The schools were staffed largely by women missionaries, the first generation of women who went into the mission field as independent mission workers rather than as wives or aides to male missionaries. While denominational funds for mission declined due to economic depressions in the 1870s and 1890s, independent women's mission organizations continued to raise increasing amounts each year. The funds raised by women and their advocacy for what were often considered unconventional methods of evangelism were critical to the success of the mission schools.[33]

The Protestant church found that while the schools brought some new members to the church, churches by themselves were largely unsuccessful in attracting Mexicans to Protestantism. The male Protestant clergy tended to remain apart from the public life of the villages they served. Teachers, on the other hand, were more integrated in the life of the village: they learned to cook and eat the same foods; they were more likely to learn some Spanish and attend local fiestas; through their students, they got to know the families and their culture. Attendance at a Protestant worship service or Sunday school was an overt, public act that meant rejection of Catholicism, their culture, and family. Social pressure and direct intervention from local Catholic priests were strong deterrents, but such restraints do not seem to have had the same impact on school participation. The desire for education was socially acceptable, even respected.

The cultural interaction between teachers and the communities where they worked brought about what might be called a movement toward "cultural conversion." The missionaries came to the Mexican villages as convinced of the superiority of their Eurocentric culture as they were of their Protestant faith, but the daily contact between teachers and the communities they served gradually eroded their prejudices. Edith Agnew and Ruth Barber wrote of the plaza teachers:

> [They] learned much from the people whom they came to serve. They were impressed by the Spanish traits of courage, courtesy, hospitality and patience. Families stayed closely together, and there was always a home for an orphan or an "Old One." . . . Mission teachers might be exasperated by their people's seeming lack of ambition, but they came to realize that there was something to be said for the lack of hurry and flurry, the want of pressures that cause ulcers, and the philosophy that happiness is not dependent on a multitude of possessions.[34]

Missionary reports reflect a distinct change in attitude and perception in those missionaries who stayed long enough. As they struggled to survive the hardships of life in the Southwest, "the vitality and tenacity of the Southwest cultures led some veteran missionaries to question (albeit usually very quietly) the assumptions that undergirded the missionary cause in which they were engaged."[35] The missionaries "defended adobe architecture, traditional New Mexican cuisine," and communal irrigation systems built by Hispano farmers. In the debate on New Mexico statehood the Presbytery of Santa Fe denounced a negative congressional report in 1888 as "untruthful and slanderous." The Presbytery took special offense, he notes, "to denigrating depictions of New Mexican social and sexual mores."[36]

A significant measure of the respect for Hispano cultural values is reflected in the changing missionary attitudes toward the *penitentes*, a Catholic lay movement that flourished in New Mexico in the absence of ordained clergy. A 1900 issue of *Home Mission Monthly* carried eyewitness accounts of *penitente* rituals, which included self-flagellation, that contrasted sharply with previous reports. Sue Zuver, a mission teacher from Penasco, wrote that the "earnestness and zeal [were] sufficient to shame some of our modern Christians."[37]

Ironically, the mission schools, which "were initiated to eradicate traditional ways . . . more often became arenas for ethnocultural interaction, where mutually held stereotypes and distrust eroded." This experience set the stage for a critical transformation within the church, so that "by the mid-twentieth century Presbyterians in the Southwest and beyond began to embrace a stance on cultural and religious pluralism that differed radically from that of their nineteenth-century predecessors."[38]

Women missionaries and their supporters in the home mission organizations also used their success in this endeavor to lobby for a more central role in the hierarchies of their denominations. In the first half of the 1900s, the success of mission schools helped determine the direction of Protestant mission expansion in other areas of social service, even as they cut back on the number of schools. Respect for Mexican culture began to erode the paternalism of Protestant missions. But the marginal status of women's missionary programs themselves blunted the potential for a more radical change in the structure of Protestant Latino missions.

1910–1960: Paternalism, Integration, Assimilation, Development

Anti-Mexican hostility increased with the turbulence of the Mexican Revolution and the resulting surge in immigration from Mexico. During the Depression of the 1930s, nearly half a million Mexicans, many U.S. born, were deported, the largest number from Texas. At the same time, the two largest Protestant denominations, Methodist and Presbyterian, began to organize separate structures and judicatories for Mexican mission in the Southwest. These efforts were often caught in a struggle between a greater need for social services and decreasing church budgets. Moreover, they often suffered from a lack of direction or long-term planning.[39]

These special structures functioned essentially as mission agencies under the direction of denominational staff, rather than as autonomous governing bodies. Organizational changes in this period were often instituted without input from the Mexican churches. Opposition to the creation of the Tex Mex presbytery in 1908, for example, prompted efforts to establish an independent Spanish-speaking Protestant church. The Independent Movement suffered from a lack of resources and leadership and eventually died out, but not before seventy members left the Presbyterian church to form five congregations.[40]

A small but growing percentage of these Latino immigrants were Protestant. Social service delivery continued to be the focus of Protestant Latino ministry, but social involvement rarely translated to political advocacy by the church. The church was largely quiet, for example, when diminished demand for labor resulted in massive deportations throughout the Depression era. "Systemic factors producing the marginalization of Mexicans in U.S. society were left unaddressed."[41]

As the Puerto Rican communities grew on the East Coast, Protestant missions in these communities followed the same model of social service ministry, brokering "a substantial flow of anti-poverty funds into the area." Despite this presence, membership in mainstream Protestant churches remained low. Pentecostal churches, much more prevalent in Puerto Rican communities, provided similar support through small, close-knit, independent communities. Both mainstream Protestant and Pentecostal churches in this period avoided political advocacy and social critique of the larger socioeconomic dynamics which created the conditions of poverty.[42]

Prior to 1960, Latino ministry in Florida centered on Key West and Tampa, home to the largest U.S. Cuban communities at that time.[43] When Cuban refugees began arriving in Miami in 1960 the church responded. Most Cuban emigrés, at least nominally Roman Catholic, first turned to the Catholic church for aid. Protestant denominations also organized to offer aid. By the latter part of 1960, representatives of the Protestant Latin American Emergency Committee (affiliated with Church World Service) were meeting each plane from Havana, along with Catholic and Jewish relief organizations, and local churches and synagogues.[44]

1960–Present: Equality or Solidarity?

With the advent of the Civil Rights movement, Latino Protestants within the church began to challenge denominational structures to reassess the status of Latinos within the church in light of their public rhetoric against racism. Both clergy and lay leadership challenged their denominations to recognize the racism within the church, and to change the structures of Latino ministry that perpetuated relationships of paternalism between Latinos and their denominations.

Latino Protestant leaders challenged their denominations to take a broader view of race and to respond to the specific concerns of the Latino community, not simply subsume them under the rubric of black-white race issues. Activists within the church echoed the themes of empowerment and self-determination voiced by activists in the Latino community.

At the same time as they challenged the church to recognize the social structures of racism and respond in solidarity to the growing political activism in Latino communities, Latinos called the church to open itself up to mutuality and solidarity within the church, to "narrow the gap between what we profess and what we do."[45]

Cultural nationalism emerged in the 1960s in virtually every minority community, as "an explicit critique of the dominant Eurocentric (white) culture." Racial and ethnic groups sought to "redefine and recapture the specificity of their minority cultures," to assert an "oppositional culture [that] could be distinguished from assimilationist practices."[46] For Latino Protestants, the church has played a key role in this process. The bilingual family who traveled across town, past the Anglo church, to worship in Spanish made a choice to worship in a particular cultural context, asserting a particular cultural identity.

The 1960s also saw the rise of national political affiliations that promoted Latino unity. Mexican Americans in the West and Puerto Ricans in the East began to recognize a common experience of discrimination. National Hispanic caucuses began to emerge in most Protestant denominations, bringing together Latinos within the church from different geographic regions. These organizations, designed to gain greater visibility and political clout at the national level, helped reinforce ethnic identity and ameliorate the sense of isolation often felt by Latino congregations.

In the last two decades, Latino Protestants have moved from organizing within their denominations to strengthening their ecumenical ties. Other trends are indicative of movement toward a more self-defined Latino Protestant church: development of new hymnals, which include more original Latino music, and Protestant services for *quincieneras* and *las posadas*. Although some of these changes may seem largely symbolic, they reflect a fundamental shift in self-perception. They can be interpreted as evidence of cultural resistance and the demand for greater openness to cultural diversity within Protestant denominations.

The role of the church as an institution of cultural resistance continues to be contested within Latino congregations. Despite the highly politicized fears of the English-only movement, the cultural hegemony of the English language guarantees that every Latino congregation struggles with the question of how to include a younger generation that speaks little or no Spanish. It is in this issue that we see most clearly the struggle within the Latino Protestant church to determine its identity and its relationship to the larger Anglo denominations of which it is a part and the community in which it ministers. This is where the church is working out whether it will function as a particular cultural expression of Protestant Christianity, taking a prophetic stance in relation to the larger denomination and the dominant culture, or whether it is to be a transitional church—a place that embraces succeeding generations of immigrants until they are integrated into the larger English-speaking church.[47]

The future trajectory of racial politics in the church will be determined in part by the way that Latino congregations respond to the issue of language, the support they receive from their respective denominations for testing out creative alternatives for ministry, and the degree to which they are willing to embrace diversity within their denominational traditions. Another critical issue that has not been addressed in this analysis is the role of Latina women within the Protestant Latino church. There is a tremendous need for research on the historical roles and contributions of women in the church, as well as explication and articulation of Latina Protestant women's faith experience and theological perspective today.

The question of self-determination is central to the future of Latino Protestant ministry. Justo González has identified three key factors which relate to the structure of Latino ministry. First, Protestant denominations have fluctuated concerning whether to maintain separate structures or to integrate Latino ministry into the main structures, with little or no input from their Latino constituencies. Looking at the Methodist church in particular, González asserts that "the production of Hispanic leadership—especially pastoral leadership—has been in direct proportion to the existence of ecclesiastical structures for Hispanic self-determination."[48]

Second, mainline Protestant denominations have traditionally organized their mission efforts and mission dollars in ways that favor mission in Latin America over mission to Latinos in the United States. González argues both for greater support of mission in the U.S. Latino community and mission structures that facilitate the kind of "give and take between U.S. Hispanics and their sisters and brothers from across the border, from whom U.S. Hispanics draw much of their inspiration and strength."[49]

Finally, mainline Protestant denominations need to confront the economic implications of their institutional requirements and expectations. Although these denominations are predominantly middle-class, many Latino churches are poor and working-class. Expectations that local congregations pay pastors standard minimum salaries and become self-sustaining within or just in a limited number of years often result in congregations whose energy is focused on meeting denominational requirements rather than on developing ministry to meet the needs of their community. It often inculcates a sense of failure and frustration within the

congregation and subtly reinforces negative stereotypes in the predominantly white denomination, perpetuating an "us"-versus-"them" relationship rather than a partnership in ministry.

The definition of race as a social construct is a relatively new approach,
still developing in the social sciences, but one that resonates deeply with
Latino experience. Racial formation takes seriously the complexity of race
as it interacts with economic structures, gender difference, and changing
political environments. The racial identity of Latinos has undergone a
number of transitions, from *espanol, indio,* and *negro* to *mestizo-mulatto* to
an evolving Latino identity that signals a growing political unity at the
same time it honors ethnic diversity. Even the use of the term *Latino*
reflects the dynamic nature of racial identity as Latinos assert a self-
defined identity over and against the projections of the dominant culture.
The interaction between the Protestant church and Latino communities
has been a critical nexus in the historical process of racial formation.
Although the Protestant church as a social institution has been a strong
bearer of Eurocentric culture, it has also created a space of political and
cultural resistance within Latino congregations, schools, and community
centers, space where Latinos have claimed, maintained, and asserted their
identity as Latinos in an Anglo culture and as Protestants in a Catholic
community.

In the dynamic processes of racial formation, the articulation of a Latino identity that unites Latinos in the common struggle for full participation in the socioeconomic and political life of this society is critical. Latino
Protestant congregations play an important role in this process as they
develop their own particular expression of what it means to be Latino and
Protestant. In this task, they face a tremendous challenge to be truly inclusive of the many diversities of ethnic heritage, religious tradition, gender,
economic class, generational difference, even language, within the Latino
community. The challenge for historical Protestant denominations is
whether they are ready to move from equality to mutuality, whether there
will be space for dialogue that can create a new mestizaje within the
church, and whether or not the church is willing to risk an uncertain
future where power is shared with those on the margins of church and
society.

Chapter 10

Mainline Hispanic Protestantism and Latino Newcomers

Harold J. Recinos

Approximately 80% of Hispanic Americans are Catholics.[1] Presently, new Latino immigrants come mostly from Central America.[2] They come to the States without the benefit of bringing their own priests or establishing parishes oriented to their issues. Conservative Protestants have been particularly active in proselytizing these new Latino immigrants, who largely reside in urban areas. Researchers offer a number of explanations for the growth of Pentecostalism in the new Latino immigrant community. Pentecostalism offers personal contact, direct services, a substitute community for those experiencing social dislocation stemming from migration, and new norms for dealing with the experience of insecurity and uprootedness.

In Latin America, the Caribbean, and the United States, Latinos came into contact with mainline and conservative Protestant missionaries about the mid–nineteenth century. For the most part, in Central America Protestant groups did not seriously challenge Catholicism. Nevertheless, in Puerto Rico and the Mexican Southwest U.S. expansionism offered the legal, political, and coercive mechanisms to redefine the religious environment. Mainline Protestantism became the religion of cultural integration in places like Puerto Rico and the Mexican Southwest. Such a religious culture served a conquest-oriented U.S. society. That Hispanic mainline Protestant churches largely reflect a Puerto Rican and Mexican American base follows from this process.

Hispanic mainline Protestantism does not operate out of a proselytizing imperative like the conservative Protestant groups. Moreover, Hispanic mainline Protestant churches have largely not been socially conscious of their more powerless brothers and sisters coming from Central America fleeing civil war and economic destitution. In my observation, Hispanic mainline Protestant tradition has too often played the role of minimizing internal doubts about the functioning of U.S. society at the local and global level. Clearly, in the United States Latino churches have been too focused on the private side of Christian faith. Faith communities spend too much time enacting liturgies and practices that fail to deal with concrete social reality.

As the Hispanic mainline Protestant church moves to include the new Latino immigrants like Salvadorans, it will discover new ways to understand its standard church traditions in relation to the challenges of social witness. Salvadoran immigrants are carriers of a culturally constituted religious symbolism capable of reshaping and amending the established belief and practices of Hispanic mainline Protestant churches. In this chapter I will discuss a form of Salvadoran religious experience that uses the public symbols of Christianity and those termed "social martyrs" to create meaning that actuates resistance to powerlessness and to construe self-identity as a response to a world of political repression.

Although Salvadoran religious experience is found in limited contexts in the United States, I hope to shed light on the political meaning of Christianity by examining the faith perspective of Salvadorans associated with a couple of Hispanic mainline Protestant churches in Washington, D.C.[3] The religious meaning articulated by Salvadorans in these faith communities equips members with symbolic structures that aid in the formation of meaningful interpretations of Christian self-identity and historical experience. Because the politics of Salvadoran faith consists of supplying new social and political values to believers, Hispanic mainline Protestant churches that come under its influence tend to organize their identity and practices around a social change agenda.

The unique faith perspective that is beginning to emerge in U.S. Latino communities where Salvadorans reside may be referred to as a variety of popular religion. By popular religion I mean belief and practices conducted within the institutional framework of a mainline denomination that both critiques standard systems of religious meaning and larger political and economic models of inequality. I have called the popular religion expressing the contentious struggle of Salvadoran newcomers "the religion of martyrology." It relates belief in a God who sides with the poor and those classified as "social martyrs" to the struggle to end human rights violations, the democratization of the state, the demilitarization of society, and the achievement of economic justice.

Social martyrs are perceived not only as those who died explicitly for the Christian faith. In Salvadoran popular religion, social martyrs also include those who gave their lives to radically change society. Social martyrs represent the symbolic structures that construct a self-identity opposed to a world of oppression. Salvadorans who interpret their lives through the popular religious symbolism of the "social martyrs" relate their belief and behavior to struggles for justice. I believe that by assimilating the political meaning of the religion of martyrology articulated by

Salvadoran newcomers in certain Hispanic mainline Protestant churches, believers will experience the progressive social witness aspect of faith in a renewed form.

For Salvadorans the popular religious symbolism of social martyrs is a construct of liberation theology that arose out of the history of the poor during a period of capitalist development. Social martyrs give voice to religious belief from the perspective of the poor; they offer a critique of society's sustaining ideologies; and they make it possible to reflect critically on the role of the church in the public order in light of efforts that promote a radical restructuring of social relations favoring exploited classes.[4] Mainline Hispanic Protestants who are open to being influenced by this variety of Christian experience may come to view their churches as a social structure with the power to build a new moral community.

The central metaphor of Salvadoran popular religion is the idea of a liberator God who offers life and freedom to the poor. Jesus, identified in liberation theology with those who suffer historical oppression, is believed to reveal this deity. Embodied in the symbol of their social martyrs, this central metaphor of a God who liberates the oppressed is contextualized in the poor's decision to narrate their life stories and the mission of the church in light of current struggles for justice and the acquired traditions of faith. Thus, for Salvadorans, belief in the "God of life" who raised the first martyr, Jesus, from death, awakens the ethic of struggle and individual sacrifice (social martyrdom) for just social change. From this vantage point, the proper role of the church is to reflect the new humanity that labors to build a just society, envisioned as a community of equals.

The religion of martyrology denies sacred legitimation to repressive forms of government and to the social forces that stand behind them, while requiring cultural actors to sustain a constant bond with the exploited poor. Mainline Hispanic Protestant churches that operate out of faith in the "social martyrs" serve the interests of radical politics by creating symbolic processes that support the insertion of the barrio poor as change agents into political settings. Salvadorans who believe in the transforming power of "social martyrs" introduce into the Hispanic mainline Protestant church a theology and religious symbols that lead directly to political activity to promote social change in the direction of the greater humanization of life.

The Ritual Process Renewing Church Identity

I believe that mainline Hispanic Protestant churches may rediscover their identity in the existential reality of Latino oppression and poverty.

This rediscovery of a social location means unfolding practices that lead to a greater inspection and comprehension of just how the people living in the barrio suffer the bitterest experiences produced by the social contradictions of capitalism. As Latino newcomers like the Salvadorans revitalize Hispanic mainline Protestant churches' belief and practices, these faith communities may be equipped to deal critically with the Latino community's history of conquest, colonization, racial oppression, poverty, family fragmentation, migration, and exile.

Latinos in the barrio need to experience life as more than a period between suffering and death. The Latino experience in the United States suggests that Hispanic mainline Protestant churches need to seek the alteration of the social structures of the barrio and steer them toward life. One significant way that Salvadorans are influencing Hispanic mainline Protestant churches in this prophetic task is reflected in ritual processes. Through ritual processes articulated by the symbolism of the social martyrs, members of two Hispanic mainline churches in Washington, D.C., are learning to live consciously in their society, observations of which I will share.

Ritual is defined as standardized behavior influenced by a symbolic system that promotes group solidarity, directs feelings, and explains the ultimate purpose of society. Popular religion conveyed as the religion of martyrology employs stereotyped behavior and uses powerful symbols of social martyrs such as Monsenor Romero, the Jesuits, or the 75,000 killed during the civil war to relate the political conflict over economic and political issues. Symbols like the social martyrs structure the meaning context of ritual events by interpreting human experience and rendering social categories for understanding complex political reality. For the Salvadoran believer, rituals signify knowledge about social relations and their place in the movement of history.

Because I am interested in the way the ritual process fashions a political theological identity that revitalizes mainline Hispanic Protestant church life, the observations focus on rituals of self-identity and subversive memory, specifically three ritual practices by which Salvadorans articulate their faith: first, the ritual practice of Bible reading; second, the formal rationality of the religion of martyrology; and third, ritual events that provide the formal structure for developing a church culture of political struggle.

The Ritual of Bible Reading

Most Salvadorans are Roman Catholic. Many do not perceive their denomination differently in the States; however, participation in the life of the church takes a distinct form.[5] While the church plays a central role in sociopolitical life in El Salvador, religious institutions are far more peripheral in the United States. In the United States some Salvadorans stop going to church, become members of Pentecostal communities, or associate with mainline Hispanic Protestant denominations. Salvadorans whose belief system is shaped by the memory of the social martyrs prefer associating with churches whose authority structure is based on addressing situations of injustice, repression, human abuse, exploitation, and establishing peace and democracy in El Salvador.

In the Lutheran parish Salvadorans engage in a ritual process that reflects the memory of the social martyrs. *La Comunidad* has about thirty members. The permanent economic crisis of most of its members impedes the steady development of group life. Men wear blue jeans, plain shirts, and sneakers or work shoes to liturgical functions and celebrations. Women wear jeans, blouse and skirt combinations, or dresses. *La Comunidad* overlooks denominational ties, although most still consider themselves Catholic. Members judge that the "real" church is identified with the poor and defends their desire for liberation from situations of exploitation and oppression.

For four months I attended weekly meetings of what is called the Bible Circle. Bible Circle meetings are ritual occasions that involve (1) prayer and singing of popular protest songs, (2) Bible reading, and (3) mutual dialogue between men and women using the Scriptures to interpret themselves and to generate social categories of understanding. Meetings are led by men and women who are named *animadores* (persons who inspire dialogue in the group). The Bible is consistently read from the perspective of the poor and used to create a context for molding a collective protest identity and a heightened sense of community.

By reading the Bible from the perspective of the poor, made concrete by their own liminal status as refugees and by the memory of their social martyrs, these Salvadorans, who associated with a mainline Hispanic Protestant church, have demarginalized themselves, erected community as an alternative response to powerlessness, and invented their refugee group as a social force in the context of the barrio. The Bible is understood to report the history of liberative struggle made by God against unjust social systems imposed by the "rich." One person in the Bible Circle observed:

> In El Salvador, Latin America and the States, the poor are kept completely marginalized. The poor are a productive vehicle for the rich. The social scheme even makes us abuse those poorer than us. There needs to be a com-

munity, a unity, so the poor as brothers and sisters who suffer the same consequences, act in unity. The important factor is a community. If one person is abused, all of us are abused.[6]

Men and women equally shared their interpretation of Scripture and experience.

Salvadorans who live in the barrio speak of experiencing their lives as removed from their meaning context and history. Bible Circles serve as a context of community that recenters identity and repositions these Latino newcomers within the larger Salvadoran struggle for political change. As a ritual document, the Bible provides the basis for forming community values based on organization and social action. One informant remarked that the Bible Circle is a place where "all the cries against this world and society could be assimilated and we, the poor, can believe in each other."

Popular songs developed in the context of Salvadoran political struggle are used to keep alive the sentiment of revolt, and the commitment to unity and organized political encounter. Popular songs function as ritual structures that generate and reinforce a political self-identity in the context of a culture of struggle. One popular song frequently intoned sees the Bible as a cultural resource for shaping an identity based on historical agency through oppositional community:

The Bible is the word of life
the Bible is the word of God
it is the word of the people
that searches and constructs liberation

La Biblia es palabra de vida
La Biblia es palabra de Dios
y es la palabra del pueblo
que busca y construye su liberacion

The Bible is a candle that illuminates
in the midst of darkness
it is the word that guides
the whole community

La Biblia es candil que ilumina
en medio de la oscuridad
y es la palabra que guia
a toda la comunidad

The Bible is like the rain
that makes our *milpas* [plots of corn] grow
and makes the seeds of
love and joy increase

La Biblia es como la lluvia
que hace crecer nuestras milpas
que hace crecer las semillas
del amor y la alegria

The Bible is like our godmother
with her we have to *chapodar* [machete-cut]
all the bitterness
that exists in our reality

La Biblia es como nuestra cuma,
con ella hay que chapodar
toditas las amarguras
que hay en nuestra realidad

The Bible is like tortillas [the bread of life]
that we make in the *comal* [cooking plate]
it exists to be shared and
to make community.

La Biblia es como las tortillas
que hacemos en el comal
porque es para compartirla
para hacer fraternidad.[7]

As a ritual context, the Bible Circles function as a mirror to represent the poor as Salvadorans to the refugee community, showing them an image of themselves as a community occupied with the struggle for justice—"justice" interpreted specifically as the negation of the repressive regime in El Salvador and the international political forces keeping it in power. Refugees who opposed the repressive regime have found their identity nourished in Bible Circles. Moreover, the Bible Circles grant *La Comunidad*'s contestational refugees a privileged place in local society from which to overcome their marginal political status and voicelessness within the larger community.

The Religious Service as an Identity Strategy

The Lutheran *La Comunidad* and United Methodist *Casa del Pueblo* both use the Salvadoran and Nicaraguan *Campesino* Mass (Liberation Mass) in religious services and for other ritual occasions. Developed in the context of political resistance, the Liberation Mass fixes the religious identity of members of these churches in a culture of opposition whose nucleus is the historical struggle of El Salvador's subaltern classes. One informant observed, "The most important part of the *Misa Campesina* [Peasant Mass] is the songs. Each song carries the expression of the pueblo [the people][8] . . . they are really the message of Christ; the message of liberation."

The Liberation Mass visualizes the poor as a unified community in which individuals define themselves by their solidarity against oppression and through class struggle against the rich.[9] As ritual, it structures knowledge and social experience by virtue of repetition, which communicates alternative values consciously rooted in social action that responds to the needs of a presumed community of resistance. For instance, the entrance song of the Salvadoran Liberation Mass equates Christian purpose with the struggle to fashion a world based on equality and the sharing of property:

> We are all going to the banquet,
> to the table of creation.
> Everyone brings a seat
> and has a place and a mission.

> *Vamos todos al banquete,*
> *a la mesa de la creacion.*
> *cada cual con su taburete*
> *tiene un puesto y una mision.*

> Today I get up very early,
> because the community is waiting for me,
> I am going up the hill very happy,
> searching for community.

> *Hoy me levanto muy temprano,*
> *y me la comunidad,*
> *voy subiendo alegre la cuesta,*
> *voy en busca de tu amistad.*

> God invites all the poor
> to this common table by faith,
> where there are no monopolizers
> and no one lacks the *conque* [the extras].

Dios invita a todos los pobres
a esta mesa comun por la fe,
donde no hay acaparadores
y a nadie le falta el conque.

We come from Soyapango,
San Antonio and Zacamil
Mejicanos, Cuidad Delgado
Santa Tecla and from Bernal.

Venimos desde Soyapango,
San Antonio y de la Zacamil,
Mejicanos, cuidad Delgado,
Santa Tecla y de Bernal.

God sends us to make of this world
a table of equality where all
work and struggle together
sharing property.

Dios nos manda a hacer de este mundo
una mesa donde haya igualdad
trabajando y luchando juntos
compartiendo la propiedad.[10]

Expounding a model of economic redistribution, this entrance song encourages the congregants to identify themselves as members of *el pueblo*, the majority poor, who occupy a privileged theological locus.[11]

The *Kyrie* (Greek for "Lord") or response of faith used in *La Comunidad* and *Casa del Pueblo* to invoke the start of the worship experience communicates class struggle and the social action of the poor. The Kyrie used in both communities comes from the Nicaraguan *Campesino* Mass. The liberative message it conveys, to use Lancaster's words, communicates "an image of the poor to themselves: the project of the poor to liberate themselves [as] a sacred undertaking."[12] The Kyrie vocalizes the poor's sense of class conflict and their dialectical reading of the causes of poverty:

Christ, Christ
Jesus identify yourself with us
Lord, Lord my God
identify yourself with us.

Cristo, Cristo Jesus
identifícate con nostros
Señor, Señor mi Dios
identifícate con nosotros.

Christ, Christ Jesus
identify yourself
not with the oppressive class
that crushes and devours
the community

Cristo, Cristo Jesus
solidarizate no con la clase opresora
que exprime y devora
a la comunidad

but with oppressed people
my very pueblo [the people] who
thirst after peace.

sino con el oprimido
con el pueblo mio
sediento de paz.[13]

In the Liberation Mass the poor conceive of themselves as historical agents of radical social change.

As ritual concerned with the cultural construction of a Christian political identity, the Liberation Mass represents the sacred memory that raises community members out of the world of oppression, injustice, and suffering by instilling values that direct attention to the power of the organized poor to radically alter the authority of the state in order to serve their social class interests. Thus, the Salvadoran *Campesino* Mass concludes the ritual experience of worship with a *Despedida* (Blessing) that vocalizes the values of the poor as an organized community overcoming injustice and establishing the conditions for their liberation:

When the poor believe in the poor
then we can sing: liberty!
When the poor believe in the poor
we will build brotherhood and sisterhood.

Cuando el pobre crea en el pobre
ya podremos cantar: ¡libertad!

Cuando el pobre crea en el pobre
construiremos la fraternidad.

The Mass is over, brothers and sisters
I'll see you later.
We've just heard what God has to say
and now we're clear that we can go ahead
we must begin the task at hand.

Hasta luego, mis hermanos,
que la Misa termino.
Ya escuchamos lo que Dios nos hablo.
Ahora si, ya estamos claros,
ya podemos caminar.
La tarea debemos continuar.

We have all committed ourselves
at the Table of the Lord
to build love in this world
and to struggle for our brothers and sisters
and to form community
as Christ is present in our solidarity.

Todos nos comprometimos
en la mesa del Señor
a construir en este mundo el Amor.
Que al luchar por los hermanos
se hace la comunidad.
Cristo vive en la solidaridad.

When the poor seek out the poor
and organization is born
that's when our liberation begins.
When the poor announce to the poor
the hope that God has given us
that's when the kingdom is born among us.

Cuando el pobre busca al pobre
y nace la organizacion
es que empieza nuestra liberacion.
Cuando el pobre anuncia al pobre
la esperanza que El nos dio
ya su reino entre nosotros nacio.[14]

The Liberation Mass provides a framework for the expression of the religion of martyrology in the context of Washington, D.C. As a liturgical vehicle, it functions as a cultural reference that molds, reinforces, and gives continuity to Salvadoran political identity in the context of Hispanic mainline Protestant church life. Through the Liberation Mass, religious identity is decisively affixed to belief in a God who clarifies the project of the poor, which means favoring life, human rights, economic redistribution, and democratic values for government.

The Liberation Mass hopes to build a social movement of the poor whose identity is based on commitment to social activism. In the message of the Liberation Mass, the poor are seen as an organized community pledged to political performance against the "oppressive classes." In contrast, both conservative Catholicism and standard Hispanic mainline Protestantism counsel against political action and view the "spiritual realm" as the key concern of the church. Although no one community can conclusively be said to have written the Liberation Mass, the poor of the base Christian communities of El Salvador and Nicaragua are seen as its creative source of originality.

Rituals of Subversive Memory

Rituals of subversive memory refer to standardized behavior in specific contexts understood as performance, verbal or in iconic representation related to the social martyrs. Through ritual, society constructs social martyrs as sacred symbols to represent its collective purpose.[15] Salvadoran popular religion constructs the memory of the social martyrs to elucidate the meaning of social change springing from conflictive political reality. As sacred symbols, the social martyrs blend religious belief with social struggle and root the fight against antidemocratic social forces in individual consciousness.

Social martyrs are sacred symbols not formed around images of " 'the state' . . . but around social and cultural oppositions that create a group or community feeling."[16] Social martyrs permit communities bonded by their resistance to oppressive forces in society to read their political struggle as a sacred text. Thus, social martyrs such as Rutilio Grande, Monsenor Romero, the Jesuits, and the tens of thousands of ordinary Christian men and women killed during the civil war in El Salvador are cultural productions that critique the dominant structures of the repressive regime. These symbols are called upon in ritual scenes to articulate contestational identity and mobilize resistance to organized state power.

Popular religious practices associated with worship, celebrations, or public demonstrations focus on the social martyrs. Several ritual events manifest the importance of the social martyrs for the construction of contestational identity and the development of social solidarity. For instance, on the occasion of the anniversaries of the deaths of the Jesuits and their two coworkers and Monsenor Romero, ritual events take place that underpin an oppositional Christian identity. Ritualized mass gatherings designed around the theme of social martyrs make symbolic statements about political inequality and struggle against oppression. Rituals of subversive memory kept at *Casa del Pueblo* and other mass gatherings communicate popular support for the struggle to alter the power of anti-democratic forces lodged within the Salvadoran state and its coercive apparatus.

At *Casa del Pueblo* a network of grassroots organizations sponsored a ritual scene termed "In Memory of the Jesuit Priests." Before the church altar, enlarged photographs of three Jesuits symbolizing the Jesuit community were placed above a large stained-glass window depicting Christ with outstretched hands. On side walls were two enlarged photographs of Elba Ramos and Celina Ramos, the Jesuit coworkers who were killed with the six members of the Jesuit community.

Two banners also hung on opposite sides of the church altar on the sanctuary walls. One banner quoted a text from the Hebrew prophet Isaiah (Isa. 2:4): "They shall beat their swords into plowshares, and their spears into pruning hooks." This ritual text identified peace as an ultimate concern of those who read their identity through the memory of the Jesuits and the social martyrs. On the other banner were words written by the poet Pablo Neruda: "Who are the ones that suffer? I do not know. But they are mine!" Both banners written in Spanish could easily be read from any part of the assembly hall.[17]

Printed in a bulletin was a short history composed in the perspective of oppositional culture describing how the armed forces killed the Jesuits and interpreting the civil war. The short history opposed established Salvadoran and North American society. For instance:

> On November 16, 1989, six Jesuit priests and their two co-workers were brutally murdered by the Salvadoran Armed Forces. To date, only one member of the military has been convicted of these murders. Jesuit leaders, human rights organizations and others are maintaining that the "intellectual authors" of these brutal crimes have not been uncovered. Also the fact that the men in the Salvadoran Armed Forces who actually pulled the trigger were not convicted because they were only "following orders" sets a very dangerous precedent for future and past human rights violations by the Salvadoran military.

The Jesuits were outspoken proponents of a negotiated solution to the conflict in El Salvador. Their stance, combined with their commitment to the poor, made them targets of the Salvadoran military. The sacrifice the Jesuits made for peace in their country is symbolic of over 75,000 Salvadorans who have died in this war—a war that the U.S. government has supported with over 4.5 billion dollars in military aid to the Salvadoran government in the past 11 years.[18]

Remembering these social martyrs associates political struggle and self-identity; meanwhile, it symbolically bestows power on opposition forces [FMLN/[19] majority poor] seeking to subvert the political regime.

Pastor Cruz provided ritual verbalization that explained the symbolic meaning of the life and death of the Jesuits. His discourse named the "structure . . . of socially approved 'proper' relations between individuals and groups" as defined by contestational culture.[20] For instance, Father Rutilio Grande was remembered as the first Jesuit to be killed by death squad members along with two peasants from his parish. The Jesuits were deemed subversive because they aided the peasants, had a social analysis of the political conflict, and made an option for the poor defined as the *pueblo* (the people), the women of the marketplace and the peasants.

Ritual discourse both reflected and constructed the authority of the Jesuit martyrs who believed in a God who sides, struggles, and walks with the poor who desire a more just way of life. The Jesuits dared to get next to the injured of El Salvador. Pastor Cruz remarked that the Jesuits knew their lives were under threat, for University of Central America Jose Simeon Canas had been bombed and they had received death threats, which caused them to sleep dispersed at times in clandestine places; yet, they always remained faithful to the Salvadoran poor. Thus, ideological language functioned as a resource linking these sacred symbols of popular religion to the formation of a protest identity.

As a ritual of subversive memory that celebrated the "living presence" of the Jesuits and their two coworkers, ritual verbalization reported and molded political meaning out of their deaths. The sacrifice of the Jesuits and their two coworkers was framed as a requirement of the struggle to overcome the repressive regime on the way toward establishing a new society. Their "living presence" was seen in the refugee communities returning to El Salvador from other Central American countries and the peace negotiations between the FMLN and the Cristiani government then taking place to end the war and promote justice in El Salvador. Finally, ritual mass gatherings often employ the words of social martyrs as sacred text to define political reality and generate a common identity. For instance, the ritual of subversive memory surrounding the anniversary of Romero's death (March 24, 1992) in *La Comunidad* included a simple worship service followed by a time of dialogue on Romero. On this occasion, members of *La Comunidad* listened to an original speech recording of Romero's last homily provided by Ramiro. Romero's homily consisted of a report on human rights violations in El Salvador, then the famous section of the sermon believed to have cost him his life:

Without the support of the people no government can be effective. Much less can it be so if it tries to impose itself by the force of blood and suffering.

I want to make a special appeal to soldiers, national guardsmen, and policemen: Brothers, each one of you is one of us. We are the same people. The *campesinos* you kill are your own brothers and sisters.

When you hear the words of a man telling you to kill, remember instead the words of God, "Thou shall not kill." God's law must prevail. No soldier is obliged to obey an order contrary to the law of God. It is time that you come to your senses and obey your conscience rather than follow a sinful command.

The church, defender of the rights of God, the law of God, and the dignity of each human being, cannot remain silent in the presence of such abominations.

We should like the government to take seriously the fact that reforms dyed by so much blood are worth nothing. In the name of God, in the name of our tormented people who have suffered so much and whose laments cry out to heaven, I beseech you, I beg you, I order you in the name of God, stop the repression![21]

In rituals of subversive memory, Romero is a focal symbol that comments on the social order by contesting it. Romero is likened to a prophet who spoke the truth and placed the government and human law under the judgment of the God of the poor and life. Ritual events constructed by the religion of martyrology remember Romero as a martyr who represented the interests of the poor and opposed the interests of the rich. Romero is frequently addressed as a "saint" and viewed as a "second Christ." As one informant observed:

Monsenor Romero is so important and significant that the pueblo (people) no longer consider him human. For the Salvadoran people Monsenor is a saint and many people with problems will even go to the tomb of Monsenor Romero to plead that he intercede on their behalf. Thus, we believe that Monsenor is the most beloved religious of El Salvador because of the courage with which he confronted danger until they killed him. He is a real example of that person who surrenders to the needs of others. When you speak of Monsenor to a Salvadoran it is to speak of something very significant and sacred.[22]

As a focal ritual symbol, Romero makes "visible, audible, and tangible beliefs, ideas, values, sentiments, and psychological dispositions that cannot be directly perceived."[23] Hence, Romero and the social martyrs focus concern on the political order as a context of cultural relations of power and domination. As sacred symbols, they give content to the oppositional ideas and behavior of Salvadorans who believe in them and are struggling against marginalization from the political and economic structures of their society. The social martyrs link symbols with specific political intentions[24] that inaugurate democratic values and change for society.

Ritual of Recommitment

Social martyrs are "guide posts and blueprints of future praxis."[25] These symbols connect the utmost concerns of social justice with politically conscious behavior. Social martyrs are popular religious symbols that function to challenge the state that represents the politically dominant classes. In the ritual events described next, the social martyrs are used to strengthen contestational identity in the service of creating a recommitment to the process of nation building in the post–Peace Accord period of El Salvador's recent history.

In the religion of martyrology, ritual behavior works to achieve both group distinctiveness and the communication of political meaning. The sacred symbols of the religion of martyrology (storehouses of contestational meaning) communicate what is known about actuality while directing human conduct within it. The social martyrs are symbols that address the large aspects of social life in the context of justice and radical political change.

A Post–Peace Accord Ritual

On January 25, 1992, a solidarity service was organized by the National Debate for Peace in El Salvador (NDPES). North Americans and Salvadorans met to celebrate the Peace Accords and ritually redefine their solidarity work as "recommitment." Ritual centered on urging the U.S. citizenry and Salvadorans in attendance to pressure Congress to change its foreign policy to state that all "U.S. aid be for peace, to change bullets to beans, bombs to blackboards, helicopters to hospitals . . . for reconstruction, reconciliation and real democracy." The gathering took place in a

Lutheran church, one of the first churches in the nation to declare itself a sanctuary for Central American refugees.

People were instructed by mail and flyers displayed in local communities to bring with them special mementos such as photos, banners, and artwork to be placed on the altar beside images of the social martyrs. The NDPES banner reading *"No Mas*/No More War-Related Aid" was draped on the church altar. As people entered the church, they were directed to two notebooks that rested on a table at the back of the sanctuary. North Americans and Salvadorans were asked to write down the specific name or names of social martyrs who were either well known or not so renowned in one of the notebooks prior to entering the church for the ritual event.

Three placards had been placed behind the altar. The signs contextualized the ritual with the words (1) REJOICING, (2) REMEMBERING, and (3) RECOMMITTING. Collectively these symbolic statements summarized the purpose of the ritual occasion. Around each sign with its single word message were placed photos depicting scenes from the civil war such as massacres, the dead (social martyrs), refugee camps, and soldiers. A photo of Monsenor Romero dressed in clerical collar was placed in the middle of each placard and surrounded by images of men, women, and children. Although not canonized a saint by the Vatican, another portrait of Romero on the altar depicted him a saint.

A placard showed a boy and the words, "Dios que hace lo justo siempre esta de parte del oprimido" (God, who works justice, is always on the side of the oppressed). The four American churchwomen, the Jesuits with their two coworkers, as well as countless others deemed social martyrs not well known to the international community but remembered by Salvadorans, were also depicted on the signs. The people who died during the civil war were simply named the "75,000 Salvadorans who gave their lives." Salvadoran popular religious ritual events always remember the 75,000 social martyrs.

Ritual recalled the sacrifice of the social martyrs who were equated with giving birth to the Peace Accords from which will come a new democratic society. Salvadorans and North Americans were reminded by words, symbols, and action that the social martyrs' deaths illuminate the Peace Accords and represent future commitment for the reconstruction of El Salvador. In this ritual context, the memory of the social martyrs was used at the service to keep alive the political vision necessary for constructing a new society based on a "justice that is favorable to the poor."

Rituals included a naming ceremony termed the "Roll Call of the Martyrs." After each martyr or incident that caused death was stated, a candle was lighted. Basically, the social martyrs were used to objectify the social criticism and political action of the contestational order in the process of producing, shaping, and reshaping meaning. By naming the martyrs and lighting the candles, the contestational culture uniting the solidarity network was illuminated and a rearticulation of the basis for a commitment to social struggle was made.

Thus, ritual action opposed the world of structured statuses of the Salvadoran experience with the alternative reality of a community of equality seeking to establish peace and justice for El Salvador. The "Roll Call of the Martyrs" instigating recommitment to democratizing struggle was read by members of *La Comunidad, Casa del Pueblo,* and representatives of social solidarity organizations. The social martyrs, which focused the ritual of recommitment, were named by the person or representative of a group (indicated by parenthesis) and included as follows,

Fr. Rutilio Grande,
and all priests and catechists
martyred in El Salvador
(Julio, *La Comunidad*)

Victims of the Sumpul and Mozote Massacres,
martyred in El Salvador
(Enrique, *Casa del Pueblo*)

Archbishop Oscar Romero
(Delmi, *La Comunidad*)

Ita Ford, Maura Clarke, Dorothy Kazel, Jean Donovan, Silvia Arriola, and
all religious women martyred in El Salvador
(Sr. Betty S., CDP, Leadership Conference of Women Religious)

Guillermo Ungo, the six FDR [Democratic Revolutionary Front] Leaders,
and all Members of popular organizations martyred in El Salvador
(Saul F., Labor)

Doctors, nurses, and all healthworkers
martyred in El Salvador
(*Clinica del Pueblo*)

Mothers of the disappeared and all women
martyred in El Salvador
(Maria, COMADRES)

Victims of the Corral de Piedra Bombing,
and all refugees and repatriated people
martyred in El Salvador
(CRECEN)

Herbert Anaya, Marianela Garcia, and all Human Rights advocates
martyred in El Salvador
(CARECEN)

Febe Elizabeth Velasquez, Tomas Marsariego, and all Labor Activists
martyred in El Salvador
William, FEASIES (Federation of Independent Associations and Unions of
El Salvador)

The Jesuit Martyrs: Ignacio Ellacuria, Segundo Montes, Ignacio Martin-
Baro, Amando Lopez, Juan Ramon Moreno, Joaquin Lopez y Lopez, and
Celina and Elba Ramos
(Fr. Joe Hacala, SJ)

For all the Heroes who have died
in the struggle for justice
(Salvador, FMLN)

For all the 75,000 who have died in these last 12 years of war
(Hector, *La Comunidad*)

For all the children,
and for new life and hope in El Salvador
(Gisela, Salvadoran child)[26]

    The heart of the ritual occasion was a letter composed by the NDPES
Washington, D.C., office. The letter was to be delivered to NDPES members located in El Salvador on February 1, 1992, on the occasion of the
inauguration of the ceasefire. North Americans and Salvadorans who
gathered for the religious service were all asked to sign the letter. Thus, ritual action served to organize the political action of the imagined opposi-

tional community and thereby link the interest of religion and politics. The letter reads:

To the National Debate for Peace in El Salvador,
San Salvador, El Salvador
From Many of Their Friends in the United States

Dear Friends,

It is with great joy and profound gratitude that we send greetings to the National Debate for Peace, to the popular organizations, to the churches, and to the Salvadoran people in general in this historic movement which announces peace and lays the foundation for building real democracy and social justice in El Salvador. We know that the New York peace accords are a victory for all the Salvadoran people, and in particular for all of you who have worked and struggled for a country where the poor have bread and shelter, land and work, education and health, and where everyone can live with dignity and freedom.

We want to especially remember the 75,000 Salvadorans who have given their lives in these twelve years of the conflict, and all that this sacrifice has meant in tears, struggle and blood. They are the heroes and martyrs of the Salvadoran people, and a light to the nations and peoples of the world. We will never forget their generosity and example.

Today with the signing of the peace accords in Mexico a new stage in the journey of the Salvadoran people begins, and we recommit ourselves with solidarity and hope to continue to accompany you in your efforts to implement the peace accords and to establish roots which will transform Salvadoran society once and for all into a society which respects life and human rights, real democracy, a thorough agrarian reform, social justice, and the self-determination of the Salvadoran people without the intervention of the U.S.

Twelve years ago, in the midst of darkness and repression which surrounded the Salvadoran people at that time, Archbishop Romero looked with hope towards the future as he preached his homily on the Feast of the Epiphany and said:

I want to reaffirm my conviction, as a person of hope, that a new stream of salvation will break through. . . . What we must save above all is the liberation process of our people. The people have undertaken a process which has cost them so much blood, and it must not be lost. We can overcome this crisis by bringing this process of liberation to its fulfillment, and this is what we must try to do.

In the name of the North American people who are in solidarity with the profoundest aspirations of all Salvadorans for a just peace, and in the name of all the churches and synagogues, humanitarian organizations and solidarity groups who have accompanied you throughout these twelve years of war and struggle for justice and peace, we rededicate ourselves to continue our work of solidarity. We want to end U.S. aid for war once and for all and convert it into aid for peace, changing bullets into beans and helicopters into tractors, so that the Salvadoran people can begin the reconstruction of your country with social justice and real democracy and the difficult task of reconciliation.

May our admiration, gratitude, prayers and solidarity accompany you always and in each moment of this new year of peace in El Salvador. Because we love peace, we work for justice.

Sincerely yours,[27]

In this letter, the religion of martyrology constitutes the "common sense" of the oppositional community. It articulates a rejection of oppression and suffering by recommitting contestational identity and the oppositional social structure forming its base to the task of undermining the social order. Almost all went to the altar to sign their names on blank sheets of paper, which would be delivered with the letter. After signing the letter each person lighted a candle and placed it beside the images of the social martyrs on the altar or offering tables. In the dark church, the altar adorned by the Household of Martyrs was lighted by the glow of candles.

Summary

Members of *La Comunidad* and *Casa del Pueblo* who experience their lives outside their homeland have learned in the barrio how to affirm self-identity in El Salvador's larger social, political, and economic struggle for democracy. By using the Liberation Mass and other rituals, these communities take a conservative coping strategy defined analytically as the preservation and amendment of their political identity under the conditions of life at the edge of U.S. society. Moreover, the Liberation Mass when enacted in Hispanic mainline Protestant communities positively transforms theological identity in the direction of a progressive social witness and politico-ethical engagement.

The Liberation Mass and popular religious symbols like the social martyrs help to create cultural spaces in North American society from which Salvadorans reinterpret the meaning of Hispanic mainline Protestantism, promote social change, and build a solidarity base. Ritual as symbolic action permits them to create meaning that transfers the purposes of social change to the larger structures of society and its political order. Local Hispanic mainline Protestant churches are not only reservoirs of internal change, but they come to act as the mediating agents of larger struggles for social justice rooted in the praxis of liberation from oppression.

Ritual events shape and amend Hispanic mainline Protestant identity by combining the history of Salvadoran oppositional struggle reflected through the social martyrs with the larger concerns for justice voiced by Latinos. Hence, popular religious discourse and social action, typified by the ritual events relating the memory of social martyrs, furnish a progressive social statement about what it means to democratize Salvadoran society and bring justice to the Latino experience. By way of these new liturgical experiences, Hispanic mainline Protestant identity is culturally constructed both by the process of social commentary on situations of political inequality and through rituals that guide actions aimed at overcoming political and economic oppression.

The larger question to be asked is, Is the mainline Hispanic Protestant church positioned by Latino newcomers to begin a new reformation?

Chapter 11

Moving from the Cathedral to Storefront Churches: Understanding Religious Growth and Decline Among Latino Protestants

Edwin I. Hernandez

Undoubtedly, one of the most profound religious movements has been and continues to be the significant religious affiliation shifts from Catholicism to conservative Protestantism occurring in Latino populations.[1] Pentecostal and evangelical Christians are by far the fastest-growing segment of Christianity: they are estimated to number around 150 million worldwide. Fully a third of these Christians come from Latin America.

A recent article in the *New York Times* reported,

> In a huge cultural transformation that is changing the face of religion in the United States, millions of Hispanic Americans have left the Roman Catholic Church for Evangelical Protestant denominations. This may be the most significant shift in religious affiliation since the Reformation, and represents a 20 percent loss of Catholic Hispanic membership in as many years.[2]

Andrew Greeley, in the first and only study to assess the Hispanic population's religious loyalties, calls the defection of Hispanic Catholics to Protestantism a "catastrophe" not only because of the estimated 60,000 people who transfer loyalties per year, but also because of the perceived indifference and lack of knowledge about what is going on among Catholic church leadership.[3] The drain is so big that it is estimated that within the past fifteen years, nearly one million Hispanic men and women in the United States have left the Catholic church.[4] This state of affairs led the recently retired director of the Catholic National Secretariat for Hispanic Affairs, Pablo Sedillo, to question whether there would still be an identifiable Catholic Latino church after the next ten years.[5]

These dramatic and unprecedented religious shifts will undoubtedly have a strong impact on the religious landscape of American religion. At stake is the reconfiguration of American Catholicism (at the present time estimated to be about 35% Latino).[6] In addition, mainline Protestantism—itself experiencing dramatic declines—has a lot to gain or lose by these seismic shifts.[7]

What accounts for the enormous growth pattern among Latinos who are embracing conservative Protestantism? Why are some Protestant denominations experiencing higher rates of growth than others? It is important to provide theoretical as well as empirical evidence for these important trends. Unfortunately, serious social science studies of the phenomenon are absent.[8] Most commentators base their judgments on anecdotal evidence that lacks verification or reliability, which leads to misinformation and confusion. As of yet, no empirical research has been conducted across denominations to understand the dynamics of conversion currently occurring among Latinos from Catholicism to Protestantism.[9]

The purpose of this chapter is to move the discussion forward by providing a sociological framework to help explain why Latinos are attracted to fundamentalist and evangelical religious groups in the United States. Through an analysis that compares and contrasts Catholicism, mainline, and conservative Protestantism, I hope to provide greater understanding of the future of Latinos within mainline Protestantism in America.[10]

Limitations and Clarifying Terms

There is a common thread of shared experience in minorities across denominations, which includes negotiating resources, institutional racism and neglect, articulating a relevant faith, and setting priorities within respective denominational hierarchies. Despite these similarities, there are distinguishable marks of religious culture, ideology, and lifestyle choices, which are created and produced by very different demographic and social configurations.[11] Although they share much in common with non-Latino believers, culture does play a differentiating role in creating a distinct Latino experience.

When referring to conservative Protestantism, I mean those sectarian groups who hold to a particular ideological core, which distinguishes them from both mainline Protestant and Catholic groups—such as certainty of God's existence, the inerrancy of the Bible, and so on.[12] Moreover, when I speak of evangelicals and fundamentalists, I will use the terms interchangeably to speak of religious communities that espouse a high degree of tension within society.[13] Given my emphasis on social basis as opposed to doctrinal differentiation, I feel justified in uniting these two religious identifications.

Understanding the Larger Context

Before an examination of the Hispanic shift itself can be made, a brief overview of the religious climate within the United States, together with a demographic picture of the Latino population, must be proffered.

The Unique Religious Landscape of the United States

Recent work in the sociology of religion has uncovered a new paradigm for understanding the role of religion in the American context.[14] The basic argument is that organized religion thrives in the United States because of the lack of structural controls favoring one religion over another: an open-market religious environment. The new paradigm is rooted in the unique American religious experience that began as a reaction against the European state-supported model. The new perspective purports to explain adequately the vitality of religious life in America in contrast to those who hold to the declining influence of religion—a process commonly called secularization.[15]

As has been recently pointed out by historians, the unique feature of American historiography is that of competition. The "open-market" lack of control and the right of free exercise of religion and protection of minority faiths has led to religious experimentation and mobilization.[16] In contrast, the European model of a controlled religious establishment has led to religious lethargy and low levels of religious participation.

When in a society there exists but one faith, a fact only possible through state coercion, devotion and commitment is dramatically reduced. Pluralism of religious faith blossoms in unregulated markets "because of the inability of a single religious firm to be at once worldly and otherworldly, strict and permissive, exclusive and inclusive, expressive and reserved, and market segments will exist with strong preferences on each of these aspects of religion."[17]

In situations where state and regulatory policies are intertwined with the religious establishment, religious devotion and commitment become dramatically weakened, particularly in public demonstrations of faith such as religious participation.[18] Even when the monopoly has resulted from immigration, the same results are borne out, prompting recent commentators to say that "even where the Catholic 'monopoly' is the informal accident of migration rather than a creature of state policy, the organizational response is one of reduced vigor with a concomitant reduction in commitment. Conversely, where the church is numerically weak, it is far more vigorous and effective."[19]

218

In fact, research shows that Latin America, notwithstanding its reputation as being a Catholic continent, is actually less Catholic than North America.[20] "Roughly speaking, 'Catholic' Latin America has fewer than 20 percent as many priests to serve its Catholic population than does 'Protestant' North America."[21] In addition, Hispanic dioceses have by far the lowest ordination rates of any diocese in the country.[22]

The question that remains is why, in the religiously pluralistic context of America where multiple denominations compete for adherents, are Latinos gravitating toward some religious groups more than others? What makes some religious communities win and others lose in the mission of evangelizing Latinos in the United States?

Church-Sect Dynamics

In 1929, H. Richard Niebuhr published *The Social Sources of Denominationalism.* The purpose of the book was to help explain why there were so many denominations. He used two basic concepts developed by Max Weber,[23] the church and the sect, to differentiate between two types of religious organizations. The churches were those groups which tended to intellectualize religious teachings and demonstrated very little emotion in public worship. Moreover, churches tended to view God as removed and somewhat unconcerned or unable to affect change in a person's daily life. Sects, on the other hand, tended to view God as present in a person's life— a perspective leading to higher spiritual awareness and free expression of emotions. Sect religious teachings were less formal and tended toward absolutism as opposed to intellectualism.

Benton Johnson provided a simple yet profound way to define the church and sect issue on the basis of one factor: the degree of tension within a particular religious group. He stated, "A church is a religious group that accepts the social environment in which it exists. A sect is a religious group that rejects the social environment in which it exists."[24] Using the concept of tension, Johnson postulated that religious groups fall along the lines of a continuum where at one end is a sect in high tension with society and at the other end is a church accommodated quite well to its sociocultural environment. It is in this sense that secularization is a self-limiting process. Secularization does not lead to irreligion, it is part of a circular pattern in which the sources of religious satisfaction shift, followed by religious revitalization and sect formation anew.

If secularization is a self-limiting process in which there is decreasing emphasis on the transcendent dimension of religious faith, then we should expect those groups in the sect category to be growing in the religious market. On the other hand, those groups who are more worldly focused will be less likely to meet the needs of their members and show signs of decline. This is exactly what is found in comparing data of church membership in the most prominent religious denominations for a thirty-year period (see Table 1).[25]

Table 1
Growth and Decline Among American Denominations

Denomination	1960	1990	% Change
Christian Church (Disciples)	10	4.1	−59
Unitarian Universalist	1	0.5	−50
United Church of Christ	12.4	6.4	−48
Episcopal Church	18.1	9.8	−46
United Methodist Church	58.9	35.8	−39
Presbyterian Church (USA)	23	15.2	−34
Evangelical Lutheran Church in America	29.3	21.1	−28
Roman Catholic	233	235.5	+1
Southern Baptist Convention	53.8	60.5	+12
Church of the Nazarene	1.7	2.3	+36
Seventh-day Adventist	1.8	2.9	+60
United Pentecostal Church	1	2	+100
Mormons	8.2	17.1	+109
Jehovah's Witnesses	1.4	3.5	+150
Church of God (Cleveland)	0.9	2.5	+177
Assemblies of God	2.8	8.8	+214
Church of God in Christ	2.2	22.1	+905

The movement to a more secularized experience of religion is precipitated by the upward mobility of the members. As Stark and Bainbridge state,

> Those with the greatest stake in the surrounding society (high status sect members) will desire to reduce these impediments by altering the sect in ways to make it more socially acceptable and thereby more socially accepting. If this is so, then, if the class composition of sect rises, they ought to move from greater to lesser tension.[26]

An Overview of the Latino Community

Demographic and Religious Trends Among Latinos

Demographic trends suggest that Latinos will become the largest minority group in the United States by the year 2015.[27] Latino population growth was more than 5 times the rate of growth for the national population as a whole (9.8%), 12 times higher than the growth rate for (non-Latino) whites (4.4%), and 4 times higher than blacks (13.2%). Half this population's startling increase is due to immigration and half to births to Latinos living in the United States. The only higher rate is seen among the Asians, who experienced 107.8% population growth.

The rapid rise in the size of the Hispanic population is even more dramatic when one compares the census figures of 1970—9.1 million—to the 1990 figure of 22.4 million: an increase of 146% in just twenty years.[28] At the present time, one of every eleven persons in the U.S. is Hispanic. They are not only the fastest-growing but also the youngest, the poorest, and the least-educated of all minority groups.[29] It is this group—the Latino population—which represents the future growth of the United States population.

Much of the population growth experienced during the last few decades has been due primarily to immigration. Undoubtedly, immigration lies at the very heart of understanding social and economic dynamics in the Hispanic population. Through disruption of community, meaningful attachments are exchanged for the isolating and alienating context of urban America. The implications of this situation on religion are significant, an issue to be explored here. One cannot understand the Latino community and the different socioeconomic levels that subgroups find themselves in without understanding that migratory dynamics have affected each Latino group in a unique way.

In terms of the religious breakdown of the Latino population, estimates vary wildly on both the percentage of Latinos within the United States Catholic or Protestant population and the percentage of Latinos who identify themselves as either Catholic or Protestant. Such divergent projections suggest that the estimates are not very reliable. In part, this is due to difficulties in estimating the undocumented Latino population.[30] National estimates of the total Catholic Latino population are based on the General Social Survey.[31] Lacking a study with an adequate sampling frame and data collection procedures, the most we can say is that the Catholic Latino population may be as high as 77% or as low as 66% and the Protestant community varies from 25% to 17%.

Exploring Differences Among Latino Religious Denominations

Identification within religious groups is shaped strongly by demographic traits. Secondary analysis of the *Latino National Political Survey* reveals the following:

Table 2

Denomination	Catholic	Mainline Protestant	Conservative Protestant
Total Respondents %	77%	4%	6%
Cuban	25%	41%	13%
Mexican	56%	44%	43%
Puerto Rican	19%	15%	44%
Religious Life			
Born-again experience	19%	60%	63%
Degree of guidance received	28%	40%	55%
Weekly church attendance	30%	47%	55%
Economic Status			
Below Poverty (< $14,999)	46%	32%	56%
Upper Middle Class (> $50,000)	7%	12%	4%
Educational Attainment			
Graduate degree	2%	4%	2%
2+ years college	15%	32%	12%

It is interesting to note the class-origin differences in religious affiliation and experience with the larger Latino population. Emerging from these findings are clear differences across the religious families in terms of their level of religious intensity. Members from sectarian religious communities are the poorest and most marginal followed by the Catholics, with the mainline Protestants enjoying the highest class status. Moreover, it is the poor and powerless who are more likely to experience religion more intensely and devoutly.

There are no differences across the religious families in terms of the ratio of women to men. Overall, women are more likely to be represented among the religious than men. They are more likely to attend church, indicate that they receive a great deal of guidance from religion, and have a born-again experience more often than men. In addition, women (52%) are more likely to be represented among the poor (those earning up to $14,999) than men (35%), even though there were no significant differences in their level of education.

The Generational Experience of Religion Among Latinos

The link between religion and ethnic identity has been examined historically and empirically.[32] As immigrant groups enter the United States, they experience culture shock, alienation, and loss of community. The role of religion in helping an immigrant group adapt and seek its identity is extremely important as the institutional mechanism for sustaining cultural values, language, and practices.[33]

Will Herberg, in *Protestant-Catholic-Jew* (1955), suggested that the declining significance of ethnicity among the second generation contributes to a declining significance in the role of religion. According to Herberg, first-generation immigrants form religio-ethnic communities in the United States as the primary means of adjusting to and maintaining community in their new social environment. The first generation usually maintains high levels of ethnic identification[34] and often seeks residence within ethnic neighborhoods as a way of dealing with the anomie created by their new status.[35] The ideological and structural pressures for assimilation bring discrimination and exclusion from mainstream society.[36] As a result, their children, the second generation, are more likely to distance themselves from their cultural roots, which include the ethnic-religious communities, as a way of integrating in society at large.[37]

While the Herberg hypothesis has generated much research and debate,[38] its importance for our purposes is the suggestion that the meaning of religious attachment changes as the meaning of ethnic identification declines among, at least, the second generation. In fact, research among Hispanics has found a decrease in religious involvement across generations.[39] Findings suggest that the more acculturated are more likely to experience religion in a more "collective-expressive" manner and that the second generation tend to experience an "individual-expressive" religion.[40]

As Herberg suggested, greater assimilation to the dominant culture results in changes in the meaning of one's ethnic identity, leading in many instances to an Anglicized identity and a loss of community.[41] To the extent that ethnic identity is tied to one's religious commitment, greater assimilation will most likely lead to lower levels of religious commitment, particularly when one's religious and ethnic identities are closely linked. On the other hand, it might be that second-generation Latinos who have experienced a resurgence of ethnic identification and meaning will seek reintegration in a religious community.

What the literature seems to point out is that second-generation Latinos, those who have experienced greater levels of acculturation, will be more likely to limit their religious commitment.[42] What impact will this have on denominations with a disproportionate number of second-generation members and a more highly acculturated membership? Which denominations attract predominantly first-generation immigrants and why? Certainly there is evidence that religious vitality is resurging primarily among first-generation, low-acculturated Latinos. Undoubtedly, the implications of these trends to denominational church growth and decline are enormously significant.

In Search of Explanations for the "Hispanic Religious Shift"

Despite the importance of religion among Latinos and the rapid growth of the population, very little attention has been given to understanding these dynamics from a sociological perspective. Most of the scholarly attention on the "Hispanic Shift" has been given primarily by Catholic theologians and sociologists, who have provided some provocative reflections on the topic.[43]

I concur with Allan F. Deck that the single most important factor in this area of study has been the complete silence and indifference to taking the "Hispanic Shift" seriously on the part of both mainline establishments.[44] Fortunately, some creative and thoughtful propositions have been put forth by both Latino and non-Latino scholars. A brief review of various theses and proposals follows.

Kenneth Davis suggests that what is occurring is not so much "a shift of institutional loyalties as an evolution in the centuries-old conflict between official Catholic, and Hispanic popular, religion."[45] Thus, the conversion of

Latinos to conservative Protestantism should be seen within the struggle between the nonofficial and official forms of Christianity—not as a denominational contest.

Echoing the earlier interpretation of Davis, Deck suggests that the key issue in understanding the "Hispanic Shift" is what he terms the "unanalyzed affinity": the close connection between popular religiosity and evangelicalism.[46] Deck suggests that exploring this affinity can help reduce the tense resistance and prejudice many mainline Catholics and Protestants hold toward conservative evangelicals and vice versa. Various elements of Catholic popular religion are found to one degree or another within the religious piety of evangelicalism and Pentecostalism. Therefore, states Deck, it shouldn't surprise anyone that the "shift" is happening, for it merely reflects continuity with the popular Catholic faith.[47]

Greeley has proposed two explanations for the defection of Latino Catholics to Protestant denominations: (1) The vacuum created by an unresponsive church that fails to reach and meet the specific needs of the poor. In contrast, sectarian groups fill the gap by providing a sense of community, fellowship that is enthusiastic, and leadership that is culturally sensitive and accessible; (2) the special appeal that sectarians have to middle-class Latinos who are seeking to break from the old traditions and become accepted into mainstream society. Sectarian groups, in this view, are vehicles for "Americanization." He finds the second explanation more credible in light of findings which show that Latino Protestants are better educated, make more money, are married, and are more likely to be managers and hold white-collar jobs.[48]

Virgilio Elizondo suggests that "Latin Americans have been asked to abandon their common roots and become Nordic Europeans in the name of the gospel! Quite often, conversion to Protestantism (from Roman Catholicism) seemed to demand an uprooting of the religious-cultural ethos that formed the deepest roots of our Hispanic culture and collective identity."[49] The perception is that the conversion experience (particularly the fundamentalist type) away from Catholicism represents an action of cultural abandonment and denial of the Ibero American religious tradition. This tradition is usually associated with popular religious celebrations of the people, which are not beholden to official pronouncements or clerical control, and which are rooted in the community's popular religious expressions.

The process of transferring loyalties to Protestant religious groups is seen as being one of the outcomes of the larger forces of modernization and Westernization that have gripped the modern world. Among Latino immigrants, the process is seen as a move toward acceptability through assimilation and accommodation. Following this line of reasoning, one would expect recent converts to evangelical groups to display a greater degree of acculturation or at least signs of cultural betrayal or distancing. Moreover, one would also expect that the longer the person has been a member of a Protestant religious group, the more likely the person will exhibit attitudes and behaviors congruent with dominant American attitudes and reflect some level of Americanization. Sociologist Caleb Rosado, in speaking about the impact of Protestantism, suggests that conversion brings with it a divorce "from the sense of community, *el pueblo.*"[50] There is an assumption that the chief motive or push factor contributing to conversion is the search for acceptance or the benefits of a new culture.

There is a general agreement among the various authors that the "Hispanic Shift," at its very core, is a movement away from "Latinonization" toward "Americanization." In searching for empirical verification of this viewpoint, what are the true reasons for the shift? What are the larger sociological forces that are contributing to this dynamic? Why are people deciding to join what at times appear to be very demanding and highly deviant religious communities? Some tentative answers to these questions are provided next.

Theoretical Perspective

Contrary to the predominant opinion, which argues that Catholic popular religion and Pentecostalism are extensions of the same phenomena (having little to do with ideological differences across religious communities), I propose the opposite. The "shift" is indebted to sociological factors of isolation, anomie, and lack of social networks within a pluralistic context in which sectarian groups compete heavily to meet demands and needs. It is precisely the unique and contrasting ideology espoused by evangelical groups that creates the degree of tension necessary to meet the religious needs of Latinos.

In building the explanatory model for the Hispanic shift, an understanding of the social experience of conversion and an exploration of the costs and benefits of high-tension religious community membership are needed before examining how specific needs of the Latino community are met by storefront churches.

Social Attachments and Rational Choice

The conversion experience is customarily understood as an experience motivated by the inspiration of a newfound truth or belief system. However, social science evidence relegates doctrinal appeal as secondary to the primary role of social attachments as the mechanisms of conversion.[51]

In understanding the dynamics of conversion, sociologists of religion call on the theoretical perspectives of control and subcultural theory.[52] Control theory states that individuals will conform to the social order as long as they have powerful bonds to the normative order. These bonds take the form of *attachments* with individuals who share similar goals, *investments* of time, energy, and talents, *involvement* in activities which promote convention, coupled with a *belief* in the task to be performed or life to be lived. When persons lack these control mechanisms, they will experiment with nonconventional alternatives even if their actions go against cultural and familial ties. From this perspective, the people most likely to convert are those who are disconnected and have experienced a strong life disruption.

Subcultural theory emphasizes the role of a group of like-minded people in creating a distinctive way of acting and thinking. The primary means of achieving group conformity is through social interaction where members provide one another with feedback, affirmation, emotions, and symbolic cues of affirmation and reward. The church functions as a subcultural group where shared experiences and like-mindedness produce strong bonding and conformity to a similar way of acting and thinking.[53]

In summary, the sociological theory of conversion I propose here states that people join a new religious group when they have stronger attachments to members of this group than to nonmembers. The key issue here is that interaction between members of the group and outsiders is crucial in order for the group to grow. Essentially, then, it is attachments and not ideology—important though this is—that lead people to convert.[54] I will return to this later.

Religion meets the universal needs of all human beings by providing answers to ultimate questions about the meaning of life and death. Dramatic changes in a person's life leave that person isolated, creating a crisis of faith. The Christian faith provides transcendent answers and offers the ultimate reward of an abundant life of eternal bliss, accessible to the faithful. These rewards function as compensators unachievable in this world. Compensators such as otherworldly beliefs in actual miracles or the intervention of the gods are more likely to attract those who live in relative deprivation—the poor and minorities—due to their class standing. Those in the upper class have the ability to achieve tangible worldly rewards of status or power. These tangible compensators will bind the upper class to certain religious groups which reject the more otherworldly beliefs. In time, the average member of a community or community itself that has experienced upward mobility will reduce the tension or cognitive dissonance of a belief system at odds with a scientific worldview. Opposite this move, those individuals who experience deprivation and who seek an otherworldly faith will feel more and more alienated and ultimately seek a community that provides clear and transcendent compensators.

I am working under the assumption that people seek to make rational choices, those which result in the greatest rewards and the least costs. With this assumption, several important questions can be answered about whether belonging to a sectarian group in high tension with its environment makes rational sense.

The Function of Communal Ritual in Religious Commitment

The primary way a risky choice becomes rational, or at least less risky, is through the social interactions and exchanges people experience in community. At the very core of religious experience is its social nature. Emile Durkheim, one of the pioneers of sociology, observed that "we tend to be moral beings to the degree that we are social beings." To the degree that we are enmeshed in close meaningful relationships with others, we are more likely to accept and live up to the expected norms and values of the group. Through rituals, religious organizations perpetuate their beliefs and traditions.[55]

Function of Testimonies

Testimonios, or testimonies, are one of the primary means whereby high tension–demanding compensators are made rational.[56] The ritual practice of testimonies varies from context to context but usually entails a period of time where members gather to share stories and experiences about how God has acted in their lives. Testimonies can differ in content from praise, petitions, and requests for deliverance to confessionals and intercessory prayers. The very nature of the testimonial experience gives further credence to the social nature of religious life. The recounting of regenerating experiences—victories over drug abuse, alcoholism, unemployment, or illness—gives evidence that high-tension beliefs really do work, making such beliefs a cost-benefit analysis bargain.

Function of Ritual Strictness in Creating Strength: "Free Riders"

Perhaps the most important function of rituals is that of controlling the "free rider" problem.[57] This refers to the people who seek to get away with the least amount of investment and contribution to the community but still receive its benefits. All organizations are affected by the problem of individuals who want membership benefits but would rather stay on the sidelines. If this happens with too much frequency, the organization will lose its sense of community and purpose. This is particularly true of voluntary organizations such as churches.

An organization's response to the problem of "free riding" is to increase the cost of membership and participation by instituting a series of demands and expectations that make it more difficult to ride the wave of indifference and still benefit from the rewards of membership. This is precisely what conservative churches do.

In 1972, Dean Kelly wrote an explosive book entitled *Why Conservative Churches Are Growing.* He documented the fact that many theologically conservative Protestant denominations have continued to add members while more liberal mainline denominations have suffered losses. The varying rates of growth and decline meant that the mainline denominations' misfortune could not be attributed to pervasive secularization. He then divided churches (congregations and denominations) into two categories: "strong" and "weak," representing growth and decline, respectively. Kelly noted that strong churches (1) are characterized by a total, closed belief system that is deemed sufficient for all purposes and needs no revision. (2) They have a distinctive code of conduct that sets their members apart from nonmembers. (3) They exercise strict discipline over their members in matters of belief and practice. (4) They demand a high commitment of time and energy from their members. (5) They maintain a missionary zeal and are eager to tell the Good News to all persons. By contrast, weak churches are characterized by relativism, permissiveness, individualism in matters of belief, tolerance of internal diversity and pluralism, lack of enforcement of doctrinal or behavioral standards, tolerance of a limited commitment to the church, little effective sharing of convictions or spiritual insights within the church, and a preference for dialogue with outsiders rather than attempts to convert them.

There are various ways in which traits of strictness strengthen an organization. Conversion and membership rituals such as adult baptism function as entry mechanisms to selectively screen out noncommitted individuals. Once in, the community monitors its members by creating alternative environments—on every level of social interaction—where the "temptation" to deviate will be significantly reduced. In addition, access to positions of leadership and responsibility are open only to those demonstrating a high degree of commitment. In reality then, the alternative of "free riding" in such a context is greatly lowered.

Another important implication to the theory is church size. Congregations that are sectarian and high-tension will tend to be smaller than those of more mainline traditions.[58] A group's ability to maintain adherence to its own norms is facilitated by its size. Small church size has the potential for enhancing the experience of community, sense of belonging, and support. Small groups can also help members become accountable to their shared values and thus discourage free riders. Thus, small-group ministries are becoming a popular way of reinvigorating congregations and volunteer organizations.[59] Even among effective, large-scale, high-tension congregations, which would seem to be evidence to the contrary, we find extensive small-group ministries. Storefront churches are on the rise.

Reasonableness of Demand and Diminishing Return

The high costs involved in high-tension religious communities increase the participation of those who decide to join, not because individual nature has somehow been transformed, but rather because the opportunities to ride free have been reduced and the benefits and rewards of involvement have been dramatically increased. Membership in these groups not only makes rational sense, but it will also be seen by many to be a "good bargain," particularly when universalized compensators—salvation and eternal life—are tied to the high demands.

However, there is a point at which greater strictness has a diminishing return, particularly among those who enjoy a higher social economic status. Farming with horses and traveling by horse and buggy may not be a terribly attractive option for many. A movement then "must maintain a certain distance or tension between itself and society. But maintaining this 'optimal gap' means walking a very fine line in adjusting to social change so as not to become too deviant, but not embracing change so fully as to lose all distinctiveness."[60]

The Hispanic Community

Every individual within the United States is affected by and through the conversion and community experiences of religion described in the preceding sections. However, it is the Latino community that is undergoing the massive change in church membership referred to as the Hispanic Shift. The basic demographic trends of the Latino population in America have already been presented: a high-poverty, relatively low-education minority. Such a profile fits readily into high-tension sect offers of other-worldly compensation. Movement into such groups is facilitated by the "quest for community" spurred on by the massive shifts in the Latino population.[61]

The Roles of Immigration and Acculturation

It has been shown that new religious movements experience revitalization and rapid growth in contexts of acute social crisis.[62] Thus, the success of sectarian movements can be aided significantly by social disruptions such as immigration. The primary reason for this social phenomenon is that social disruption of networks weakens the ties individuals have with their religious communities, providing the space for sects to meet a market niche through aggressive evangelism.[63]

O'Dea and Poblete's classic study "Anomie and the 'Quest for Community'" sought to explain the dramatic growth of Protestant sects among Puerto Ricans in New York.[64] They hypothesized that the development of sectarianism was a response to anomie. They further theorized that immigrants experience loss of community, which results in increased isolation and alienation. This state of affairs leads immigrants to seek community, which many find in storefront churches. They argued that sectarian groups provide a truer experience of community. Conversion to such groups is an attempt at re-creating the community lost through immigration. Unfortunately, no one has furthered the "anomie-to-community" hypothesis proposed by O'Dea and Poblete.

Meaninglessness results from detachment. As Stark and Iannaccone state, "When the average member of a group suffers a substantial loss of attachments, social disorganization occurs and conformity to the conventional moral order declines. In this sense, disasters free many members of a group to adopt a new culture."[65] In the barrio, where there is a large proportion of newcomers, the situation is ripe for new attachments to high-tension religious groups who are readily accessible and eager to welcome new members.

Sects: The Culture-Denying Hypothesis

As noted in the review of professional literature, an important argument among those seeking to understand the Hispanic Shift is the notion that part of the attraction for many Latinos to conservative Protestant groups is a desire to abandon their cultural identity and traditions. Perhaps the most significant issue in this discussion is that of the cultural assimilation assumed to result from conversion to Protestantism. Recent findings from the *Latino National Political Survey* (LNPS) provide some important insights on this issue.[66] In reviewing the recent findings from the study, Garcia, Falcon, and de la Garza conclude that

> there is no residual cultural characteristic that explains Latino attitudes. That is, once obvious ethnic attributes such as language ability and nativity are accounted for, there are no significant differences between Anglos and either Puerto Ricans or Mexican Americans. Contrary to the claims of nativists and cultural nationalists, in other words, there is no evidence that either group reproduces a set of political values and orientations that is unique to them and keeps them apart from the American political mainstream.[67]

It appears that Latinos, despite their very distinct cultural values and traditions, act, think, and behave very similarly to the dominant group. What recent findings further show is that "distinctive cultural variables do not have a major significant impact on Latinos" and that "as a whole, Latinos are much more like non-Latinos in the United States than had previously been realized."[68]

Does religion make any difference? According to the culture-denying-effect hypothesis, conservative Protestants should exhibit more conservative sociopolitical attitudes and behaviors, thus showing the inclination of those members to embrace the prevailing conservative political mood of America.

Contrary to expectations, conservative Protestants (19%) are as likely to see themselves as liberals as are Catholics (16%) and mainline Protestants (17%) (figures based on secondary analysis of the LNPS). This is further confirmed by the fact that conservative Protestants are just as likely to be Democrats (35%) as are Catholics (33%) and mainline Protestants (36%). In fact, mainline Protestants have the largest number of Republicans (27%) compared with 15% of conservative Protestants and 13% of Catholics. Moreover, conservative Protestants were just as likely to vote for the Democratic presidential candidate as were Catholics and mainline Protestants.[69]

When one examines the social attitudes of the three religious families, all three are equally apt to adopt an individualistic ideology, a strong work ethic, and have a strong patriotic sentiment. In fact, on some items, conservative Protestants expressed less patriotic sentiments than the others. For example, on a question having to do with how much the respondents loved the United States, conservative Protestants were the least likely to say that they did (only 26%), compared with 33% of Catholics and 50% of mainline Protestants. Moreover, on several important social issues which affect the Latino community—such as bilingual education, health, welfare, public education, affirmative action, and job security—conservative Protestants were as likely to support increased public funding as were Catholics and mainline Protestants. In addition, conservative Protestants were more likely to be involved in charitable organizations and to volunteer. Only on a few items such as attending public meetings, political rallies, and general political activities such as voting were conservative Protestants less involved.

Perhaps most important was the finding based on a question concerning whether the respondents personally supported and promoted Latino cultural issues. The findings show that there were no significant differences across the religious groups. Conservative Protestants were as likely to support and promote cultural issues as were Catholics and mainline Protestants. On the issue of the role of women in society, the findings show that conservative Protestants were just as likely as Catholics and mainline Protestants to support a more inclusive view. To assume that Catholicism, whether popular or official, is the sole protector and vehicle of cultural transmission and affirmation is to fail to recognize how "American" American Catholicism has become, as I have shown.[70]

An alternative explanation to the culture-denying hypothesis can involve two parallel arguments. Initial attraction and connection to another religious ideology has nothing to do with a desire to reject one's cultural roots. In fact, quite the opposite takes place. There is a redefinition of one's ethnic identity, or rather the symbolic expressions of that identity. What is really going on is not cultural abandonment but rather abandonment of practices and traditions that appear to go against the desire to maintain what is judged to be a purer or higher-tension religious experience. To reduce culture-affirming practices and values to participation in certain types of festivities or traditional celebrations is to have a myopic view of the way cultural values adapt and redefine themselves in new situations.

Storefront congregations' styles, forms, and rhetoric very often reproduce those of a congregation in the originating country. Life in these communities of like-minded individuals is patterned after the old country precisely to provide the meaning and community that has been lost. It is a way to retain the past in a new context. The manner in which life is lived within the religious community is highly affirming of one's ethnic identity and culture. Life within a sectarian community becomes a refuge from the otherwise dreary and often threatening world.

Upward social mobility is the primary factor that leads people to embrace the cultural values of the dominant culture. This is primarily done through education.[71] There are some Protestant groups that have a strong educational tradition and, as a result, maintain a large network of educational institutions from kindergarten through university, increasing the social standing of their members.[72] Among Latino Seventh-day Adventists, recent research has shown that participation in parochial education has a very significant effect in promoting higher educational aspirations and achievements.[73] The potential "Americanizing" effect of parochial education is an issue within fundamentalism and Catholicism.[74]

In summary, these preliminary findings show that Latino Catholics and mainline Protestants are as likely as conservative Protestants to embrace core American values. Moreover, they show that conservative Latino Protestants are as likely as mainline Latino Protestants and Catholics to be engaged in promoting sociopolitical agendas that support the Latino community and culture. Any future discussion about the supposed "Americanizing" influence of conservative Protestantism on the Latino population will need to be highly nuanced with appropriate documentation and evidence. To describe the conservative Protestant community as an accommodationist movement which distances people from their cultural roots and community is simply misguided and misinformed.[75]

Although the evidence is not exhaustive or rigorous and certainly not without its limitations, for the moment I would like to suggest that fundamentalism is not a destroyer of culture any more than popular or official forms of Catholicism or mainline Protestantism.

Conclusion

The proposed theory to explain the sociological basis of the Hispanic Shift is based on the assumption of the disestablishment of religion. The capacity of a single religious group to provide for the religious needs of a people is reduced significantly in a monopolistic setting. As a result, religious vitality is greatly reduced. The religious impulse may manifest itself in such a situation noninstitutionally, through popular sentiments, mores, and values. When the coercive forces are eliminated, pluralistic religious movements of renovation and revitalization will proliferate.

The concepts of church and sect are used to define two types of religious organization on the basis of the level of tension existing between the group and the larger culture. Tension refers to the ideological, behavioral, and stigmatizing moral demands that make the group stand against the larger culture. Human beings by nature seek spiritual meaning and a sense of greater purpose, as well as compensators, whether material (of this world) or spiritual (otherworldly). These sentiments differ by socioeconomic strata such that persons will seek rewards compatible to their own interests and status. Thus, people of higher social status will seek tangible, worldly compensators and greatly reduce otherworldly compensators. Those who are poor and lack power and are thus unable to receive rewards in this world will be attracted to a high-tension community that provides universalized rewards.

Sectarian groups, therefore, are more likely to attract followers who are powerless and who have experienced a severe crisis in their lives, such as immigration. The benefits and rewards of belonging to such a religious group arise from the social experience of a living, vibrant, energizing, creative, empathizing, affirming, and hoping community. Through attachments and social networks, people become converted to new communities of faith even though they may not fully understand the doctrines. A meaningful community is created where the newly converted have stronger attachments within the new group than with those outside. Moreover, the oppressive conditions of the poor and those experiencing marginality lead people to seek hope and tangible benefits that will help them deal with present living conditions. High-tension religions provide a religious faith where miracles, the resurrection, life after death, the sense of God's presence in the here and now, and a unique sense of calling are real and true. Public rituals such as testimonies function to make credible the claims of the community and to create social bonding.

Because religion is a socially constructed reality, benefits are received in direct proportion to a person's depth of involvement. People generally seek to maximize benefits and reduce costs. In order to prevent "free riders" from debilitating and weakening the group, a series of high claims, which may include strict lifestyle standards, are introduced. In addition, some public rituals such as baptism function as entry mechanisms to screen the "true believer."

Discussions related to understanding the great "religious shift" and its consequences occurring in the Latino religious community can be greatly enhanced by social science theory and research. The social scientific study of Latino religious communities has barely begun. There are numerous issues and concerns, which require the careful attention of scholars committed to an inclusive view of the research process.[76] The utility of the perspective offered here will ultimately be demonstrated through qualitative, historical, and quantitative analysis of the real-life experience of the Latino religious community. As a result, the community will be richer, more informed, and benevolent, provided that scholars reassess their theories and opinions in light of empirical evidence.

Part IV

Ministry and Congregational Realities

Chapter 12

The Protestant Hispanic Congregation: Identity

Rubén P. Armendáriz

Hispanic mainline or historical Protestant congregations generally tend to be small in number. It is, indeed, rare to encounter a congregation characterized as a "mega" church among this group. However, being a small church is not unique to Hispanic Protestant congregations. Carl S. Dudley observes that in mainline denominations, at least 60% of the congregations are included in the "small church" category.[1] As such, Hispanic Protestant congregations share general characteristics consistent with mainline "small" churches. Dudley describes them as primary groups that in most cases behave in the manner of folk societies within urban areas. These groups tend to be familial and live as extended families providing territorial identity, cultural and ethnic continuity where their particular faith is transmitted. It is here also that personal relationships are nourished and persons supported during critical moments in their lives.[2] The characterization of "small" churches as folk societies is supported by Anthony G. Pappas, who provides a list of nineteen qualities of such a society.

> A Folk Society is composed of a group of people who, (1) are small in number, (2) have a long-term association, (3) know each other well, and (4) have a strong sense of belonging. The group is (5) isolated from other groups in neighboring areas and conversely has a (6) high identification with the territory it occupies. It often functions as if it is (7) "in a little world off by itself." There is a strong (8) coincidence of wisdom, prestige and authority with the age of the individual which is enhanced by the fact that (9) each generation goes through a similar sequence of life events. There is a (10) simplicity of roles, (11) a primacy of oral over written communications, and a (12) straight-forward level of technology. (13) The individual's position in the folk society determines his or her rights and duties, (14) behavior is as much expressive as it is effective, and (15) relationships are ends in themselves not a means of achieving an external object. (16) Social recognition in the Folk Society is a greater motivator of behavior than material gain. (17) Qualities which contribute to stability, not change, over time are valued. (18) Tradition determines actions and (19) moral worth attaches to the traditional way of doing things. The term "folk society" and those nineteen specific qualities serve to objectify what we might loosely call "a tribe."[3]

The small, mainline Hispanic Protestant congregation shares some aspects of a "folk-society" as described by Anthony G. Pappas. His description suggests a closed and self-contained society. However, this description does not apply in its totality to the congregations in this study. Though small and unique, they maintain, for example: (1) a complex organizational structure consistent with that of their respective denominations; (2) while respecting oral tradition, they depend on and use and produce written sources; and (3) relationships are not an end in themselves but more often become a vehicle for extending the congregation to other communities and social entities. Often they reflect a "small scale society" as described by Ulf Hannerz: "People in this kind of society also know one another not only segmentally from particular kinds of activities, but as wholes, familiar more or less from the entire round of life."[4]

Although there exist congregational studies of mainline-historical Protestant English-speaking (Anglo) small churches, such studies have not included small Hispanic Protestant congregations. The observation that Hispanic Protestant congregations share qualities or characteristics of "small churches" in their respective denominations provides a framework for addressing the question of identity. The method employed in the study outlined here was to examine the life of eight Hispanic Protestant congregations from five Protestant mainline denominations. Those represented were Episcopalian, Lutheran, Methodist, Presbyterian, and United Church of Christ. Through contact with pastors and governing boards of these congregations, focus groups were selected from their congregation. An attempt was made to have representation from all aspects of the life of the congregation. Focus groups selected from each congregation were asked to respond to the following questions.

1) What is Hispanic about your congregation?
2) What is Protestant about your congregation?
3) What is different from your Anglo counterpart in your denomination?
4) How are you different from Roman Catholics?
5) What relationship do you have with other Hispanic congregations?
6) Who are your key heroes and saints? Where are your sacred places, symbols, and events or rituals?
7) Can you trace your roots in Hispanic Protestantism to Mexico or other Latin countries?

In addition to these questions, worship and other congregational activities were observed, and documentation of church life was obtained wherever possible. The results of information gathered from "focus groups," from observing church life, and gathering of documentation, have provided a yet unfinished but fairly adequate description of the Hispanic Protestant or mainline-historical congregation. The information gathered and results of observation have been organized in this chapter into six categories, which, for the sake of clarity and direction, have been labeled the marks of a Hispanic Protestant congregation. These categories are, in order of presentation, the Family *(La Familia)*, the Language *(El Lenguaje)*, Protestant *(Protestante)*, Minority Within a Minority *(Minoría entre Minoría)*, Culture *(Cultura)*, and Worship *(Adoración)*. It was observed at the beginning that Hispanic Protestant congregations embody generally the characteristic of any small congregation. The results of investigation with Hispanic Protestants, while showing these general characteristics shared with others, also reveal the uniqueness and particularity of the Hispanic Protestant church through its congregational life.

The Family (La Familia)

The Hispanic Protestant congregation can be accurately described as a family group. The membership of the congregation is usually composed of from one to three identifiable large families who are related to one another through marriages. Other smaller family units also join those large families either through marriages or through what is known as *padrinos* or *madrinas* (godfathers or godmothers) or *compadres y comadres* (coparents). These persons become part of the family, forming what is known as the extended family through sacramental participation in baptisms but also through participation in such rituals as *quinciañeras* (the celebration of a young woman's fifteenth birthday) and weddings. Here the existence of kinship relationships within the congregation goes beyond the immediate nuclear family—father, mother, and children. The congregation looks and behaves as an extended family, which is characteristic of families in the Hispanic culture. Here the elder members of the extended family take on importance, attributed to both their contributions and commitment to the family. They are labeled heroes or saints who have been, if they are deceased, or who continue to be, if they are still living, pillars and inspiration to younger generations. Oftentimes, the heroes or saints are pastors who are revered and who take on the role of father figure. William Madsen describes the sometimes complex relations of the extended family.[5] The extended family consists of father, mother, and children, and their children; the grandparents of the father and mother (with the grandparents of the father being the most important in most

241

cases); the uncles and aunts of the father and the mother; the first cousins, who may also be considered brothers and sisters; the coparents or *compadres,* who are related through baptisms, marriages, and sometimes other rituals such as *quinciañeras.*

The system of compadres is a highly respected tradition among Hispanics. The compadres system is parental, supportive, and advisory. Compadres very often provide emotional support. Although there are many considerations at play as parents choose compadres for their children, it is not unusual and sometimes highly probable that relatives will be chosen as the children's compadres. This choice guarantees continuity to the family and stronger bonds. The extended family identifies itself, not by individuals' names primarily but by dominant family last name, which comes from the male side of the family. For the Hispanic person, family is security and support in hostile and threatening environments. Through the family, the Hispanic individuals know they are not alone, do not lack shelter or food, and can find counsel and support in times of need. One Hispanic describes the family this way: "Our home was like a mighty rock in a stormy sea. It was fun to swim and fight the waves. It was also fun to return to the rock. It was a remarkable rock. It could even reach out and pluck you from the sea as you were going down."[6]

It is remarkable and perhaps not so unusual that Hispanic Protestant congregations behave and act as extended families. Research and observation of events and worship among the congregations participating in this study revealed that the Hispanic congregation considers itself a family, not so much in a theological sense as it does in a cultural sense. The hospitality offered and experienced in these congregations is that experienced in a family. Terms used to describe themselves when asked, "What is Hispanic about your congregation?" were consistent with this definition: we are *familia.* The family unit is very important and is described in the extended family sense. Within this family, youth and children are valued as representing continuity and the future. Older persons are respected because of their wisdom. Members describe themselves as informal yet respecting the authority of their elders and persons in designated positions of leadership. Warmth and affection, physical contact and physical proximity as experienced in the culture are expressed in the congregation by the familial *abrazo*—which is more than a hug! At least three of the congregations observed in this study during their worship service welcomed their visitors to their family by assuring visitors that "they are no longer strangers or visitors but from now on considered family members."[7]

This familial relationship is also expressed in familial words. Persons address one another in endearing terms—*hermano* and *hermana* (brother and sister). These terms are well known among Hispanic Protestants as defining their relationship of faith. In some quarters, Hispanic Protestants are referred to as *hermanos* because they are Protestant as opposed to being Roman Catholic. At a gathering of several Hispanic Protestant congregations, a gathering that is held quarterly and known as Convenciones,[8] persons identify themselves as members of the family of a particular congregation, and pride is taken by the family (congregation) having the largest number attending. As in a small-scale society, the group is composed of people who are few in number, have a long-term association, and have a strong sense of belonging—characteristics strengthened by strong familial relationships.

The trait of church as family finds its roots deeply embedded in the larger Hispanic culture. Eldin Villafañe quotes a number of sources who describe familism among Hispanics, among them Joseph P. Fitzpatrick:

> Commitment to family is one of the salient characteristics of Latin American culture. . . . The individual in Latin America has a deep consciousness of his membership in a family. He thinks of his importance in terms of his family membership. . . . It is as strong among the families of the very poor as it is among those of the very wealthy. The world to a Latin consists of a pattern of intimate personal relationships, and the basic relationships are those of his family. His confidence, his sense of security and identity are perceived in his relationship to others who are his family.[9]

As a result of this research, one may conclude that one of the predominant marks of the Hispanic Protestant congregation is that of a family in the sense of the Hispanic cultural concept of family. Understanding family value in Hispanic culture is important in understanding the Hispanic Protestant church as a family. Here, the individual is respected, but the family unit is more important than the individual. Here the individual finds meaning, not in the sense of rugged individualism as defined in U.S. American culture, but in relationship to his or her family.

Although we find that the concept of *familia* describes the Hispanic Protestant congregation, we must not idealize the concept. We are aware that patterns are changing with regard to the Hispanic family in the United States. Patricia Montgomery reports on the family composition of Hispanics:

The proportion of married couples among Hispanic families decreased between 1983 and 1993. About 72 percent of Hispanic families were maintained by married couples in 1983 compared with 69.1 percent in 1993. While there was an increase in Hispanic male householders with no wife present between 1983 (5.0 percent) and in 1993 (7.7 percent), there was no significant change in the proportion of Hispanic female householders with no husband present (about 23 percent at both points in time).[10]

The same report indicates that, with regard to household composition, "Hispanic households were more likely to be family households than were non-Hispanic households (80.3 percent for Hispanics as compared to 69.6 percent for non-Hispanic Whites)."[11] While the trend indicates a growing single-parent population among Hispanics, the household as family is still strong. The understanding of the concept of *familia* in the Hispanic culture has great implications for pastoral ministry, and though this concern is not within the scope of this chapter, it is a topic for future consideration.

Language (Lenguaje)

Although it may be assumed that Hispanic Protestant congregations carry out their congregational life using the Spanish language exclusively, the reality is that most Hispanic Protestant congregations are bilingual in English and Spanish. This bilingual condition and experience is a natural expression and a reality with which they live daily. Rubem Alves states: "Knowledge of the world is crystallized in language. . . . Language is always interpretation. In interpretation objects fuse with emotions, the world and human being embrace. . . . Talk about the world, then, is always interpretation of the world."[12]

For most Hispanics, English is the spoken language in the workplace and Spanish is the language of the home. This reality carries over into their church and religious life. Rodolfo de la Garza and others in *The Mexican American Experience* have observed that

> although practically all ethnic groups in America have attempted to maintain their native languages, the general pattern—despite some variations—has been for the use of ancestral tongue to decline noticeably as the generations pass and for English to become the principal language among third and subsequent generations. While the number of speakers of other non-English languages in America has been declining, the number of Spanish speakers has been growing.[13]

Hispanics are unique, as an immigrant group and as native-born, in contrast to other immigrant groups in the United States of America. They have maintained their language. *Mexican American Experience* observes that

> the Mexican Americans afford a marked contrast to this usual pattern. While the number of speakers of other non-English languages in America has been declining, the number of Spanish speakers has been growing. The Mexican American group is not, of course, the only Spanish-speaking group on the scene; but it is definitely the largest and surely has been the primary contributor to the survival of Spanish in the United States.[14]

Grebler, Moore, and Guzmán

> studied samples of Mexican Americans living in different residential areas within Los Angeles and San Antonio [and] gathered information on this question. The researchers found, first, that a majority of the people interviewed in both cities were bilingual. They found, second, that those with higher incomes were more fluent in English than those with lower incomes and they found, third, that while Spanish was frequently used in the home of lower-income groups, sizable numbers of all income groups prefer to use Spanish when speaking to their children.[15]

Although this study of Hispanic Protestant congregations did not examine the educational or income level of the members, it is assumed that these Hispanic Protestants reflect the views expressed by Grebler, Moore, and Guzmán with regard to language use. When congregations participating in this study were asked about their preference concerning language use, Spanish or English, in their congregational life and in particular their worship life, they all responded that they are bilingual (English and Spanish). They shared the fact that in their meetings of governing bodies and committees, in their informal and social gatherings, as well as in their worship services, English and Spanish are used automatically, first one and then the other, alternately. When asked about their bilingualism, the response also reflected their generational realities. The older persons speak more Spanish than the younger. Some members of Hispanic Protestant congregations can still trace their Protestant roots to Mexico and other Caribbean and Latin American countries.

What has influenced the continued use of the Spanish language by Hispanic Protestants other than general immigration patterns is the added religious dimension. Clifton L. Holland, in *The Religious Dimension in Hispanic Los Angeles: A Protestant Case Study,* observes that Protestantism has its origins in the period of 1852–1910. "The states with the strongest Protestant activity were Chihuahua, Coahuila, Jalisco, Nuevo León, San Luis Potosí, Sonora and the Federal District. The Strength of the Protestant work was notably in the northern states along the U.S. border and the fringes of the Central Mesa."[16] Hispanic Protestants from countries other than Mexico, but in particular Mexico, continue to immigrate and join Hispanic Protestant congregations in the U.S. Thus, the continued influence and need to use the Spanish language. Second, first-generation immigrants and nonimmigrants as well as second-generation U.S.-born Hispanics in Protestant churches are fluent in the Spanish language. It is the third and newly growing fourth generations that have declined in the use of Spanish. Accordingly, all groups have added English as a second or first language. Consequently, it is not surprising to find Hispanic Protestant congregations using both languages and calling themselves bilingual. By the use of both languages, English and Spanish, the Hispanic Protestant church can minister to and serve all generations of Hispanics. Without bilingualism, entire families would be forced to divide their loyalties. This is a real concern voiced by those who advocate a bilingual ministry instead of a monolingual ministry, Spanish or English. The second mark of a Hispanic Protestant congregation today is their bilingualism, English and Spanish.

Protestant (Protestante)

The word *Protestant* is no longer commonly used by Hispanic Protestants in order to define themselves within the Christian tradition. Rather, the word *evangélico* (evangelical) is the commonly used term of definition. The sense and meaning in English refers to evangelical churches. The meaning grows out of an understanding of the act of evangelizing, communicating the *evangélio* (gospel), and converting persons to Protestantism. This is a word enclosed in a legacy inherited from nineteenth-century missionaries who initiated Protestant mission with Hispanics. When congregations were requested to respond to the question, "What is Protestant about your congregation?" the answers, although they reflected a strong understanding of Protestant faith and beliefs, nevertheless were often couched in terms of being different from Hispanic Roman Catholics. This is not surprising when we understand some of the motifs in the expansion of Protestantism to Mexico and Hispanics. The first three chapters of *Iglesia Presbiteriana,* cowritten by Douglas Brackenridge and Francisco García-Treto, describe this legacy in great detail. The titles of the chapters themselves give indication of this inheritance—"On the Papal Frontier, Texas 1830–1910," "Teaching the Children of Mexican Papists,

246

New Mexico, 1870–1910," and "They Surely Need the Gospel, Colorado, Arizona, and California, 1850–1910." Chapter 1, in an excerpt from The Annual Report of the Board of Foreign Missions of the Presbyterian Church (USA), 1841, captures this sentiment.

> Although this mission is for the present located in Texas, it is properly a mission to Mexico. The day is not distant when intolerance of popery will no longer be able to retain in seclusion and darkness the millions of Mexico and South America. As well may the attempt be made to stem the current of the Mississippi as to arrest in our hemisphere the progress of civil and religious liberty which already, by the independence of Texas, has reached the borders of Mexico.[17]

Other sources remind us of this inherited legacy of present Protestants. Linna E. Bresette, conducting a survey on Mexicans for the National Catholic Welfare Conference, 1928, makes the following observations in her report.

> Anti-catholic activity is evident throughout the Southwest. Protestant proselytizing agencies in the United States and representatives of the Mexican government take advantage of the situation of the Catholic Church in Mexico to spread false propaganda about the Church. One of the priests in a western state where there has been much of such activity says, "Lies about the ignorance of the Mexicans and the condition of the Catholic Church in Mexico have been told to Mexicans." The Mexican Pastor of a Presbyterian church in the West has publicly stated: "The Catholic Church is the greatest enemy Mexico has ever had."[18]

In at least the last four decades there has been growing tolerance and understanding between Roman Catholics and Hispanic Protestants. While there does not seem to be overt antipathy, however, the differences are clearly marked by how Hispanics articulate their Protestantism. The contribution by the sample congregations as to their faith and belief as Protestants is articulated in this manner:

The Bible is central and normative for our faith.
The Bible leads us to understand that we are justified and saved by faith alone.
The Bible commands us to observe only two sacraments: Baptism and The Lord's Supper.
The Bible teaches a personal relationship with God.
The Bible teaches that Jesus Christ is our only savior and the only inter-

mediary between us and God.

Prayer is a means of personal relationship with God.

All people are sinful and confession is to God alone and pardon comes from God.

All people have an equal relationship with God.

The study indicates that the role of the Bible is central to their understanding of being a *Protestante*. When this observation is considered along with the question, "Can you trace your Hispanic Protestant roots to Mexico or Latin America?" if answered in the affirmative, the element of conversion takes on a very special meaning. Although conversion may mean accepting Protestant tenets of faith, the deeper meaning is found in leaving a Roman Catholic way of life and adhering to a Protestant way of life. David Stoll, in *Rethinking Protestantism in Latin America,* suggests that this conversion is to a "Protestant ideal of self-discipline."[19] The question not addressed in this study but certainly growing out of it is, "Is there a Hispanic Protestant Religiosity?" Stoll's suggestion has led me to consider that the Protestant ideal of self-discipline can be an expression of Hispanic Protestant religiosity. Through Bible reading, Bible study, Bible-centered instruction, and preaching, Protestant Hispanics convert to a disciplined way of life that has been defined as puritan in content and action.

This self-discipline involves a change in behavior. Sin is identified with certain cultural activities that are defined as "of the world." Self-discipline in the Hispanic Protestant experience finds narrow and strict expressions as well as more liberal ones. The introduction of ideals such as self-discipline can be traced to early missionary enterprises with Hispanics from North America. Brackenridge and García-Treto quote the covenant "My Engagement to Be the Lord's" (1896), for Mexicans who would become members of a Protestant church:

> Being one of a lost and ruined race, and convinced that I am a sinner by nature and practice, I betake myself with sincere repentance to the mercy of God in Christ, and yield myself up to the government and guidance of the Holy Spirit, speaking to me in the inspired word which He has given me; trusting now in the help which Christ, my Lord and Savior, offers me, I promise that I will live for Him who died for me; that I will renounce a life of sin in all its forms; that I will pray in secret every day and read, if able to do so, some part of the Word of God; that I will keep holy the Lord's Day; that I will avoid amusements and entertainments of a frivolous and worldly character as well as are brutal and criminal; that I will always speak the truth and will fulfill the engagements I made; that I will keep aloof from

impure and corrupting conversations; that I will use all possible effort to become a useful Christian.[20]

This example of discipline, imposed at first, has perhaps become the basis for an ideal of self-disciplined behavior, which is a mark with some modifications today, to be sure, of a Hispanic Protestant popular religiosity. While responses to faith and belief statements reflected a Protestant perspective, so did other elements that marked other differences from Roman Catholics. Most respondents in the study reflected their governance and participation in the life of the church. Most responded that they are governed by broad representation and have important input on decision making that affects their lives. The important differentiation articulated was the fact that women can be ordained. In a church culture and where women are numerically stronger, this seemed to them to be a proper response to the ordination of women. The third mark of a Hispanic Protestant congregation is being *Protestante*, and being *Protestante* is to be Bible-centered, with the Bible being normative for their beliefs and practices together with some code of self-disciplined behavior which sets them apart from Hispanic Roman Catholics.

Minority Within a Minority (Minoría entre Minoría)

What is the difference between a Hispanic Protestant congregation and its denominational Anglo counterpart? This question was posed to all participating congregations. The responses revealed a consistent pattern characterized by a feeling that corresponds to the reality that Hispanic Protestants are a minority within a minority. Added to this is that most Hispanics are Roman Catholic, at least nominally, making the Hispanic constituency of mainline denominations quite small when compared with the overall membership. For example, in the Presbyterian Church (USA), people of color, the term for all members who are nonwhite, including Asian, African American, Middle Eastern, and so forth, and Hispanic, represent only .05% of the total membership. In the United States, there are estimated to be between 22 to 24 million Hispanics; thus, if indeed the general majority are Roman Catholic, the Hispanic Protestant is certainly a minority within a minority. This leads them to a certain perception of themselves which may coincide with the general self-perception of minorities living within majority groups. They may sense that as a minority they are voiceless and powerless. They tend to participate at the fringes of society, not because of choice or lack of ability but simply because of being a minority.

Those congregations participating in this study believe and perceive themselves to be small compared with all Anglo congregations in their respective denominations. Yet, they are not aware that they fall into the 60% category of all Protestant denominations. "The term suggests that small churches are congregations with less than average membership. Strange, that is not the way the phrase is used. In most mainline denominations, at least 60% of the congregations are included among the 'small' churches. Small is something more than numerical description."[21] They, in fact, are not the unusual but the usual in terms of numbers. However, they also perceive of themselves as small in terms of resources, both human and financial. In this regard, their perceptions are correct. According to Carl S. Dudley, small churches are not small just in number but in access to resources. The sense and feeling of smallness in this sense, therefore, is confirmed by the fact that a large number of Hispanic Protestant congregations are small numerically and depend on financial support, either through local regional or national Anglo denominational bodies.

The Hispanic Protestant congregations also expressed the feeling of "Us versus Them" with respect to their Anglo counterparts. While most Protestant Hispanic congregations belong and participate in denominational structures, it is only and mostly a formality. There are and have been exceptions to this relationship where congregations belong or have been a part of an all-Hispanic governing body; however, one senses that the feeling of "Us versus Them" is still in effect. The United Methodist Church has an all-Hispanic Rio Grande Annual Conference with its own Board and District Superintendents, sharing a Bishop with the Anglo Southwest Conference. The Presbyterian Church (U.S.) established the Texas Mexican Presbytery July 30, 1908, which was dissolved in 1954 by The Synod of Texas, Presbyterian Church U.S. Brackenridge and García-Treto in their book devote a chapter to this governing body, which amply describes it as "not quite a standard judicatory."[22] As participants, the Hispanic Protestant congregation feels that they are underrepresented due to numbers and resources, which leads, as some have expressed it, to a sense of inadequacy, not with themselves as persons, but "because they have more and we have less."

They sense another difference, which is related to geography and location. Congregations are located in predominantly Hispanic communities. Generally, these congregations do not deal efficiently with the communities in which they are located. One particular survey in one of the participating congregations indicated, overwhelmingly, that its own members recognize their lack of involvement in the issues affecting the community. Part of the reason is that most members of these congregations do not actually live in the community. A large majority of the members of these sample congregations live outside and thus become commuters to church activities. In a sense, they are Hispanic Protestant religious aliens in their own communities and aliens to the neighborhood to which they commute for church activities.

Although the study yields negative feelings, there are also some very positive aspects to being a minority within a minority in congregational life. Smallness can spell "culturally wonderful" in terms of ministry. The positive side to being small, according to these congregations, is described in words that communicate closeness and familiarity. These congregations feel and act friendlier and everyone including visitors is given a sense of belonging, which allows for spontaneity, and less formality, as is found in the family. They can be supportive of one another, particularly in times of conflict and crisis. Leadership is fluid and many are able to participate in the life of the congregation. Carl S. Dudley likens these small congregations to primary family groups.

> Like the primary family group, the small church offers intimacy and reassurance among those who can be trusted. Like the extended family, many small churches have a territorial identity with a particular place. Its turf may be the rural crossroads or the urban barrio or the old neighborhood or even the developing suburb. Like the family-clan, the church family often carries the food, rhythm, and culture of a particular ethnic, racial or national group. The faith is transmitted through the cultural artifacts.[23]

In this sense, being different from their Anglo counterpart has a positive side. Within these Hispanic Protestant congregations lives a pride in being bilingual and bicultural, even as a minority. They make every attempt to preserve this uniqueness and not only wish to continue but share this experience with others.

Culture (Cultura)

Hispanic congregations continue to hold on to some aspects of the Hispanic culture, particularly in their religious and communal life. Virgilio Elizondo reminds us that for Hispanics, "No aspect of life was separated from religion. Numerous rites, prayers, rituals and ceremonies accompanied not only every moment of each day, but also the seasons and yearly cycles."[24] The religious-cultural aspects gathered from the participating congregations in this study can be identified in three areas: *sacramental, liturgical,* and *communal.*

For the *sacramental,* we observe the practice of infant baptism. While infant baptism is common to most Christian denominations, such baptism among Hispanics reflects their cultural heritage. In this sacramental event, during the worship service, the child not only receives a personal as well as family name, but also becomes a member of an extended family, particularly through the participation of *padrinos.* The *padrinos* become the second parents who together with the parents assume full responsibility for the child. The event of baptism does not conclude with the church ceremony but culminates with a celebration, a fiesta where all the extended family gathers, usually in the parents' home. Baptism rites at the church, especially infant baptism, during worship services, offer another expression of creating the extended family, and the "after baptism celebration" in the home extends the meaning of baptism as an act of the whole community of faith.

For the *liturgical,* we observe the practice of celebrating *Quinciañeras* (a celebration of fifteen years). Quinciañeras were traditionally celebrated only by Roman Catholics, but recently they have become popular in Hispanic Protestant congregations. Liturgies have been written from a Protestant Hispanic perspective and used in these congregations for this celebration. Although the Quinciañera today is reserved for the young woman who celebrates her fifteenth birthday, it has not always been so.

> A tradition that is gaining popularity among many Mexican American communities is that when a young lady reaches the age of 15 years, she has a celebration called *quince años,* which means 15 years. The custom probably dates back to a custom of the Mayas and the Toltecs. It was considered that the *muchacho* was not a person until he reached the age of 15. It was at this time that he was presented to the tribe community. It was then that he became a warrior. At this time he was given his *escudo* and *espada.* Now, he legally belonged to the community. The young lady was also presented to the community because she was looked upon as a vital force of the tribe. Because of her power of motherhood, she gave warriors to the community. For the young lady, the ceremony included the commitment and responsibility she had to the community. The community in turn accepted her as a committed and responsible member.[25]

The original purpose and meaning of this cultural event is no longer the same; however, incorporated into the liturgical life of the church, its celebration is both a celebration of a significant day and the taking on of commitments and responsibilities to family and church.

A second liturgical event is known as Las Posadas. Traditionally, this event was celebrated exclusively by Roman Catholics; however, it has gained acceptance in Hispanic Protestant congregations, with small changes to reflect a Protestant perspective.[26] Jennifer Fast provides a brief description of the origin of the Posadas: "In 1580 St. John of the Cross made a religious pageant out of the proceedings, which were later introduced to Mexico by Spanish missionaries. The practice eventually let the church to be held in private homes and as a community event."[27] The term *posada* here means a manger, and the event is centered on the birth of Jesus when Mary and Joseph are seeking lodging. Having been rejected in several places, the holy couple finds lodging in a stable, where Jesus is born. The celebration includes a procession, which stops and knocks at three homes where Mary and Joseph seek lodging and are rejected. Finally, the fourth home opens its doors to admit them, and a *fiesta* begins with food and drink. The whole celebration is accompanied with appropriate music and scripture readings. Special persons are selected to play the roles of Mary and Joseph.

For the *communal* aspect of culture in the Hispanic Protestant congregations, one need only observe how often their activities on special religious days revolve around eating together. Traditions have been formed in these congregations mostly but not exclusively around Thanksgiving, Christmas, and Easter. While the majority of Protestants congregate to worship on those days and then separate to their own homes and family for the traditional meal, Hispanic congregations celebrate both worship and breaking of bread together.

As we have observed, these three aspects of Hispanic Protestant congregations reflect the blending of culture with religious life. Thus, the fourth mark of the Hispanic Protestant congregation is their expression of their cultural heritage.

Worship (Adoración)

Generally speaking, worship in the Hispanic Protestant congregation is often largely a carbon copy of its Anglo Protestant denominational counterpart. Sunday worship with its order of worship or bulletins reflects that the area of worship has not been challenged with the development of liturgy reflecting the culture. Most Protestant denominations have historical liturgies and orders of worship that have been translated into Spanish. Perhaps the only area where one observes a Hispanic contribution is hymnology. Historically, the hymns used in Hispanic Protestant congregations have been translations of hymns composed in English. The most popular hymnal among Hispanic Protestant churches has been *El Himnario*, produced ecumenically by the Council on Spanish American Work of the National Council of Churches in 1964. The majority of these hymns are translations; however, there are some Hispanic contributions, such as "Jesús Es Mi Rey Soberano," "Hosanna," "Tiernas Canciones Alzad Al Señor," hymns composed by Hispanics and generally known throughout all Hispanic congregations. More recently, Latin American, South and Central American, as well as Caribbean influences have affected both content and music in the creation of songbooks, hymnbooks, and musical resources that reflect the Hispanic reality. One must not overlook the contribution the Roman Catholic Church has made in this area and which is accepted and used by many Hispanic Protestant congregations. Some Protestant denominations have produced hymnals in Spanish such as *Mil Voces Para Celebrar-Himnario Metodista,* and the Presbyterians are in the process of completing a *Himnario* in Spanish. It has been observed that while worship follows the denominational patterns, there seems to be a larger place for informality, where congregational concerns may interrupt, without any lack of reverence, the regular flow of the worship experience. And though it may be viewed as informal, prayers and expressions of joy and concern are still voiced by the participants during worship by coming forward for pastoral prayers. The center of worship for Hispanic Protestant congregations continues to be the preaching event. Central to their understanding of their faith is the Bible and its interpretation through the sermon.

With regard to symbols in the worship space, Hispanic Protestant congregations, who have preferred a very austere setting, are now making greater use of them. Candles and crosses at the altar or communion table are now usual where once only the Bible occupied a sacred space. Communion cloths, such as *sarapes,* covering the communion table are often colorful. Banners depicting several liturgical themes are ever-present. The place of worship still embodies the presence of God. It is a sacred place and observed as such.

Although worship in the Hispanic Protestant congregations has not been thoroughly examined, *¡Alabadle!*[28] the book edited by Justo L. González, is recommended as a significant contribution in this area.

Protestant Hispanic congregations of historical mainline traditions are shaped in their congregational life, not so much by theological tradition as by elements characteristic of Hispanic culture in general. Congregational life centers on cultural values important to their culture as well as historical realities in which they exercise their lives. Although they may mirror their respective dominant denominational traditions, their life as a congregation will ultimately reflect their cultural customs and values. This reality must be of primary consideration for those engaging in ministry with and among Hispanics.

Chapter 13

A Profile of Hispanic Protestant Pastors

Jorgé Lara-Braud

Introductory Remarks

The pastor is a crucial actor in interpreting, molding, and passing on the tradition of the congregation. This has been an issue of special professional interest to me as a longtime theological educator, and more recently as a pastor. Over the years, I have kept vivid memories and extensive notes of conversations and interviews with pastors of a wide variety of backgrounds and denominations, particularly Hispanic pastors who serve congregations within so-called mainline Protestant denominations.

More recently, I have devised and used a questionnaire which seeks to elicit from Hispanic pastors of mainline denominations their understanding of themselves and their congregations as heirs of a peculiar past. By peculiar past I mean the eclectic appropriation of the legacy of Catholic Indo-Hispanic Latin America and a Protestant experience shaped by revivalism, sectarianism, and marginality, within the ecclesiastical forms of classical English-speaking Protestantism.

The questionnaire is also meant to elicit from the pastors assessments of their present and future role as citizens, community leaders, denominational agents, and pastors of churches, which are becoming more and more bilingual and multicultural. Both the informal notes I have kept through the years and the questionnaire I have prepared for this study form the basis of the profile I have drawn of the Hispanic Protestant pastors.

I have used the questionnaire with fifteen Hispanic pastors representing a variety of Protestant denominational identities. The sample is certainly diverse enough to be representative of the denominations we call mainline.

Who Is a Hispanic Pastor?

The designation "Hispanic pastor" includes a surprising variety of persons. The recent practice by the U.S. Census specifying that "Hispanics" may be of any race is quite applicable to Hispanic pastors. One has only to attend one of their conventions to see a rainbow of pigmentations. If race does not define, who then is a Hispanic pastor? In the interest of common sense, we might define a Hispanic pastor simply as one who serves a Hispanic congregation as spiritual and administrative leader. The advantage of such a definition is that it does justice to the reality we observe among Hispanic pastors across the denominational landscape of the United States. For example, a Peruvian immigrant, who could be *mestizo,* Indian, black, white, or Asian, who serves as a spiritual and administrative leader of a Hispanic congregation anywhere in the nation, would qualify as a Hispanic pastor. The same would be true for an "Anglo ethnic" who meets the same criteria—serving a Hispanic congregation as a spiritual and administrative leader.

If we adhere to this broad definition, there are bound to be cases hard to classify. What, for instance, of the Hispanic pastor who serves as an institutional chaplain or as a denominational officer? Or what about a Hispanic ethnic who is a full-time pastor serving a predominantly Anglo congregation which houses a "Hispanic mission," one that he or she serves on an optional-time basis? These examples are not so exceptional. They become more numerous as more and more Hispanics become professionally trained pastors, with gifts and skills for ministry suitable in a multiplicity of settings.

What is essential to keep in mind is the wide-ranging diversity found among Hispanic pastors. That is the only way to do justice to the complexity of this group. Also to be noted, practically every Hispanic congregation reflects the diversity represented by the pastors as a group.

Of course, there are regional variations. As one might expect, Mexican dominates in the Southwest, Caribbean in the Northeast, Central American in the Washington, D.C., area, Cuban in South Florida, and a combination of all of these in the Midwest. At the same time, the diversity of subethnicities and national origins among the pastors often bears no correlation to geography.

From the turn of the century to the sixties and even seventies, it was not rare for a Hispanic Protestant church to be served by a pastor from Mexico, the Caribbean, some other place in Latin America, or Spain. Often that pastor came from an area where the U.S.-based denomination had carried out missionary work. That trend continues in a number of areas to this day, especially in the Northeast, where proximity to the Caribbean makes it natural for Puerto Ricans, Cubans, and Dominicans to serve congregations predominantly composed of people of their national origin.

The time-honored practice of relying on imported pastors is a reflection of the difficulty denominations have had finding and training pastors born and raised in the United States. The exception among mainline denominations is found where the denomination has allowed the retention of a Hispanic judicatory, as in the case of The United Methodist Church with its Rio Grande Conference.

Although it is not within the scope of this chapter to enter into the complexities of pastoral training and recruiting practices, we must at least suggest why the personnel picture in Hispanic Protestant sectors differs so clearly from the denomination's mainstream. Specifically, if we examine why recruiting and training candidates for Hispanic pastoral ministry has been so difficult for mainline denominations, the primary reason is that denominational leaders for a long time looked upon the Hispanic congregation as a passing phenomenon, a kind of halfway house for people on the road to Americanization.

The analogy was drawn from the experience of "other immigrant communities." That proved to be a seriously flawed analogy. To begin with, Hispanics were living in what is now the United States long before the arrival of Pilgrims and Puritans. That means Spanish has been spoken in the U.S. *for more than four centuries, without interruption.* The analogy was also flawed because it ignored the fact that movement north and south of the U.S.-Mexico border never stopped, prior or subsequent to the Mexican War (1846–48). Instead, the human traffic grew and grew in both directions, until it became *legally* the most crossed border in the history of nations. And there is no end in sight.

Nor is the movement restricted to the "border areas." Mexicans, Caribbeans, Central Americans, and South Americans visit every nook and cranny of the nation every year in significant numbers. As one would expect, the largest number are attracted to magnet areas like San Antonio, Houston, Los Angeles, Miami, New York, and Chicago. Meanwhile, thousands upon thousands of Latin Americans are becoming *legal* immigrants and citizens, some with residence in places like Hoboken, New Jersey, the Yakima Valley of the State of Washington, Peoria, Illinois, Holland, Michigan, and, of course, the magnet cities mentioned.

Halfway house? No. The analogy with "other immigrant communities" does not hold true at all. The Hispanic Protestant church in this nation is now enormous, especially in its Pentecostal variety. Hispanic Protestantism as a whole has a future comparable to that of the Hispanic Catholic church. The pity is that the miscalculation of the halfway house has proved very costly to Hispanic communities of mainline denominations.

It has been a heroic accomplishment for congregations to survive the years of neglect, prejudice, and sheer wrongheadedness of denominational decision-makers. This explains why highly qualified men and women who could have entered the pastoral ministry instead chose other careers to serve their communities more effectively. Many of these women and men, who became professionals in secular careers, would, however, acknowledge that their passion for excellence and service came to them directly from the inspiration of their hometown church, which kept dignity and hope alive in the worst of times. I have heard this acknowledgment time and again from young and old. The wonder is that, having been defined for so long as virtually futureless by the denominational summits, these churches continue to offer a viable ministry to recent arrivals from south of the border and the Caribbean, as well as to families that have been part of the same congregation for four, five, or six generations.

Contextual Issues That Affect the Identity and Ministry of Hispanic Pastors

An important sign of hope we need to emphasize is that when speaking of Hispanic pastors, we now use the language of "he or she." Even if Hispanic males still outnumber females 10 or 15 to 1 in the pastorate, Hispanic females are attending seminaries in growing numbers. Pastoral ministry that models the full partnership and equality of men and women bears strong potential for energizing the congregation, the denomination, and the communities they serve.

But any talk of hope needs to be judicious. There are still too many legacies from the time of "futurelessness." Some denominations tend to recruit pastors in a way that reflects the legacy of the years when more pastors came directly from south of the Rio Grande and the Caribbean Islands than from the U.S. mainland. Some have significant numbers of pastors serving who are not only imported but who have functioned previously as clergy in another denomination. Fortunately, others show unmistakable signs of heralding a new day. For instance, the Rio Grande Conference of The United Methodist Church has in recent years attracted a fresh contingent of *native* U.S. Hispanic women and men, lowering reliance on imported pastors.

Many of the pastors I interviewed, while expressing a cautious sense of optimism about the future of Hispanic Protestant ministries, pointed frequently to the growing presence of Hispanics at denominational headquarters, on the staff of judicatories, and on seminary faculties. It is in these places that a fresh and more deliberate long-range policy for Hispanic ministry is being articulated. In this regard, it is significant that many of those Hispanics who exercise national or regional leadership in their denominations are ordained ministers. Many of these women and men found the local congregation too confined by the legacies of the past, but, rather than give up, sought to make themselves more useful by helping to create at the level of policy-making a more promising future for Hispanic ministry as a whole.

This larger participation of Hispanics in denominational policy-making, a phenomenon of the last decade or so, has begun to yield promising results. The main result is that Hispanic ministry is now integral to the overall agenda of the denomination. But as the pastors interviewed pointed out, it would be naive to assume that every denomination has given priority status to Hispanic ministry.

There is yet a great deal of ground to cover before the more influential decision-makers in church and society let go of the illusion that Hispanics will assimilate on the model of "other immigrant communities." As the pastors told me, those with influence in both church and society must come to terms with the fact that inevitably there will be in this nation large, robust, viable communities and institutions of Spanish-English bilinguals, made up of Hispanics and non-Hispanics. Until those with influence grasp that vision of the future, they told me, Hispanic ministry will continue to be hampered by hesitancy and halfway measures.

In the face of a future seen by some as hopeful and barely seen by others or not seen at all, the recruiting and training of pastors goes on. At least now, there is a vital minority of Hispanics and non-Hispanics in church and society who share the vision of a truly pluralistic society. Candidates for the ministry are generally more confident about the fruitfulness of their future pastorates and are being led and taught not only by non-Hispanics but also by able Hispanics.

In sum, it is difficult to make generalizations about people as diverse as Hispanic pastors. Yet, there are commonalities which they share precisely because they are Hispanic pastors of mainline denominations. For example, by now, a large number of Hispanic pastors of mainline churches are bilingual and seminary-trained, including the foreign-born. Most have been trained in U.S. theological seminaries. It is also true that a large number of other pastors have completed their seminary training somewhere in Latin America or Spain, but have taken additional courses in U.S. seminaries to meet denominational requirements for ordination.

Before touching on other contextual factors, we need to take up a rather sensitive issue that has emerged recently which goes to the heart of the self-understanding and practice of pastoral ministry. It is the fact that an increasing number of Hispanic pastors have become fully credentialed, like their mainstream counterparts. As one might expect, this has not been an unmixed blessing. It has brought a new sense of confidence and status with it, but it has also placed unusual burdens on most Hispanic pastors, especially if they are married while still in seminary, or if the spouse brings in no income, once they are in the pastorate. For one thing, the idea of the spouse putting the seminarian through school is a departure from the most basic traditions of Hispanic family life. For another, there is a burdensome debt future pastors incur, given the long years of training required (a college degree and a master of divinity degree). This burden is likely to last a long time because most Hispanic pastors can hope to earn salaries only close to a required denominational minimum.

Hispanic pastors recognize the danger that this kind of professionalization of the ministry will change the character of the Hispanic Protestant pastor and the congregation. The danger is twofold. One is that laypeople may no longer see as much need for their participation, since the fully credentialed pastor is seen as the authority in all facets of church life, whether it be administration, fund-raising, pedagogy, the mending of broken hearts, or the repair of leaking pipes. The second is that most of the income of the congregation may now have to be devoted to pay for a "well-educated" pastor. This is certainly not just a theoretical danger in denominations that require *all* their congregations to pay pastors a "minimum package" of salary and perquisites. For the typical small Hispanic congregation this can pose an impossible dilemma. The choices may be no full-time pastor or one whose "package" leaves the congregation with no means for its educational task, ministry to the community, or maintenance of church property. Of course, there is another choice: becoming or remaining a "mission church," subject to an induced sense of inferiority, and subject also to the moods of denominational executives or the financial vagaries of the ecclesiastical system.

Practically every pastor I interviewed felt with some anxiety the realities of this dilemma of professionalization and remuneration, no matter how it had been managed by congregation or denomination. Certainly, the pastors wished not to let the dilemma interfere with the call to compassion and self-sacrifice. Yet every pastor, ethnic or nonethnic, mainline or noline, is put in the position of having to be anxious about raising sufficient revenues.

Besides, as pastors acknowledged, in recent years achieving solvency in congregational finances has come to be regarded by congregation, denomination, and colleagues as the *sine qua non* of pastoral effectiveness. This was a fact deplored by every pastor I interviewed, yet they saw it as inevitable for pastoral ministry modeled on the assumption that congregations have the means to treat their pastors like any other well-educated professional who is entitled to fair remuneration.

The dilemma is really not resolved by the provision of supplementary aid from judicatories. Congregations which for too long have known the condescension that goes with being "mission churches" are not likely to want to remain in that position; yet, even if by great exertion they can raise enough to afford their professional pastor, they wonder if this is why churches exist.

In the view of many of the pastors interviewed, the way out of the dilemma does not lie in the deprofessionalization of the pastor. One possible way out is for the professional pastor to have the blessing of the congregation and the judicatory to earn part of his or her income in a secular occupation, until such a time as the congregation grows sufficiently to be able to pay the ministerial minimum, no longer at the expense of the basic congregational ministries, like proclamation, nurture, evangelization, and the works of justice. The other way out of the dilemma is to follow the example of the free churches, which tend to grow at a much greater rate than mainline congregations (Hispanic or non-Hispanic). In the free churches, if the pastor serves full time, he or she does so without the protection of a minimum salary. It is remarkable how many Hispanic pastors would be willing to exercise this option, if it were not for the heavy financial obligation with which they emerge from a residential seminary education, especially if they are married, have children, and the spouse is unable to work for pay.

It is only fair here to point out something that emerged in response to my questionnaire. There is growing evidence that in Hispanic pastoral households of mainline denominations, where the spouse earns a separate income and the pastor earns an assured minimum, the combination of incomes places the family in a comfortable middle-class situation ("middle class" as it is generally understood among Anglo families).

As might be expected, mainstream credentials and relative financial security raise questions of identity and vocation for any pastor serving a congregation of limited means. For the Hispanic pastor, these questions are quite existential, as they told me. For one thing, by former standards, the pastor is in a situation of advantage, yet the Hispanic pastor is still seen by the larger public as a member of a marginal community, serving a congregation also of marginals or near-marginals, and living in close solidarity with them. This stereotypical image magnifies ambiguities, when in reality the typical Hispanic pastor of a mainline denomination is no longer under-credentialed or seriously disadvantaged. Moreover, there may be at work here an image of the Hispanic congregation that may not be nuanced enough. The fact of the matter is that like their pastors, many Hispanic congregations of mainline denominations are no longer at the lowest end of the socioeconomic scale.

To be sure, the so-called middle-class Hispanic Protestant rarely has as large a proportion of financially secure families as does the comparable Anglo church, yet it tends to behave as though it did. Quite likely there is no one in the congregation who is illiterate in the language of the home, while many are bilinguals with a high school education and even one or two years of college, and those who have jobs typically earn more than the minimum salary.

To put it provocatively, a large number of Hispanic Protestant churches prove that Max Weber was not entirely wrong when he wrote *The Protestant Ethic and the Spirit of Capitalism.* The mistake we must not make is to assume that those who go on to get college degrees and well-paying jobs stay in the Hispanic congregation. Especially in well-established congregations—congregations whose members represent the continuity of three, four, or more generations—many among the better educated or the more successful in business ventures, transfer their membership to Anglo churches. This is particularly the case with Baby Boomers and their children, who no longer speak or understand any variety of Spanish with ease.

Many who remain in the Hispanic congregation, as soon as they can afford to, move out to more integrated residential areas and become commuters—a great loss of testimonial presence and work in the community that surrounds the congregation. Fortunately, as the pastors pointed out, there is a growing trend among these "success types" to stay, even if there is no reverse flow from suburb to the barrio. One reason is the growing number of congregations that are led by a more versatile pastoral professional, who is more bilingual and more multicultural. This in turn brings with it a better-educated lay leadership. "Success types" also tend to stay because in many places throughout the nation it is becoming quite respectable to be bilingual and to associate with others who are, too.

As one might expect, the self-understanding of the Hispanic pastor is significantly influenced by whether one is male or female, older or younger, foreign-born or native-born, of Mexican extraction or Cuban extraction, a former Roman Catholic or a native Protestant, a pietist or an activist, and so forth. But the impact of the congregation and of the ethos of the community on the pastor cannot be underestimated. Generally, the impact of the congregation on the Hispanic pastor is so strong that it tends to relativize personal idiosyncrasies.

Such relativization of the pastor's idiosyncrasies happens because the congregation has retained from the ancestors the evocative power of language, music, rituals, and symbols. These distinctives remain permanent features of even highly *Gringoized* Hispanic churches. Here is power that transcends boundaries of every sort, because it is the power of the sacred incarnate in a hemispheric culture. Here lies the greatest challenge for the Hispanic pastor: how to honor the traditions of forebears in a way that leads to a vital synthesis of past and present, not a hybridization that settles just for what "works" in the convergence of the worlds of Hispanic America and the United States. This leads us to anticipations of the future.

What Kind of Future Do Hispanic Pastors See?

From all the responses I have received, the question of the future is the most filled with hope and perplexity, irrespective of gender, age, national origin, or confessional origin of the Hispanic pastor.

For a long time, the Hispanic Protestant congregation in the United States was a replica of its counterpart in Mexico or the Caribbean. To complicate matters, the Mexican or the Caribbean version of the Protestant church was not indigenous. It was modeled after church life in nineteenth-century New England and the American Bible Belt. The main detectable difference of a Methodist church in Mexico and a Hispanic Methodist church in Dallas in the 1950s was language. Spanish was still dominant both places, but becoming less and less so among the young. The "Gringo" world was making its inevitable inroads, especially as people had more years of schooling in the United States, and more social contact with the mainstream. Still, preaching in Dallas in the 1950s was virtually the same as in Mexico; so were the liturgy, the hymnody, and the adult Sunday school class. Of course, discriminatory practices in church and society had much to do with the protracted retention of "foreign" (Mexican) characteristics.

The traditionalists in Hispanic churches made a virtue out of necessity, and became even more devoted to models of church life prevalent south of the Rio Grande and in the Caribbean. The denominational authorities by and large let this happen. As long as these churches were kept alive and did not ask for too much "mission," no one could really object. It is no wonder that for at least the first half of this century, U.S. Hispanic churches depended to a large degree on imported pastors. They were not expensive, and they were orthodox, certain of the abyss that separated the

Church of Rome from the true Church of Jesus Christ ("la Iglesia Evangéli-ca"). These imported pastors set the tone for Hispanic Protestant church life in the United States, often in inspiring ways, and yet keeping their con-gregations alien from the American situation, retaining a great deal of anti-Catholicism, and driving away into Anglo churches Hispanic Protes-tants who could no longer wait for another generation to become tolerant or acculturated.

What is truly perplexing to the Hispanic Protestant pastor is how this tradition of the forebears can be honored for its enormous contributions to the faith and life of several generations. How does one honor the tradition and build on it, at a time when a large proportion of the members speak English as the first language, when because of much larger access to pub-lic education, and because of the massive influence of television, most members are more "American" than they have ever been? How does one honor and build on the tradition of the forebears in a way that capitalizes on the recent rebirth of Spanish in American society and the massive waves of visitors and immigrants from Latin America without becoming "foreign" again and losing an entire generation of children, young people, young adults, and middle-aged professionals?

The dominant note I have heard from Hispanic pastors is one of hope that will require a large dose of common sense and fresh commitment by everyone who has any role to play in building the future of these church-es. What there seems to be no doubt about is that the future of the His-panic Protestant churches lies in their becoming more bilingual and more culturally adaptive to the peculiar ethos of the different regions of the United States. That means that in east Los Angeles the Hispanic church will consciously remain close to the cultural traditions of Mexico and Cen-tral America, in south Florida to those of Cuba, in the Northeast to those of the Caribbean, and so on.

What pastors have also told me is that they want to lead their congrega-tions toward a model of church life that is home as much for the immigrant who speaks no English, as for the acculturated member who barely speaks Spanish. I sensed no naivete in the responses. No one underestimates how difficult this is going to be. It requires a bilingual proficiency not many pas-tors possess, and there is no agreement as to what "bilingual" means. Is it the proper English and the proper Spanish of the classroom? Or is it the combination of both languages so prevalent in social and home life? And if we are to be bilingual, are we going to divide the congregation for worship on the basis of language? Will we carry out the educational program with two completely separate sets of people and curriculum?

The reason why these difficult questions do not seem to dampen the hope of the pastors is that there is a sense now that these are "our" problems, that "we" have a lot of gifted people in the congregation, in the seminary, in the judicatory, and at headquarters who can work together with "us" to make the difference. There is also a new sense of loyalty to the denomination, precisely because "we" are not absent from it, where it counts, and because the decision-makers are much more available for dialogue than were their former counterparts.

Another source of hope among these pastors is that they represent a new generation of people not determined by the anti-Catholicism of their congregations. Many of these pastors have been trained in denominational seminaries that have become quite ecumenical in terms of the denominational diversity of their students, and in terms of theological scholarship that knows no boundaries of separation, certainly not from the Roman Catholic Church. Also many pastors are finding the most effective way to do the works of justice in their communities is in cooperation with local Roman Catholics. Curiously, when pastors were asked what for them was the principal difference between a Hispanic Catholic congregation and theirs, the response tended to be a bit vague, and when not vague, it pointed to an ostensible difference that appeared to be not peculiarly Protestant or Hispanic. I am referring to responses such as, "We believe in grace," "We use the laity more than they do," "We are less authoritarian," "Our worship services are more joyful," "We give more attention to preaching," and so forth. But could we not get the same responses from Roman Catholics or Pentecostals?

To the specific question, "What would the Church of Jesus Christ in this country lose if there were no ministry of the kind provided by your church?" the answers tended to be equally vague, and, if not vague, the "distinctive" contribution of the Hispanic church did not appear to be either distinctive or particularly Hispanic Protestant.

Most often the pastors interviewed mentioned cultural contributions like the Spanish language, and the color, art, and "style" of Mexico, of the Caribbean, and of the rest of Latin America. But they themselves acknowledged that few Hispanic churches of mainline Protestantism seriously reflect, in their way of being, authentic Mexican, Caribbean, or Central or South American color, art, or style. These pastors admit that even now the identity of their congregations has developed little that is original, unless by original they mean the adaptation of translated liturgies, translated theology, or "translated" rituals. Perhaps the most symptomatic concern in all my research among Hispanic pastors of mainline Protestant churches lies here. I am referring to what the pastors themselves consider distinctive of Hispanic Protestantism as practiced by their congregations, now that the vast majority of their church members live, move, and have their being in the overlap of the ethnic community and the larger society.

I kept asking the pastors what they thought was their role in the new situation where fast-growing Hispanic churches, like Southern Baptists and Pentecostals, have massively taken over the sectarian role played until recently by Hispanic Methodists, Presbyterians, Lutherans, Disciples, and Congregationalists. Their answers tended to be nostalgic ("Ah, if we could only be the way we used to be!"), or defensive ("We have been orphans in our denomination"), or wistful ("We could do a lot better if . . . , if . . . , if . . . .").

I asked as well how mainline Latino congregations might respond to the challenge of the evangelical renewal of the Catholic church, which makes the Bible central, Christ's grace uppermost, congregational singing a regular practice, and the participation of the laity more prominent than ever—all still considered Protestant distinctives in Hispanic Protestant congregations. By and large, the pastors seemed a bit unsure there has been that much of an evangelical revival in the Roman Catholic Church. Those who were more convinced it was happening considered it a hope for the future, because it might cause their congregations to be less "over-against" and more pro-active in joining Roman Catholics in ventures of justice, without a sense of betrayal of their forebears.

The reason for these questions about both other Protestant groups and Catholics was not apparent to some, until it came time for the interviews. During interviews, these pastors said the way they could see a future for their congregation was by "reviving" it, but it was not hard to perceive they had in mind a slightly updated version of the recent sectarian past. Those who were aware that the sectarian past has been preempted by Baptists and Pentecostals and by the Catholic renewal were hard-pressed to articulate what kind of future awaits their ministry. But they had the capacity to express a firm hope and willingness to let the Spirit of God reshape their ministry in the light of a rich legacy from the sectarian past and the promise of the new situation. By the new situation they meant principally that Hispanic churches of mainline Protestantism have a new degree of self-determination at a time when being bilingual and multicultural is no longer an oddity in this nation, but rather the future of millions.

Meanwhile, practically all the pastors I interviewed recently and many of those whom I have consulted through the years, retain a strong confidence that what is peculiarly Protestant and peculiarly Hispanic in Hispanic Protestantism is invaluable to shaping Christian faith and life. Again, they are thinking of a "new situation" in which the ethnic and religious community is no longer invisible to the national and religious mainstream, and in which Hispanics are being recognized more and more for outstanding contributions in practically every sphere of American society.

I am left with the impression that even though it is difficult at this time for Hispanic Protestant pastors to articulate clearly what is the singular contribution that Hispanic churches of Protestant denominations can make in the future, the pastors with whom I have talked see themselves as carriers of a gospel way of life that merits renewed commitment. They know that their way of life has withstood neglect, marginality, prejudice, poverty, injustice, and the wrongheaded forecasts of friends and enemies.

In the end, the Hispanic Protestant way of life inherited from forebears is reliable because at the same time that it has proclaimed Good News, it has also practiced compassion and built lives of extraordinary usefulness. Surely, what these pastors are saying is, "Don't hold us to the words, hold us to the deeds."

Chapter 14

Hispanic Protestant Clergy:
A Profile of Experience and Perspectives

David Maldonado, Jr.

Introduction

Little is known about the Hispanic population within mainline Protestant denominations, due to the limited research conducted on this population. Latinos are generally overlooked or briefly touched upon in studies of U.S. Protestant populations. Likewise, when Hispanic religious life is examined, Protestants are commonly overlooked. Studies of Hispanic Protestant clergy are even more rare. Very little is known about this population of religious leaders. No denominational studies on Hispanic Protestant clergy are known to exist. Thus, basic information about Hispanic clergy within historical Protestant denominations is extremely limited and important questions have never been asked. For example, what is a basic profile of this population? What do we know about the ethnicity, religious orientations, and sociopolitical perspectives of Hispanic Protestant clergy? What has been its experience in ministry and how are important issues for the Hispanic church and community perceived? Few efforts have been made to collect basic information on this group on a systematic and multidenominational level. As a result, denominational policy and planning, ministerial recruitment, and theological education have often been based on impressions, stereotypes, and personal observation. This chapter intends to present an initial introduction to the profile, experience, and perspectives reflected among Hispanic clergy within mainline or "old-line" Protestant denominations in the United States.

Several Protestant denominations cooperated in a national survey. These included the United Methodist Church, the Disciples of Christ, the Presbyterian Church (U.S.A.), and the Lutheran Evangelical Church of America. These denominations provided mailing lists of Hispanic pastors and clergy members for the purpose of surveying this population. Nearly 300 clergy, approximately one-third, responded. Survey instruments in both English and Spanish were mailed to all persons on the lists provided by the denominations.

A Profile

The purpose of a profile is to provide a sense of what a particular population is like in order to better understand that group. However, such a profile is always risky. It could easily generate new stereotypes or perpetuate old ones. This chapter is written with these concerns in mind. It does not claim to present an exhaustive profile. It only claims to report the responses of those who chose to participate in this study. Yet, it does represent a significant first step in the collection of broad-based data on selected areas of interest regarding Hispanic clergy within old-line Protestant denominations.

Immigration. Although the Hispanic population has historical roots within the continental United States predating the arrival of the pilgrims on the East coast, in recent years it has been associated with significant immigration from Mexico, Central America, South America, and other Caribbean countries. In addition, Puerto Ricans have continued their long-established migratory patterns. For a number of years, Mexican Americans in the Southwest and Puerto Ricans in the Northeast constituted the bulk of the Hispanic population. However, the Cuban revolution caused a large number of Cubans to relocate in the United States, especially in southern Florida. More recent political struggles in Central America added another layer of immigrants in Florida, California, and throughout the nation. Likewise, recent economic difficulties in Mexico have resulted in increased migration into the United States. As a result of such immigration and high fertility rates, the Hispanic population has emerged as a significant U.S. population with an increased diversity from various national origins. Needless to say, internal migration within the United States has occurred. Large concentrations can be found in most major urban areas throughout the United States.

The question is whether the Hispanic clergy reflects the immigration and diversity of the Hispanic population as a whole. If it does, the clergy would be composed of a significant number of immigrants and a broad range of national origins. The data indicates that, indeed, 59% of the respondents were born outside the mainland United States. This is a significant percentage, and a higher proportion of foreign birth is apparent among Protestant clergy than in the Hispanic population as a whole. In addition, this sample of clergy reports a higher percentage of foreign-born parents—59% indicating that their mothers were foreign-born and 62% reporting that their fathers were foreign-born. What this suggests is that members of Hispanic Protestant clergy have close, personal ties with immigration. They are immigrants themselves, or are children of immigrants. This raises important questions about cultural formation, acculturation into the life of the United States, political perspectives, attitudes toward immigration, and readiness to lead congregations within the context of living in the United States.

With regard to the nativity of those not born within the United States mainland, this sample represented traditional places of origin: Puerto Rico, Mexico, and Cuba, and to a lesser extent, other Latin American nations. Clearly, Puerto Ricans composed the largest group born outside the U.S. mainland with 32.2%, and Mexicans were next with 22.1%. The third largest group of foreign-born clergy were Cubans with 15.3%, and the fourth Central Americans, who composed 11.3% of the foreign-born among the clergy. The rest (19%) were born in other Latin American or Caribbean countries. Of these, Colombia was the largest with 5.6%. These numbers suggest that Hispanic clergy come from the native countries of the main Hispanic populations, and that they also represent the diversification of the population as a whole. However, their diversity does present one important variation. Although the Mexican American population is the largest Hispanic population in the United States, they are not the largest among the foreign-born clergy. One explanation may be that it is easier for Puerto Rican pastors to migrate to the United States than it is for Mexican pastors. Another possibility might be the higher percentage of Protestants in Puerto Rico and that the theological education (M.Div.) available in Puerto Rico is recognized by church structures in the United States, while theological education in Mexico and other Latin American nations may not have the same recognition.

Race and Ethnicity. Closely related to nativity and foreign birth, but not identical, is the question of race and ethnicity. Ethnic identity and race have long been significant in the United States because they influence social status, social mobility, economic opportunities, and other crucial aspects of life in this country. For people of color, race and ethnicity have long been associated with "minority" status and marginal treatment. In this country, Hispanics have been defined as ethnically different from the dominant population and thus subject to the many social and economic consequences of minority status. Race and ethnicity affect external perception and treatment, but also internal or self-identity. They are factors influencing self-understanding at the individual and group levels. Thus, race and ethnicity are serious considerations and are the subject of much discussion and debate. Debate includes questions of naming, ethnic identity maintenance, and acculturation.

Ethnicity can be defined as the shared sense of peoplehood usually associated with a common national origin, history, language, and culture.

Race refers to biologically determined physiological characteristics which also are shared. The two are separate and distinct categories. Sometimes, however, they are combined. In this country, for example, Hispanic populations are described as white populations of Hispanic origins. However, some Hispanics also reflect African origins. Racially, Hispanics tend to be *mestizo* or a blending of peoples. Among Mexicans, Mexican Americans, Central Americans, and many South Americans, *mestizaje* refers to the blending of native peoples with Spanish or European stock; among the Caribbean populations there is also a mixture of African heritage. This blending is commonly referred to as *mulatez*.

The sample of the clergy surveyed provides interesting information about racial identity among the clergy. With regard to racial identification, 43.5% identify themselves as white, 30.4% as mestizo, 8.8% as Indio (native), 3.2% as mulatto, 2.1% as black, and the rest (12%) as "other." These responses suggest that the largest number identify themselves as white, consistent with the practice and racial attitudes in the United States. Next are the blended identities (mestizo and mulatto combined), reflective of the blending which has actually occurred in the hemisphere. The racial identity with the lowest selection rate is black identity.

Sociologists have established that Hispanics tend to identify more strongly with nations of origin than with race, or with terms such as "Hispanic" or "Latino," which have been popularized as umbrella terms to include all Hispanics. This means, for example, that a Puerto Rican Hispanic would identify first with being a Puerto Rican, and second, as a Latino or Hispanic. Responding to the question of heritage in the survey, 61.9% identified with their nation of origin. The rest (38.1%) chose a cluster term, such as Hispanic, Latino, and so on. Again, this is consistent with other studies of the Hispanic population.

However, when asked for their identity with the terms "Latino" and "Hispanic," 77.6% indicated strong identification with the term Hispanic, while 53.5% identified with the term "Latino." Apparently, the term Hispanic is more acceptable among this group of religious leaders when there is the need to use an umbrella term.

The question of the ethnic breakdown of the clergy is more difficult to assess. This is due to the selection of Hispanic or Latino by 38% of the sample. However, of those who did select a specific Spanish heritage identity, 45% were of Mexican heritage, 42% Puerto Rican, and 12% of Cuban heritage.

Language. The question of language is an important issue for Hispanics. In a context in which Spanish is a strong cultural symbol and element, immigration a significant experience, and acculturation a social reality, the question of language is paramount for issues related to ministry. The clergy must speak the languages of the people—Spanish and English. They must speak Spanish well if they are to lead a congregation of Spanish-speaking people and to reach out to immigrants. The clergy must also be able to communicate with the English-speaking segments of the congregation. These include many of the youth and acculturated adults. It is also important that pastors speak the language of the broader context, in this case English. Hispanic pastors should be able to understand and engage in dialogue with the general culture. Thus one question asks about the language capabilities of the clergy in both Spanish and English. Not surprisingly, 92.9% of the respondents reported "good" to "excellent" Spanish-speaking ability. Less than 3% had difficulties with Spanish. It is clear that Spanish language capability is a strong characteristic among Hispanic clergy. But what about their English capabilities? A strong proportion (78.9%) reported good to excellent English skills. Only 3.7% reported poor English-speaking capability and less than 3% could read only Spanish. These numbers suggest that the Hispanic clergy perceive themselves as well equipped linguistically for Hispanic ministry in this context. They possess the necessary language skills for both the internal and external needs of the Hispanic church.

Education. The question of education is an important one, indicating the level of formal training and preparation the clergy have for ministry. Of special importance is the question of theological education. One of the chief characteristics of old-line Protestant denominations is the educational requirements for ministry. Because Hispanic clergy are expected to meet all such requirements, it is anticipated that the Hispanic clergy will be a well-educated group. The responses to the survey indicate that this is the case. Eighty-five percent of the respondents had completed all or part of their education in the United States. Well over half of these clergy had graduate theological degrees or were pursuing such a degree. Thirty-five had earned doctor of ministry degrees and 14 had earned Ph.D.'s. This data suggests that Hispanic clergy within old-line Protestant traditions are well educated, reflecting an educational profile much higher than that of the general Hispanic population.

Employment and Income. Because of their high educational attainment it could be expected that Hispanic clergy would also reflect higher income levels. Again, such is the case. Over 21% had yearly incomes in excess of $50,000 and 42.1% had annual incomes between $30,000 and $49,999. Only 8.8% earned less than $15,000. This can partly be explained by the fact that 8.1% of the sample were retired pastors. With regard to employment, Hispanic pastors are generally full-time church employees. Nearly 82% of the sample were employed full-time in the church. Nonetheless, 6% were employed full-time in a secular job and nearly 10% held part-time secular jobs. Overall, Hispanic clergy seem to earn more than what is typical for most Hispanics. Hispanic clergy of the old-line Protestant denominations are middle class.

Personal Profile: Gender, Age, and Household Size. Of the 298 respondents, 35 or 11.8% were women. Clearly this does not represent the gender distribution of the Hispanic population. What is not known is whether this gender ratio among the clergy is significantly different from that of other populations. In terms of marital status, 74.5% of the total sample were married to their first spouse, and 14.1% were remarried. This means that 88.6% of this sample were married. Almost 4% had never married, and 4.4% were single due to death or divorce. Ninety-one percent were parents and 70% still had children living at home. Forty-nine percent had one or two children living at home and only 6.9% had four or more children still living at home. Twenty percent housed other persons in addition to their children.

Overview. This profile suggests that old-line Protestant Hispanic clergy tend to be well educated, bilingual persons with close ties to immigration. Those who were born abroad come from the traditional countries of origin for the U.S. Hispanic population, but there is higher proportion of Puerto Ricans. These clergy identify strongly with their native lands and also with the term "Hispanic." They received part of their education in the United Sates and earn middle-class incomes. They tend to be married and have relatively few children still living at home. An important observation is that women are significantly underrepresented in this population.

Ministry and Religious Profiles

Questions concerning the ministry, religious profile, and orientation of the Hispanic clergy address issues of religious beliefs and perspectives, as well as religious experiences and backgrounds. What do we know about the Hispanic clergy within old-line traditions with regard to their religiosity and religious worldviews? What is their religious heritage and how do they view other religious traditions? These questions are important in that they reflect the religious orientations of the ministerial leadership of Hispanic Protestant churches and may well shape the views and theology offered. Thus, it is important to explore such aspects of the Hispanic clergy; understanding the clergy may help us understand the broader Hispanic church. These pastors, as congregational and religious leaders, play crucial roles in shaping, forming, and educating the Hispanic church. Likewise, they represent the church in the community and within the life and structures of the denomination. Their religious attitudes, perceptions, experiences, and understandings influence the church through preaching, teaching, counseling, administrative leadership, and modeling. What has been the religious experience of these persons? What are their religious orientations and attitudes toward other churches within the Hispanic community, such as the Catholic church and the Pentecostal churches? How do they feel toward ecumenical concerns? These and other questions will be explored in order to gain a better understanding of these religious leaders.

Experiences in Ministry. Slightly fewer than half (45%) of the respondents had other careers prior to entering the ministry. Of these, two-thirds were in professions or white-collar employment. This means that more than half understand ministry as being their lifelong profession. Over 30% have been in ministry more than twenty-five years, and 28% ten years or less. Over half (58%) have been in ministry less than twenty years. These figures suggest a healthy distribution of service and experience in ministry. When combined with the age distribution, the Hispanic clergy reflects a balanced distribution of age and experience.

Interestingly, among this sample of Hispanic clergy, 17.6% were ordained in a denomination other than the one with which they are presently affiliated. In addition, 25.6% have been employed by another denomination in the past. These figures suggest that among the Hispanic clergy within old-line denominations, relationships with other denominations are not uncommon. It also suggests flexibility in doctrine.

The current ministerial role of these members of the clergy is primarily pastoral. Close to three-fourths (74%) are presently serving as pastors; slightly more than 4% are associate pastors. Apparently, the vast majority find their work as clergy satisfying (43%) or highly satisfying (53.1%). Only 1.7% find the work unsatisfying. In addition, two-thirds feel extremely close to God (66.3%) and one-third (32%) somewhat close to God. Only 1.6% described their situation as not feeling close to God. These figures suggest that Hispanic clergy are quite satisfied with their work and feel close to God.

Religious Background. The majority of Hispanic Protestant clergy within old-line traditions are rooted in Protestant traditions, yet, an important proportion have Roman Catholic roots. For example, 32.8% indicated that their fathers were Catholic and 27.2% reported that their mothers were Catholic. Nineteen percent indicated that they themselves had been

Catholic at one time. Thus between one-fifth and one-third had either been Catholic or had Catholic parents. This suggests that they were reared in Catholic homes. On the other hand, it also indicates that between four-fifths to two-thirds were reared in Protestant homes. The majority are not converts to Protestantism, but have been lifelong Protestants.

Denominational Affiliations: Past and Present. An interesting characteristic of the Hispanic clergy seems to be that they have experienced changes in denominational affiliation. Approximately 47% have apparently held membership in another Protestant denomination in the past. Among the most significant previous Protestant affiliations are the United Methodist (12.3%), Reformed (9.2%), Presbyterian (7.4%), American Baptist (6.7%), and the Lutheran (Missouri Synod) (6.7%) churches. This suggests that there is significant denominational movement among those who become Protestant clergy both from Catholic to Protestant and among different Protestant denominations. There seems to be greater movement among Protestant denominations.

A related and important question concerns age at the time of changing denominations. This question was asked in terms of when they joined their current denomination. It is important because it can provide insight into denominational identity and formation. Approximately 19% had joined their current denomination by the age of 10. Half had joined by age 18, and 75% had joined by the time they were 29 years old. This means that half joined their current denomination when they were young adults and 25% joined at the age of 30 and later. In fact, 10% joined their current denominations at 39 years of age or later. These findings suggest that denominational changes are experienced throughout middle age. They hold important implications for training and orientation in denomination-al history, doctrine, polity, and identity.

The findings also suggest that among Hispanic Protestants, denomina-tional boundaries among Protestant churches are not considered very important, especially among the old-line denominations, or at least they are not formidable barriers to movement. Hispanic Protestants do not find it problematic to move among the various Protestant denominations. Although data is not available on the movement from Protestant to Catholic, it is suggested here that "Protestant" identity may be stronger than denominational identity. Finally, if the clergy are able to change denominations without much problem, it might follow that an equal or larger movement might occur among the laity.

Religious Orientation. The religious orientation of Hispanics has been the topic of many informal conversations, especially in light of the growth of evangelical-conservative churches and the gradual decline of mainline churches. Some suggest that Hispanic Protestants are theologically conservative and thus more in tune with evangelical-conservative churches than with their own denominations, which tend to be moderate to liberal in their orientation. The respondents in this study provide us with an interesting profile. Approximately 52% identify their orientation as "moderate." However, when subdivided, the moderate-to-very-liberal group constitutes 70.8% of the sample, while the moderate-to-very conservative constitutes 81.1%. Slightly more than 25% consider themselves conservative, and 16.5% see themselves as liberal. Only 2.4% view themselves as very liberal and 3.8% very conservative. Overall, there is a slight leaning toward moderate-conservative; however, it is questionable whether moderates and conservatives would identify with each other. It might be that moderates and liberals are more likely to identify with each other than are the moderates and conservatives. It is probably more helpful to describe the Hispanic Protestant clergy as moderate with a conservative tilt.

Religious Opinions. The question of religious and theological orientations involves questions about specific beliefs and understandings about key religious questions and issues. Two of these relate to the understanding of the Bible. Is it understood as God's literal word, as the inspired word of God, as a historical book, or as a human expression of faith? Are specific biblical stories accepted as literally true? The dominant response (69.6%) of this sample of Hispanic clergy was an understanding of the Bible as a book written by people inspired by God, but containing human and historical dimensions. Slightly more than 26% held a literal understanding of the Bible. When asked whether God created the world in six 24-hour days, 47.6% responded definitely not, 6.6% said they leaned toward not, and 5.5% said they were not sure. Only 24.8% said definitely yes. This specific question indicates a more liberal understanding of the Bible and its contents.

Questions relating to theological interpretation are also helpful in understanding the Hispanic Protestant clergy. When asked about the extent of their agreement with the statement that Jesus will come back and take the righteous to heaven, more than 75% definitely agreed. This is a strong level of agreement with a statement generally considered theologically conservative. More than 86% also strongly agreed that the Ten Commandments still apply. Slightly more than 77% disagreed that all religions are equally true, suggesting a low level of openness toward other religions. Combined, these responses suggest that though the Hispanic clergy tend to hold a liberal understanding of the Bible, they lean toward the more conservative theologically.

Hispanic Theology. The theological field has witnessed an energetic emergence of Hispanic theology within both Catholic and Protestant traditions during the last decade. Of special interest is the production of Hispanic theology in the context of the United States. Although Latin American theology has had a global impact including the United States for a number of years, U.S. Hispanic theology is more recent and particular to the life situation of Hispanics within the U.S. Such theology addresses the realities of daily life, religious experience, and faith of Hispanics within the U.S. The assumption is that life within the United States is quite different from life in a Latin American country. The Hispanic experience within the U.S. includes social marginality, racism, and acculturation. In the study, the question concerned the attitudes of Hispanic Protestant clergy toward such theologies. How do they view Latin American theologies of liberation and U.S. Hispanic theology? Are the clergy familiar with this theology? Do they read it? What attitudes can be identified?

A strong majority (71.7%) of the respondents agreed or strongly agreed that it was important to develop Hispanic theology. Only 15.5% responded in the negative. With regard to whether they read Hispanic theology, 40.3% described themselves as active readers, and another 53.6% said they were occasional readers. This means that 93.9% have read or are readers of Hispanic theology. Six percent said that they never read such theology.

The question remaining is whether these clergy view liberation theology as appropriate for Hispanics in the United States. Liberation theology is the product of the Latin American context, and especially of Catholic theologians. The responses reflect a stronger distribution. While 31.9% agreed or strongly agreed, 41% disagreed or strongly disagreed. Slightly more than 27% were not sure. This reflects a wide-ranging opinion among Hispanic Protestant clergy on the appropriateness of liberation theology. While there is definitely a group that sees the usefulness of such theology in the U.S. context, there remains a large group that disagrees or is not sure. These responses reflect a clear interest in Hispanic theologies, which reflect the U.S. context, and a continuing debate on Latin American liberation theologies.

Attitudes Toward the Catholic Church. Most Hispanic Protestants have had significant experiences because of their ethnicity and Protestant identity. They are Protestants in cultures historically associated with Roman Catholicism. Hispanic cultures are deeply imbued with Catholic symbols, meanings, and events. Hispanic Protestants have been unavoidably influenced by Catholicism in one way or another, including family, friendships, and daily life, and these experiences have not always been positive. To be Protestant in a Hispanic context is to be different and to some extent in tension or conflict with Catholic identity and the accepted way of life in the Hispanic environment. Many Hispanics have paid a heavy price to become Protestant. Doing so may have involved loss of friendships, splits in families, and social marginalization.

At the root of such negative experiences is the religious conflict and competition between Catholics and Protestants. Strong anti-Catholic and anti-Protestant feelings have been openly expressed and manifested in this country as well as in Latin America. Such sentiments and activity continue in many places. An important question is the extent to which such attitudes are present among the Hispanic Protestant clergy. How do they view the Catholic church and relations between the two traditions? Attitudes toward the Catholic church have important implications for ministry within the Hispanic community, especially in developing appropriate strategies and goals for Protestant Hispanic ministries.

A high proportion (over 73%) of Hispanic Protestant clergy agree that Catholics and Protestants have many things in common. Another 73% agree or strongly agree that Catholics are as Christian as Protestants. More than 73% agree or strongly agree that some Catholic practices (liturgies) from the Catholic tradition can be used in the Protestant traditions. More than half (53.6%) agree that Catholics and Protestants are working toward the same goals. Such a high percentage of agreement with statements which articulate commonalities between Catholicism and Protestantism suggests an openness among these Hispanic clergy toward Catholics.

With regard to the existence of anti-Protestant and anti-Catholic attitudes, there is some diversity of opinion. The largest percentage is among those who do not perceive anti-Catholic (46.9%) and anti-Protestant (44.1%) attitudes, while half as many believe that there are anti-Catholic (24.6%) and anti-Protestant (23.1%) sentiments. It is interesting to note that 32.8% are not sure whether there are any anti-Protestant attitudes among Catholics, and 28.5% are not sure whether there are anti-Catholic attitudes among Protestants. If those "not sure" responses are combined with those who see no negative attitudes between the two religious populations, the overall impression is very positive about Catholic-Protestant attitudes.

However, there are some reservations reflected in the responses. Two-thirds agree that it does matter whether one is Catholic or Protestant. More than 56% do not believe that Catholics and Protestants are becoming more alike. Attitudes toward the Virgin Mary of Guadalupe, a dominant Catholic symbol among Hispanic Catholics, also indicate reservations. More than 55% do not see her as an important symbol, and more than 83% do not recognize the Virgin to have any special powers.

Attitudes Toward Pentecostal Churches. The energetic growth of Pentecostal churches among Hispanics in the United States has brought a new element into Hispanic religious life. Although Hispanic Protestantism originated in relationship to historical Protestant denominations, such as the Methodists and Presbyterians, recent growth has been observed or perceived to be strongest among the Pentecostal groups. In fact, some might suggest that Hispanic Protestant churches associated with old-line denominations have reached a plateau, while the Pentecostals have taken the lead in church growth. An important question asked about the attitudes of mainline Protestant Hispanic pastors toward Pentecostals. What perceptions are held toward this movement? Are Pentecostals viewed in the same vein as other Protestant churches? What differences are perceived? How can these be understood? What implications can be drawn?

Because well over half (62.5%) agreed that Hispanic Protestants are more similar to one another than they are to Anglos within their own traditions, we might expect that mainline clergy would find much similarity with Hispanic Pentecostals. However, more than half (57%) of the clergy responding indicated that they disagreed or strongly disagreed with the statement that their denominations were similar to the Pentecostals. Slightly more than a fourth (26%) perceived Pentecostals and their own denominations to be similar. This suggests that the majority of Latino Protestant clergy within old-line denominations perceive Pentecostals as different and distinct from their own Protestant traditions. Could it be that the similarities are perceived to exist primarily among mainline denominations and not necessarily between them and Pentecostals?

In exploring attitudes toward Pentecostalism further, the question was asked whether Pentecostalism misleads people. While 41.8% responded in the negative, well over half (58.2%) were not sure or agreed. Slightly more than 29% were not sure that Pentecostalism misled people, and slightly more than 28% agreed that Pentecostalism did mislead people.

Attitudes were also examined in regard to the form of worship among Pentecostal churches. Is it perceived as a good model of worship? Half (50.1%) disagreed that Pentecostalism offered a good model of worship, while only one fourth (24.2%) agreed. Another fourth (25.6%) were not sure whether it was a good model or not. It can be deduced that approximately 75% could not affirm that Pentecostalism offered a good model of worship.

On a positive note, mainline Hispanic clergy seem to perceive outreach efforts among Pentecostals as better than those among old-line denominations. Slightly more than 75% agreed or strongly agreed that Pentecostals have better outreach than their own traditions.

All of this suggests that Hispanic clergy within old-line traditions are cautious and do not agree with several aspects of Pentecostalism. It questions the popular notion that Hispanic Protestants share a strong sense of commonality. Pentecostals are perceived as different, not offering an appropriate model of worship, and possibly misleading people. However, Pentecostals are recognized for their effective outreach.

Ecumenism. The foregoing discussions raise the question of ecumenism. How aware of are the Hispanic clergy and how important to them are ecumenical relations and participation? Most (87.5%) reported knowledge of some form of ecumenical or ministerial alliance in their communities, including more than one-third (35.9%) who were aware of a Hispanic ministerial alliance. One-fourth (26.1%) indicated that they participated in a Hispanic ministerial alliance and two-thirds (67.4%) reported involvement in some form of ecumenical or ministerial organization. When asked about the importance of ecumenical activities, a large majority (85.3%) responded positively and only 7.5% said they were not important. With regard to supporting such activities, 87.5% indicated that they supported ecumenical activities. These responses suggest that Hispanic Protestant clergy are ecumenically minded and supportive of such activities.

With regard to areas in which they see significant differences among Hispanic Protestant denominations, the following order ranks differences in descending order, with the first being the most significant: (1) theology, (2) worship, (3) socio-economic class, and ecclesiastical structures, and (4) acculturation. This suggests that theology and styles of worship are important to Hispanic clergy and are considered significant differences among the various Protestant denominations. On the other hand, differences in such matters as socioeconomic class and acculturation are not given much importance.

Attitudes Toward Folk Beliefs and Practices. Among most of the Hispanic ethnic groups, several folk practices and beliefs can be identified as quasireligious in nature. Many of these are related to medicine and to some Catholic symbols and traditions; some suggest that they are also grounded in African or indigenous cultures. Nonetheless, they have become important or at least common among Hispanic populations. These include *curanderismo,* especially among the Mexican heritage populations, and "spiritualists" among other Latino populations. When asked whether it was appropriate for Christians to consult a curandero, 89.4% said no. Another 96.6% also said that Christians should not consult a spiritualist. When asked whether they themselves had ever consulted a curandero, only 3.4% reported they had done so. These responses suggest that Hispanic clergy are not sympathetic to folk practices or beliefs such as curanderismo.

Issues in Ministry and the Church

The memberships and neighborhoods of most Hispanic congregations reflect a broad range of cultural manifestations. They may include immigrants who just arrived last week, and persons whose roots in this country go back for many generations including the period prior to annexation. The Hispanic church and community most likely reflect many levels of acculturation and cultural profiles. In addition, many of its families reflect important cultural differences between generations. Some congregations may even include persons from different Hispanic origins, customs, and traditions. Such internal and environmental diversity can lead to many linguistic and cultural issues. These issues are simply a function of being a Hispanic congregation in a Hispanic community. Not surprisingly, Hispanic congregations wrestle with cultural questions such as language. What language shall be used in a congregation in which members range from monolingual English speakers to monolingual Spanish speakers? Is bilingualism a useful option? What language should it use in worship, Christian education, church literature?

Of special concern is the question of language and the ability of the Hispanic church to attract and keep certain constituencies. How does language influence the youth and immigrants? Is bilingualism viewed as an attraction or a barrier? Of special concern is the impact of acculturation on the youth and their relationship to the church. How do the clergy view acculturation and its impact on the church?

Acculturation, Ethnic Identity, and the Church. Acculturation refers to the process in which a smaller or immigrant population assimilates into the culture of the host and dominant population. It involves taking on cultural elements such as language, religion, worldviews, and values. As immigrants with cultures different from the culture of the dominant population, Hispanics have experienced acculturation in varying degrees and ways. Most acculturation occurs through normal structures of socialization such as educational systems, the mass media, and other aspects of social life. It is a natural and unavoidable process. As might be expected, acculturation varies along generational lines, reflecting different exposures to systems of acculturation depending on age group. Thus, adult immigrants can generally be expected to reflect lower levels of acculturation while younger generations, especially those born in the U. S. or who immigrated as infants and were thus educated in this country, reflect higher levels of acculturation. For example, it can be expected that Spanish is spoken and preferred by adults while English might be the language of the young. Such differences in acculturation can be very challenging to Hispanic congregations. What language will be used in worship, church school, and in the general life of the church? Can the pastor speak both languages? What attitudes exist toward acculturation in general and with regard to language in particular?

Of particular importance are the attitudes and opinions held by Hispanic clergy toward acculturation itself. Do they view it as natural and thus acceptable? Is acculturation viewed as a problem for Hispanics and the church in particular? More than half (55.3%) of the respondents seem to perceive acculturation as inevitable. One-fourth do not see it as inevitable. When asked whether the acculturation of Latinos into Anglo culture is good, one-fourth (25.4%) agreed or strongly agreed, while 44.4% disagreed or strongly disagreed. Slightly more than 30% were not sure. These responses suggest that Hispanic clergy see acculturation as inevitable, but hold reservations about it and tend to lean toward a negative perspective with regard to its desirability for Hispanics. Such attitudes may hold implications for their openness toward activities in the church that might reflect acculturation processes. For example, how open would a pastor be to bilingual worship services?

An important aspect of acculturation is that of ethnic identity. Ethnic self-identity is maintained as long as there is a sense of difference. When those differences are eliminated, an acculturated person takes on the identity of the host population. This would mean that as Hispanics become acculturated they tend to lose their ethnic sense of identity as Hispanics. When the clergy were asked whether Hispanics should maintain their sense of ethnic self-identity, 86.8% answered in the affirmative, while only 5.1% indicated that Hispanics ought not to maintain their ethnic identity. Implications of this finding include concerns for the ethnic identification of the congregation as a whole and the manner in which the ministry of the church supports or promotes the ethnic identity of the members.

It is reasonable to question why Hispanic clergy would hold reservations about acculturation and ethnic identity. Do they see it affecting the life of the church? how? When asked whether acculturation had changed the sense of ethnic identity of Hispanic congregations, more than half (55.4%) indicated that it had done so. Twenty-three percent were not certain and 20.7% said that acculturation had not affected the church's ethnic identity. These responses suggest that pastors have observed acculturation within their congregations and that it has influenced the church's ethnic self-understanding.

Worship: Bilingualism and the Use of Spanish. Worship holds a central and special place in the life of a congregation. It is a corporate event in which the people celebrate, affirm, and articulate their faith and religious experience. It is an act of affirmation of God and God's presence in their lives. It reflects the lives and experience of the people. This suggests that worship is closely connected to the self-understanding of the worshipers and perceptions of their experience. More concretely, worship in a Hispanic church reflects the Hispanic people, their religious faith and religious experience. This involves their symbols, language, and culture. How does this apply when a people reflect various levels and forms of acculturation?

An important question concerns consequences of acculturation in the life of the church and its ministry. When asked whether acculturation had changed the worship style of their congregations, 55.4% indicated that it had done so. Twenty-two percent said no, and another 22% were not sure. Although the clergy might hold reservations about acculturation, it is their observation that Hispanic congregations have been affected by the realities of acculturation.

When asked whether their congregations worshiped bilingually, 36.2% said never, and 18.4% indicated that they do so all of the time. The largest group (45.4%) reported that they worshiped bilingually some of the time. These responses suggest that 63.8% of the congregations represented by these clergy celebrate worship bilingually either all the time or some of the time. This confirms the impression of the clergy that acculturation is having an impact on Hispanic congregations. By the same token, it also suggests that Hispanic congregations are responding to the realities of acculturation among members.

An important question concerns the impact that bilingual worship might have on key segments of the congregation such as the youth, who may be limited in Spanish, and the immigrants, who may be limited in English skills. The question is, Do the clergy believe that bilingual worship services alienate Hispanic youth and immigrants? The responses suggest that there is significant concern among the clergy. Nearly two in five (39.7%) believe that bilingual services alienate immigrants and 35.2% think that they alienate the youth. On the other hand, 44.7% disagree that they alienate youth and 34.2% disagree that they alienate the immigrant. It seems that a larger proportion believe that bilingualism will alienate immigrants more than youth.

It is interesting to note that when asked directly if worship should be totally in Spanish, 44.9% disagreed, but nearly 40% agreed. This suggests that Hispanic clergy do not agree on the question of bilingualism in worship or its impact on some segments of the congregation.

A related question concerns the use of other Hispanic cultural elements in addition to the Spanish language. For example, are Latino rhythms and sounds appropriate for the Hispanic Protestant church? To what extent is the liturgy and music used in the church of Hispanic origin? A large proportion (89.2%) agreed or strongly agreed that Latino rhythms are proper for the church. Only 3.7% disagreed. When asked the extent to which the liturgy in their churches was of Hispanic origin, 44.1% reported that it was all or mostly Hispanic in origin. An additional 23.8% reported an equal mix of Hispanic and non-Hispanic origins. Nonetheless, 32% indicated that their worship services were either all or mostly non-Hispanic.

What about the question of language in other aspects of the life of the church such as Christian education? Responses were split with regard to the question of the language of Christian education material. Thirty-two percent indicated that their material was in English and 29% reported their material to be in Spanish. Thirty-eight percent described their material as bilingual.

What about the theology of the church? Acculturation involves changes and adaptations in worldviews, values, and myth. Does acculturation also influence the theology of the Hispanic church? Forty-six percent believed that it did, while nearly 30% did not believe that acculturation influenced the theology of the church. These responses suggest that Hispanic congregations are perceived by the clergy to reflect a broad range of theological perspectives associated with levels of acculturation. The connections between acculturation and theological perspectives remain unclear to Hispanic clergy.

Although acculturation is perceived as inevitable, there is concern about its impact on the church. The clergy are concerned about the loss of ethnic identity, especially as a congregation. They have observed that acculturation carries significant consequences for the church, including its worship, and are not in agreement as to the direction the church ought to go. Much research, experimentation, discussion, and reflection still must be done.

Reading the Bible in Spanish. Language is not simply a functional tool for the purpose of communication. It is also a cultural element, connecting people within cultural and ethnic groups. Language takes on meanings beyond the utilitarian. Language becomes an ethnic symbol, a distinguishing factor, a defended cultural right, and as such, it has special value. Its use in the religious life of a community can also have special meanings and value. Because religion reflects and speaks to the human experience of a people, their language becomes a principal means of articulating their religious experience and faith. It is thus not surprising that reading the

Bible in Spanish is an important cultural, congregational, and theological issue among Hispanics.

When asked whether reading the Bible in Spanish was important, a large majority responded in the affirmative. More than 88% agreed or strongly agreed that it was important to read the Bible in Spanish. Only 5.4% disagreed. But why do they believe that reading the Bible in Spanish is important? The possible responses varied. The two most popular responses were that reading the Bible in Spanish produces special insights (32.3%) and that it provides cultural affirmation (28.1%). The first reflects the significance of the language of the people to articulate and reflect their religious experience and faith. The second affirms the experience of the people as a people. The next two popular responses tend to reflect other cultural reasons. Slightly more than 11.2% indicated that it was important for reasons of tradition, and 10.4% believed that by doing so, it preserved the language. Another 9.6% indicated that it was important to read the Bible in Spanish because it was a symbol of ethnic identity. The smallest proportion of responses identified the value of reading the Bible in Spanish as a way to enhance spiritual life. This information suggests that reading the Bible in Spanish is important for the clergy primarily because of its connection to Hispanic cultures and its value for understanding and articulating the religious experience and faith of the people.

Acculturation and Hispanic Youth. A continuing debate is the impact of acculturation on the younger generation and the challenges it presents to the Hispanic church. There are those who are concerned that acculturation is affecting the involvement of the youth in the life of the church. As the youth become acculturated, able to speak more English and less Spanish, it is expected that they will leave the Hispanic church and join an Anglo church or drop out altogether from any church participation. More than half (54.9%) of the clergy believed that as Hispanic youth acculturate into the larger culture, they become less involved in Hispanic churches. Twenty-seven percent were not certain, and 25.4% disagreed. Whether in fact acculturated Hispanic youth are less involved or not in the Hispanic church, there is a sizable proportion of clergy who believe that is the case.

Part of the debate is whether acculturated Hispanic youth are moving on to Anglo churches or whether they are dropping out of church involvement altogether. Slightly more than half (51.5%) of the clergy believe that the youth are going to Anglo churches. One-fourth do not believe that this is the case, and 22.7% are not sure. When asked separately whether Hispanic youth become increasingly unchurched as they acculturate, 45.5% agreed. Approximately one-fourth disagreed. Slightly more than 29% are not certain about this question. These responses suggest that a significant proportion of the Hispanic clergy feel that the Hispanic church is losing its youth as a consequence of acculturation. The youth are either going to Anglo churches or are not attending any church. Yet, a fourth of the sample seems consistently to disagree that the Hispanic church is losing its youth.

Immigrants and the Church. Although Hispanics have been present in the land now known as the United States for many generations, including years before the pilgrims arrived, Hispanic populations have been associated historically and more recently with immigrant populations from Latin America. An important question is the reception that newer Hispanic immigrants are receiving in Hispanic churches. Are immigrants being received and made comfortable in these Latino churches? Are there any apparent issues or concerns? A large proportion (71.2%) of the respondents indicated that their churches welcome immigrants. Only 12.3% said that their churches did not welcome such persons. In fact, 61.9% reported they had recent immigrants in their congregations. However, it is interesting to note that fewer than half (46.6%) of these clergy were able to respond in the affirmative when asked whether they agreed that immigrants feel comfortable in their churches; 34.6% disagreed that immigrants feel comfortable in their churches and 27% were not sure. Although a large proportion felt that their churches welcomed immigrants and an equally large percentage had recent immigrants already in their membership, more than half of the clergy are not sure or do not believe that immigrants are comfortable in their churches.

Remembering that a significant proportion of these pastors had a personal connection with immigration themselves and the widespread assumption that Hispanic churches exist to serve the Hispanic population, these responses raised considerable concern about the Hispanic churches and their ministry to the Hispanic immigrant. That more than half (52.5%) agreed that there were too many immigrants further raises concerns about this question.

Community Ministries. In addition to the influence of acculturation on self-identity and worship, does acculturation affect how the Hispanic church provides ministry to its community? In response to the question whether acculturation had changed the relationship between the church and the larger Hispanic community, 47.1% said yes, while 20.8% indicated that it had not. A significant 32.1% were not sure. However, 83.1% reported that their congregations were involved in the community surrounding the church. If most of these congregations are situated in Hispanic barrios, this information suggests that Hispanic churches have maintained a ministry to the Hispanic population, especially among those who live around the church.

Women Clergy. Most old-line Protestant denominations ordain women. However, many congregations and some male clergy continue to struggle with this new reality. What is the perceived situation of women clergy within Hispanic churches and the attitudes held toward them as clergy? More than 87% of the respondents affirmed that their denominations ordained women. Slightly more than 12% indicated that their denomination did not ordain women. Whether Hispanic congregations welcomed clergywomen is another question. More than 64% of the respondents perceived Hispanic congregations as welcoming women clergy; however, 17.7% did not agree that women were welcomed. Thus, although the denominations are open to women clergy, there continues to be a perception that they are not welcomed by some congregations.

Of importance however, are the attitudes held by the clergy themselves. How do they feel about the ordination of women, their effectiveness and contribution? Almost 82% support the ordination of women; 13% indicated that they were not in favor. With regard to the perceived effectiveness of women clergy, 76% felt that women clergy were effective and 9.2% did not agree. As to whether women clergy had made positive contributions to the church, 67.3% agreed and 8.2% disagreed.

These responses suggest that a fairly large proportion of the clergy agree that women should be ordained. However, fewer agree that clergywomen are effective and have made positive contributions to the church. These responses indicate that Hispanic women continue to struggle with a considerable segment of congregations and clergy to gain acceptance and respect.

Social and Political Perspectives

Settings. Hispanic congregations are usually found in settings challenged by many social, economic, cultural, and political issues. One such setting is the established *barrio*. These areas have been home to Hispanics for generations. It is not uncommon for barrios to serve as the arrival point for recent immigrants. Barrios have traditionally had distinct cultures and identities. They may reflect well-established power structures and socioeconomic systems. Their relationship with the larger city has normally been one of social, economic, and political marginality.

Hispanic congregations are also found in transitional neighborhoods. These are residential areas experiencing the emigration of one population and the immigration of another. It might be a neighborhood going through white flight and the entry of Hispanics. Many times, these situations reflect an older white population being replaced by a younger Latino or Hispanic population. In some cases, it might be an African American neighborhood being replaced by a newer Hispanic population. These neighborhoods tend to experience ethnic or racial tensions, rapid changes in the quality and pattern of housing, and other social stresses. Some of these Hispanic congregations in transitional neighborhoods may be found in older Anglo church buildings. They may have inherited the old facilities or they may be sharing the church facilities. In either case, these congregations face the many tensions and issues of poor neighborhoods going through rapid social change.

Some Hispanic congregations may be found in older suburbs where Hispanics have moved. In many of these cases the Hispanic population is dispersed throughout the area. There may be no definable Hispanic barrio. Thus the congregation could exist almost anywhere and its constituents scattered.

Other congregations are found in older parts of the central business districts of cities and towns. Some may call these areas the inner city. Many times these churches are found in what used to be a barrio but is now a commercial area. Office and industrial buildings along with parking lots have replaced old Hispanic residential neighborhoods. These churches serve a dispersed congregation. There is no neighborhood to serve. Its ministry is to a population scattered, and their concerns are citywide issues.

All of this suggests that Hispanic congregations can be found in diverse settings, each with unique sets of social issues. However, whether the setting be an inner city, an older established barrio, a suburb, or a transitional community, Hispanic churches face many similar types of challenges. These include issues particular to the Hispanic community whether it be concentrated or dispersed: racism and race relations, and socioeconomic and political concerns. The question in the study concerned the understanding and perceptions held by Hispanic Protestant clergy as they serve and lead Hispanic congregations in such settings. What social issues do they consider important for the Hispanic community? How do they perceive racial relations? Do they address these and other issues from the pulpit? Should the Hispanic church be involved? These are important questions in understanding how the Hispanic church is led to respond to its environment and address issues critical for Hispanics.

Issues in the Hispanic Community. There are many social issues or concerns facing Hispanics in communities such as the ones in which Hispanic congregations are located. These issues may be so many and complex that they can overwhelm congregations desiring to be in ministry to their communities. Which issues or concerns are more important? How do the clergy rank these issues and are they addressed by the church? Respondents were asked to rank selected issues and to add others.

The issue given the highest ranking was poverty. It seems that these clergy perceive poverty as central to the multiple challenges facing Hispanics in their communities. This observation reflects the reality of Hispanics in this country and defines the economic reality in which Hispanics live and the Hispanic church ministers. Hispanic congregations minister in settings perceived and defined as poor. These churches are surrounded by poverty, and ministry to their communities is ministry to the poor.

Tied for second were three issues: school dropouts, unemployment and underemployment, and gangs. All are closely related. The first two—school dropouts and unemployment or underemployment—are certainly connected to poverty. Without a strong educational foundation employment is a serious problem. Poverty is the result of the lack of education and employment. Gangs are also related to school-dropout and employment issues. School dropouts and unemployed youth find community and support within their gangs. They have time on their hands and gang activity can become a source of income.

The next two issues were ranked in the following order: immigration and racism. It is interesting to note that these two issues tend to reflect dynamics beyond the U.S. Hispanic community. They involve economic and political situations in Latin American countries and attitudes held by other populations in this country. In a sense, they are issues imposed upon the Hispanic populations in this country. It may well be that the two issues are related. To what extent is the immigration debate motivated by racial attitudes? Nonetheless, these clergy seem to rank these as important issues affecting the lives of their communities.

The issues ranked next were crime and drug abuse, in that order. Again, it is interesting to note the relationship between these two issues so closely ranked. It is well known that drug addiction requires large sums of money and that many drug addicts must rely on crime to maintain their addiction. It is unfortunate that many of these addicts turn on their own neighbors in their crime. As a result poor communities such as Hispanic barrios live in fear and amid the consequences of such crime.

The two issues ranked lowest were teenage pregnancy and health care. This does not mean that these issues are not considered important. It may well be that they are more manageable through existing systems such as the family, public hospitals, and other public social programs.

The Church and Social Issues. The foregoing discussion suggests that Hispanic clergy are well aware of the many social issues within their communities and appear to have an opinion as to the order of their significance for the Hispanic community. The question is whether and how do these clergy address such issues within the context of the ministry of the church. Another question is whether these clergy try to apply their faith to political and social issues. When asked, 90.5% agreed or strongly agreed that they try to apply their faith to such issues. Only 5.4% reported in the negative. But do they address such community issues from the pulpit and sermons? A slightly lower proportion (87.8%) indicated that they do so. Yet, this is a significant proportion that do address such issues in their sermons. Only 6.4% reported not doing so.

A remaining question is whether Hispanic congregations represented by these clergy are involved in the communities surrounding the church. More than 83% indicated that their churches were indeed involved with their communities. A much lower number (8%) were reported not to be involved with their communities. At a higher level, should the church attempt to influence public officials on the various social issues affecting the community? More than 85% of the clergy agreed or strongly agreed that the church should do so. Slightly more than 7% were of the opinion that it should not (they disagreed or strongly disagreed).

The overall impression is that Hispanic clergy are aware of the many social issues facing their communities and are able to rank them in a meaningful way. In addition, they report connecting their social awareness to their religious faith. This is further demonstrated in the high proportion which tie the teachings of faith to social problems and concerns affecting their neighborhoods. They report that their congregations are involved with their surrounding communities and that they should seek to influence officials on the many social issues in their communities.

Racism in the Community. The Hispanic population is commonly perceived and treated as a racial group. Although it is officially defined as "white or Caucasian," it is treated as nonwhite. In reality, the Hispanic populations incorporate the racial and many ethnic groups, including Caucasians, Negroid, Native American, and Asian. Within the Hispanic world, *mestizaje* is popularly used as a term of self-definition, referring to the blending of the many European, African, and Native peoples. Because Hispanics have been defined and treated as nonwhite they have been subject to many forms of racism. The study question dealt with the perception of Hispanic clergy concerning racism in their communities. Such perceptions can influence congregational ministry and action.

Well over 87% of the clergy agreed or strongly agreed that racism and prejudice were alive and well in their communities. Slightly more than 6% disagreed. When asked in a slightly different way, almost 68% of the respondents disagreed that racism was not a problem. The two sets of responses are consistent with the perception that racism is indeed a real issue. This is further manifested in responses specific to the Hispanic population. For example, 91.7% agreed or strongly agreed that racism affected Hispanics. Only 5.5% did not agree that racism affected this population. Furthermore, 65.2% agreed or strongly agreed that the police do not respect Hispanics as much as they respect Anglos. Slightly more than 15% were not sure if this was the case. When asked about anti-Hispanic attitudes in their communities, 48.9% agreed or strongly agreed that they existed and 22.4% were not sure.

An important question is whether progress in race relations is perceived by the clergy. Is there any hope? It is interesting to note that 53.7% seem to see race relations improving. Nonetheless, this discussion suggests that Hispanic clergy perceive racism to be a real issue and one that clearly affects Hispanics.

Concluding Reflections

This study of the Hispanic clergy within old-line denominations projects a profile which in many ways differs from the population it serves and yet reflects the many issues and concerns of that population. Like the Hispanic populations served, Hispanic clergy reflect diversity of national origin, acculturation, language utilization, and ethnic identity. However, from there forward, interesting differences emerge. Although the clergy are dedicated to serving a socially and economically marginal population, the clergy are well educated and possess a middle-class profile. They seem to have a higher level of immigration and an apparently successful rate of social and economic mobility.

Nonetheless, the Hispanic clergy within old-line Protestant denominations is a group clearly connected to and concerned about the many critical issues confronting the Hispanic population and communities. These range from the impact of acculturation, ethnic identity, and racism, to survival issues of poverty, education, and employment. They perceive poor communities struggling with poverty, employment, education, and crime.

Understandably, the Hispanic clergy are also concerned about the Hispanic Protestant church. They perceive a church wrestling with questions of identity and being. The clergy see the church affected by acculturation and reflecting a diverse people, including immigrants, acculturated youth, and bilingual-bicultural adults. What is the Hispanic Protestant church to be? How should it deal with dynamics of acculturation? Should the church support and promote ethnic identity and Hispanic cultures? Should it promote and encourage acculturation? The question of the nature and future of the Hispanic Protestant church will be answered by the Hispanic church itself and its ministerial leaders as they examine together their identity, their community, and their mission.

There are many issues yet to be addressed. This study presents a snapshot of the attitudes and perceptions of the clergy. Obviously, these do not necessarily reflect a profile of the laity and the whole church. However, the study does offer a beginning point for the search for a better understanding of Hispanic Christianity within old-line Protestant traditions.

Postscript

Hanging on an Empty Cross: The Hispanic Mainline Experience

Justo L. González

This book represents some of the results of an ongoing conversation of over two years' duration. In that conversation, one of the recurrent themes has been the difficulty in defining exactly what we mean by "mainline" denominations. We have mentioned the historical origin of the term, to refer to those churches that developed along the main railroad lines. We have mentioned and discussed a number of sociological and theological criteria for determining who and what are "mainline." In the end, we have simply come to the conclusion that, although we have a fairly clear idea of what we mean, it is virtually impossible to arrive at a working definition that sets clear boundaries between those churches that are "mainline" and those that are not.

One way to describe the "mainline" churches, at least as Hispanics first experienced them, is through the centrality of the symbol of the empty cross. Many of us remember sermons in which we were told that one of the hallmarks of Protestantism was the empty cross. To this day, the most common symbol in church buildings in most of our denominations, both Latino and not, is the empty cross. It is true that at one end of the "mainline" spectrum there are churches that still use crucifixes, and that at the other end of the same spectrum there are churches that refuse to use even the empty cross. But by and large, the empty cross is the most common symbol of the churches represented in our dialogue—and even in those "mainline" Protestant churches that use the crucifix, as well as in those that refuse to use any crosses at all, the most common theology could be described as a theology of the empty cross.

The empty cross stands for much of what has come to characterize Latino "mainline" Protestantism. Among such characteristics, the most obvious is that we have been taught to define ourselves—and many of us still do—in terms of opposition to Roman Catholicism. Roman Catholicism is the faith of the crucifix; therefore, we must reject the crucifix and cling to the empty cross. At an earlier time, Hispanic Protestantism, even in its "mainline" manifestations, was radically anti-Catholic. What characterized our churches, and an important point of pride, was precisely that we got rid of everything that was in the least suspect of "popery." We had no images, no candles, no vestments, and only vestiges of the liturgical year—usually no more than Christmas, Epiphany, and Holy Week. The empty cross, precisely because it was empty, reminded us of all that was no longer there, and thus became for us a powerful symbol of difference.

Second, the empty cross became for us a symbol of victory over the powers of death that have so long prevailed in our communities and our histories. As the early Protestant missionaries and preachers constantly inculcated in us, the empty cross is a reminder of the resurrection, of life, of victory. In many ways, the empty cross symbolizes much of what Latinos and Latinas in the early days found attractive in Protestantism.

Protestantism came to us as a liberating force. In many Latin American countries, the first successful Protestant missionary enterprises came in the wake of independence, and allied themselves with those elements in society that at that time were progressive. Protestantism came waving the banner of freedom of conscience, freedom to study Scripture, participatory worship in the vernacular, public education, and free enterprise. Its main opponents were the conservatives who represented the older landed aristocracy, the Catholic hierarchy, and the old ideals promulgated first by the Council of Trent and then reiterated and even accentuated by Pius IX. Its main allies were the liberals who represented the new intellectual and commercial elite, the professionals, and the governments that sought to break the stranglehold of the old ideals on the peoples and the nations. It was thus that James Thomson, usually considered the founder of Protestant missions to Latin America, was well received and supported by a number of Latin American governments. And it was for the same reason that liberal President Justo Rufino Barrios came to New York to ask that Presbyterian missionaries be sent to Guatemala.

Similar episodes may be found at various points in the history of Hispanic Protestantism in the United States. In his essay for this book, Tomás Atencio tells the story of Antonio José Martínez—el cura de Taos (the Taos priest)—which serves to illustrate the point. A Mexican who loved his country, and at the same time a man of advanced ideas who bemoaned the way traditional Mexican culture and religiosity had been used to oppress his people and to hold them back, Martínez was not sympathetic to the American invasion, but welcomed the new ideas of freedom and wider democracy that came in with the invaders. Ironically, as New Mexico became an American territory, the person sent to be the first American bishop of Santa Fe did not understand any of this, and tried to force

Martínez and his followers into a mold that was a mixture of Tridentine theology and American superiority—a mixture whose two components were diametrically opposed to Martínez's more liberal theology and profound sense of Mexican dignity. The result was a clash which has been amply documented by others, and which it is not necessary to rehearse here. What is significant for our purposes is that out of that clash Martínez emerged with sympathies toward the newly arrived Anglo Protestant missionaries, to the point that he advised that his grandchildren attend a Protestant school. One of his children became the first Hispanic Presbyterian pastor in New Mexico. To Martínez and many of his followers, as to many liberals throughout Latin America, Protestantism was an ally against the obscurantism and the authoritarianism of the Roman Catholic Church. (Significantly, neither Martínez nor most of those Latin American liberals ceased being Catholics *a su manera*—after their own fashion.)

The story of José Ynez Perea is similar, although he took the actual step of becoming a Protestant. Atencio accurately describes that story as a "transition from Mexican to American." For Perea, becoming a Protestant was part of a process of liberation from an oppressive form of Christianity—one that for long had supported the status quo and kept the masses in ignorance both of the Bible and of their own rights.

For these early Hispanic Protestants, the contrast between the crucifix and the empty cross was central. The crucifix, with its dead Christ, both symbolized and glorified the suffering of the masses. The masses were attracted to it precisely because they saw there a suffering similar to and even greater than their own. But the same masses were also mollified by it, as if suffering—and even unmerited suffering—were the highest form of obedience to God's will, and as if resistance or rebellion against suffering were resistance or rebellion against that will. The empty cross, on the other hand, spoke of victory even over death, of an order in which evil, injustice, and oppression do not have the last word. Thus, in embracing the empty cross and rejecting the crucifix, those early Latino Protestants were also claiming all the freedoms, and even the iconoclastic tendencies, that are usually associated with American Protestantism and democracy.

At the same time, there was a high price to pay. The crucifix is not only a religious symbol; it also stands at the very center of a culture and a tradition. Atencio rightly states that Perea's conversion to Protestantism was part of the process whereby he became Americanized and de-Mexicanized. Much of what Protestant missionaries said in criticism of the crucifix was also derogatory toward our culture—we were a people fixed on gore and suffering; we did not know how to leave death behind, but must constantly meditate on it; we were much given to thinking in terms of images and examples, rather than in terms of ideas and principles. As a result, to reject the crucifix and to embrace the empty cross was also to reject and be rejected by much of one's own culture and even family. (Stories abound of Protestant converts evicted from their parents' home, or ostracized by their community.) To reject the crucifix was also to reject the traditional celebrations of saints' days and *romerías* around which individuals, villages, and towns developed their identity. Traditionally, children were usually named after one of the saints on whose day they were born, and every year, on the anniversary of their birth, people celebrated their "santo." On a certain saint's day, all the people with the same name celebrated their birth as well as their "santo"—and often, those born on a different date, still celebrated their "santo." To this day, most traditional birthday songs do not refer to one's birthday ("cumpleaños"), but to one's saint's day ("el día de tu santo"), and in common parlance people speak of one's birthday as one's "santo." Most Protestants felt compelled to reject this tradition alongside the crucifix, with the result that Hispanic Protestants were limited to celebrating birthdays, and to singing "Happy birthday to you," or some reasonable facsimile thereof. The same may be said of the patron saint of a village or town—often the saint after whom the town was named, such as "Santa Barbara," "San Agustin," or "San Antonio." That saint's day was also the community's celebration of its own identity and history. This too Protestants had to leave behind, thus often becoming foreigners in their own towns and communities. Likewise, when one embraced the empty cross of Protestantism, several traditional rites of passage, of bonding, and of communication (such as *quinceañeras, compadrazgos, romerías,* etc.) had to go the way of the crucifix. (Certainly, some of those traditions had to be corrected by the message of the gospel. For instance, *quinceañeras* were traditionally rites of puberty which perpetuated the notion that a young woman's role in life was primarily to mate and procreate. Yet, rather than seeking to understand and transform such ritual traditions, mainline Protestantism simply cast them out—and with them cast out also most of the culture that had sustained us for generations.) In short, the price for the empty cross was the emptying of culture—the loss of many of the rites and traditions by which a culture lives and passes itself from generation to generation. This may be one of the reasons why, while David Maldonado reports that Hispanic mainline Protestants seek to be involved in their communities, Rubén Armendáriz indicates that such involvement is seldom efficient. In other words, although the theology we have been taught calls us to be involved in our barrios and communities, our own distancing from our traditional culture, as symbolized by the empty cross, makes it difficult for us to be productive in that involvement. (It is also at this point that Harold Recino's essay brings in a note of hope, for the newly arrived immigrants, particularly those from Central America, are bringing with them a living of the faith that is profoundly engaged in issues of culture and politics.)

The result of all this is that the phrase "hanging on an empty cross" has both a positive and a negative meaning. On the positive side, we hang from an empty cross in the sense that we cling to it. In the empty cross we have found liberation, not only from sin and death, but also from much that was sinful and deathful in our own culture and environment. We cling to the empty cross as a symbol of Christ's victory over sin and death, which is also our own.

But there is also a negative side to the empty cross. We hang on an empty cross in the sense that we hang from it, that it is we who have been and are being crucified on it—if not individually, at least in our culture, tradition, and identity. The danger of an empty cross is that it will not remain empty for long. In the crucifix, Jesus hangs in our stead. In the empty cross, there is always the danger that it will be our people, our culture and tradition that will hang in Jesus' stead!

This may be seen in the story of New Mexican Protestantism as told by Atencio. What is both ironic and frightening in that story is that Hispanic Presbyterianism in New Mexico received a boost from the manner in which Lamy and the Anglo leadership of the Roman Catholic Church dealt with the recently conquered Neomexicans; and then Anglo Presbyterians dealt with Neomexican Presbyterianism in the same fashion. Little wonder, then, that the story is one of original enthusiasm and success, followed by diffidence and decline.

What took place in New Mexico is illustrative of a story repeated many times over. That is why the category of *border,* explored in different ways by both Sylvest and Machado, is so important for Hispanic Protestantism. Sylvest is right in comparing and connecting British "borderer" religion with Mexican American "borderer" religion. The relationship is both causal and parallel: causal, in that the form of Protestantism that was preached to Latinos in the borderlands was mostly that which had developed centuries earlier in the British borderlands; parallel, in that the conditions of Hispanics living in the borderlands were similar to those in the earlier British borderlands. Machado shows that, although times have changed, the typical manner in which "mainline" Protestant churches have related to their Hispanic work in Texas is as the center relating to the periphery—the borders.

This is the paradox of our very identity as Hispanic mainline Protestants. We belong to churches that call themselves "mainline," and which therefore claim to represent the mainstream of North American life and society. But we are Hispanics, and thus by definition—by definition by others, but definition nevertheless—people at the margins of this society. As "mainline," we are people of the empty cross. As Hispanics, we are people of the crucifix. As mainline Hispanics, we often find our entire community hanging from a cross that is supposed to be empty. Significantly, at each meeting of our working groups for this project, the matter of identity kept surfacing—not primarily, as is often the case in the dominant culture, as an individual question, but rather as a communal question: Who are we as Hispanic mainline Protestants? Are we really Hispanic? Are we really Protestant? What does it mean to be both?

In some ways, the ambiguity of our experience with the empty cross parallels what José David Rodriguez says about confessions and confessing the faith in Spanish. A confession is both an act and a document; both an event and an institution. The Augsburg Confession, for instance, is both a brave deed on the part of the German nobility in 1530, and a document that has often been used to determine who is and who is not a Lutheran—which is the reason behind the bitter struggles around any attempt to modify it. As an act, the Confession of Augsburg marked a watershed in which the German people—or rather, their princes—claimed the right and the duty to read Scripture for themselves. As a document and an institution, the Confession of Augsburg has repeatedly been used to pressure others into reading Scripture, not for themselves, but as the Germanic leaders of Lutheranism believe it should be read. Likewise, there is the emptying of the cross as an act, and the empty cross as a doctrine and an institution. As an act, the emptying of the cross was a liberating experience for José Ynez Perea and for many at a later date—and it continues to be such for many Hispanics to this day. As an institution, the empty cross is a symbol of the manner in which mainline Protestantism has demanded that its Hispanic adherents either remain at the margins of the various denominations or cease being Hispanics.

This is why in his essay Pedraja rightly suggests that both the empty cross and the crucifix have a place in Hispanic piety—even in Hispanic Protestant piety—and that both are to be kept. It is in the presence and from the experience of the crucifix that the empty cross comes as a word of assurance and liberation. Without the crucifix, the empty cross risks becoming a symbol of triumphalism for those who already stand atop the social pyramid, and a means of oppression, subjugation, and denial of identity for those who do not. Without the empty cross, the crucifix risks becoming a symbol of fatalism and a call to acquiescence in the face of suffering and injustice. As Hispanics, we are acutely aware of the manner in which this functions in the majority culture. The churches whose missionaries told us that our minds and emotions were too fixed on the suffering Christ of the crucifix have evolved along those lines to such a point that today many of them do not even gather for worship on Good Friday. They glide easily from Palm Sunday to Easter, as if the agony in Gethsemane, the betrayal, the trial, and the crucifixion were merely a series of unfortunate events on the way to the empty tomb. Little wonder, then, that so many preachers have little to say about Easter beyond the common springtime platitudes about nature being reborn and butterflies springing from cocoons! Little wonder that churchgoers find it so difficult to speak of their suffering and failures. And little wonder that there is such malaise in most of the mainline Protestant denominations. Without the correction of the crucifix, the empty cross has led many to an "all is O.K." sort of religion—and the irony is that such a religion is certainly not O.K.!

It is at this point that Pedraja's suggestion, that we need both the empty cross and the crucifix, becomes poignantly relevant, not only for Hispanics, but for all Protestants in this country.

To many Hispanic Protestants, such a suggestion may sound alien and even heretical, accustomed as we are to think that the crucifix is a "popish" symbol, and that the empty cross is more biblical. But in fact our faith and our piety have always maintained many of the dimensions of the crucifix, even while excluding the actual symbol from our churches and devotions. In spite of all we have been told—and even in spite of all we have said, because we were taught to say it—we are still a people of the crucifix. All that its exclusion from our churches achieves is a cultural dissonance and a religious schizophrenia. (The fact that much of the criticism and rejection of the crucifix has to do with criticism and rejection of the culture that uses the crucifix becomes even clearer when one realizes that many Hispanic Protestant churches that would never allow a crucifix to be displayed in church have no such qualms about other images coming primarily from the dominant culture. Thus, in many Hispanic churches one sees a famous, Anglo-like portrait of Jesus, or the equally famous painting of Jesus knocking at the door, or Jesus teaching the children. All of these are acceptable, because they come from the same culture that told us that the crucifix, so central to our traditional culture, was not acceptable.)

The persistent importance of the crucifix—or of what it stands for—may be seen in many of the features of Hispanic worship and piety. One such feature is the popularity of hymns having to do with the cross and its suffering. Such hymns—some of them translated from English, and coming from an earlier time in Anglo Protestant Christianity—hold a central place in the heart of many believers. They are not reserved for Good Friday. On the contrary, they are sung at Sunday worship, in midweek Bible studies, in home gatherings, and at just about any other occasion in which believers gather and sing. Most of these hymns, with their description of the Lord hanging from the cross, remind one much more of a crucifix than an empty cross. And even when we sing about the cross, we are not singing about a symbol, but rather about the events traditionally depicted and summarized in the crucifix. The words may be about the cross; the mental images are about the crucifixion.

Another such feature in Hispanic worship is the place and nature of the requests for prayer, and the testimonials about prayer answered. As is customary in many Anglo churches, at a certain point in the worship service in many Latino congregations, the leader asks for concerns for prayer. In many of those congregations—especially those that are less acculturated, and less shaped by middle-class standards—the concerns raised are often both very personal and very painful. People are quite willing to express their fears, to describe their diseases and their symptoms, and to declare their failures—after all, if Jesus himself failed in Jerusalem, if he did sweat blood at Gethsemane, and if he suffered on the cross, there is no failure or suffering which is unspeakable within the family of Christ. (This, in contrast with many Anglo mainline congregations, where one seldom hears petitions for prayer by those who cannot pay the mortgage, who are unemployed, or who are suffering from a dreaded disease. In Hispanic congregations, such petitions and prayers are often followed [sometimes preceded] by *testimonios*—acts in which believers witness to what God has done for them. Although often ridiculed by those who consider them unsophisticated—and although at times they do descend to the level of the ridiculous—*testimonios* may be considered a literary genre with its own structure. That structure is patterned—although not consciously—after the transition from Good Friday (and sometimes Palm Sunday) to Easter. The speaker may begin by telling of high hopes for success (Palm Sunday), often to the point of relying on his or her own wisdom, prowess, or persistence. Then comes failure to the point of impossibility: as in Good Friday, there is nothing but death and hopelessness. For instance, one's disease was declared incurable, another had come to the end of all financial resources, someone's children had become incorrigible delinquents, another's drug habit had taken control, and so on. Finally (as in Easter

Sunday) there is a witness to new life out of death, to new possibility out of impossibility, by the power of God. Obviously, the Easter-like event—one could say, the empty cross—is the point of the entire *testimonio*. But one can only arrive at it through Friday-like, crucifixlike pain and hopelessness.

At a deeper level, what Ismael García says about the manner in which Hispanics tend to approach ethics and moral decision may also be connected to the contrast between the empty cross and the crucifix. At the risk of oversimplifying García's carefully nuanced essay, one could say that, while Protestants in the dominant culture tend to make decisions on the basis of the "ethics of principle," Hispanics tend to soften the edges of such principles on the basis of the "ethics of care" and personal relation. At this point too, Hispanics have been criticized by many in the dominant culture—and sometimes also by other Hispanics—for allowing personal considerations to sway our moral judgment. We are told that ethics is a matter of principles, and that to be moral means to live by those principles. And yet, that is not the manner in which we actually function. We know the principles, and in general use them as guidance when there are no other considerations, or when it is necessary to make decisions in an almost automatic manner; but for us it is more important to know the persons involved, and to make decisions on the basis of care and personal relations. And I suspect that here again there is an example of the contrast between the religion of the empty cross and the piety of the crucifix. The empty cross is a principle; the crucifix is a person. One thinks about the empty cross, and applies it to one's life, much as one thinks about a principle or an ideal and applies it to one's life. But one cares about the crucifix, much as one cares for the many who today are crucified in the name of principles and ideals!

From the foregoing it should be obvious that I am convinced that as Hispanic mainline Protestants we have much to contribute to the larger churches to which we belong. Moving as I do within several denominations, and both among their Hispanic and their Anglo constituencies, I am very much aware of significant differences between the two. Certainly, there is still much that Hispanic mainline Protestantism can learn from its non-Hispanic counterpart. Yet, I choose not to emphasize that particular direction of learning, for given the present structure of power and of resources, it is to be expected that Hispanic mainline Protestants will continue learning much—both good and bad—from their Anglo brothers and sisters. It is learning in the other direction—from the minority to the majority, from the periphery to the center, from the relatively powerless to the more powerful—that is always in danger of not taking place, and therefore I choose to emphasize here the source of learning that we as Hispanic Protestants can be for the church at large. There is no need to repeat or to prove what the members of those churches themselves are saying: mainline Protestantism is in crisis. It is not just a crisis of growth; it is a crisis of identity, a crisis of nerve, a crisis of mission, a crisis of faith. By and large, mainline Protestantism no longer knows what it is about. Sometimes one even wonders if it knows what it is!

It is at this juncture that Hispanic Protestantism—not just the Protestantism of the empty cross, but the Protestantism of the empty cross *and* the crucifix—may prove to be an invaluable resource for the renewal of the churches. This became clear to me a few years ago, partly through a personal experience. I was undergoing a series of medical tests, trying to discover the cause of some disturbing symptoms. On that particular week, I had occasion to spend some time with both Hispanic and Anglo sisters and brothers. At the end of the week, I commented to an Anglo brother, somewhat facetiously, but also quite seriously, "You know what I have discovered this week? When you are sick, Hispanics *pray* for you; Anglos *think* about you!" Naturally, I knew—or at least hoped—that what my Anglo friends meant when they said they would be "thinking" about me was that they would be praying. Yet, the very words used made it clear that to them it was embarrassing to say in so many words that they would be praying for me. Part of this may be due to the manner in which the white middle class in this country values its privacy, and finds it embarrassing to speak about matters that are supposed to be private—most notably, sex, money, and prayer. Part may be due to the pervading influence of a mechanistic view of the universe, which leaves no place for atavistic customs such as prayers of petition. But also part of it may be due to the excessive emphasis on the empty cross. One *thinks* about the cross; one *prays* to the one who hangs from the cross. The empty cross, as a principle, may lead to significant reflection; the crucifix, at the center of which is a person, leads to personal relation, including prayer. If mainline Protestantism in this country does not learn to pray, to speak openly about prayer, and to give testimony to answered prayer, if all the community of faith can do for its members is to *think* about them, there is more than ample reason for the current crisis in mainline Protestantism.

In his study of some selected pastors and congregations, Jorge Lara-Braud declares that one of the difficulties that mainline Hispanic Protestant churches encounter in recruiting Hispanics for ordained ministry is the "futurelessness" of the enterprise. Such futurelessness is connected both with the current crisis in mainline Protestantism at large, and with the crisis of identity within Hispanic mainline Protestantism, which here I have sought to illustrate by means of the contrast and tension between the crucifix and the empty cross. In this last connection, "futurelessness" is the counterpart of "pastlessness": we do not know what future to project, because we do not know what past to affirm. Is it the past that we were encouraged to reject as the empty cross was preached among us—a past culturally akin to us, but theologically alien? Or is it the past of the churches of the empty cross—a past theologically akin to us, but culturally alien? Until we come to terms with those two pasts in their tension and complementarity, and with the issues of identity posed by them, Hispanic mainline Protestants will have difficulty, not only recruiting persons for ordained ministry, but also making their potentially very significant contribution to the rest of the church and society.

All of this points to the need for future studies. Most of the essays included in this volume are probes into particular instances or episodes within Hispanic mainline Protestantism. Each of them could be multiplied tenfold, expanded into the subject for a book or a doctoral dissertation, or explored with reference to its implications for church policies. My hope is that one by-product of the present volume will be to convince researchers as well as church leaders that Hispanic mainline Protestantism is a worthy and urgent subject for research, not only on the part of Hispanics themselves, but also on the part of the entire community of faith as it seeks to fulfill its mission.

Notes

Chapter 1: Bordering Cultures and the Origins of Hispanic Protestant Christianity

1. David Hackett Fischer, *Albion's Seed: Four British Folkways in America* (New York: Oxford University Press, 1989).

2. A. Gordon Kinder, *Casiodoro de Reina: Spanish Reformer of the Sixteenth Century* (London: Tamesis Books, 1975). Cf. Henry Kamen, *Inquisition and Society in Spain in the Sixteenth and Seventeenth Centuries* (Bloomington: Indiana University Press, 1975), 62-100.

3. W. H. Rule, *Memoir of a Mission to Gibraltar and Spain* (London: John Mason, 1844).

4. Virgil Elizondo, *Galilean Journey: The Mexican-American Promise* (Maryknoll, N.Y.: Orbis, 1983).

5. Moíses Sandoval, ed., *Fronteras: A History of the Latin American Church in the USA Since 1513* (San Antonio: MACC, 1983).

6. Fischer, *Albion's Seed*, 605.

7. David Martin, *Tongues of Fire: The Explosion of Protestantism in Latin America* (Cambridge, Mass.: Blackwell, 1990).

8. Fischer, *Albion's Seed*, 621.

9. Ibid., 629.

10. Ibid., 630.

11. Ibid., 633-34.

12. Weber, David J., *The Spanish Frontier in North America* (New Haven, Conn.: Yale University Press, 1992), 272.

13. Grady McWhiney, *Cracker Culture: Celtic Ways in the Old South* (Tuscaloosa: University of Alabama Press, 1988), 268; cf. also Fischer, *Albion's Seed*, 605-782, and the chart, pp. 813-15.

14. Fischer, *Albion's Seed*, 708.

15. Deborah Vansau McCauley, *Appalachian Mountain Religion* (Urbana: University of Illinois Press, 1995).

16. A fruitful direction for investigation, among several suggested by the reality just defined, will be to compare and contrast the history of Appalachian mountain religion with that of Hispanic Protestants in the Southwest. Many of the internal dynamics are similar, the principal, defining Christian traditions are the same (though intersecting with the two cultures at differing points in their evolution), and relations between the two groups and the mainline denominations are also similar.

17. Fischer, *Albion's Seed*, 615.

18. Ibid., 616.

19. Ibid., 618.

20. Leigh Eric Schmidt, *Holy Fairs: Scottish Communions and American Revivals in the Early Modern Period* (Princeton, N.J.: Princeton University Press, 1989), 11-32; Marilyn J. Westerkamp, *Triumph of the Laity: Scots-Irish Piety and the Great Awakening, 1625–1760* (New York: Oxford University Press, 1988), 15-42.

21. Westerkamp, *Triumph of the Laity*, 187.

22. Schmidt, *Holy Fairs*, 59-68; McCauley, *Appalachian Mountain Religion*, 190.

23. Timothy M. Matovina, *Tejano Religion and Ethnicity: San Antonio, 1821–1860* (Austin: University of Texas Press, 1995), 39-40. N.b. the earlier work of the *colporteurs*, pp. 14-15.

24. Juan Gómez-Quiñones, *Roots of Chicano Politics, 1600–1940* (Albuquerque: University of New Mexico Press, 1994), 69.

25. Ibid., 61.

26. Ibid.

27. Nettie Lee Benson, "Texas as Viewed from Mexico, 1820–1834," *Southwestern Historical Quarterly* 90/3 (January 1987): 242.

28. Reginald Horsman, *Race and Manifest Destiny: The Origins of American Racial Anglo-Saxonism* (Cambridge, Mass.: Harvard University Press, 1981), 82-83.

29. Ibid., 86.

30. Actually, no less a figure than Thomas Jefferson, himself, had begun to entertain doubts about the equality of blacks, and had decided that it would be impossible to incorporate blacks into white society. Cf. Horsman, *Race and Manifest Destiny*, 101.

31. Horsman, *Race and Manifest Destiny*, 103-15.

32. Ibid., 102.

33. Ibid., 103-4.

34. Ibid., 109.

35. Ibid., 157. See pp. 116-57 for a helpful analysis of the process by which this scientific perspective, so convenient for the interests of expansion, came to prevail.

36. Ibid., 208.

37. Ibid., 209.

38. Ibid., 210.

39. Ibid., 255-56.

40. Ibid., 251.

41. Ibid., 253.

42. Cf. Paul Horgan, *Lamy of Santa Fe: His Life and Times* (New York: Farrar, Straus, and Giroux, 1975).

43. Cf. R. Douglas Brackenridge and Francisco O. García-Treto, *Iglesia Presbiteriana: A History of Presbyterians and Mexican Americans in the Southwest*, 2nd ed. (San Antonio: Trinity University Press, 1987), 2-4; Walter Vernon et al., *The*

Methodist Excitement in Texas (Dallas: Texas United Methodist Historical Society, 1984), 106; William Stuart Red, *Texas Colonists and Religion, 1821–1836* (Austin: E. L. Shettles, 1924), 71, 138-40.

44. Melinda Rankin, *Texas in 1850* (Boston: Damrell & Moore, 1850), 55.

45. Ibid., 56.

46. Melinda Rankin, *Twenty Years Among the Mexicans* (Cincinnati: Chase & Hall, 1875), 38.

47. Ibid., 42.

48. Ibid., 97-119.

49. Nannie Emory Holding, *A Decade of Mission Life in Mexican Mission Homes* (Nashville: Publishing House Methodist Episcopal Church, South, 1895), 9.

50. Cf. Perry Miller, *Errand into the Wilderness* (Cambridge, Mass.: Belknap Press of Harvard University Press, 1956), pp. 1-16.

51. Holding, *Decade of Mission Life*, 141.

52. Ibid., 144-45.

53. Matovina, *Tejano Religion*, 14; cf. also Red, *Texas Colonists and Religion*, 80-85.

54. Red, *Texas Colonists and Religion*, 80-81.

55. New Mexican Protestantism began under the aegis of "northern" Methodists and Presbyterians, who were somewhat less revivalistic and somewhat more "puritan" in their approach to mission. There are significant differences of style and values between Rio Grande Conference churches in New Mexico and in Texas. Some of those differences are a function of the differing Hispanic cultures of the states, others, a function of the differing characteristics of Anglo-Celtic culture from the South and that of the Midwest.

Chapter 2: The Empty Cross: The First Hispano Presbyterians in Northern New Mexico and Southern Colorado

1. E. A. "Tony" Mares, a Padre Martínez scholar and professor of creative writing in the English Department at the University of New Mexico, and Padre Luis Jaramillo, pastor of Our Lady of the Assumption in Albuquerque, read this paper and made invaluable contributions.

2. Alfredo Padilla, interview with author, Truchas, N.M., July 1996.

3. Epifanio Romero, TC #36, April 1982, Albuquerque, N.M., in Menaul Historical Library of the Southwest audiotape archive; Epifanio Romero, interview with author, Truchas, N.M., July 1996.

4. Thomas J. Steele and Rowena A. Rivera, *Penitente Self-Government* (Santa Fe: Ancient City Press, 1985). Joann Martínez Atencio, interview with author, Dixon, N.M., August 1996.

5. Steele and Rivera, *Penitente*, 17.

6. Andrés Segura, "Continuidad de la tradicion filosofica Nahuatl en las danzas de Concheros," in *El Cuaderno* (de vez en cuando) 3 (1973): 22-23.

7. Steele and Rivera, *Penitente*, 46. Padre Luis Jaramillo, interview by author, September 1996. Steele and Rivera emphasize the approximation of the crucifix to the Eucharist in terms of the place where the two are kept while Jaramillo emphasizes the symbolic meaning of the crucifix as a part of the Eucharist.

8. Mark T. Banker, *Presbyterian Missions and Cultural Interaction in the Far Southwest, 1850–1950* (Urbana and Chicago: University of Illinois Press, 1993), xi.

9. Randi J. Walker, "Protestantism in the Sangre de Cristos: Factors in the Growth and Decline of Hispanic Protestant Churches in Northern New Mexico and Southern Colorado" (Ph.D. diss., Claremont Graduate School, 1983), 7.

10. An "order" is a juridical group, or congregation of priests, who have taken the vow of poverty and have a superior, or head, within the order to whom they are responsible. They are distinguished from priests who do not take such a vow and who are directly under the diocesan bishop. They are known as secular or diocesan priests. Their parishes are known as diocesan or secular churches.

11. Fry Angélico Chávez, *But Time and Chance* (Santa Fe: Sunstone Press, 1981), 87-88; Thomas Harwood, *History of New Mexico Spanish Missions of the Methodist Episcopal Church from 1850 to 1910 in Decades*, vol. 1 (Albuquerque, N.M.: newly edited by Committee on Archives and History of the First United Methodist Church, 1983; Albuquerque, N.M.: El Abogado Press, 1908), 30.

12. Chávez, *But Time and Chance*, 159. E. A. Mares, "The Many Faces of Padre Antonio José Martínez: A Historiographic Essay," in *Padre Martínez: New Perspectives from Taos*, ed. E. A. Mares (Taos, N.M.: Millicent Rogers Museum, 1988), 18-45.

13. Chávez, *But Time and Chance*, 17-24.

14. Steele and Rivera, *Penitente*, 19-23, 39, 46.

15. Steele and Rivera, *Penitente*, 8-9. Padre Luis Jaramillo suggested Padre Martínez was de facto pastor-at-large for the large landholding peasant community of northern New Mexico. Padre Jaramillo also contributed to the doctrinal analysis of the Brotherhood. For an explanation of Penitente organization, see Steele and Rivera, *Penitente*, 1985, 13-75.

16. Chávez, *But Time and Chance*, 53. The "later authors" referred to in the narrative are Willa Cather, *Death Comes for the Archbishop* (New York: Knopf, 1927), and Paul Horgan, *Lamy of Santa Fe* (Farrar, Straus, and Giroux, 1975). See also E. A. Mares, *Padre Martínez: New Perspectives from Taos*.

17. Penitentes' involvement in the rebellion is reminiscent of the behavior of the peasant groups described by Eric Hobsbawn. Those groups were faced with conditions similar to those of northern New Mexico during the Mexican and Territorial periods. Penitentes had also another role: to protect the values

and way of life of an isolated peasant community. E. J. Hobsbawm, *Primitive Rebels* (New York: Norton, 1959), 1-12.

18. D. W. Meinig, *Southwest* (New York: Oxford University Press, 1976), 17-20.

19. Mares, "The Many Faces of Padre Martinez," 41-45.

20. Chávez, *But Time and Chance,* 92-100.

21. Ibid., 98, 140-44; Harwood, *History of New Mexico Spanish Missions,* 29.

22. Padre Luis Jaramillo, interview with author, Albuquerque, N.M., September 1996.

23. Chávez, *But Time and Chance,* 108-13.

24. Thomas J. Steele, "A View from the Rectory," in *Padre Martínez: New Perspectives from Taos,* 71-96.

25. Mares, "The Many Faces of Padre Martínez," 34.

26. Chávez, *But Time and Chance,* 159; Gabino Rendón, as told to Edith Agnew, *Hand on My Shoulder* (New York: Board of National Missions of the Presbyterian Church in the U.S.A., 1993), 54.

27. J. A. Schufle, *Preparing the Way: History of the First 100 Years of Las Vegas Presbyterian Church* (Las Vegas, N.M.: First United Presbyterian Church, 1970), 5; "Francisco Perea's Obituary," *Morning Journal,* 22 May 1913, personal papers of Elizabeth Romero, Ranchos de Taos, N.M.

28. R. Douglas Brackenridge and Francisco O. García-Treto, *Iglesia Presbiteriana* (San Antonio: Trinity University Press, 1987), 39.

29. Elizabeth Romero, interview with author, Ranchos de Taos, N.M., August 1996.

30. Schufle, *Preparing the Way,* 8.

31. "Perea's Obituary," *Morning Journal;* Chávez, *But Time and Chance,* 144.

32. Jane Atkins Grainger, ed., *El Centenario de la Palabra* (Chacón: El Rito Presbyterian Church, 1979), 9.

33. Rendón, *Hand on My Shoulder,* 18; Ruth K. Barber and Edith J. Agnew, *Sowers Went Forth* (Albuquerque: Menaul Historical Library of the Southwest, 1981), 19; J. A. Schufle, *Preparing the Way,* 24.

34. Rendón, *Hand on My Shoulder,* 24.

35. Ibid., 42-43.

36. Brackenridge and García-Treto, *Iglesia Presbiteriana,* 58; Barber and Agnew, *Sowers Went Forth,* 23-25.

37. Barber and Agnew, *Sowers Went Forth,* 25, 62.

38. Ibid., 26.

39. Grainger, *El Centenario de la Palabra,* 11-13.

40. Alexander M. Darley, *Passionists of the Southwest* (Glorieta, N.M.: Rio Grande Press, 1968). Marianne L. Stoller and Thomas J. Steele, S.J., eds., *Diary of the Jesuit Residence of Our Lady of Guadalupe Parish, Conejos, Colorado, December 1871–December 1875* (Colorado Springs: Colorado College Studies, 1982), 10-20, 144-45.

41. Rendón, *Hand on My Shoulder*, 75.

42. Barber and Agnew, *Sowers Went Forth*, 30.

43. Stoller and Steele, *Diary of the Jesuit Residence*, 11.

44. Victor Westphall, "History of Albuquerque, 1870–1880" (master's thesis, University of New Mexico, 1947), 99, quoting the *Albuquerque Review*, 24 April 1880.

45. Harwood, *History of New Mexico Spanish Missions*, 20.

46. George I. Sánchez, *Forgotten People* (Albuquerque, N.M.: Calvin Horn Publisher, 1967).

47. Susan M. Yohn, *A Conquest of Faiths: Missionary Women and Pluralism in the American Southwest* (Ithaca, N.Y.: Cornell University Press, 1995), 7-8.

48. Brackenridge and García-Treto, *Iglesia Presbiteriana*, 17, 48.

49. For Gabino Rendón's complete story, see Rendon, *Hand on My Shoulder*, 1-105.

50. Barber and Agnew, *Sowers Went Forth*, 56, 57; Elizabeth Romero, interview with author, August 1996.

51. Rendón, *Hand on My Shoulder*, 93.

52. "Menaul School, Albuquerque, N.M.: Seventy-five Years of Service in the Southwest, 1881–1956" (Personal papers of the author), 12-13.

53. Alfonso Esquibel to J. A. Schufle, *Vaquero to Dominie: The Nine Lives of Alfonso Esquibel* (Las Vegas, N.M.: n.p., n.d.).

54. José L. Medina, interview with author, Albuquerque, N.M., April 1996. Others of Medina's cohort group who were interviewed are Moicelio Cruz, Porfirio Romero, and Epifanio Romero, Tomás C. Gonzales, and José Adelaido Medina.

55. Minutes of La Iglesia Betel, 1921–1949, La Cebolla, N.M., Menaul Historical Library of the Southwest archives, Albuquerque, N.M.

56. Schufle, *Preparing the Way*, 93.

57. Barber and Agnew, *Sowers Went Forth*, 87-98.

58. Brackenridge and García-Treto, *Iglesia Presbiteriana*, 185.

59. Interagency Council for Area Development, *Embudo: A Pilot Planning Project for the Embudo Watershed of New Mexico* (New Mexico Planning Office, n.d.), 43-44.

60. Richard L. Nostrand, *The Hispano Homeland* (Norman: University of Oklahoma Press, 1992), 222-23.

61. Padre Luis Jaramillo, interview with author, September 1996.

62. For an excellent discussion of the meaning of myth and archetypes applicable to the discussion on the archetypal foundations of the crucifix introduced at the beginning of the essay, see Erich Neumann, *The Origins and History of Consciousness* (Princeton, N.J.: Princeton University Press, 1954). Cf. Steele and Rivera, *Penitente*, 16-18.

63. Crypto-Judaism, or *conversos*, was a religious phenomenon in Spain

from the late fourteenth century up to the expulsion of Jews in 1492. Crypto-Judaism arose when observing Jews were forced to convert under threat of death, but remained loyal to Judaism and observed rituals in secret. There is evidence that some crypto-Jews or their immediate heirs, known as *conversos nuevos,* migrated to Mexico. It is assumed that some settled in New Mexico. In a study under way, I am examining the crypto-Jewish remnants in New Mexico *manito* (New Mexico Indohispano) society and culture.

Chapter 3: Inter-ethnic Relations Between Mexican American and Anglo American Methodists in the U.S. Southwest, 1836–1938

1. Major Horace Bell remarked about Manifest Destiny and filibustering in the early 1850s:

> The theory of filibustering, or manifest destiny, was "First, that the earth is the Lord's and the fullness thereof, and we are the Lord's people; second, that all Spanish American governments are worthless, and should be reconstructed and that such is our mission." . . . To sympathize with filibustering at the time was popular. An actual filibuster was a lion—a hero.

(E. C. Orozco, *Republican Protestantism in Aztlán* [N.p.: Petereins Press, 1980], 94, quoting from Horace Bell, *Reminiscences of a Ranger, or Early Times in Southern California* [Santa Barbara: Wallace Hebberd, 1927], 214-15).

2. The Protestant Mission Boards viewed California as providentially reserved for Anglo American Protestants. Peter G. Mode, in *The Frontier Spirit in American Christianity,* cites correspondence in the *Home Missionary:*

> The growing ascendency of the English in China and the Asiatic Islands simultaneously with the transfer of California to our people completes the control of the four great coast lines of the Northern Hemisphere, by two Protestant nations, speaking the same language, and one in all the great features of their character. . . . And the circumstances that precede and have followed our possession of California, show that herein a great trust is committed to us by Providence, for the benefit of a new empire, about to arise in the Pacific world, God kept that coast for a people of the Pilgrim blood; He would not permit any other to be fully developed there. The Spaniard came thither a hundred years before our fathers landed at Plymouth; but though he came for treasure, his eyes were holden that he should not find it. But in the fulness of time, when a Protestant people have been brought to this continent, and are nourished up to strength by the requisite training, God commits to their possession, that Western Shore.

Peter G. Mode, *The Frontier Spirit in American Christianity* (New York: MacMillan Co., 1923), 36-37, quoting from correspondence in the *Home Missionary* (June 1849).

3. Daniel R. Rodríguez-Díaz, "Los Movimientos Misioneros y el Establecimiento de Ideologías Dominantes: 1800–1940," *Apuntes: Reflexiones Teológicas desde el Margen Hispano.* 13/1 (Spring 1993): 67.

4. Expressions of the sense of racial superiority prevalent among Anglo Americans can be seen in the letters published in American newspapers. A letter published in the Washington *Daily Union* referred to the war as "the religious execution of our country's glorious mission, under the direction of Divine Providence, to civilize and Christianize, and raise up from anarchy and degradation a most ignorant, indolent, wicked and unhappy people" (Edwin Sylvest, "Hispanic American Protestantism in the United States," in *Fronteras: A History of the Latin American Church in the USA since 1513,* ed. Moíses Sandoval [San Antonio: Mexican American Cultural Center, 1983], 279-338, quoted from Albert K. Weinberg, *Manifest Destiny and Mission in American History: A Reinterpretation* [New York: Vintage, 1963], 162). David Weber writes, "One circumstance that colored Anglo American attitudes toward Hispanics was racial mixture. . . . Anglo Americans were shocked to meet a predominantly mestizo population [throughout the Southwest]. Through much of the nineteenth century, Anglo Americans generally regarded racial mixture as a violation of the laws of nature." For instance, Thomas Jefferson Farnham, a New England attorney, wrote that a child from parents of different races suffered from "a constitution less robust than that of either race from which he sprang." After having toured California in the 1840s, Farnham expressed commonly held views of Hispanics in the Southwest. He stated that racial blending of Spaniards and Indians in California had created "an imbecile, pusillanimous, race of men . . . unfit to control the destinies of that beautiful country" (David Weber, "The Spanish Legacy in North America and the Historical Imagination," *The Western Historical Quarterly* 23 [February 1992]: 7, quoting Thomas Jefferson Farnham, *Travels in California* [Oakland, Calif.: Biobooks, 1947], 161).

5. Reginald Horsman, *Race and Manifest Destiny: The Origins of American Racial Anglo-Saxonism* (Cambridge, Mass.: Harvard University Press, 1981), 211.

6. Ibid., 209. Horsman's quotation of Bushnell is from Horace Bushnell's *An Oration, Pronounced Before the Society of Phi Beta Kappa, at New Haven, on the Principles of National Greatness* (August 15, 1837), 5, 9, 11, 16.

When Horace Bushnell, in August 1837, delivered an oration on the principles of national greatness, he used old and familiar arguments concerning America as a land saved for events of world significance; however, he used a new precision in writing of the origin of the people for whom the New World had been preserved. "Out of all the inhabitants of the world," he said, "a select stock, the Saxon, and out of this the British family, the noblest of the stock, was chosen to people our country." In contrast, the Mexican state, he said, had started with fundamental disadvantages in the character of its immigrants. Josiah Strong (in *Our Country: Its Possible Future and Its Present Crisis*, rev. ed. [New York: Doubleday, Page, and Co., 1912], 222-23) supported Bushnell's miscegenational views. He predicts a time when the Anglo-Saxon race will vie with the other races of the world for supremacy:

> Long before the thousand millions are here, the mighty *centrifugal* tendency, inherent in this [Anglo-Saxon] stock and strengthened in the United States, will assert itself. Then this race of unequaled energy, with all the majesty of numbers and the might of wealth behind it—the representative, let us hope, of the largest liberty, the purest Christianity, the highest civilization—having developed peculiarly aggressive traits calculated to impress its institutions upon mankind, will spread itself over the earth. If I read not amiss, this powerful race will move down upon Mexico, down upon Central and South America, out upon the islands of the sea, over upon Africa and beyond. And can any one doubt that the result of this competition of races will be the "survival of the fittest"?

7. Macum Phelan, *A History of Early Methodists in Texas, 1817–1866* (Nashville, Tenn.: Cokesbury Press, 1924), 70.

8. Ibid., 149.

9. William Stuart Red, *A History of the Presbyterian Church in Texas* (N.p.: Steck Co., 1936), 31-33.

10. Thomas H. Campbell, *History of the Cumberland Presbyterian Church in Texas* (Nashville, Tenn.: Cumberland Presbyterian Publishing House, 1936), 29.

11. Sylvest, "Hispanic American Protestantism," 294.

12. Some authors have used the theory of colonialism to study the social relationship between ethnic and racial minorities and Anglo American society in the United States. See Robert Blauner, "Internal Colonialism and Ghetto Revolt," *Social Problems* 16 (Spring 1969): 393-408. Others have used the theoretical framework of colonialism as a means of interpreting the religious condition of Mexican Americans in the Southwest. See David Maldonado, "Hispanic Protestants: Reflections on History," *Apuntes* 11/1 (Spring 1991): 3-16. E. C. Orozco's *Republican Protestantism in Aztlán* relies on the concept of colonialism as well. I have chosen to use the concept of marginalization instead of colonialism.

13. For an account of the first Protestant efforts to minister to the Spanish-speaking in the Southwest, see Sylvest, "Hispanic American Protestantism," 279-338.

14. Ibid., 293.

15. Alfredo Nañez, *History of the Rio Grande Conference of the United Methodist Church* (Dallas: Bridwell Library, Southern Methodist University, 1980), 3.

16. Olin W. Nail, *The First Hundred Years of the Southwest Texas Conference of the Methodist Church 1858–1958* (San Antonio: Southwest Texas Conference, Methodist Church, 1958), 120. See also H. G. Horton, "Beginnings of the Mexican Work," *Texas Methodist Historical Quarterly* 1/3 (January 1910): 291.

17. R. Douglas Brackenridge and Francisco O. García-Treto, *Iglesia Presbiteriana: A History of Presbyterians and Mexican Americans in the Southwest*, 2nd ed. (San Antonio: Trinity University Press, 1987), 6-7, quoting *The Annual Report of the Board of Foreign Missions of the Presbyterian Church in the United States of America* (New York, 1841), 8.

18. Nañez, *History of the Rio Grande Conference*, 58.

19. Ibid.

20. Thomas Harwood, *History of Spanish and English Missions of the New Mexico Methodist Episcopal Church from 1850–1910,* vol. 1 (Albuquerque, N.M.: El Abogado Press, 1908), 25-26.

21. Ibid., 26.

22. Ibid.

23. Ibid., 33-34, quoting J. P. Durbin, the Mission Secretary, in his report to the Mission Board of the Methodist Episcopal Church in 1855.

24. Harwood, *History of Spanish and English Missions,* 46.

25. Sylvest, "Hispanic American Protestantism," 302.

26. E. C. Orozco asserts that "organized proselytism" of Mexicans in Texas began in the 1880s, when the railroads arrived. In the footnote to this remark, he cites the organization of the first Mexican church in San Antonio in 1888. He overlooks the Methodists, who organized a Mexican district in 1874, which eventually became a Mexican Border Mission Conference in 1885. Orozco, *Republican Protestantism in Aztlán,* 109, 128n. 12.

27. Various authors note that the first Protestant churches in Texas and New Mexico had one or a few Spanish-speaking members. True integration of the groups, however, never materialized. Among some of the first Spanish-speaking members of Protestant churches: Mrs. William G. Cook (Angela María de Jesús Navarro), daughter of a hero of the Alamo, José Antonio Navarro, was one of the 13 charter members of First Baptist Church in San Antonio, organized January 20, 1861 (Joshua Grijalva, *A History of Mexican Baptists in Texas, 1881–1981* [Dallas: Office of Language Missions, Baptist General Convention of Texas, in cooperation with the Mexican Baptist Convention of Texas, 1982], 12). H. G. Horton also claims the daughters of José Antonio Navarro as members of the Soledad Street Methodist Episcopal Church, South, in San Antonio. He adds that José Antonio Navarro himself joined the church. Horton states,

"When I was pastor there in the early part of 1862 I found a number of Mexicans as members, and the Navarro girls were teachers of Mexican classes in our Sunday School." Horton tells of other conversions of Mexican Americans attending preaching services in Texas. (H. G. Horton, "Beginnings of the Mexican Work," *Texas Methodist Historical Quarterly* 1/3 (1910): 289-90. Matovina disputes the accuracy of Horton's claim about the Navarro family's affiliation with the Methodist Episcopal Church (Timothy M. Matovina, *Tejano Religion and Ethnicity: San Antonio, 1821–1860* [Austin: University of Texas Press, 1995], 62). In New Mexico, the first Presbyterian church organized in Santa Fe in 1867 received a *Nuevomexicano*, Anastacio Gonzáles, on May 9, 1869 (Brackenridge and García-Treto, *Iglesia Presbiteriana*, 37).

28. *Actas de la Conferencia Fronteriza Misionera Mexicana* (San Antonio, October 28–November 2, 1885). *Actas de la Conferencia Fronteriza Misionera Mexicana* (Chihuahua, Mexico, October 15-19, 1890).

29. Roger Loyd, "Alexander H. Sutherland: Prophet of the Lord," paper submitted for a course at Perkins School of Theology, April 22, 1971, Appendix: "Alexander H. Sutherland—Chronology."

30. Nañez, *History of the Rio Grande Conference*, 19-20.

31. "Statistical Report for the New Mexico Spanish Mission," in *Minutes of the Annual Conferences of the Methodist Episcopal Church. Fall Conferences of 1891* (New York: Hunt & Eaton, 1891), 568. "Statistical Report for the New Mexico Spanish Mission," in *Minutes of the Annual Conferences of the Methodist Episcopal Church. Fall Conferences, 1907* (New York: Eaton & Mains, 1907), 818.

32. Walter M. Vernon, "Some Thoughts on the Historic Methodist Mission to Mexican Americans" (Dallas, Tex.: Perkins School of Theology, February 1975), 3. Quoting from Alexander Sutherland's missionary report in *Annual Report, Board of Missions, Methodist Episcopal Church, South, 1883*, 70.

33. R. W. Roundy, "The Mexican in Our Midst," *Missionary Review of the World* 44 (May 1921): 367.

34. Vernon, "Some Thoughts," 10. Quoting from Alexander Sutherland in *Annual Report, Board of Missions, Methodist Episcopal Church, South, 1884*, 72.

35. Thomas Harwood, "Mission Report," *Sixty-fourth Annual Report of the Missionary Society of the Methodist Episcopal Church (for the Year 1882)* (New York: Missionary Society of the Methodist Episcopal Church, January 1883): 201.

36. Nañez, *History of the Rio Grande Conference*, 19.

37. Ibid., 54.

38. Alfredo Nañez, "The Transition from Anglo to Mexican-American Leadership in the Rio Grande Conference," *Methodist History* 16 (January 1978): 68.

39. *Minutes of the Conferencia Fronteriza Misionera Mexicana of the Methodist Episcopal Church, South* (Monclova, Mexico: Nov. 10-14, 1887), 18-19.

40. Ibid., 19.

41. *Minutes of the Conferencia Fronteriza Misionera Mexicana of the Methodist Episcopal Church, South* (San Antonio: Oct. 16-21, 1889), 14.

42. *Minutes of the Conferencia Fronteriza Misionera Mexicana of the Methodist Episcopal Church, South* (Chihuahua, Mexico: Oct. 15-19, 1890).

43. *Minutes of the Conferencia Fronteriza Misionera Mexicana of the Methodist Episcopal Church, South* (Laredo, Tex.: Feb. 12-14, 1914), 34.

44. This information was obtained from the annual minutes of all of the Spanish-speaking missions and conferences of the Methodist Episcopal Church, South, operating along the U.S.-Mexico border from 1885–1939, including the following institutions: Conferencia Fronteriza Misionera Mexicana (Mexican Border Mission Conference), Conferencia Noroeste Misionera Mexicana (Northwest Mexican Mission Conference), Conferencia Mexicana (The Annual Conference of Mexico), Misión Mexicana de Texas (Texas Mexican Mission), Misión Mexicana del Pacifico (Pacific Mexican Mission), Misión Mexicana del Occidente (Western Mexican Mission), Conferencia Mexicana del Occidente (Western Mexican Conference), and Conferencia Mexicana de Texas (Texas Mexican Conference).

45. The typical labels do not apply to Tafolla. It would not be accurate to refer to him simply as Spanish-speaking since he was fully fluent in English and Spanish. His ability to speak fluent English was probably a factor in his appointment as a presiding elder.

46. Tafolla, *Nearing the End.*

47. *Minutes of the Conferencia Fronteriza Misionera Mexicana of the Methodist Episcopal Church.* List of appointments for 1885–89 and 1890–94.

48. Nañez, *History of the Rio Grande Conference,* 92.

49. As an example, appropriations made by the Missionary Society of the Methodist Episcopal Church for the New Mexico Mission in 1880 show that the missions pastored by Anglo American missionaries made at least $200 more than those pastored by *nuevomexicano* pastors. Thomas Harwood, "Mission Report," in *Sixty-second Annual Report of the Missionary Society of the Methodist Episcopal Church (for the Year 1880)* (New York: Missionary Society of the Methodist Episcopal Church, January 1881), 228. The appropriations made for 1881 continue the practice of unequal financial compensation. Anglo American missionaries received compensation ranging from $600 to $1,000; *nuevomexicano* pastors received compensation ranging from $300 to $450. Thomas Harwood, "Mission Report," *Sixty-third Annual Report of the Missionary Society of the Methodist Episcopal Church (for the Year 1881)* (New York: Missionary Society of the Methodist Episcopal Church, January 1881), 284.

50. Loyd, "Alexander H. Sutherland," 11.

51. Randi Jones Walker, *Protestantism in the Sangre de Cristos, 1850–1920* (Albuquerque: University of New Mexico Press, 1991), 83.

52. Loyd, "Alexander H. Sutherland," 18.

53. *Minutes of the Conferencia Fronteriza Misionera Mexicana of the Methodist Episcopal Church, South* (Laredo, Tex.: November 5-9, 1891), 9 (translation mine).

54. *Minutes of the Mission Board of the Methodist Episcopal Church, South* (Nashville, Tenn.: May 7, 1913), 6.

55. Until 1914, the Spanish-speaking missions and conferences of the Methodist Episcopal Church, South, operating without regard for the U.S.-Mexico border, spanned both sides of the border.

56. The memorial states: "Resolved, That this Board memorialize the next General Conference to take such action as will transfer that part of the work of the Mexican Border Conference which lies in Texas to the Home Department of the Board of Missions or to the Annual Conferences within which the work falls" (*Minutes of the Mission Board*, 6).

57. Nañez, *History of the Rio Grande Conference*, 63.

58. *Minutes of the Conferencia Fronteriza Misionera Mexicana of the Methodist Episcopal Church, South* (Laredo, Tex.: February 12-14, 1914), 32.

59. Ibid., 35 (translation mine).

60. The 1914 General Conference established the boundaries of the two missions: "The Pacific Mexican Mission shall include the work in Spanish in California and Arizona and in the States of Sonora and Sinaloa and the territories of Tepic and Baja California in Mexico. . . . The Texas Mexican Mission shall embrace all the work for Mexicans in Texas east of the Pecos River" (*Journal of the Seventeenth General Conference of the Methodist Episcopal Church, South*, held in Oklahoma City, May 6-23, 1914 [Nashville, Tenn.: Publishing House Methodist Episcopal Church, South], 375). Nañez notes the boundaries of the reorganized conference of which the two missions were a part: "The Mexican Border Conference . . . was to include the states of Tamaulipas, Nuevo León, Coahuila, Chihuahua, and Durango in Mexico and in the United States, Texas west of the Pecos River and New Mexico" (Nañez, *History of the Rio Grande Conference*, 65).

61. *Minutes of the Conferencia Fronteriza Misionera Mexicana of the Methodist Episcopal Church, South* (Laredo, Tex.: February 12-14, 1914), 34, author's translation.

62. Nañez, "Leadership," 69.

63. *Journal of the Twenty-second General Conference of the Methodist Episcopal Church, South* (Jackson, Miss.: April 26–May 8, 1934), 314.

64. Alfredo Nañez, "Interview with Alfredo Nañez," conducted by Roy Barton (N.p., n.d.), 23.

65. Ibid. Nañez argues that the Anglo American delegates from the two Texas and Western Mexican Conferences were responsible for inserting the exemption on the tenure of district superintendents, in "Leadership," 70. The delegates to General Conference were the Reverend F. S. Onderdonk, a presiding elder in the Texas Mexican Conference, and his wife, Mrs. F. S. Onderdonk, and the Reverend Laurence Reynods, a presiding elder in the Western

Mexican Conference, and Mrs. R. J. Parker ("Tentative Committee Assignments," *Daily Christian Advocate* [1934]: 4-5). There is no documentary evidence that the delegates from the two Mexican conferences were actually responsible for including the two conferences in the exemption for the legislation, but Nañez' attribution of the exemption to these delegates is the most plausible account.

66. Minutes of the *Conferencia Mexicana del Occidente of the Methodist Episcopal Church, South* (Nogales, Ariz.: November 6-8, 1934), 13. Nañez attributes the vote of 22 to 8 in favor of the amendment by the Texas Mexican Conference to the members' concern for the status of F. S. Onderdonk. He states, "By 1934 there was only one minister with missionary status, and that was the dearly beloved Dr. Onderdonk. He had been in ill health for some time, and if the amendment had not passed, he would have to leave the district. This explains the favorable vote to the amendment" (Nañez, *History of the Rio Grande Conference*, 92). After Onderdonk died in 1936, the Texas Mexican Conference sent a memorial to General Conference in 1937 requesting an end to the exemption.

67. *Minutes of the Conferencia Mexicana de Texas of the Methodist Episcopal Church, South* (San Antonio: October 14-17, 1937), 14.

68. Nañez, *History of the Rio Grande Conference*, 83-84.

69. Joel Martínez, "The South Central Jurisdiction," in *Each in Our Own Tongue: A History of Hispanic United Methodism*, Justo L. González, ed. (Nashville: Abingdon Press, 1991), 51.

70. Nañez, *History of the Rio Grande Conference*, 83.

71. Ibid.

72. Ibid.

73. *Minutes of the Conferencia Mexicana Suroeste of the Methodist Episcopal Church, South* (Dallas: November 2-5, 1939), Statistical Chart; *Minutes of the Conferencia Anual Rio Grande of the Methodist Church* (El Paso: June 8-11, 1950), Statistical Chart. The "Disciplinary Questions" section of the report of the Conferencia Suroeste Mexicana in the *General Minutes of the Methodist Church* reports 6,397 in 1939, while the statistical chart in the *Minutes of the Conferencia Suroeste Mexicana of the Methodist Church*, in Dallas, November 2-5, 1939, reports 6,903.

74. Nañez, *History of the Rio Grande Conference*, 30.

75. Ibid., 32.

76. *Minutes of the Conferencia Mexicana Suroeste of the Methodist Episcopal Church, South* (Dallas: November 2-5, 1939), Statistical Chart. Randi Jones Walker states in *Protestantism in the Sangre de Cristos* that there were even fewer members than this report indicates. She states that "there were only 480 Hispanic members and six Hispanic ministers in New Mexico" (*Protestantism in the Sangre de Cristos*, 43). The *Minutes of the New Mexico Mission, 1939*, which records the last annual meeting of the Spanish-speaking churches as part of

the English-speaking mission, held in Albuquerque, June 1-4, 1939, shows that there were 493 members. This number is taken from the statistical chart. Although the district superintendent's report lists twelve churches on p. 20, only six of these churches are listed in the statistical chart on p. 101. They are Albuquerque, Deming (Circuit), El Paso–El Buen Pastor, Las Cruces, Socorro (Circuit), and Wagon Mound.

Chapter 4: Latinos in the Protestant Establishment: Is There a Place for Us at the Feast Table?

1. Robert Wuthnow, *Christianity in the Twenty-first Century: Reflections on the Challenges Ahead* (New York: Oxford University Press, 1993), 4.

2. Ibid., 8.

3. Ibid.

4. Ibid.

5. Peter Kivisto, "Religion and the New Immigrants" in William H. Swatos, Jr., ed., *A Future for Religion? New Paradigms for Social Analysis* (Newbury Park, N.Y.: Sage Publications, 1993), 92.

6. Anthony E. Healy, "The Age of Migration," *Cutting Edge,* Board of Church Extension, Christian Church (Disciples of Christ) 24 (1995): 1.

7. Ibid., 94.

8. Pastora San Juan Cafferty and William C. McCready, *Hispanics in the United States* (New Brunswick, N.J.: Transaction Books, 1985), 25. This figure may be dated, yet the authors point out that, "while most demographers who have analyzed illegal immigration from Hispanic countries had concluded that the *stock* of illegal immigrants is not so large as the speculated 5-6 million, there is a large *flow* of undocumented immigrants." For the purposes of this paper this means that mainstream denominations have an even greater challenge to develop viable ministries in the Latino communities in the United States.

9. Jayadeva Uyangoda, "Understanding Ethnicity and Nationalism," *Ecumenical Review* 47 (April 1995): 193.

10. Ibid., 191.

11. Ibid.

12. Arnoldo De León, *They Called Them Greasers: Anglo Attitudes Toward Mexicans in Texas, 1821–1900* (Austin: University of Texas Press, 1983), 1.

13. Ibid., 2.

14. Ibid., 3.

15. Ibid., 5.

16. Ibid., 8-9.

17. Ibid., 15.

18. Ibid., 13.

19. William Stuart Red, *The Texas Colonists and Religion, 1821–1836* (Austin: E. L. Shuttles, 1924), 75.

20. Ibid., 74.

21. W. R. Estep, "Religion in the Lone Star State: An Historical Perspective," *International Review of Mission* 78 (April 1989): 181.

22. Colby D. Hall, *Texas Disciples* (Fort Worth: Texas Christian University Press, 1953), 38.

23. Red, *Texas Colonists and Religion*, 84; Hall, *Texas Disciples*, 38.

24. Hall, *Texas Disciples*, 33.

25. Ibid., 89.

26. See Richard Griswold del Castillo, *The Treaty of Guadalupe-Hidalgo: A Legacy of Conflict* (Norman: University of Oklahoma Press, 1990); Arnoldo De León, *Mexican Americans in Texas* (Arlington Heights, Ill.: Harlan Davidson, 1993).

27. The terms "Mexican," "Mexican-Texan," and "Tejano" are used interchangeably throughout this essay. Although it is accurate to distinguish a Mexican as someone born in Mexico and a Mexican-Texan or Tejano as a U.S. citizen of Mexican ancestry, for the missionaries of the late 1800s and early 1900s these distinctions were not important. The issue was that whether Mexican or Tejano these folks were *Other*.

28. Arnoldo De León and Kenneth L. Stewart, *Tejanos and the Numbers Game, A Socio-Historical Interpretation from the Federal Censuses, 1850–1900* (Albuquerque: University of New Mexico Press, 1989), 4.

29. "Mexican Americans," *Survey of Service*, The United Christian Missionary Society (St. Louis: Christian Board of Publication, 1928), 127 (emphasis mine).

30. Joshua Grijalva, *A History of Mexican Baptists in Texas, 1881–1981* (Dallas: Office of Language Missions, Baptist General Convention of Texas, 1982), 27 (emphasis mine).

31. For a history of how the Presbyterians perceived their work in Texas, see R. Douglas Brackenridge and Francisco O. García-Treto, *Iglesia Presbiteriana: A History of Presbyterians and Mexicans in the Southwest* (San Antonio: Trinity University Press, 1987). Like other mainstream Protestants, the Presbyterians perceived Christianization as an important component in the process of the Americanization of the Mexican.

32. "Hispanic Ministries: Challenge and Opportunity," a report to the General Conference of The United Methodist Church (1992), 39.

33. Grijalva, *History of Mexican Baptists in Texas*, 13.

34. "Mexican Americans," *Survey of Service*, 121.

35. William McKinney, "Of Centers and Margins," *Cutting Edge*, Board of Church Extension, Christian Church (Disciples of Christ) 18 (1989): 2.

36. Wade Clark Roof and William McKinney, *American Mainline Religion* (New Brunswick, N.J.: Rutgers University Press, 1987), 33-39.

37. Ibid., 34.

38. Ibid.

39. Ibid., 25-26.

40. Jorge Lara-Braud, "Hispanic Ministry: Fidelity to Christ," *Pacific Theological Review* 19 (Winter 1986): 13.

41. McKinney, "Of Centers and Margins," 4.

42. Isidro Lucas, *The Browning of America: The Hispanic Revolution in the American Church* (Chicago: Fides/Claretian, 1981), ix.

43. McKinney, "Of Centers and Margins," 1, 2.

44. Ibid., 3.

45. Ibid.

46. Ibid.

47. Though estimates vary, U.S. Department of Commerce, Bureau of the Census, "News release on 1990 Census Counts on Hispanic Population Groups" (June 12, 1991), gives an "official" total U.S. population for persons of "Hispanic Origin" of 22.3 million. These figures are often hotly disputed among Latinos who argue that the official figures do not include the undocumented segment of the Latino population, which some say raises the total to over 25 million persons of Hispanic origin residing in the United States.

48. David A. Vargas, "Toward a Liberating Ecumenical Church," paper presented at the Christian Church (Disciples of Christ) Churchwide Planning Conference, Lexington, Kentucky, June 1-5, 1988, 8.

49. General Assembly of the Christian Church, Business Docket, 318-19.

50. Joel N. Martínez, "Hispanic Ministry: More Than 'Add-on,'" *Christian Social Action* 7 (February 1994): 35.

51. Ibid., 34.

52. U.S. Department of Commerce, Bureau of the Census. "News release on 1990 Census Counts on Hispanic Population Groups" (June 12, 1991), Table 3B.

53. Ibid., Table 3A.

54. Martínez, "Hispanic Ministry: More Than 'Add-on,'" 35.

55. Vargas, "Toward a Liberating Ecumenical Church," 5.

56. Martínez, "Hispanic Ministry: More Than 'Add-on,'" 35.

57. Daniel M. Long, "Toward Effective Ministry with Hispanics," *Word & World I* (Winter 1985): 33.

58. Stephen B. Bevans, *Models of Contextual Theology* (Maryknoll, N.Y.: Orbis, 1992), 63-80.

Chapter 5: Confessing the Faith from a Hispanic Perspective

1. Fortunately, most faculty members at the seminary and other institutions of higher learning are beginning to revise their old courses and teaching

practices making more significant references to Hispanic scholarship and the religious experience of our people.

2. Here I use the term "catholic" to mean "according to the whole." For a more elaborate examination of this point, see Justo L. González, *Out of Every Tribe and Nation: Christian Theology at the Ethnic Roundtable* (Nashville: Abingdon Press, 1992), 18-27. Also by the same author, *Santa Biblia: The Bible Through Hispanic Eyes* (Nashville: Abingdon Press, 1996), 16-21.

3. It is important to clarify that this prophetic function is produced by the witness of Roman Catholic and Protestant Hispanics on the tradition of faith that we share in common. This prophetic witness creates the conditions for a new ecumenical foundation for dialogue and ministry for the church as a whole, as we strive to be faithful in our understanding and witness to the gospel. For an eloquent articulation of this point, see Justo L. González, *Mañana: Christian Theology from a Hispanic Perspective* (Nashville: Abingdon Press, 1990), 9-74.

4. González refers to these events as "macroevents"—events so large and far-reaching that we only become aware of them when we stand back from daily events and try to see the trends of the last few centuries. In *Mañana* he examines three of these macroevents: (1) the end of the Constantinean era, (2) the failure of the North in promising a new era of prosperity for humankind, and (3) the growing self-consciousness of many who were mostly silent until fairly recent times. He also points out that these macroevents might bring more drastic changes than those which took place in the sixteenth century. Ibid., 43.

5. Ibid., 43-48.

6. Ibid., 51.

7. For a more elaborate understanding of this statement, see José D. Rodríguez, "Confessing the Faith in Spanish: Challenge or Promise," in *Hispanic Theology: Challenge or Promise*, Ada María Isasi-Diaz and Fernando F. Segovia, eds. (Minneapolis: Fortress, 1995), 351-66.

8. González, *Mañana*, 48-53.

9. This article was written for the celebration of the tenth anniversary of *Apuntes*. See José D. Rodríguez, "De 'apuntes' a 'esbozo': Diez años de reflexión," *Apuntes* 10/3 (winter 1990): 75-83. In it, I examined the relationship of this perspective to Latin American theology, I explored its emphasis on the sociohistorical and religious marginalization experienced by our community, I analyzed the use of marginality and mestizaje as its central hermeneutical keys, and I provided examples of basic themes examined by its main exponents. I also suggested areas in need of development.

10. This experience of struggle is very common in the life of Hispanics and other ethnic groups in the United States. For a more extensive exploration of the history and social experience of Hispanics in the United States, see the

studies by other writers in this volume. For an interesting description of this struggle in the context of theological education and scholarship, see Fernando F. Segovia, "Theological Education and Scholarship as Struggle: The Life of Racial/Ethnic Minorities in the Profession," *Journal of Hispanic/Latino Theology* 2/2 (November 1994): 2-25.

11. For a more recent article in which I articulate this more fully, see n. 7 above.

12. I am pleased that these efforts are contributing to clarifying and deepening the impact of this perspective in a wider context. In another study I briefly examine some important works in this area. See José D. Rodriguez, "On Doing Hispanic Theology," lecture presented at the First Encuentro on Theology and Ethics at Princeton Theological Seminary, Princeton, New Jersey, June 1995 (Louisville: John Knox/Westminster, forthcoming). This encuentro was sponsored by the Asociación de Educación Teológica Hispana.

13. One of the most important early works in this area is *Fronteras: A History of the Latin American Church in the USA Since 1513* (San Antonio: Mexican American Cultural Center, 1983). This study, produced by mostly Hispanic American Roman Catholic authors in the U.S., is also part of the collection of CEHILA (Commission for the Study of the History of the Church in Latin America). A more recent effort to document the religious history of Hispanics from a Protestant perspective is *Hidden Stories: Unveiling the History of the Latino Church,* Daniel Rodríguez and David Cortés-Fuentes, eds. (Decatur: AETH, 1994).

14. Virgilio Elizondo describes this religious perspective as a *mestizo* Christianity, which is both in communion with the universal church and its traditions, as well as with our own historical and cultural uniqueness. For a more detailed examination of this topic, see Virgilio Elizondo, *The Galilean Journey* (New York: Orbis, 1983).

15. Piri Thomas, *Savior, Savior, Hold My Hand* (New York: Doubleday, 1972), 260.

16. Victor Codina, "Credo Oficial y credo popular," *Revista Latinoamericana de teología* 26/9 (mayo-agosto 1992): 243-52.

17. The true purpose of the story is not to bring people to venerate an image of the virgin, but to challenge people then, as well as now, to join in an ancient biblical tradition that the early Christian community attributed to the virgin Mary (Luke 1:46-55). It is the tradition of a God who loves all human beings. To express this love, God "scatters the proud, puts down the mighty from their thrones, and exalts those of low degree." For a more detailed account of this important religious symbol and its relationship to the conversion to Christianity of indigenous people in Latin America, see Elizondo, *Galilean Journey,* 11-13. For a Protestant perspective on this event, see José D. Rodriguez and Colleen Nelson, "The Virgin of Guadalupe," in *Currents in Theology and Mission* 13/6 (December

1986): 368-69. One of the most recent and valuable studies of this subject is Jeanette Rodríguez, *Our Lady of Guadalupe: Faith and Empowerment Among Mexican-American Women* (Austin: University of Texas Press, 1994).

18. While the names of Montecinos and Las Casas are well known as protectors of indigenous people in America, Epifanio de Moirans and Francisco de Jaca should also be mentioned for their advocacy of African slaves. See José Tomás López García, "Dos defensores de los esclavos negros," in *Raices de la teología Latinoamericana*, Pablo Richard, ed. (San José, Costa Rica: Departamento Ecuménico de Investigaciones, 1985), 67-71. Among these prophetic witnesses, Antonio de Valdivieso deserves a special mention for being the first great ecclesial martyr murdered in 1550 for his compelling preaching in defense of the native people. For an interesting study on sixteenth-century bishops who protected indigenous people in America, see Enrique Dussel, *El episcopado Latinoamericano y la liberación de los pobres 1504–1620* (México: Centro de Reflexión Teológica, A.C., 1979).

19. According to Codina, this popular faith, while at times it becomes the expression of religious alienation—false resignation, passivity, and anti-Protestant and anti-communist apologetics—it nevertheless constitutes the basis for the renewal of the church's theology and praxis. Codina, "Credo Oficial y credo popular," 251.

20. For a valuable discussion of the biblical, historical, and theological origins of this confessional dimension of faith, see *Confessing One Faith*, G. W. Forell and J. F. McCue, eds. (Minneapolis: Augsburg Publishing House, 1982). Carl Braaten argues that the confessional principle of Luther and Lutheran theology is the product of the basic act of faith, for a nonconfessional Christianity is a contradiction in terms. He further contends that the confessional datum of faith is most clearly seen in the baptismal formulae and eucharistic hymns that made up the most primitive creeds of Christianity. Carl E. Braaten, *Principles of Lutheran Theology* (Philadelphia: Fortress, 1983), 27-28.

21. An interesting exception to this trend is the work of Justo L. González. In one of his numerous publications, he provides the historical development and sociopolitical context of three theological perspectives that characterized the early development of Christian theology and the significant role they played in the theological formulation of their originators. González, *Christian Thought Revisited: Three Types of Theology* (Nashville: Abingdon Press, 1989).

22. See González, *Mañana*, 21-30.

23. In 1988, Justo L. González published a report on the theological education of Hispanics in the U.S., Puerto Rico, and Canada. This study, commissioned by The Fund for Theological Education, showed the value of the effort and further recommended the creation of a National Hispanic Summer Program. See González, *The Theological Education of Hispanics* (New York: Fund for Theological Education, 1988).

24. For those interested in a more elaborate exposition of these various biblical reading strategies, see Fernando F. Segovia, "Hispanic American Theology and the Bible: Effective Weapon and Faithful Ally," in *We Are a People! Initiatives in Hispanic American Theology,* Roberto Goizueta, ed. (Minneapolis: Fortress, 1992), 21-49; also Jean Pierre Ruiz, "Beginning to Read the Bible in Spanish," *Journal of Hispanic/Latino Theology* 1/2 (February 1994): 28-50.

25. González, *Mañana,* 84.

26. Ibid., 75-77.

27. "We know that we are born out of an act of violence of cosmic proportions in which our Spanish forefathers raped our Indian foremothers. We have no skeletons in our closet. Our skeletons are at the very heart of our history and our reality as a people. Therefore, we are comforted when we read the genealogy of Jesus and find there not only a Gentile like ourselves but also incest and what amounts to David's rape of Bathsheba. The Gospel writer did not hide the skeletons in Jesus' closet but listed them, so that we may know that the Savior has really come to be one of us—not just one of the high and the mighty, the aristocratic with impeccable blood lines, but one of *us*" (ibid., 77-78).

28. Ibid., 75-87.

29. Fernando F. Segovia, "Reading the Bible as Hispanic Americans," in *The New Interpreter's Bible* vol. 1 (Nashville: Abingdon Press, 1994), 170-71.

30. Ibid., 85-87. In a recent publication González argues that, given the diversity of Hispanic perspectives in reading the Bible, even in the context of the Protestant Hispanic community, it is better to provide different paradigms to help clarify what is meant by reading it "through Hispanic eyes." In this study, he explores five themes or paradigms (marginality, poverty, *mestizaje, mulatez,* and solidarity) characteristic of Hispanic hermeneutics. He also provides concrete examples of the way these paradigms are employed by leaders of our community (González, *Santa Biblia,* 31-33). The book was the product of the collective work of pastors, professors, and other church leaders at the Hispanic Instructors Program. The program, offered by the Mexican American Program at Perkins School of Theology, was designed as a program providing nurture and support for people who are ministering in various Hispanic settings.

31. Harold J. Recinos, *Hear the Cry! A Latino Pastor Challenges the Church* (Louisville: Westminster/John Knox Press, 1989), 65-81. In another publication Recinos explores this topic as it relates to the multicultural and global experience in the urban centers of the United States. His ability to hear and dialogue with other voices enables us to find God in the crucified humanity of the city, challenging the whole church to fulfill its call of delivering good news in its mission and ministry. See Recinos, *Jesus Weeps: Global Encounters on Our Doorsteps* (Nashville: Abingdon Press, 1992).

32. Marta Sotomayor-Chávez, "Latin American Migration," *Apuntes* 2/1 (1982): 8-14.

33. Rebeca Radillo, "The Migrant Family," *Apuntes* 5/1 (1985): 16-19.

34. González, "Sanctuary: Historical, Legal, and Biblical Considerations," *Apuntes* 5/2 (1985): 36-47. Also Francisco O. García-Treto, "El Señor guarda a los emigrantes," *Apuntes* 1/4 (1981): 3-9.

35. González, "The Apostles' Creed and the Sanctuary Movement," *Apuntes* 6/1 (1986): 12-20. Jorge Lara-Braud, "Reflexiones teológicas sobre la migración," *Apuntes* 2/1 (1982): 3-7. Hugo L. López, "Towards a Theology of Migration," *Apuntes* 2/3 (1982): 68-71, and by the same author, "El divino migrante," *Apuntes* 4/1 (1984): 14-19.

36. Sociopolitical problems challenging ministry with migrants include discussion of the economic and political interests which affect state and federal legislation of migration in the United States, paying equal regard to the costly human suffering created by this legislation.

37. García-Treto, "El Señor guarda," 8.

38. González, "The Apostles' Creed and the Sanctuary Movement," 19.

39. For an interesting examination of the significance of preaching in the period of the sixteenth-century Reformation, see Bernard Cooke, *Ministry to Word and Sacraments: History and Theology* (Philadelphia: Fortress, 1980), 285-303.

40. Justo L. González and Catherine G. González, *Liberation Preaching: The Pulpit and the Oppressed* (Nashville: Abingdon, 1980).

41. Their analysis of preaching seeks to provide a description of the theological perspective of traditionally powerless sectors of society. "When we speak here of 'liberation theology,' we are referring to theology done from the perspective of those who have been traditionally powerless in society and voiceless in the church. In the United States, this means blacks, Hispanics, Asian Americans, and others" (ibid., 11-12).

42. Ibid., 29-93.

43. In this book they examine four other pointers: (1) reassigning the cast of characters, (2) imagining a different setting, (3) considering the direction of the action, and (4) avoiding avoidance (ibid., 69-93).

44. The basis of this hermeneutic circle is drawn from the works of the Latin American theologian Juan Luis Segundo (ibid., 31-33).

45. Ibid., 33.

46. *Pulpito Cristiano y justicia social,* Daniel Rodríguez and Rodolfo Espinosa, eds. (México: Publicaciones El Faro S.A. de C.V., 1994). This book also provides a valuable examination of some of the most important issues in the area of preaching by representatives of our people both in the United States and in Latin America. An earlier collection on this subject is *Voces del púlpito hispano,* ed. Angel L. Gutiérrez (Valley Forge, Pa.: Judson Press, 1989).

47. *Pulpito Cristiano,* 221-27. In another section of the book, Margarita Sánchez de León reflects on the deeper and more complex character of this prejudice and exclusion imposed on black women (ibid., 113-21).

48. Ibid., 187-94.

49. José D. Rodriguez, *El precio de la vocación profética* (México: Publicaciones El Faro, S.A. de C.V., 1994). The author of this book is my father.

50. Ibid., 7-12.

51. Edwin D. Aponte, "*Coritos* as Active Symbol in Latino Protestant Popular Religion," in *Journal of Hispanic/Latino Theology* 2/3 (February 1995): 57-66.

52. Gómez, who teaches in the Mexican American Program at Perkins School of Theology, argues that for the mestizo Protestant who has "doctrinal problems with the idea of the virgin," the celebration of *el día de las madres* may be the one remaining link, albeit an unconscious one, to the Virgin of Guadalupe (Roberto Gómez, "Mestizo Spirituality: Motifs of Sacrifice, Transformation, Thanksgiving, and Family in Four Mexican-American Rituals," *Apuntes* 11/4 [winter 1991]: 86).

53. María Santillán Baert, "Worship in the Hispanic United Methodist Church," in *¡Alabadle! Hispanic Christian Worship,* ed. Justo L. González (Nashville: Abingdon Press, 1996), 57-71.

54. Pablo A. Jiménez, "Worship Resources," in *¡Alabadle!*, 111-23.

55. Teresa Chávez Sauceda, "Becoming a Mestizo Church," in *¡Alabadle!*, 89-99.

56. Miguel A. Darino, "What Is Different About Hispanic Baptist Worship," in *¡Alabadle!*, 73-88.

57. Indigenous elements include celebrations of *the quinceañeras, las posadas, via crucis,* or the use of the music and instruments of our people like maracas, guitarras, and Caribbean-style drums.

58. My friend also told me that as a consequence of this and other negative experiences during his campaign, the candidate lost his race for election.

59. For a further exploration of this topic see Rodríguez' reflection on Matthew 20:1-16 in "The Parable of the Affirmative Action Employer," *Apuntes* 8/3 (fall 1988): 51-59.

60. There is a large bibliography of these contributions. Some of the prominent writers are José Míguez Bonino, Julio de Santa Ana, Elsa Tamez, Medardo Gómez, Ofelia Ortega, Walter Altmann, Wanda Deifelt, and Vitor Westhelle.

61. Elsa Tamez, *The Amnesty of Grace: Justification by Faith from a Latin American Perspective* (Nashville: Abingdon Press, 1993).

62. Ibid., 21.

63. In her study, Tamez provides a compelling articulation of the biblical basis for the relationship between the doctrine of justification and the notion of justice. She also provides a good summary of the contribution of Latin American scholars on this topic.

64. Justo L. González, *The Story of Christianity, Vol. 1: The Early Church to the Dawn of the Reformation* (San Francisco: Harper & Row, 1984), 31.

65. Ibid., 39-48.

66. González, *Mañana,* 93.

67. This is a faith stance that I find closely related to what Paul Tillich and Jaroslav Pelikan describe as the particular contribution of Lutheranism by their characterization of this confessional movement within the church catholic as emphasizing a "Catholic substance" and a "Protestant principle." I part company with these distinguished theologians when they make reference to philosophical concepts that may provide a "static" or "essentialist" view of what I consider to be a more dynamic and participatory experience of faith that continues to evolve and be enriched by the contribution of the faithful throughout time, space, gender, culture, etc. See Paul Tillich, *The Protestant Era* (Chicago: University of Chicago Press, 1957).

Chapter 6: Guideposts Along the Journey: Mapping North American Hispanic Theology

1. Alfred North Whitehead, *Modes of Thought* (New York: Free Press, 1938), 52-55. For Whitehead, meaning and value occur in the interplay between the infinite (indeterminate) relatedness of things and their concrete embodiment. *The Philosophy of Alfred North Whitehead,* Paul Arthur Schilpp, ed. (New York: Tudor Publishing, 1951), 674-75.

2. Alfred North Whitehead, *Process and Reality,* corrected edition (New York: Free Press, 1978), 15.

3. Jürgen Moltmann, in *Theology of Hope* (San Francisco: Harper San Francisco, 1967/1991), argues that a theology grounded in eschatology does not form judgments which nail reality down to what it is, but forms anticipations which show reality its prospects and future possibilities. Theological concepts do not give a fixed form to reality, but they are expanded by hope and anticipate future being (pp. 35-36). Hispanic theologies share this fluidity and anticipation of the future in their liberative vision, preventing fixed theological concepts.

4. As Roberto S. Goizueta notes in *Caminemos con Jesús: Toward a Hispanic/Latino Theology of Accompaniment* (Maryknoll, N.Y.: Orbis, 1995), 137.

5. Jacques Derrida, of *Grammatology,* Gayatri Chakravorty Spivak, trans. (Baltimore: John Hopkins University Press, 1976), 50-57.

6. See Derrida's article, "Différance" in *Speech and Phenomena and Other Essays on Husserl's Theory of Signs.* David B. Allison and Newton Garber, trans. (Evanston: Northwestern University Press, 1973), 129-31.

7. Ibid., Derrida writes: "The trace is not a presence but is rather the simulacrum of a presence that dislocates, displaces, and refers beyond itself. The trace has, properly speaking, no place, for effacement belongs to the very structure of the trace. Effacement must always be able to overtake the trace, otherwise it would not be a trace but an indestructible and monumental substance," p. 156.

8. Emmanuel Levinas, *Otherwise Than Being or Beyond Essence,* Alphonso Lingis, trans. (Boston: Martinus Nijhoff Publishers, 1981), 12.

9. See Goizueta, chap. 6.

10. Goizueta, *Caminemos con Jesús,* 164-65.

11. Postmodernism rejects the modern idea of an abstract, absolute, universe in favor of a multi-verse that values diversity and difference as noted by Stanley J. Grenz in *A Primer on Postmodernism* (Grand Rapids: Eerdmans, 1996), 49.

12. Goizueta notes this danger in "In Defense of Reason," *Journal of Hispanic/Latino Theology* 3/2 (February 1996): 16-26. David Abalos also laments this detached reasoning in *Latinos in the United States: The Sacred and the Political* (Notre Dame, Ind.: Notre Dame Press, 1986), 2.

13. Ada Maria Isasi-Diaz, *En la Lucha/In the Struggle: A Hispanic Women's Liberation Theology* (Minneapolis: Fortress, 1993), 170.

14. Justo L. González, *Mañana: Christian Theology from a Hispanic Perspective* (Nashville: Abingdon Press, 1990), 129.

15. Ibid.

16. See Sixto Garcia's article, "Sources and Loci of Hispanic Theology," in the *Journal of Hispanic/Latino Theology* 1/1 (November 1993): 40-41, and Maria Pilar Aquino's article, "Directions and Foundations of Hispanic/Latino Theology: Towards a Mestiza Theology of Liberation," in the same volume, 18-19.

17. Enrique Dussel, in the appendix of *History and the Theology of Liberation* (Maryknoll, N.Y.: Orbis, 1976).

18. Gustavo Gutiérrez, *A Theology of Liberation,* 15th anniversary edition (Maryknoll, N.Y.: Orbis, 1988), xxvii.

19. González, *Mañana,* 85.

20. Justo L. González, *Santa Biblia: The Bible Through Hispanic Eyes* (Nashville: Abingdon Press, 1996), 58-59.

21. Ibid., 26.

22. Gutiérrez, *Theology of Liberation,* 56.

23. See Goizueta's use of Vasconcelos in *"La Raza Cosmica?* The Vision of José Vasconcelos," *Journal of Hispanic/Latino Theology* 1/2 (February 1994): 5-27.

24. See, e.g., Elizondo's understanding of mestizaje in *The Future Is Mestizo: Life Where Cultures Meet* (New York: Crossroads, 1992), esp. pp. 82-86.

25. Elizondo, *Galilean Journey,* 100, identifies the mestizo as those who have suffered and been rejected, and as the "poor" in a broader sense of the word, p. 95.

26. Ibid., 100-101.

27. See further, Leonardo F. Astride's article, "Comunidades Latinas en los Estados Unidos: Su presente y su futuro," in *Apuntes* 15/2 (Summer 1995): 37-43.

28. See David Maldonado's article, "El Pueblo Latino and Its Identity: The Next Generation?" in *Apuntes* 15/2 (Summer 1995): 45-57.

29. González addresses this type of marginalization in his own life in *Mañana*, 22-23.

30. Elizondo, *Future Is Mestizo*, 20.

31. Ilan Stavans, in *The Hispanic Condition: Reflections on Culture and Identity in America* (New York: HarperCollins, 1995), notes that history texts do not mention that 10,000 Mexican Americans fought in the Civil War; that the first permanent European settlement in the New World was St. Augustine, Florida; that Mexican land was taken in the Mexican-American war; nor the Hispanics killed in resistance movements of the early twentieth century (p. 23).

32. Isasi-Diaz, *En la Lucha*, 52-54.

33. See Elizondo's treatment of "Galilean identity" and God's election in *The Galilean Journey: The Mexican American Promise* (Maryknoll, N.Y.: Orbis, 1983), 94-102.

34. González, *Mañana*, 26.

35. Roberto Goizueta, "Rediscovering Praxis," in *We Are a People: Initiatives in Hispanic American Theology* (Minneapolis: Fortress, 1992), 63-64.

36. See Orlando Espín's article "Tradition and Popular Religion: An Understanding of the Sensus Fidelium" in *Frontiers of Hispanic Theology in the United States*, Allan Figueroa Deck, ed. (Maryknoll, N.Y.: Orbis, 1992), 62-87, and Sixto Garcia's article "Sources and Loci of Hispanic Theology."

37. See Anthony M. Stevens-Arroyo's definition in the introduction to *Discovering Latino Religion: A Comprehensive Social Science Bibliography* (New York: Bildner Center Publications, 1995), 28-29.

38. Ibid., 64-65.

39. Gustavo Benavides writes in "Resistance and Accommodation in Latin American Popular Religion," that popular religion is a symbolic act of protest against the elite that excludes the practitioners. *An Enduring Flame: Studies on Latino Popular Religion*, Anthony M. Stevens-Arroyo and Ana Maria Diaz-Stevens, eds. (New York: Bildner Center Publications, 1994), 39.

40. Espín, "Tradition and Popular Religion." Espín notes that popular religion can be perceived as a source of embarrassment for the Catholic Church causing some Catholic theologians to either ignore or reject it (p. 62).

41. Edwin Aponte, "Coritos as Active Symbols in Latino Protestant Popular Religion," *Journal of Hispanic/Latino Theology* 2/3 (February 1995): 62-65.

42. Ibid., 63. Words in a particular corito can change to address those in the audience.

43. González, *Santa Biblia* (Nashville: Abingdon Press, 1996), 117-18.

44. For instance, Isasi-Diaz writes that the Bible plays a limited role in Hispanic Christianity, and a marginal role in the lives of Latinas (*En la Lucha*, 46).

45. C. Gilbert Romero, *Hispanic Devotional Practice: Tracing the Biblical Roots* (Maryknoll, N.Y.: Orbis, 1991), 20.

46. Ibid., 21-33.

47. Elizondo, *Galilean Journey*, 41-42.
48. C. Gilbert Romero links traditions and symbols with the role of the Bible in Hispanic theologies in "Tradition and Symbol as Biblical Keys for a United States Hispanic Theology," in *Frontiers of Hispanic Theology in the United States*, 41-61.
49. González, *Mañana*, 22.
50. Ibid., 85.
51. See Garcia's article "Sources and Loci of Hispanic Theology," 28-30.
52. Roberto Goizueta refers to it in *Caminemos con Jesús*, 31.
53. The Hispanic Instructors provide essential direction, feedback, and dialogue on the books' topics. In the preface of *Santa Biblia*, González acknowledges this community's dialogue and influence (p. 7). González's earlier book *Mañana* also is indebted indirectly to that community (pp. 7, 29).
54. González, *Mañana*, 28-30.
55. For instance, see Isasi-Diaz's acknowledgments in *En la Lucha: A Hispanic Women's Liberation Theology*, p. xiii, where she writes that she "cannot do theology and will not do theology apart from a community of support and accountability."
56. See Virgilio Elizondo's foreword to *Mañana*, p. 19, on how this new ecumenism enriches our understanding of God by allowing differences, and González's discussion of it as both a shared struggle and faith in a new liberative vision of the Gospels, 73-74.
57. Elizondo, *Future Is Mestizo*, 102-3.
58. González, *Mañana*, 164.
59. Elizondo, *Galilean Journey*, 115.
60. Ibid., 114.

Chapter 7: Hispanic Experience and the Protestant Ethic

1. Anthony Cortese, *Ethnic Ethics: The Restructuring of Moral Theory* (Albany: State University of New York Press, 1990), 91.
2. This mode of ethical thinking is known by the technical name "deontological ethics" or the ethics of duty. The classical formulation of this ethic was given by Immanuel Kant. An influential Protestant formulation of the theory is present in the work of Paul Ramsey. See his *Basic Christian Ethics* (Louisville: Westminster/John Knox Press, 1993); *Deeds and Rules in Christian Ethics* (New York: Charles Scribner's Sons, 1967); and *War and the Christian Conscience* (Durham, N.C.: Duke University Press, 1961).
3. This point is equally recognized by Iris Marion Young, *Justice and the Politics of Difference,* and Annette C. Baier, *Moral Prejudices: Essays on Ethics* (Cambridge, Mass.: Harvard University Press, 1995).
4. The classical expression of Utilitarian Ethics is presented by John Stu-

art Mill and Jeremy Bentham. A Christian advocate of this ethics is Joseph Fletcher, *Situation Ethics: A New Morality* (Philadelphia: Westminster, 1966).

5. Aristotle and Plato provide the classical expression of the ethics of character. Thomas Aquinas and Augustine deal with character formation from a theological point of view. Alasdair MacIntyre is one of its strongest present philosophical advocates. See his *After Virtue* (Notre Dame, Ind.: Notre Dame University Press, 1980) and *Three Rival Versions of Moral Inquiry: Encyclopedia, Genealogy, and Tradition* (Notre Dame, Ind.: University of Notre Dame Press, 1990). Among today's theologians, the work of Stanley Hauerwas is representative of this point of view. See his *Community of Character* (Notre Dame, Ind.: University of Notre Dame Press, 1981) and *Vision and Virtue* (Notre Dame, Ind.: University of Notre Dame Press, 1974). And William Bennett, the former Secretary of Education and Drug Czar, has made concern for character formation a part of political debate.

6. Justo González makes this point in *Mañana: Christian Theology from a Hispanic Perspective* (Nashville: Abingdon Press, 1970), 72.

7. Bruce C. Birch and Larry L. Rasmussen quote James Fallow, a speechwriter for President Jimmy Carter, who claims that while President Carter is a person of strong moral character and moral commitment, both of which are revealed by his commitment to homeless people and other international and national charity and justice commitments he is engaged in, he was a poor decision maker and problem solver (*Bible and Ethics in the Christian Life* [Minneapolis: Augsburg, 1989], 95).

8. It is this point that I believe has made Hauerwas' work attractive to many church leaders. One of the challenges Christians confront today is clarifying for themselves and others what difference it makes to look at the world from the perspective of Christian commitment. It is a matter of defining and clarifying one's religious identity, as well as the space where one's identity is shaped. Hispanics who seek to clarify aspects of their religious, social, and cultural identity, also find character ethics quite persuasive and attractive.

9. Eldin Villafañe and other Pentecostal thinkers emphasize the reality of evil and oppression represented by the terminology of powers and principalities. See his *Liberating Spirit: Towards an Hispanic American Pentecostal Social Ethics* (New York: University Press of America, 1992). See also John H. Yoder, *The Politics of Jesus* (Grand Rapids: Eerdmans, 1972), 135-62; and Stephen C. Mott, *Biblical Ethics and Social Change* (New York: Oxford University Press, 1982), 3-21.

Chapter 8: Reading the Hyphens: An Emerging Biblical Hermeneutics for Latino/Hispanic U.S. Protestants

1. The title of this paper is derived from the title—and the concept behind it—of Cuban American critic and poet Gustavo Pérez Firmat's *Life on the*

Hyphen, a 1994 volume of critical essays concerning what may be called the social location of Cuban Americans, and by extension and *mutatis mutandis,* of all U.S. Hispanics.

2. See Stanley Fish, *Is There a Text in This Class? The Authority of Interpretive Communities* (Cambridge, Mass.: Harvard University Press, 1980), esp. pp. 167-73.

3. A particularly helpful collection of articles detailing "social location" readings is found in Fernando F. Segovia and Mary Ann Tolbert, eds., *Reading from This Place, volume 1: Social Location and Biblical Interpretation in the United States* and *volume 2: Social Location and Biblical Interpretation in Global Perspective* (Minneapolis: Augsburg Fortress, 1995). A third volume was published in 1996. See also my review of the first volume in *Journal of Hispanic/Latino Theology* (1996), vol. 3, no. 3, 71-74.

4. The *Journal of Hispanic/Latino Theology* is the publication of ACHTUS, the Academy of Catholic Hispanic Theologians of the U.S., but counts a number of mainline Protestant academics among the members of its Editorial Board and Board of Contributing Editors.

5. Justo L. González, *Mañana: Christian Theology from a Hispanic Perspective* (Nashville: Abingdon Press, 1990), 41-42.

6. Ibid., 41.

7. Fernando F. Segovia, "Toward a Hermeneutics of the Diaspora: A Hermeneutics of Otherness and Engagement," in Segovia and Tolbert, eds., *Reading from This Place,* vol. 1, 66.

8. Fish, *Is There a Text,* 173.

9. See González, *Mañana,* 73-74, for a concise and cogent statement of the dimensions of that ecumenism.

10. Virgilio P. Elizondo, "Foreword," in González, *Mañana,* 9-20.

11. Justo González, "Hispanics in the New Reformation," 238-59; Harold Recinos, "Mission: A Latino Pastoral Theology," 133-45; Samuel Soliván-Román, "The Need for a North American Hispanic Theology," 45-52; Eldin Villafañe, "An Evangelical Call to a Social Spirituality: Confronting Evil in Urban Society," 210-23. In Arturo J. Bañuelas, ed., *Mestizo Christianity: Theology from the Latino Perspective* (Maryknoll, N.Y.: Orbis, 1995).

12. *Apuntes: reflexiones teológicas desde el margen hispano,* currently in its fifteenth year of publication, is the journal of the Mexican American Program at Perkins School of Theology, Southern Methodist University. For a representative collection of articles from its first ten years, see Justo L. González, ed., *Voces: Voices from the Hispanic Church* (Nashville: Abingdon Press, 1992).

13. Leander E. Keck et al., eds., *New Interpreter's Bible* (Nashville: Abingdon Press, 1994–). There are two Hispanics listed among the Consultants (Minerva Carcaño and Juan G. Feliciano) and five among the authors (Francisco O. García-Treto, Justo L. González, Samuel Pagán, Fernando F. Segovia, and Moisés Silva) of this 12-volume work.

14. Justo González, "Historia de la Interpretación Bíblica," in Pablo A. Jiménez, ed., *Lumbrera a Nuestro Camino* (Miami: Editorial Caribe, 1994), 117.

15. Ibid. (translation mine). The Spanish reads:

> Aunque frecuentemente se oye decir que nuestro pueblo rechaza el método histórico-crítico porque le quita autoridad a la Biblia, cabe preguntarnos si otra razón, quizá más profunda, de ese rechazo no sea quizá que el método mismo, y el modo en que se emplea, le quita autoridad al pueblo, a la comunidad hermenéutica, que es la iglesia toda.

16. See Justo L. González, *Santa Biblia: The Bible Through Hispanic Eyes* (Nashville: Abingdon Press, 1996), 28.

17. See pp. 125-87 of vol. 1 of the *New Interpreter's Bible* for a series of articles on these topics by James Earl Massey, Chan-Hie Kim, Fernando F. Segovia, George E. Tinker, and Carolyn Osiek, respectively.

18. Fernando F. Segovia, "Hispanic American Theology and the Bible: Effective Weapon and Faithful Ally," in Roberto S. Goizueta, ed., *We Are a People! Initiatives in Hispanic American Theology* (Minneapolis: Fortress, 1992), 21-49.

19. Fernando F. Segovia, "Toward Intercultural Criticism: A Reading Strategy from the Diaspora," in Segovia and Tolbert, eds., *Reading from This Place,* vol. 2, 303-30.

20. Ibid., 306.

21. Ibid.

22. Segovia, "Hispanic American Theology and the Bible," 34.

23. Ibid.

24. Ibid.

25. Ibid., 35.

26. Harold Recinos, "Militarism and the Poor," in González, ed., *Voces,* 159-65, p. 163. For the parable of the rich young ruler, see Luke 18:18-30.

27. See n. 16.

28. See, e.g., Virgilio Elizondo, *Galilean Journey: The Mexican-American Promise* (Maryknoll, N.Y.: Orbis, 1983).

29. Roberto S. Goizueta, *Caminemos con Jesús: Toward a Hispanic/Latino Theology of Accompaniment* (Maryknoll, N.Y.: Orbis, 1995).

30. González, *Mañana,* 75-87.

31. Ibid., 79.

32. Ibid., 77-78.

33. Ibid., 85-87.

34. Segovia, "Hispanic American Theology and the Bible," 45.

35. González, *Santa Biblia,* 32.

36. Ibid., 33.

37. See also Justo L. González, *Hechos* (Miami: Editorial Caribe, 1992) *Comentario Bíblico Hispanoamericano, passim;* and "Reading from My Bicultural Place: Acts 6:1-7," in Segovia and Tolbert, eds., *Reading from This Place,* vol. 1, 139-47.

38. González, *Santa Biblia,* 51.

39. Ibid., 55.

40. Ibid., 57.

41. Ibid., 58.

42. Ibid., 59.

43. Ibid., 74.

44. Ibid., 75.

45. Ibid., 78.

46. Ibid., 79-80.

47. Ibid., 80.

48. Ibid., 84.

49. Ibid., 90.

50. Ibid., 93.

51. Francisco García-Treto, "El Señor guarda a los emigrantes," *Apuntes* 1/4 (winter 1981). Republished in González, ed., *Voces,* 35-39.

52. Jorge Lara-Braud, "Reflexiones teológicas sobre la migración," *Apuntes* 2/1 (spring 1982). Republished in González, ed., *Voces,* 87-91.

53. In "Hyphenating Joseph," a paper I read at the November 1996 national meeting of the Society of Biblical Literature, I presented a Cuban exile's reading of Joseph the Hebrew exile.

54. González, *Santa Biblia,* 103.

55. Ibid., 108.

56. Ibid., 109.

57. See the analysis of my article on the Gibeonites in Fernando Segovia's "Toward Intercultural Criticism," in Segovia and Tolbert, eds., *Reading from This Place,* vol. 2, 303-30. Both the article and another one extending the theme to biblical scenes where characters directly argue with God appear in the third volume of *Reading from This Place* (*Teaching the Bible* [Orbis, 1998]).

58. Justo L. González, "Historia de la interpretación bíblica," in Pablo A. Jiménez, ed., *Lumbrera a nuestro camino* (Miami: Editorial Caribe, 1994), 118 (translation mine). The Spanish original reads:

Y es precisamente eso lo que somos nosotros: una nueva comunidad hermenéutica. Gentes que leemos la Biblia como se nos enseñó y que por ello encontramos en ella lo que se nos enseñó. Pero si llega el día en que de veras nos atrevamos a enfrentarnos a la Biblia, no como se nos enseñó, sino con plena apertura al texto, afirmando y reconociendo nuestra perspectiva y nuestras experiencias particulares, y confiando en el Espíritu Santo para que nos conduzca a la verdad, lo que hemos de encontrar en el texto sagrado bien podrá sorprendernos, y quizá sorprenderá también a la comunidad hermenéutica universal, que tendrá que reconocer en el texto los elementos que nosotros, desde nuestra propia perspectiva, habremos descubierto.

Chapter 9: *Race, Religion, and la Raza: An Exploration of the Racialization of Latinos in the United States and the Role of the Protestant Church*

1. David Maldonado, "Hispanic Protestantism: Historical Reflections," *Apuntes* year 11, no. 1 (spring 1991): 14.

2. These three groups have been chosen on the basis of their historical presence as the earliest and largest U.S. Latino populations. The term "Latino" includes a growing number of immigrants from other parts of Latin America, especially Central America. My supposition at this point, particularly with reference to Central American refugees, is that they enter the United States as an already racialized people.

3. Tomas Almaguer, *Racial Faultlines: The Historical Origins of White Supremacy in California* (Berkeley: University of California Press, 1994), 57.

4. Michael Omi and Howard Winant, *Racial Formation in the United States: From the 1960's to the 1980's,* 2nd ed. (New York: Routledge, 1994), 55.

5. Ibid., 194 n. 1, 54-55.

6. Ibid., 66, 81.

7. Ibid., 51.

8. Ramon A. Gutierrez, *When Jesus Came, the Corn Mothers Went Away: Marriage, Sexuality, and Power in New Mexico, 1500–1846* (Stanford, Calif.: Stanford University Press, 1991), 192-97. In some instances in New Mexico the term "mulatto" is applied to persons of Spanish and Indian ancestry. *Coyote* refers to someone of mixed ancestry born to an Indian slave woman and *genizaro* refers to detribalized Indian slaves.

9. Almaguer, *Racial Faultlines,* 2-3, 56-57, 82.

10. Ibid., 73.

11. Genaro M. Padilla, *My History, Not Yours: The Formation of Mexican American Autobiography* (Madison: University of Wisconsin Press, 1993), 3-41.

12. James Jennings, "The Puerto Rican Community: Its Political Background," in *Latinos and the Political System,* ed. F. Chris Garcia (Notre Dame, Ind.: University of Notre Dame Press, 1988), 67; and Virginia E. Sanchez Korrol, *From Colonia to Community: The History of Puerto Ricans in New York City,* 2nd ed. (Berkeley: UCB Press, 1994), 4, 20, 31-32, 54.

13. Korrol, *From Colonia to Community,* 85-86, 100. Korrol describes *compadrazgo* as ritual kinship, which provided godparents or companion parents. "Within this

relationship the parties developed a deep sense of obligation, support, encouragement, commitment, and even financial assistance toward one another."

14. Ibid., 4, 132ff.

15. Clara Rodriguez, "Puerto Rican: Between Black and White," in Clara Rodriguez et al., eds., *The Puerto Rican Struggle* (New York: Puerto Rican Migration Research Consortium, 1980), 25, 28. Quoted in Eldin Villafane, *The Liberating Spirit: Toward an Hispanic American Pentecostal Social Ethic* (Grand Rapids: Eerdmans, 1993), 23.

16. Jennings, "The Puerto Rican Community," 69.

17. Angelo Falcon, "Black and Latino Politics in New York City: Race and Ethnicity in a Changing Urban Context," in *Latinos and the Political System*, 176.

18. Maria Cristina Garcia, *Havana USA: Cuban Exiles and Cuban Americans in South Florida, 1959–1994* (Berkeley: UCB Press, 1996), 19.

19. Ibid., 28-29.

20. Ibid., 40.

21. Ibid., 43.

22. Ibid., 68-69.

23. Ibid., 108.

24. Ibid., 281-83, 317.

25. Reginald Horsman, *Race and Manifest Destiny: The Origins of American Racial Anglo-Saxonism* (Cambridge: Harvard University Press, 1981), 1-6.

26. Ibid., 44-45, 117ff.

27. By "cultural convert" I do not want to suggest that these early missionaries became acculturated into Latino culture, but rather that there is a significant change in their perceptions and relationship to the Latino community, similar to the "conversion to the poor" in liberation theology, representing a movement toward solidarity with the Latino community.

28. Edwin Sylvest, "Hispanic American Protestantism in the United States," in *Fronteras: A History of the Latin American Church in the USA since 1513*, ed. Moíses Sandoval (San Antonio: Mexican American Cultural Center, 1983), 291.

29. R. Douglas Brackenridge and Francisco O. García-Treto, *Iglesia Presbiteriana: A History of Presbyterians and Mexican Americans in the Southwest*, 2nd ed. (San Antonio: Trinity University Press, 1987), 2-3.

30. Joel N. Martinez, "The South Central Jurisdiction," in *Each in Our Own Tongue: A History of Hispanic United Methodism*, ed. Justo L. González (Nashville: Abingdon Press, 1991), 40-42.

31. Almaguer, *Racial Faultlines*, 62.

32. Sylvest, "Hispanic American Protestantism," 294-95.

33. Susan M. Yohn, *A Contest of Faiths: Missionary Women and Pluralism in the American Southwest* (Ithaca, N.Y.: Cornell University Press, 1995), 17-30; Mark T. Banker, *Presbyterian Missions and Cultural Interaction in the Far Southwest, 1850–1950* (Chicago: University of Illinois Press, 1993), 151.

34. *The Missionary Magazine* (March, 1909), 123-24; quoted in Brackenridge and García-Treto, *Iglesia Presbiteriana,* 50-51.

35. Banker, *Presbyterian Missions,* xiii.

36. Ibid., 131.

37. Ibid. The *penitentes* began as a lay brotherhood, which, in the absence of clerical presence in northern New Mexico, "maintained church buildings, assisted needy community members, and conducted services and performed rituals that clearly reflected the persistent legacy of medieval Catholicism," 6.

38. Ibid., xii.

39. Martinez, "South Central Jurisdiction," 50.

40. Brackenridge and García-Treto, *Iglesia Presbiteriana,* 90.

41. Sylvest, "Hispanic American Protestantism," 322.

42. Mercer L. Sullivan, "Puerto Ricans in Sunset Park, Brooklyn: Poverty Amidst Ethnic and Economic Diversity," in *In the Barrios: Latinos and the Underclass Debate,* Joan Moore and Raquel Pinderhughes, eds. (New York: Russell Sage Foundation, 1993), 13.

43. Humberto Carrazana, "The Southeastern Jurisdiction," in *Each in Our Own Tongue,* 92-94.

44. Garcia, *Havana,* 19.

45. Ibid., 205-7.

46. Omi and Winant, *Racial Formation,* 109.

47. Justo L. González, "Hispanic Worship: An Introduction," *¡Alabadle!* (Nashville: Abingdon Press, 1996), 11. González quotes Luis Madrigal, Executive Dir. of the Hispanic Assoc. of Bilingual Bicultural Ministries, who describes the generational conflict: "These young people are frustrated because most Hispanic churches are Spanish-only and dominated by their parents' culture. . . . Pastors, on the other hand, . . . often don't understand why these young people—even their own children—are so different from them" (125 n. 2).

48. González, "Overview," *Each in Our Own Tongue,* 33-34.

49. Ibid., 31.

Chapter 10: Mainline Hispanic Protestantism and Latino Newcomers

1. See Barry A. Kosmin and Seymour P. Lachman, *One Nation Under God: Religion in Contemporary American Society* (New York: Random House, 1993).

2. See Alejandro Portes and Ruben G. Rumbaut, *Immigrant America: A Portrait* (Berkeley: University of California Press, 1990).

3. See Harold J. Recinos, *The Politics of Salvadoran Refugee Popular Religion* (Ph.D. dissertation, American University, Washington, D.C., 1993).

4. Phillip Berryman, *Liberation Theology: The Essential Facts About the Revolutionary Movement* (Oak Park, Ill.: Meyer Stone Press, 1984), 6.

5. See Thomas Ward, *The Price of Fear: Salvadoran Refugees in the City of Angels* (Ph.D. dissertation, Department of Anthropology, University of California, Los Angeles, 1987).

6. Harold J. Recinos, Fieldnotes, Washington, D.C., 1992.

7. My translation.

8. In El Salvador, *pueblo* (the people) is largely understood as a reference to the majority poor.

9. See esp. Roger Lancaster, *Thanks to God and the Revolution: Popular Religion and Class Consciousness in the New Nicaragua* (New York: Columbia University Press, 1988).

10. My translation.

11. Ibid.

12. Ibid.

13. My translation.

14. My translation.

15. See David Kertzer, *Comrades and Christians: Religion and Political Struggle in Communist Italy* (Cambridge: Cambridge University Press, 1980), and *Ritual, Politics, and Power* (New Haven and London: Yale University Press, 1988).

16. William Roseberry, *Anthropologies and Histories: Essays in Culture, History, and Political Economy* (New Brunswick, N.J.: Rutgers University Press, 1989), 226.

17. Words written on banner in the Sanctuary of Casa del Pueblo, Washington, D.C.

18. See esp. Jon Sobrino, *Jesus the Liberator: A Historical-Theological View* (Maryknoll, N.Y.: Orbis, 1993).

19. Farabundo Marti National Liberation Front. Until 1994 the FMLN was constituted by five groups. The FMLN is now a legal political party in El Salvador.

20. E. R. Leach, *Political Systems of Highland Burma: A Study of Kachin Social Structure* (Atlantic Highlands, N.J.: Athlone Press, 1986; 1964), 15. Cruz is a Salvadoran Lutheran pastor now living in Washington, D.C., from the Department of La Union, El Salvador.

21. See Jon Sobrino and Ignacio Martin-Baro, eds., *Archbishop Oscar Romero: Voice of the Voiceless* (Maryknoll, N.Y.: Orbis, 1990).

22. Harold J. Recinos, Fieldnotes, Washington, D.C., 1991. See esp. Anna L. Peterson, *Martyrdom and the Politics of Religion* (New York: State University of New York, 1997).

23. Victor Turner, *The Forest of Symbols: Aspects of Ndembu Ritual* (Ithaca, N.Y.: Cornell University Press, 1967), 50.

24. Kertzer, *Ritual, Politics, and Power,* 120.

25. Lancaster, *Thanks to God and the Revolution,* 133.

26. Interfaith Service Bulletin, January 25, 1992.

27. NDPES Letter, January 25, 1992.

Chapter 11: *Moving from the Cathedral to Storefront Churches: Understanding Religious Growth and Decline Among Latino Protestants*

1. David Martin, *Tongues of Fire: The Explosion of Protestantism in Latin America* (Oxford: Basil Blackwell, 1990).

2. Quoted in Barry A. Kosmin, *The National Survey of Religious Identification 1989–1990* (New York: City University of New York, 1991).

3. Andrew Greeley, *The Catholic Myth* (New York: Charles Scribner's Sons, 1990), 120-25. It should be pointed out that there are weaknesses to the General Social Science survey upon which these findings are based. In the first place, the survey is not based on a Hispanic sampling frame, which would require a stratified sample by region. In addition, it is very likely that the sample misses the very poorest respondents.

4. Andrew Greeley, "Defection Among Hispanics," *America* (July 30, 1988), 61-62.

5. Quoted in Kenneth Davis, "The Hispanic Shift: Continuity Rather Than Conversion?" *Journal of Hispanic/Latino Theology* 1/3 (1994): 68.

6. Allan Figueroa Deck, *The Second Wave: Hispanic Ministry and the Evangelization of Cultures* (New York: Paulist Press, 1989), 61.

7. The church growth and decline literature among mainline Protestants is enormous. The following are a representative sample: Dean R. Hoge, Benton Johnson, and Donald A. Luidens, *Vanishing Boundaries: The Religion of Mainline Protestant Baby Boomers* (Louisville: Westminster/John Knox, 1994); C. Kirk Hadaway and David Roozen, *Rerouting the Protestant Mainstream: Sources of Growth and Opportunities for Change* (Nashville: Abingdon Press, 1995); David A. Roozen and C. Kirk Hadaway, eds., *Church and Denominational Growth: What Does (and Does Not) Cause Growth or Decline* (Nashville: Abingdon Press, 1993); Wade Clark Roof and William McKinney, *American Mainline Religion: Its Changing Shape and Future* (New Brunswick, N.J.: Rutgers University Press, 1987).

8. The first and only serious attempt at understanding this dynamic was presented three decades ago by Thomas O'Dea and Roberto Poblete in their classic exploratory study "Anomie and the 'Quest for Community': The Formation of Sects Among the Puerto Ricans of New York," in Thomas F. O'Dea, *Sociology and the Study of Religion* (New York: Basic Books, 1970), 180-98. Since then no attempt other than the present chapter has provided a sociological explanation for these dramatic and significant trends.

9. The only exception limited to one religious group is the AVANCE research. See my article, "The Browning of American Adventism," *Spectrum* 25/2 (1995): 29-50.

10. Like any attempt at providing an explanation to a very complex and multidimensional phenomenon, my argument will need to be subjected to

critical analysis and empirical verification. Theories are only as good as their ability to correspond with the lived social reality of a community. Second, as a sociological argument, matters related to the verifiability, correctness, or relevancy of a particular belief statement are not a primary concern, except insofar as understanding the role that a particular religious discourse plays in affecting human behavior and collective action.

11. This was the main point of the now classic study by H. Richard Niebuhr who posited that denominational variations and proliferation were caused by differences across social lines—age, income, education, race (*The Social Sources of Denominationalism* [New York: Henry Holt, 1929]).

12. Robert Wuthnow and Matthew P. Lawson, "Sources of Christian Fundamentalism in the United States," in *Accounting for Fundamentalism,* ed. Martin E. Marty and R. Scott Appleby (Chicago: University of Chicago Press, 1994), 23.

13. In the discussion I will develop more fully the concept of tension borrowed from Rodney Stark and William S. Bainbridge, *The Future of Religion: Secularization, Revival, and Cult Formation* (Berkeley: University of California Press, 1985), 48.

14. R. Stephen Warner, "Work in Progress Toward a New Paradigm for the Sociological Study of Religion in the United States," *American Journal of Sociology* 98/5 (March 1993): 1044-93.

15. The main proponents of the classical formulation of the secularization theory are Bryan Wilson, *Religion in Sociological Perspective* (New York: Oxford University Press, 1982), and *Religion in Secular Society* (London: C. A. Watts, 1966); Peter Berger, *The Sacred Canopy: Elements of a Sociological Theory of Religion* (Garden City, N.Y.: Anchor, 1969), and *A Rumor of Angels: Modern Society and the Rediscovery of the Supernatural* (Garden City, N.Y.: Anchor, 1970).

16. For a recent application of this theoretical perspective, see Roger Finke, Avery M. Guest, and Rodney Stark, "Religious Pluralism in New York State, 1855 to 1865," *American Sociological Review* 61/2 (April 1996): 203-18.

17. Rodney Stark and Laurence R. Iannaccone. "A Supply-Side Reinterpretation of the 'Secularization' of Europe," *Journal for the Scientific Study of Religion* 33/3 (1994): 233.

18. Rodney Stark, "Do Catholic Societies Really Exist?" *Rationality and Society* 4:261-71.

19. Rodney Stark and James C. McCann, "Market Forces and Catholic Commitment: Exploring the New Paradigm," *Journal for the Scientific Study of Religion* 32/2 (1993): 121.

20. Stark, "Do Catholic Societies Really Exist?" 261-71.

21. Stark and McCann, "Market Forces and Catholic Commitment," 111-24.

22. Ibid., 118. Of course there are other explanations for this phenomenon including the institutional exclusion or discrimination of Latinos from enter-

ing the priesthood and the important value of the family that may mitigate against young men seeking the priesthood.

23. Max Weber, *The Protestant Ethic and the Spirit of Capitalism* (New York: Scribners, reprint, 1995).

24. Benton Johnson, "On Church and Sect," *American Sociological Review* 28 (1963): 539-49.

25. Ibid., 541.

26. Stark and Bainbridge, *Future of Religion*, 157.

27. Jorge Chapa and Richard R. Valencia, "Latino Population Growth, Demographic Characteristics, and Education Stagnation: An Examination of Recent Trends," *Hispanic Journal of Behavioral Sciences* 15/2 (May 1993): 165-87.

28. U.S. Department of Commerce, Bureau of the Census, *Hispanic Americans Today*, Current Population Reports, series P-23, no. 183 (Washington, D.C.: U.S. Government Printing Office, 1993).

29. Joan Moore and Raquel Pinderhughes, *In the Barrios: Latinos and the Underclass Debate* (New York: Russell Sage Foundation, 1993).

30. For a discussion of this issue, see Frank D. Bean and Marta Tienda, *The Hispanic Population of the United States* (New York: Russell Sage Foundation, 1990), 104-36.

31. Lacking a national survey of the religious identity of Latinos in the United States, we are dependent on data sets based on accumulated numbers over decades, such as the General Social Survey, which did not have a specific Latino sampling frame, its data collection process did not include the Spanish-speaking population, and the survey did not take all of the possible Latino or religious subgroups into account.

32. Marcus Lee Hansen, "The Problem of the Third-generation Immigrant," *Commentary* 14 (1952): 492-500; Will Herberg, *Protestant-Catholic-Jew* (New York: Doubleday, 1955); Milton Gordon, *Assimilation in American Life* (New York: Oxford University Press, 1964); Andrew Greeley, *Why Can't They Be Like Us?* (New York: E. P. Dutton & Co., 1971); Martin Marty, "Ethnicity: the Skeleton of Religion in America," *Church History* 41 (1972): 5-21.

33. Allen E. Richardson, *Strangers in This Land* (New York: Pilgrim Press, 1988).

34. Margaret Clark, Sharon Kaufman, and Robert C. Peirce, "Explorations of Acculturation: Toward a Model of Ethnic Identity," *Human Organization* 35 (1976): 231-38.

35. Douglas S. Massey and Nancy A. Denton, "Spatial Assimilation as a Socioeconomic Outcome," *American Sociological Review* 50 (1985): 94-106; Alejandro Portes and Ruben G. Rumbaut, *Immigrant America: A Portrait* (Berkeley and Los Angeles: University of California Press, 1990).

36. Richardson, *Strangers in This Land*, 1-44.

37. W. W. Isajiw and T. Makabe, *Socialization as Factor in the Ethnic Identity*

Retention (Toronto: University of Toronto Center for Urban and Community Studies, 1982); David Abalos, *Latinos in the United States* (South Bend, Ind.: University of Notre Dame Press, 1986).

38. J. Alan Winter, *Continuities in the Sociology of Religion: Creed, Congregation, and Community* (New York: Harper & Row, 1977), 197-229.

39. Harold J. Abramson, "The Religioethnic Factor and the American Experience: Another Look at the Three-generations Hypothesis," *Ethnicity* 2 (1975): 163-77; Roberto O. Gonzalez and Michael J. LaVelle, *The Hispanic Catholic in the United States: A Socio-Cultural and Religious Profile*, Hispanic American Pastoral Investigations, vol. 1 (New York: Northeast Catholic Pastoral Center for Hispanics, 1985).

40. Phillip E. Hammond, "Religion and the Persistence of Identity," *Journal for the Scientific Study of Religion* 27 (March 1988): 1-11; *Religion and Personal Autonomy* (Columbia: University of South Carolina, 1992).

41. Armado M. Padilla, ed., *Acculturation* (Boulder, Colo.: Westview Press, 1980); Richard Rodriguez, *Hunger of Memory* (Boston: C. R. Godine, 1982); Susan E. Keefe and Amado M. Padilla, *Chicano Ethnicity* (Albuquerque: University of New Mexico Press, 1987).

42. The recent AVANCE study found evidence for a declining effect in some aspects of religious commitment among the more highly acculturated Latinos. See my article "Browning of American Adventism."

43. Mark Christensen, "Coming to Grips with the Losses: The Migration of Catholics into Conservative Protestantism," *America* (January 26, 1991): 58-59; Kenneth Davis, "The Hispanic Shift: Continuity Rather Than Conversion?" *Journal of Hispanic/Latino Theology* 1/3 (1994): 68-79. Allan F. Deck, "The Challenge of Evangelical/Pentecostal Christianity to Hispanic Catholicism," *Hispanic Catholic Culture in the U.S.: Issues and Concerns*, ed. Jay P. Dolan and Allan F. Deck (Notre Dame: University of Notre Dame Press, 1994), 409-39; Andrew Greeley, "Defection Among Hispanics," *America* (July 30, 1988): 61-62; Andrew Greeley, *The Catholic Myth* (New York: Charles Scribner's Sons, 1990).

44. Deck, "Challenge of Evangelical/Pentecostal Christianity," 418.

45. Davis, "The Hispanic Shift," 70-71.

46. Deck, "Challenge of Evangelical/Pentecostal Christianity," 421. For a recent treatment of this same issue, see Orlando Espín, "Pentecostalism and Popular Catholicism: The Poor and *Traditio*," *Journal of Hispanic/Latino Theology* 3/2 (1995): 14-43.

47. Ibid.

48. I caution the reader to the limitations of the data Greeley analyzed. It is very possible that these trends do not reflect the actual situation. We await further confirmation of these important issues.

49. Virgilio P. Elizondo, "Foreword," in *Mañana: Christian Theology from a Hispanic Perspective* (Nashville: Abingdon Press, 1990), 14.

50. Caleb Rosado, "The Concept of *Pueblo* as a Paradigm of Explaining the Religious Experience of Latinos," in *Old Masks, New Faces: Religion and Latino Identities*, ed. Anthony M. Stevens-Arroyo and Gilbert R. Cadena (New York: Bildner Center for Western Hemisphere Studies, 1995), 77-91.

51. Rodney Stark, *Sociology*, 6th ed. (Belmont, Calif.: Wadsworth, 1996).

52. The following discussion is taken from William S. Bainbridge, "The Sociology of Conversion," in *Handbook of Religious Conversion*, ed. H. Newton Malony and Samuel Southard (Birmingham, Ala.: Religious Education Press, 1992), 178-91.

53. Ibid., 183.

54. John Lofland and Rodney Stark, "Becoming a World-Saver: A Theory of Conversion to a Deviant Perspective," *American Sociological Review* 30: 862-75.

55. Ibid.

56. Rodney Stark and Laurence R. Iannaccone, "Rational Choice Propositions About Religious Movements," *Religion and the Social Order* 3A (1993): 241-61.

57. Mancur Olson, *The Logic of Collective Action: Public Goods and the Theory of Groups* (Cambridge, Mass.: Harvard University Press, 1971).

58. Ibid., 250.

59. For a thorough discussion on the extent, function, and impact of small groups in America, see Robert Wuthnow, *Sharing the Journey: Support Groups and America's New Quest for Community* (New York: Free Press, 1994).

60. Laurence R. Iannaccone, "Why Strict Churches Are Strong," *American Journal of Sociology* 99/5 (March 1994): 1203.

61. O'Dea and Poblete, "Anomie and the 'Quest for Community.'"

62. A. F. C. Wallace, "Revitalization Movements," *American Anthropologist* 58 (1956): 264-81.

63. Stark and Iannaccone, "Rational Choice Propositions About Religious Movements," 257.

64. O'Dea and Poblete, "Anomie and the 'Quest for Community.'"

65. Stark and Iannaccone, "Rational Choice Propositions About Religious Movements," 257.

66. Rodolfo de la Garza, et al., *Latino Voices: Mexican, Puerto Rican, and Cuban Perspectives on American Politics* (Boulder, Colo.: Westview Press, 1992).

67. F. Chris Garcia, Angelo Falcon, and Rodolfo de la Garza, "Introduction: Ethnicity and Politics: Evidence from the Latino National Political Survey," *Hispanic Journal of Behavioral Sciences* 18/21 (May 1996): 93.

68. Ibid., 102.

69. For a thorough discussion of the elusive relationship between conservative religion and politics, see Roger Dudley and Edwin I. Hernández, *Citizens of Two Worlds: Religion and Politics Among American Seventh-day Adventists* (Berrien Springs, Mich.: Andrews University Press, 1992).

70. See Greeley, *Catholic Myth.*

71. Stark and Bainbridge, *Future of Religion;* James Davison Hunter, *The Coming Generation* (Chicago: Chicago University Press, 1987).

72. This is true for Mormons as well as Seventh-day Adventists. See Malcolm Bull and Keith Lockhart, *Seeking a Sanctuary: Seventh-day Adventism and the American Dream* (San Francisco: Harper and Row, 1989). See also the findings that show African American Adventists experiencing significant upward mobility in Barry A. Kosmin and Seymour P. Lachman, *One Nation Under God* (New York: Random House, 1993).

73. See my article "Browning of American Adventism."

74. Philip Lampe, *Comparative Study of the Assimilation of Mexican Americans: Parochial Schools Versus Public Schools* (San Francisco: R and E Research Associates, 1975).

75. This is not to say that there are not religious movements from either the conservative or liberal theological spectrum which promote cultural assimilation, an escapist ideology, or oppressiveness. No religious movement is monolithic. What these findings begin to show is that common stereotypes about conservative religious movements should no longer be accepted without serious questioning, and are not sufficient to form the basis of large-scale generalizations.

76. For a discussion of this perspective, see my chapter, "Relocating the Sacred Among Latinos: Reflections on Methodology," in *Old Masks, New Faces: Religion and Latino Identities,* ed. Anthony M. Stevens-Arroyo and Gilbert R. Cadena (New York: Bildner Center for Western Hemisphere Studies, 1995), 61-76.

Chapter 12: The Protestant Hispanic Congregation: Identity

1. Carl S. Dudley, *Making the Small Church Effective* (Nashville: Abingdon, 1978), 19.

2. Ibid., 32-33.

3. Anthony G. Pappas, *Entering the World of the Small Church* (Alban Institute, 1988), 9.

4. Ulf Hannerz, *Culture Complexity* (N.Y.: Columbia University Press, 1992), 41-42.

5. William Madsen, *Mexican-Americans of South Texas* (New York: Holt, Rinehart and Winston, 1964), 44-45.

6. Ibid., 44.

7. These congregations are Emmanuel Presbyterian Church, San Antonio, Texas; Santa Fe Episcopal Church, San Antonio, Texas; Monte Sinai Methodist Church, San Antonio, Texas.

8. In full, Convencion de Mission Presbytery, Synod of Sun, Presbyterian Church (USA).

9. Eldin Villafañe, *The Liberating Spirit* (Grand Rapids: Eerdmans, 1993), 13.

10. Patricia A. Montgomery, *The Hispanic Population in the U.S.* (U.S. Department of Commerce, March 1993), 3.

11. Ibid., 4.

12. Rubem A. Alves, in Villafañe, *Liberating Spirit,* 16.

13. Rodolfo O. de la Garza, et al., eds., *The Mexican American Experience* (Austin: University of Texas Press, 1985), 24ff.

14. Ibid., 24.

15. Ibid.

16. Clifton L. Holland, *The Religious Dimension in Hispanic Los Angeles: A Protestant Case Study* (Pasadena, Calif.: William Carey Library, 1974), 34.

17. R. Douglas Brackenridge and Francisco O. García-Treto, *Iglesia Presbiteriana: A History of Presbyterians and Mexican Americans in the Southwest* (San Antonio: Trinity University Press, 1974), 6.

18. Carlos E. Cortes, ed., *The Mexican American* (New York: Arno Press, 1974), 38.

19. Virginia Garrad-Burnet and David Stoll, *Rethinking Protestantism in Latin America* (Philadelphia: Temple University Press, 1993), 4.

20. Brackenridge and García-Treto, *Iglesia Presbiteriana,* 28.

21. Carl S. Dudley, *Sacred Worship in Small Churches,* Reformed Liturgy and Worship (Presbyterian Church, U.S. & USA) xvii/2 (spring 1983).

22. Brackenridge and García-Treto, *Iglesia Presbiteriana.*

23. Carl S. Dudley, *Making the Small Church Effective* (Nashville: Abingdon, 1978), 32-33.

24. Virgilio P. Elizondo, *Christianity and Culture,* Our Sunday Visitor (Huntington, Ind., 1975), 116.

25. Angela Erevia, *Quinciañera* (San Antonio: Mexican American Cultural Center, 1980), 3.

26. Rubén P. Armendáriz, *Las Posadas,* Reformed Liturgy and Music, Presbyterian Church (USA) (autumn 1984).

27. Jennifer Fast, ed., *La Posada* (Minneapolis: Augsburg Publishing House, 1987), 7.

28. Justo L. González, ed., *¡Alabadle!* (Nashville: Abingdon Press, 1996).

Contributors

Rubén P. Armendáriz is former Professor of Ministry and Vice President for Seminary Operations and Relations of McCormick Theological Seminary in Chicago. He is a graduate of the University of Texas and Austin Presbyterian Theological Seminary. A native Texan, he resides in San Antonio and is a member of the Presbyterian Church (USA).

Tomás Atencio is a Lecturer in Sociology at the University of New Mexico, where he completed his doctoral studies. He is a native of New Mexico and member and elder at Second Presbyterian Church (USA) in Albuquerque.

Paul Barton has been appointed Director of Hispanic Ministries with teaching responsibilities in church history at the Episcopal Theological Seminary of the Southwest, Austin, Texas (as of Fall 1999). He is a member of the Rio Grande Conference of The United Methodist Church.

Ismael García is Professor of Christian Ethics at the Austin Presbyterian Theological Seminary in Austin, Texas. He did his doctoral work at the Universiy of Chicago and is a member of the United Church of Christ. He is a native of Puerto Rico.

Francisco García-Treto is Professor of Religion at Trinity University in San Antonio, Texas. He completed his graduate studies at Princeton Theological Seminary and is a native of Cuba. He is a member of the Presbyterian Church (USA).

Justo L. González is Director of the Hispanic Summer Program and the Hispanic Theological Initiative, the latter based at Emory University. He completed his graduate work at Yale University and taught at Candler School of Theology. He is a native of Cuba and a member of The United Methodist Church.

Edwin I. Hernandez is Vice President for Academic Affairs at Antillean Adventist University in Puerto Rico. He completed his doctoral studies in sociology at the University of Notre Dame. He is a native of Puerto Rico and ordained in the Seventh-day Adventist Church.

Jorgé Lara-Braud has spent most of his professional life as a theological educator. He holds degrees from Austin College, Austin Presbyterian Seminary, and Princeton Seminary. He resides in Austin and is a Visiting Scholar at the Institute of Latin American Studies of the University of Texas, and an Adjunct Professor of Mission and Evangelism at Austin Presbyterian Seminary.

Daisy L. Machado is Program Director of the Hispanic Theological Initiative based at Emory University. She did her doctoral studies at the University of Chicago and taught at Brite Divinity School. She is a native of Cuba and a member of the Christian Church (Disciples of Christ).

David Maldonado, Jr., is Professor of Church and Society at Perkins School of Theology. His doctoral work was completed at the University of California, Berkeley. He is a native of Texas and a member of The United Methodist Church.

Luis Pedraja is Assistant Professor of Systematic Theology at Perkins School of Theology. He is a graduate of the University of Virginia and a native of Cuba. He is a member of the Baptist Church.

Harold Recinos is Professor of Theology, Culture, and Urban Ministry at Wesley Theological Seminary in Washington, D.C. He holds a Ph.D. in Cultural Anthropology completed at the American University. He is a native of New York and a member of The United Methodist Church.

José David Rodriguez is Associate Professor of Systematic Theology and Director of the Hispanic Ministry Program at the Lutheran School of Theology in Chicago.

Teresa Chávez Sauceda is completing her doctoral work in Religion and Society (Ethics) at the Graduate Theological Union in Berkeley. She is a native of California and a member of the Presbyterian Church (USA).

Ed Sylvest is Associate Professor of History of Christianity at Perkins School of Theology. He completed his graduate work at Southern Methodist University. He is a native of Louisiana and a member of the Rio Grande Conference of The United Methodist Church.

Index

acculturation, 224, 226, 232, 282-87
Anglo
  Anglo Americans, 60-84
  Anglo Celtic, 21-28, 36-37
  Anglo Saxonism, 31-34
annual conferences, 63-65, 67, 68, 70-73, 76-83
Aponte, Edwin, 133, 134
assimilation, 88-90, 96
anti-Catholicism, 247, 266, 279. *See also* Roman Catholic Church

Baptists, 91, 93, 94, 98
barrio/neighborhood, 288-89
Bible, 48-50, 58, 59, 129, 130, 135-38, 163-65, 167-79, 248-58
  reading in Spanish. *See* Spanish
  reading of, 198-300
  See also scripture
border (U.S./Mexican), 29, 30, 34-37

Cardenas, Benigno, 34, 41, 44, 65-67
clergy
  native/indigenous, 39, 41, 43, 48, 56, 64-66, 69-81
  See also ministers/pastors
Colorado, 49-50, 56
community, 148-55, 158
confessing/confession of, 109-13, 115, 120, 122
  the faith in Spanish. *See* Spanish
congregations, 246-47, 251-54, 264
  as family, 242-45
  members, 263
  small, 240-41, 251-54
conversion, 40-41, 51, 53, 57, 111, 186-89, 249, 296-97

Hispanic shift, 212, 224-28, 231, 235
converts. *See* conversion
Cuba/Cubans, 183-85, 190
culture, 252-54, 296-99

demographics, 221-23, 233-34
denominations
  denominational affiliation, 276
  denominational growth, 220-21
Disciples of Christ, 91, 93, 94, 98, 100-102

ecumenism, 137-38, 141, 164, 281
El Salvador/Salvadoran, 195-203, 205-14
Elizondo, Virgilio, 97-98, 132, 135, 162, 168, 170
ethics
  character ethics, 149-52, 155
  duty ethics, 142-45, 149, 150, 154
  ethics of care, 153-59
  ethics of consequence, 142, 146-48
  principle ethics, 142-51
  See also moral thinking/reflection
ethnic relations, 64, 67, 68, 70, 73-84
ethnicity, 11-12, 271-72. *See also* identity, ethnic
ethnocentrism, 179
exiles/aliens, 162, 171, 172

Goizueta, Roberto, 126
González, Justo L., 109, 113-16, 120, 121, 127, 129, 135-37, 162, 164, 165-73, 192

hermeneutics (Hispanic), 160-61, 163-73. *See also* interpretative community

349